The Incredible Internet Guide™ to
STAR WARS

The Complete Guide to Everything Star Wars Online

By Peter J. Weber

Cover Art by Erin Cristall

©1999 By Peter J. Weber &
Facts on Demand Press
1971 E Fifth Street, Suite 101
Tempe, AZ 85281
(800) 929-3811
www.brbpub.com

Dedicated to Ivy.

The Incredible Internet Guide™ to Star Wars
The Complete Guide to Everything Star Wars Online

©1999 By Peter J Weber and Facts on Demand Press
1971 E Fifth Street, Suite 101
Tempe, AZ 85281
(800) 929-3811

ISBN 1-889150-12-6
Graphic Design by Robin Fox & Associates
Cover Art by Erin Cristall
Edited by James R. Flowers, Peter J. Weber

Cataloging-in-Publication Data

791.43 Weber, Peter J. (Peter Julius), 1952-
WEB   The incredible Internet guide to Star Wars : the
        Complete guide to everything Star Wars online / by Peter
        J. Weber ; cover art by Erin Cristall. -- 1st ed.
            p. cm. -- (The incredible internet guide)
            ISBN: 1-889150-12-6

            1.Star Wars films--Computer network resources. 2.
        Web sites--Directories. I. Title.

        PN1995.9.S695W43 1999   791.43'75
                            QBI99-5000405

All rights reserved. Printed in the United States of America. No part of this book may be used or reproduced in any form or by any means, or stored in a database or retrieval system without the prior written permission of the publisher, except in the case of brief quotations embodied in critical articles or reviews. Making copies of any part of this book for any purpose other than your own personal use is a violation of United States copyright laws. Entering any of the contents into a computer for mailing list or database purposes is strictly prohibited unless written authorization is obtained from Facts on Demand Press.
Star Wars and all its film titles and character names are copyrighted © by and trademarked ™ by Lucasfilms Ltd. This book was in no way authorized, sanctioned, endorsed, or produced by Lucasfilms Ltd. or any of its employees. *The Incredible Internet Guide Series* is a trademark ™ of BRB Publications Inc. Artwork used in *The Incredible Internet Guide to Star Wars* is found online on the Internet using web search tools, and is intended as examples only. Readers are encouraged to patronize these artwork sites, where noted. Screen capture images are author property, purchased using an ISP for hire, and found on the author's computer.
This book is sold as is, without warranty of any kind, either express or implied, respecting the contents of this book, including but not limited to implied warranties for the book's quality, performance, merchantability, or fitness for any particular purpose. Neither the authors, the publisher nor its dealers or distributors shall be liable to the purchaser or any other person or entity with respect to any liability, loss, or damage caused or alleged to be caused directly or indirectly by this book.

Contents

Introduction 1
The Cast & Characters of Star Wars 5
    The Jedi 5
    Obi-Wan/Alec Guinness & Ewan McGregor 6
    Yoda/Frank Oz 7
    Luke Skywalker/Mark Hamill 8
    Princess Leia/Carrie Fisher 10
    Windu/Samuel L Jackson 11
    Young Anakin/Jake Lloyd 12
    Qui-Gon/Liam Neeson 12
    Padme/Queen Amidala/Natalie Portman 13
    Han Solo/Harrison Ford 14
    Lando Calrissian/Billy Dee Williams 16
    Chewbacca/Peter Mayhew 16
    Aliens, Creatures, & Things Oh My 17
    Ewoks 18
    Droids, C-3PO, & R2-D2 19
    Villains, Emperor Palpatine, & Jabba the Hut 20
    Darth Vader/David Prowse & James Earl Jones 23
    Boba Fett -- Coolest of the Bounty Hunters 25
    Other Major & Minor Characters 27

Star Wars in Entertainment 29
    The Films 29
        Cast Lists & Cast Filmographies 29
        The Phantom Menace (Episode 1) & Prequels 32
        A New Hope (Episode 4) 37
        Empire Strikes Back (Episode 5) 38
        Return of the Jedi (Episode 6) 39
        Trilogy Special Editions 40
        Flix -- Other Notable Films 41

    The Mediums & The Media 42
        Comics, First & Foremost! 42
        Moviemakers, Executives, Studios 44
        George Lucas 45
        Productions & FX 45
        TV/Radio 47

Star Wars Discussion -- Talk it Up, Fuzzball! 49
    Chat Rooms 49
    Fan Clubs 52
    Forums & Message Boards 53
    Mailing Lists 57
    Newsgroups 59
    Quizzes, Trivia, & Knowledge Games 61

Surveys, Polls, & Where Your Opinion Counts 63

Star Wars Multimedia 65
A Multimedia Potpourri 65
Videos 72
AVIs 72
MPEGs 75
QuickTime Movies (MOV Files) 75
Real Video 78
Videos -- Miscellaneous 79
Audio 86
MIDIs 86
MP3s 88
Real Audio 89
WAVs 90
Audio -- Miscellaneous 94

Star Wars Image Galleries 101
3D Images & Stereovision 101
Animations -- Images That Move 103
Cover Images 105
GIFs 105
JPEGs 108
Logo Images 114
Original Artwork, Paintings, Sketches, etc. ... 115
Photos & Photgraphy 118
Poster Images 122

Star Wars Fun, Games, & Lifestyle Topics 123
Merchandise 123
Collectibles 123
Toys 125
Trading Cards 127
Electronic Gear for Your Home 128
Stores Online 128
Lifestyle 129
News 129
Events & Schedules 133
Humor -- The Light & The Dark Side 134
Parties -- Where to Find Masks, Costumes, Novelties, & Gear 139
Games, Video Games, & Simulators of All Types 140
Collectible Card Games (CCGs) 147
Electronic Greeting Cards 147
Sci-Fi Fandom 148
Modeling 149
Dioramas 151
Educational Material 151
Roleplaying 153
MUSH 153
Resources 154

Star Wars Reference Points 159
    Databases 159
    Directories 160
    FAQs 161
    Link Lists 163
    Portals 165
    Search Engines & Finders 166
    Timelines & Chronologies 167
    Webrings 167

Star Wars Software 173
    Accessories 173
    Fonts 174
    Free e-mail Systems 175
    Icons & Cursors 175
    Screensavers 177
    Themes 178
    Wallpaper 179

Written in the Stars 181
    Scripts & Storylines 181
    Commentary & Essays 182
    Quotes 184
    Reviews 185
    Articles 186
    Editorials 188
    Interviews 189
    Books 189
    Fiction & Fan Fiction 192
    Song Lyrics 194
    Rumors 195

Star Wars Locations, Spacecraft, & Hardware 197
    The Cantina 197
    Planets, generally Bespin, Dagobah, or Naboo 198
    Tatooine -- Mos Eisley, Jundland Wastes, The Pit 199
    Endor -- Actually, the Forest Moon of Endor 200
    Coruscant -- The Imperial City 200

Spacecraft 201
    Alliance Spacecraft 201
    Millenium Falcon 202
    Star Fighters 202
    TIE Fighters 203
    Imperial Spacecraft 204
    The Death Star 205
    Specs, Diagrams, & Secret Information 206

Hardware 207
    Equipment Found in the Star Wars Universe 207
    Weapons & Lightsabers 207
    Vehicles (Excluding Spacecraft) 210

Star Wars Site Profiles 211

Introduction

There's a tremor in the Force...

The online universe is a two-edged sword – or should we say, a dual light saber? On one hand, the Internet gives us almost unlimited access to published material. On the other hand, how can we possibly keep track of all the Star Wars pages, especially when new ones are popping up faster than the rate Ewoks, like rabbits, multiply? Which sites are the best – which have the most to offer and are worth visiting? And, how do we get to them quickly?

Whether you measure it in parsecs or minutes, time is our most precious commodity, and many of us don't want to waste time surfing around the big 3W. Many have found that the standard search engines are not adequate. The big search engines give us only lists, and these lists are usually based on the popularity of a web site, not on the actual quality of it, and not the "details" of it. In our own exploration of the hundreds and hundreds of Star Wars web sites, we've found that it's not how big or expansive a web site is that interests us – instead, it's what that web site *has* that holds our interest.

And Star Wars fans' interests are varied. Look at all the aspects of what we call the Star Wars lifestyle. Foremost is the movies themselves, the lore of the characters and places in them as well as information about who makes the movies, what's ahead, the inside stories, and all that. But there are also Star Wars web sites functioning as online avenues for Star Wars games and roleplaying. There are Star Wars merchandisers, auctions, newsgroups, message boards, and model builders. There are inter-connected Star Wars webrings that you can page through much like an electronic storybook journey, and there are galleries, humor sites, and news. Star Wars sites are put up by any and all kinds of people – students, professionals, artists, moviemakers, pirates – all with one thing in common: a basic love for participation in the myth of Star Wars.

It's a Modern Phenomenon

We estimate that there are more than 10,000 individual Star Wars-related web sites. Most of these sites consist of more than one web page. Some of the bigger Star Wars sites, the force.net for example, have over one hundred "sub-pages" under their domains. The exact number of Star Wars sites changes daily.

With this book, we estimate that you are, at most, two web pages away from 80% to 90% of all the Star Wars web pages in existence.

So, if you've never heard of Star Wars, you can use this book to locate web sites that have the actual scripts of the movies. If you have an affinity or a special love in your heart for a Star Wars character, then you can use this book to make quick online connections with people who share the same ideas and interests. And if you want to find details, well, this book is the place to look for specialized Star Wars web sites!

In fact, it is ALL quite exciting. And, it was exciting to put together a book – a virtual list – of as many Star Wars web sites as we could gather with our computers so that you could quickly get to all the sites that interest you. We trust that you'll find that we've done a pretty good job of collecting the best sites in the Star Wars universe.

Using this Book is as Easy as 1 - 2 - 3

1

First, decide who or what you are looking for. Then, search the table of contents to find a chapter and section to look in. For example,

- ➢ *If you're looking for a web site for a person in a particular movie, look in the first chapter -- Cast & Characters.*
- ➢ *If you're looking for activities, check out the Lifestyle chapter.*
- ➢ *If you want to talk online about your interests, see the chapter called Discussion.*

2

Once you find the page number for a section that interests you, turn to that section and read through the list of sites and their descriptions. Or simply browse them all.

3

To get more information on a site, look it up in the back half of the book (where web sites are listed in alphabetical order, like a dictionary)

~Or~

Go online and type in the URL of the site you want to see.

A big question is: are web sites listed under more than one chapter and category? The answer is: does a Wookiee have hair!? Of course! There are many sites that are listed under more than one category. For instance, the Harrison Ford Newsgroup appears in the Cast & Characters chapter, underneath the heading "Han Solo/Harrison Ford," but it also appears in the Discussion Chapter as part of the "Newsgroups" list.

If you are new on the Web, you'll soon discover that there's one basic truth about the Internet clickstream: there are a lot of different things that can be found on a Star Wars web site. So, in **the second half** of the *Incredible Internet Guide to Star Wars* you'll find an alphabetical listing of all the sites – over 1100 of them. Here, each site has its URL, but also a description of what's on that site. We call it the site "profile." So, if you want to know ahead of time what to expect at a site, read the profile.

Introduction

In this book, there are images that are clearly screen captures. Other images were plucked from fans' web sites. These are presented as examples of what you'll see on your computer screen in order to help you find your way around the Internet. If you would like copies of any of these pictures, go to the web site itself. For images that appear as part of the screen captures in this book, read the URL address pictured in the browser window, then type it in the address bar of your own browser, which will take you to that web page.

I can't find a page -- what's wrong?

There are a number of things you should be aware of, which this book has no control over. First, some web sites simply "die" off – disappear. Also, web sites do change addresses – they move around. Generally, the page author will set up a link that takes you to the new location, but not always.

Some sites are only accessible through their main page. One way to try to find a site that won't open is to "truncate" the URL. This is done by deleting the last section of the address. For example, if www.starwars.com/droids would not open for you, then try using only www.starwars.com as the address. Once you are at the "main page" or an "index page," you should then be able to use links to navigate to the specific page you need.

Lastly, some sites are FTP sites, and they will not be accessible to you unless you use an FTP access utility – a program that is designed to handle FTP files. Usually, the FTP utility program can be downloaded for free, you store it on your computer, and use it when you encounter an FTP music or video file.

Keeping the Star Wars universe safe for children.

In our searching of Star Wars sites, not once did we stumble upon a pornographic site (although there may be some out there). Additionally, when we found a site that we felt had slightly objectionable material, we marked it in as having "adult content" in the profiles. In order to protect your children from objectionable material, you may wish to visit and use a "child protection" software site, such as NetNanny (www.netnanny.com) or CYBERsitter (www.cybersitter.com).

How to save something off a web site onto your computer

There are a number of ways to do this – downloading, screen capture, etc.

To download an item, simply right click (using your right mouse button) on the link to the file. Then choose "Save target as..."

To capture a screen, simply press the Alt key simultaneously with the Print Screen button. Then, you must open a word processing document (or something comparable) and paste your capture, and then save the file.

To use an image as wallpaper, right click on it and choose "Set as wallpaper."

To copy/paste text, use your mouse to simply highlight the area you want. Then, choose copy from the Edit menu of your browser, and then choose paste from the Edit menu of your word processing program.

To save a web page's text and/or links, choose "Save file as . . ." from your browser's File menu. You can save the page as plain text (which will eliminate all graphics and links), or you can save it as HTML (which will retain the links if you open it in a program capable of viewing HTML files).

Remember, too, that when you find a site you like and you want to return to it later, use the "Bookmarks" (on Netscape Navigator) or "Favorites" (on Internet Explorer) to remember the site location for you. We suggest that you create an exclusive Star Wars folder in your Bookmarks or Favorites just for your Star Wars sites.

Another way to return to a site is to enter your browser's "Properties" section and find the field that says "Show History." Most browsers automatically add the web sites you visit to a history list, usually arranging the lists in weekly segments. This is also a good way to check on the places your computer and the others who use it have been.

How do you write to us?

We'd certainly like to hear from you, and we'd be especially interested in hearing about anything new or original regarding Star Wars on the Internet. We're not too excited about new web pages that consist mainly of links to other sites. There are plenty of these already. Star Wars fan fiction sites are especially interesting as are sites that have original or derivative artwork, or even rare pictures or rare merchandise. Sites with sound or video clips are also of interest to us.

Additionally, if you find an error in this edition of the *Incredible Internet Guide to Star Wars,* feel free to e-mail us a correction.

Our e-mail address is `websitecentral@naboo.zzn.com`

Sorry, we cannot respond to all e-mail, but we especially like to hear good ideas and good words about Star Wars and our book.

Visit the Incredible Internet Guide to Star Wars online.

You may find the *Incredible Internet Guide to Star Wars* at www.brbpub.com/iig/starwars. You will find interesting Star wars stuff, including a place to sign up for your own Naboo E-mail address. Our web site also links to the *Incredible Internet Guide For Trekkers* and others in the Incredible Internet Guide series.

Cast & Characters
of Star Wars

Are you interested in the characters in the Star Wars story, or the actors who played them? Here you will find sections for the characters/actors, also sections for minor characters, creatures, droids, starting with...

The Jedi

The Jedi are the shining knights of the Galaxy. The sites below explain much about them, their powers and purpose. See also the individual Jedi's in the sections that follow, including Yoda. Young Anakin is listed separately. You'll find more Darth Vader in his section under Villains.

Darth Vader
www.starwars.com/characters/darth_vader/
Official jumping-off site for the series' most imposing character.

Force Powers
www.wcug.wwu.edu/~paradox/force.html
Descriptions of the known Force Powers.

Jedi Academy
www.jediacademy.com/force.htm
Jedi training and info site for the serious Jedi.

Jedi Domain
www.geocities.com/Area51/Shadowlands/3543/
Multi-presentation site: Jedi flavor, Kenners, Jedi of the month.

Jedi Knight Clan Legacy
www.starwarz.com/swlegacy/clan/frameset.html
Jedi Clan plays games & makes videos.

Jedi Knight Game Newsgroup
alt.games.jedi-knight

Jedi Knight LucasArts Game Newsgroup
alt.games.lucas-arts.star-wars.jedi-knight

Jedi Knights Homepage
http://members.aol.com/Myau84/jedi.html
Click on the book of Jedi knowledge; it has enlightening pix!

Jedi Society
http://members.aol.com/Myau84/society.html
Links to Star Wars sites that display cool new banners.

JediKnight.net
www.jediknight.net/
Jedi's on the gaming circuits! Game resources & news.

Kevin's Angle On Things - Why . . . Be a Jedi Knight
http://orion.it.luc.edu/~kriorda/angle.html
All Jedi need to check Kevin's 6th & final paragraph.

Obi-wan Kenobi
www.starwars.com/characters/ben_kenobi/
Official Star Wars Ben Kenobi page.

Religion, Star Wars The
http://hamp.hampshire.edu/~elwF94/planet/test.html
14 religion-like lessons for Jedi or anyone.

Yoda
www.starwars.com/characters/yoda/index.html
Yoda's official Lucasfilms page.

Obi-Wan/Alec Guinness & Ewan McGregor

Obi-wan Kenobi has been played by two actors: Sir Alec Guinness (Episodes 4, 5, 6) and Ewan MacGregor (Episode 1). MacGregor is likely to play the role in Episodes 2 & 3. Here are web sites for all three names.

Alec Guinness - All-Media Guide
http://allmovie.com/cg/x.dll?UID=9:01:46|PM&p=avg&sql=B29203
Filmography & biography of Sir Alec Guinness.

Duel of Darth Vader & Obi-wan Kenobi Video
www.telecom.csuhayward.edu/~aleung/dv_ken.mov
Clip of Darth & ol' Ben wearing out batteries on their sabres.

Etcetera (Virtual McGregor)
www.enter.net/~cybernut/ewanlinx.htm
The truth about Ewan - don't worry, it's good.

Ewan MacGregor
    `http://ucs.orst.edu/~harraha/`
        Good Tribute to Ewan - largely his Star Wars contributions.

Ewan McGregor (Lycos Network)
    `www.lycos.com/entertainment/celebrities/celebs/McGregor_Ewan.html`
        Basic Ewan unplugged.

Ewan McGregor Gallery
    `www.geocities.com/~ewanmcgregor/gallery/`
        More Ewan images than your eyes can stand.

Ewan Multimedia
    `http://ucs.orst.edu/~harraha/multi.htm`
        Ewan McGregor collection - Sounds, Images, Videos.

Ewanspotting
    `www.ewanspotting.com`
        Ewan is going to like this.

Hello There Video of Obi-Wan Kenobi
    `http://users.why.net/radrock/sounds/hello.avi`
        It's a video of the first time we hear Obi-Wan speak.

Obi-wan Kenobi
    `www.starwars.com/characters/ben_kenobi/`
        Official Star Wars Ben Kenobi page.

Virtual McGregor
    `www.enter.net/~cybernut/articles.htm`
        Ewan has some of the best fan web sites. Visit this one.

Yoda/Frank Oz

Mechanical Puppet or Jedi Master? – you decide. Frank Oz is the creator and voice of Yoda.

Dagobah Official Site
    `www.starwars.com/locations/dagobah/`
        This swamp really isn't that bad; official site.

Frank Oz - IMDb
    `http://us.imdb.com/Name?Oz,+Frank`
        Frank Oz - Yoda's voice - his career from the Internet Movie Database.

Prequel Yoda
    `http://members.aol.com/CapeMan69/yoda.html`
        Pix of Yoda model-making for The Phantom Menace.

Taz's Yoda Archives
    `http://seconn4.yoda.com/~vader97/yoda/yoda.html`
        Yoda JPEG image archive.

Yoda
    `www.starwars.com/characters/yoda/index.html`
        Yoda's official Lucasfilms page.

Yoda - Online Psychic
    `www.sun-sentinel.com/graphics/entertainment/yoda.htm`
        Shockwave Yoda - Online Psychic

Yoda's Hooked On Phonics, Help You It Can
http://pweb.netcom.com/~fragger/Phonics.html
Why don't we all talk like Yoda?

Yoda's Star Wars Webring
www.geocities.com/Area51/Cavern/1783/webring.htm
Yoda's Webring actually has great sites!

Yoda's Swamp
http://www2.netdoor.com/~broberts/yodapg.html
Tribute to Yoda; his favorite sayings and pix.

Luke Skywalker/Mark Hamill

Luke Skywalker, played by actor Mark Hamill, is the hero of the Star Wars Trilogy (Episodes 4, 5, 6). There is a little of Luke in all of us, and a lot of Luke in the following sites.

Dreaming of Mark Hamill
http://members.xoom.com/DreamingofMH/
This Mark fan site is inactive - would you like to take over?

Hear Mark
www.chez.com/jedinat/sounds.html
Mark speaks! WAV sound files of his quotes.

House of Skywalker Luke & Leia Paper Dolls
www.flyingarmadillo.com/cantina/fashion/leia/leia.htm
Cut out Luke, Leia, clothes, then dress 'em to impress.

The Jedi say "May the force be with you," but few know that Imperial's say "Serve the Emperor above all others."

Characters — Luke Skywalker/Mark Hamill — 9

IMHFC International Mark Hamill Fan Club (*Photo Album Page Shown Above*)
   www.markhamill.com/home.htm
      Info, pix, schedules, bios for Mark.

Lars Family, The
   http://seconn4.yoda.com/~vader97/lars/lars.html
      The Lars family met an unfortunate end.

Luke Skywalker
   www.starwars.com/characters/luke_skywalker/
      Luke Skywalker's Official Lucasfilms screen page.

Luke Skywalker Galleries (Taz's)
   http://seconn4.yoda.com/~vader97/luke/luke.html
      Luke pix galleries arranged by movie.

Luke Skywalker Movie Theme
   www.winfiles.com/apps/98/themes-movie-q.html
      Luke Skywalker "Theme" for your computer with Windows.

Luke Skywalker Ring of Dreams
   www.webring.org/cgi-bin/webring?ring=lukefans;index
      Basically, this is the "We Love Luke" webring.

Mark Hamill (Lycos Network)
   www.lycos.com/entertainment/celebrities/celebs/markhamill.html
      Lycos Network Mark Hamill interest page and links.

Mark Hamill - All-Media Guide
   http://allmovie.com/cg/x.dll?UID=9:01:46|PM&p=avg&sql=B29931
      Mark Hamill bio & filmography uncluttered by special effects.

Mark Hamill Mailing List
www.chez.com/jedinat/list.html
Mailing list & message board dedicated to Hamill.

Mark Hamill Quotes
www.chez.com/jedinat/quotes.html
Collection of Luke Quotes from everywhere.

Mark Hamill Rare Images (Gothic Skywalker's)
www.geocities.com/TimesSquare/Dungeon/3913/mark.html
Mark Hamill wonder years? Are they authentic?

Natalie's Mark Hamill Homepage
www.chez.com/jedinat/site1.html
Hamill unplugged - sounds, pix, and fun!

Sylvia Christina's Special Thoughts for Mark Hamill A Very Special Person
www.yggdrasill.demon.nl/Serie01/MHHome2.htm
A great fan site with Mark's bio, slides, fan fiction.

Why Luke Stinks
www.silcom.com/~pruth/luke.html
Downside of Luke - what little there is to berate.

Princess Leia/Carrie Fisher

Carrie Fisher plays Princess Leia in the Trilogy (Episodes 4, 5, 6). Her official web page is among these favorite Princess Leia/Carrie Fisher sites:

A Feminine Perspective
http://members.aol.com/bananie42/index.html
Solid! None of that really mushy stuff.

Carrie Books
www.saunalahti.fi/~margot/books.htm
Pix of Carrie's book covers along with comments.

Carrie Fisher (Lycos Network)
www.lycos.com/entertainment/celebrities/celebs/Fisher_Carrie.html
Things you need to know about Carrie - & links to more.

Carrie Fisher Web Site
www.carriefisher.com/
Carrie's pages are "must sees!"

Carrie Photographs (Unofficial Carrie Fisher Homepage)
www.offsoho.com/carrie/html/8photographs.html
Unofficial Carrie photo pix collection.

Carrie Videos (Unofficial Carrie Fisher Homepage)
www.offsoho.com/carrie/html/8video.html
Fun MOV video clips featuring Carrie.

late night with you kung fu colt daddy L Silky
www.toshistation.com/lizard.htm
Oh Baby (as said by Barry White)

Leia Quiz
www.saunalahti.fi/~margot/quiz.htm

Leia's Gown Museum Piece
www.geocities.com/Area51/Vault/3227/smithsonian/27.htm
Leia's original dress displayed at the Smithsonian exhibit.

Margot's Carrie Fisher Page
www.saunalahti.fi/~margot/cf.htm
Very stylish Carrie tribute site!

Princess Leia
www.starwars.com/characters/princess_leia/
Official Princess Leia site, recommended for Fisher's pix.

Ultimate Carrie Fisher Shrine
www.angelfire.com/ca/princessleia2/
Mystery site in development.

Unofficial Carrie Fisher Homepage
www.offsoho.com/carrie/html/86home.html
It's Unofficial but it's very stellar. Big Carrie pix sections.

Wig Outlet
www.wigs.com/plist.html
Find a Princess Leia wig - or wig for almost any occasion.

World's Best Star Wars Web Site Pics
www.geocities.com/Area51/Nebula/6259/
Assorted JPEG pix, with 14 of Leia.

Windu/Samuel L Jackson

Samuel L. Jackson wanted to be in Star Wars, and he got his wish, playing the role of a Jedi councilman. Here are biographical sites and one for his breakout movie Pulp Fiction.

Best Samuel L Jackson Home Page
http://member.aol.com/gifhack/main.html
Sounds & images from Samuel L Jackson's many movies.

Entertainment Weekly's Top 25 Actors of the 90s - Samuel L Jackson
http://cgi.pathfinder.com/ew/features/minisite/90s_actors/0,2566,16-16,jackson.html
Biographical material on Jackson from an EW write-up

Nocturne's Pulp Fiction
www.skipnet.com/~nocturne/pulpfiction.html
We had to include Samuel L. Jackson's most memorable movie.

Samuel L Jackson (Lycos Network)
www.lycos.com/entertainment/celebrities/celebs/Jackson_Samuel.html
Claims to fame plus good links to his major web sites.

Young Anakin/Jake Lloyd

Here are a few web sites with information about Jake Lloyd, who plays young Anakin Skywalker, our favorite hero in Episode 1: The Phantom Menace. We expect new web sites will be created for this budding young star.

Anakin Skywalker, Slave Boy
http://meltingpot.fortunecity.com/greenwood/487/char/anakin.html
Text info about Young Anakin, played by Jake Lloyd.

Jake Lloyd (1) - IMDb
http://us.imdb.com/M/person-exact?Jake+Lloyd
IMDb vitals and filmography site for Our Man Jake.

Qui-Gon Jinn/Liam Neeson

The web provides a number of sites for actor Liam Neeson, who plays the heroic Jedi Master Qui-gon Jinn in Episode 1: The Phantom Menace.

Jedi Knight Qui-Gon Jinn
http://meltingpot.fortunecity.com/greenwood/487/char/quigon.html
Vital information about Qui-Gon Jinn.

Liam Neeson
http://starwars.com/cast/neeson/index.html
Official Star Wars cast site for Liam, mostly text.

Liam Neeson (Lycos Network)
www.lycos.com/entertainment/celebrities/celebs/Neeson_Liam.html
A basic info page on Liam - a good place to start.

Liam Neeson - All-Media Guide
http://allmovie.com/cg/x.dll?UID=9:01:46|PM&p=avg&sql=B52070
Bio & filmography of Qui-Gon/Liam Neeson.

Liam Neeson Appreciation Pages
www.geocities.com/Hollywood/Set/6510/index2.html
Neeson info, filmography. E-mail him a message, maybe.

| Characters | Padme/Queen Amidala/Natalie Portman | 13 |

Liam Neeson Fact Sheet
> www.eonline.com/Facts/People/Bio/0,128,157,00.html
> E-Online Fact Sheet for Liam Neeson - personal & career.

Liam, Liam, Liam!!!!
> http://members.tripod.com/~BASKERTON/Liam.html
> So, you wanted to see a celebrity "un-tribute" web site?

Padme/Queen Amidala/Natalie Portman

Natalie Portman surprises us in the female lead role in The Phantom Menace. She has a number of good fan sites, and her own official web site.

Ask A Question - Natalie Portman
> www.allexperts.com/moviestars/oz/portman.shtml
> Have a Hollywood insider answer your Natalie questions.

Natalie Portman Filmography
> www.geocities.com/Hollywood/Lot/7181/filmography.html
> Great Natalie filmography with pix from each movie.

Natalie Portman Image Gallery
> www.natportman.com/images/
> Literally hundreds of Natalie pix!

Natalie Portman Photo Gallery
> www.geocities.com/Hollywood/Lot/7181/natpics.html
> 100-plus photos of Natalie.

Natalie Portman's Hang Out
> http://ucsu.colorado.edu/~vuong/Natalie.html
> Biographical info on Natalie & youthful images of her.

NatPortman.com
www.natportman.com/
All About Natalie Portman, plus images, video.

Phantom Menace Site, The
www.users.wineasy.se/doot/starwars/index.html
Prequel site focusing mostly on main actors and Nat Portman.

QueenAmidala.Com
www.queenamidala.com

Queen Amidala, Monarch of Naboo
http://meltingpot.fortunecity.com/greenwood/487/char/amidala.html
So, this is the famous Queen Amidala.

Stakawaka's Natalie Portman Page
www.geocities.com/Hollywood/Lot/7181/natalie.html
Collection of Natalie info and poses over the years.

Liam Neeson is so tall – 6" 4' - he could play a wookie or Darth Vader if he wasn't already a Jedi.

Han Solo/Harrison Ford

After playing Han Solo in Star Wars Episodes 4, 5, and 6, Harrison Ford went on to become one of the premier actors of the big screen. Among the tribute and database sites below are sites for a number of his movies.

Air Force One
www.spe.sony.com/movies/airforceone/home_swf.html
Wasn't Harrison The Prez in this One?

Audio Booth, The
www.smartlink.net/~deej7/audio.htm
Harrison sound clips in RealAudio. Player downloads, too.

Bria's Retribution, Flagship of the Rebel Commander
www.geocities.com/Area51/Nebula/8247/sum.html
Explore more - a variety site.

FTP Directory Bladerunner
ftp://ftp.sunet.se/pub/pictures/tv.film/Bladerunner/
Harrison in Bladerunner pix - by the dozens.

Han Solo
www.starwars.com/characters/han_solo/
Official Han Solo page from Lucasfilms Ltd.

Han Solo Archive
http://seconn4.yoda.com/~vader97/han/han.html
Han (Harrison Ford) in five galleries - in living color.

Characters — Han Solo/Harrison Ford

Han Solo-Ists
www.hansolo-ists.freeservers.com
In love with Han Solo, or would you rather kiss a Wookiee?

Harrison Ford (1)
http://us.imdb.com/Name?Ford,+Harrison
Want to check out Harrison's professional career credits?

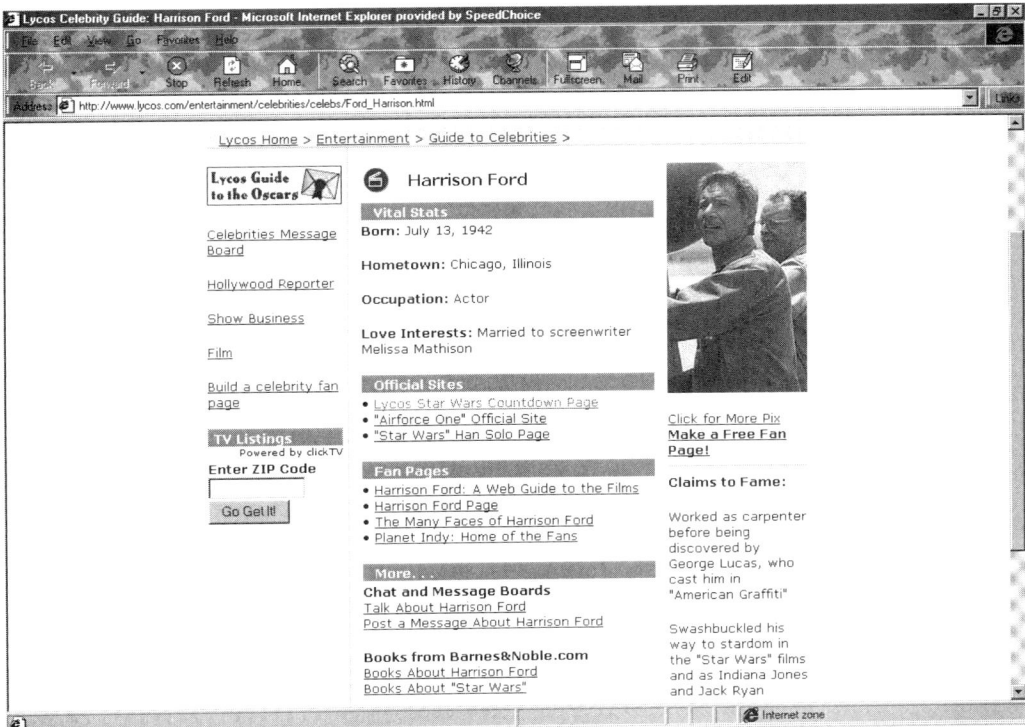

Harrison Ford (Lycos Network)
www.lycos.com/entertainment/celebrities/celebs/Ford_Harrison.html
Lycos' big Harrison Ford info page.

Harrison Ford - A Web Guide to the Films
www.smartlink.net/~deej7/harrison_ford.html

Harrison Ford - Viewing Room
www.smartlink.net/~deej7/pix.htm
Oh yeah - this is the place for Ford pix!

Harrison Ford Newsgroup
alt.fan.harrison-ford

Many Faces of Harrison Ford
www.geocities.com/Hollywood/Hills/2080/ford.html
Everything you should know about Harrison.

Planet Indy - Home of the Fans
http://indyjones.simplenet.com/
Han, meet Indy. Mr. Jones, meet Mr. Solo.

Lando Calrissian/Billy Dee Williams

The most suave of the Star Wars Trilogy characters, Lando Calrissian was aptly played by actor Billy Dee Williams. Sites below include books, humor, and tributes about Lando.

Bespin
www.starwars.com/locations/bespin/
A planet like Venus and/or Jupiter.

Cloud City
www.starwars.com/locations/cloud_city/
Afloat above Planet Bespin.

Lando Calrissian
www.starwars.com/characters/lando_calrissian/index.html
Soldier of Fortune & High Stakes Player - that's Lando.

Lando Calrissian - The Suavest Man In Space
www.geocities.com/Area51/3642/lando.htm
Lando tribute page with an obvious humor slant!

Lando Calrissian Adventures
www.ozemail.com.au/~alkenned/starwars/swlcst.htm
Lando & Han adventure books are linked here.

Lando Calrissian, Boba Fett, & Jabba The Hutt Books
www.geocities.com/Area51/Portal/7365/swpages/Lando.htm
Lando, Boba Fett & Jabba books - and links to others.

Lando's Star Wars Galaxy
www.geocities.com/Area51/Chamber/5094/index.html
A solid Lando fan site that is worth exploring.

Chewbacca/Peter Mayhew

Chewbacca the Wookiee – or Chewie – is the big furry lug played by actor Peter Mayhew. Find many favorite Chewie sites in the section below as well as a Peter Mayhew data site.

Absolute Chewbacca
www.xs4all.nl/~evdz/chewie/bio.html

Chewbacca Galleries (Taz's)
http://seconn4.yoda.com/~vader97/chewie/chewie.html
Chewie in glorious Wookiee-color!

Chewbacca Homepage, The New
http://users.ids.net/~mtavares/chewie.html
Cool Java tricks onboard - high tech for a Wookiee super site.

Chewbacca the Wookiee
www.starwars.com/characters/chewbacca/
Official Chewbacca Lucasfilm page.

Chewie's Web Page
www.music.uh.edu/~chewie/
Upbeat Chewie portal with sights, sounds, & fun.

Peter Mayhew - All-Media Guide
http://allmovie.com/cg/x.dll?UID=9:01:46|PM&p=avg&sql=EPeter|Mayhew
Peter Mayhew - Chewbacca - his AMG database page.

World 'O Chewbacca
http://members.aol.com/andrewm675/chewbacca/chewie.html
Chewie tribute site with videos, sounds, survey, & his bio.

Aliens, Creatures, & Things Oh My

Star Wars is full of aliens and creatures – some amusing, some alarming, some just plain cute. The Ewoks are not here; they have a section to themselves, later. Also, later, you will find the droids section.

Admiral Ackbar For President
www.geocities.com/Hollywood/Studio/6290/
Ackbar's a lot like Ronald Reagan, isn't he?

Alien Vocalizations
http://buteo.colorado.edu/~yosh/psi/system2/sounds/
A few alien AIFFs - but we need more!

Disgruntled Ewok & Malcontent Jawas Page
http://netdial.caribe.net/~orinoco/jae.html
Is life (& Star Wars browsing) too serious? While away time here.

Gammy's Altar
www.toshistation.com/gammy.htm
Pig, Gammy, Mork icons, sick humor. Twisted, Bent.

Gungan Forest
www.geocities.com/Hollywood/Club/5212

Jar Jar Binks, Gungan Outcast
http://meltingpot.fortunecity.com/greenwood/487/char/jarjar.html
Read about Jar Jar, but don't let him kiss you.

jawafortress.com
www.jawafortress.com/index2.html
Want to help build a good looking site? Check this...

Mysterious Characters
www.fortunecity.com/tattooine/lucas/66/bio-index.html

Official Creatures
www.starwars.com/creatures/
Official subject directory of Star Wars creatures.

Race & Species Descriptions
www.civila.com/hispania/obi-juan/species.htm
Inside info on alien species from A to Z to)"(.

Rogue 9's Animations
www.geocities.com/Baja/Mesa/4807/index2.html
Animations of Imperial craft, also B-wings & more.

Sand People
www.starwars.com/aliens/sandpeople/
Easily scared, but annoying!

Star Wars Movie Art
http://empire.res.wabash.edu/art/movies/index.htm
Paintings & pix used for movie production.

Tauntauns
www.starwars.com/creatures/tauntauns/
Afraid of the cold? Tauntauns can brave it.

Zaphoids MS Plus Themes
http://synergy.foo.net/~zaphoid/starwars/ms_plus_themes/
Themes for MSPlus; one for each day o' the month.

Ewoks

Ewoks are either loved or hated by Star Wars fans. Regardless, these furry forest-dwelling critters have had their own TV cartoon show and TV movies. Here's a number of Ewok sites.

Daisy Hill Village
www.angelfire.com/fl/yubcantina/daisyhill.html
Ewok village that's forming in England.

Ewok Adventure, The (1984)
http://uk.imdb.com/Title?0087225
Cast and specifics about the great Ewok Adventure movie.

Ewok Warrior Headquarters
www.angelfire.com/al/cybertrees/dwf.html
Ewok version of World News & War Report.

Ewoks
www.starwars.com/aliens/ewoks/
Ewoks according to Lucasfilms.

Ewoks - Star (Marvel) Comic Books Series
http://207.237.121.181/starwars/ewok01-06.html
15 Ewok Comic Book Covers in full color.

Ewoks [Star Wars: various titles] - TV Series 1985-87
http://us.imdb.com/Title?0088515
Tells us info about the Ewok TV series & its other titles.

Ewoks Photo Archive
www.geocities.com/Area51/Corridor/4307/ewoks.html
Small but colorful JPEG image gallery of Ewoks.

Ewoks Stink - What Ought to Happen to Ewoks
www.silcom.com/~pruth/ewok.html
Ewoks don't stink - do they? Whiner complains about Ewoks.

Ewoks Story
www.foxhome.com/animated/html/ewstory.htm
Children's story & activity book online - Fun with Ewoks.

Ewoks: The Battle For Endor (TV/Movie, 1985)
http://us.imdb.com/Title?0089110
Ewok TV movie that spawned the Ewok cartoons.

Guide to the Ewoks Cartoon Series
www.mvhs.srvusd.k12.ca.us/~ehall/ewoks.html
Ewok Cartoons listings: plots, author & date.

Droids, C-3PO, & R2-D2

When we think of droids – robots – in Star Wars, most people think of C-3PO and little R2-D2. Here's web sites for them, also sites describing other droids like Gonk and Threadwells.

Anthony Daniels - All-Media Guide
http://allmovie.com/cg/x.dll?UID=9:01:46|PM&p=avg&sql=B16857
Filmography of Anthony Daniels - golden droid with the silver leg.

C-3PO
www.starwars.com/characters/c-3p0/
C-3PO Official page.

C-3PO's Starpages
www.surfnet.fi/~zargon/swchan/c3pos.html
C-3PO continues to dispense dribble.

Droidcentric Art & Fan Fiction
http://members.aol.com/candyfish/gateway.htm
Fan fiction & pix in honor of 2 droids who've been 'round the block.

Droids
www.starwars.com/droids/
Official find-a-droid page.

Droidshrine - Oh, Thank The Maker
http://members.aol.com/candyfish/droidshrine.htm
Droids-R-Us (at least, R2 & C-3PO!)

Droidstuff
http://members.aol.com/fishdroid/Droidstuff.htm
Worth a quick look and quick laugh.

Essential Guide To Droids - Review
http://theforce.net/books/reviews/guidedroids.shtml
Online review of Essential Guide to Droids book.

Gonkite's Groovy Grotto & Glossary
http://members.aol.com/gonkite/index.htm
A get-you-acquainted glossary and Gonk info pages.

Kenny Baker - All-Media Guide
http://allmovie.com/cg/x.dll?UID=9:01:46|PM&p=avg&sql=B3418
There really was an actor named Kenny in that R2 unit!

R2-D2
www.starwars.com/characters/r2-d2/
Official R2-D2 page - the perfect little hero!

Star Wars Index to Characters
http://index.echostation.com/char.html
Information on ALL known characters & droids.

Threadwell's Techdome
www.jax-inter.net/users/datalore/starwars/
Techdome looks at Star Wars production "tek-nek-lee"

Most people don't know the name for the spider-like droids that roll along in Star Wars. Their true technical name is Threadwells.

Villains, Emperor Palpatine, & Jabba the Hut

There's no shortage of villains in Star Wars – there's Imperial officers, bounty hunters, criminal creatures, and others filled with the power of the Dark Side. Except for Darth Vader and Boba Fett who are listed in a separate sections, below you will find web sites that include such characters as the Emperor, Darth Maul, Jabba, etc. and the actors who played them.

2nd Empire - The Emperor's Wrath
http://members.tripod.com/~Dolmyn/empire.htm
Imperial database and mission statement at its worst.

Biker Scouts
www.starwars.com/characters/biker_scouts/
Official page for another Star Wars wild ride.

Boba Fett
http://members.aol.com/Fett15m/Fett.html
Almost everything you wanted to know about Boba Fett and friends.

Boba Fett & Darth Vader Galleries
www.geocities.com/Area51/Shadowlands/4918/gallery.html
Picture gallery of villains Boba Fett & Darth Vader.

Boba Fett Fan Club
www.bobafettfanclub.com
Everything else you wanted to know about Boba Fett and friends.

Boba Fett's Awesome Homepage
www.geocities.com/Area51/Lair/2192/Home.html
Fett & bounty hunter eye-candy & commentary.

Bossk's Homepage
www.geocities.com/Area51/Dimension/9216/
Info on bounty-hunter Bossk, also Star Wars images for wallpaper.

Bounty Hunters
http://people.a2000.nl/tvdbrink/
Searchable Bounty Hunter collection with pix.

Cult of Piett Member Sites
www.piett.org/link.html
Cult of Piett! His following is as great as it is humble.

Daala's Quarters
www.geocities.com/Area51/Chamber/4182/admiral.html
Ms. Admiral Daala - unifier of the Imperials.

Dark Hunters
www.homestead.com/DarkHunters/index.html
Bounty Hunter mini-portal.

Dark Lords of Sith
www.geocities.com/Hollywood/Location/1657/darthandexar.html
Feel the dark side. Webring site and Lords of Sith mini-portal.

Dark Side, The - Jedi Academy Lesson
www.jediacademy.com/dark.htm
Know thy enemy. Be good not evil. Here's why.

Darth Vader
www.starwars.com/characters/darth_vader/
Official jumping-off site for the series' most imposing character.

Emperor Palpatine
www.starwars.com/characters/palpatine/
So much evil, so little time.

Emperor Palpatine Archive
http://seconn4.yoda.com/~vader97/emperor/emperor.html
Emperor Palpatine in all his living (or deathly) color.

Evil Has a New Face - Darth Maul Galleries
www.dbmedia.org/maul/maultimedia/
It's intimidating just to look at this page; there's evil humor, too.

Fett Net
www.bobafett.net/page1.htm
Boba Fett news, views & more.

How to Build a Stormtrooper Costume
www.studiocreations.com/stormtrooper/
Wanna build your own stormtrooper uniform? Here's how.

Imperial Officers
www.geocities.com/Area51/Corridor/8727/imperial_officers.html
Big pix of big villains.

Imperial Pictures
www.geocities.com/Area51/Corridor/4312/imperial.html
Big JPEG pictures of Darth, basically.

Imperial TIE Fighter Hangar Bay, The
www.geocities.com/Area51/Shadowlands/4918/
Multimedia from the Imperial perspective.

Jabba The Hutt
www.starwars.com/characters/jabba_the_hutt/
Not a perfect date.

Jabba The Hutt Archives
http://seconn4.yoda.com/~vader97/jabba/jabba.html
Pictures, pictures & more pictures of Jabba

Jabba's Palace
www.starwars.com/locations/jabbas_palace/
A very unpleasant place; did you squirm in your theatre seat?

Jabba's Palace - Outer-Rim Multimedia
http://outer-rim.net/multimedia/sounds/Palace
"I will not give up my favorite decoration...Han Solo!" - Jabba.

Jabba's Palace Movie
www.telecom.csuhayward.edu/~aleung/jabba's.mov
QuickTime video of Jabba's Palace.

Lando Calrissian, Boba Fett, & Jabba The Hutt Books
www.geocities.com/Area51/Portal/7365/swpages/Lando.htm
Lando, Boba Fett & Jabba books - and links to others.

Mandalorian Portfolio
http://scifi.simplenet.com/starwars/prequels/portfolio/mand/mand.html
Like an spreading cancerous evil - these Mandalorians!

MaulNet.Com
www.maultnet.com
dbmedia's Darth Maul super site - evil, evil, evil (and recommended)

Official Dave Prowse Web Site
www.daveprowse.com/
Dave Prowse DESERVES to win an academy award.

Palpatine Portfolio
http://scifi.simplenet.com/starwars/prequels/portfolio/pal/palpatine.html
Watch out for this fellow - there's no end to evil!

Peter Cushing - All-Media Guide
http://allmovie.com/cg/x.dll?UID=9:01:46|PM&p=avg&sql=B16338
Films & biography of the horror icon & A New Hope villain.

Ryan's Star Wars Pictures
> http://members.spree.com/sci-fi/swrealm/Pictures.htm
> Pix in all shapes, sizes, & sorts - cruise on through!

Salacious Crumb
> http://cs.wilpaterson.edu/~led/Sand/main/Crumb/Crumb
> Salacious Crumb's influence on US History.

Salacious Crumb Homepage
> www.madbbs.com/~salaciouscrumb/INDEX.HTM
> Salacious Crumb - a character, a band, a Sword of Chaos gamer, a legend!

Sith Lords
> www.geocities.com/Hollywood/Location/1657/dvek.html
> Bios of favorite villains.

Sith Lords Star Wars Quiz
> www.geocities.com/Hollywood/Location/1657/quiz.html
> You think you know your trivia? See what you know about bad guys.

Sith Powers
> www.wcug.wwu.edu/~paradox/sithpowers.html
> Villains should at least know what they're doing.

Star Wars Gear
> www.gogs32.freeserve.co.uk/gear.htm
> Imperial craft animations, lightsaber lore. Different.

Star Wars Sounds (Imperial)
> www.aaronklaassen.com/starwars/swwavs.htm
> Quotes from villains/Imperials in WAV sound format.

Stormtrooper HQ
> http://www.ausnet.net.au/~jaseod/stormtrooper/stormtrooper.htm
> Stormtrooper gear JPEG images.

Ways of the Sith, The
> www.geocities.com/Hollywood/Location/1657/sith.html
> Monthly online magazine featuring the dark side's perspective.

Welcome to the Mandalorian Sector
> www.geocities.com/Area51/Cavern/5723/index2.html
> Early Fett site draws heavily from comic book information.

Zaphoids MS Plus Themes
> http://synergy.foo.net/~zaphoid/starwars/ms_plus_themes/
> Themes for MSPlus; one for each day o' the month.

Darth Vader/David Prowse & James Earl Jones

Played on screen by David Prowse, but using the dominating voice of James Earl Jones, the character of Darth Vader needs no introduction. Can you believe that cute little Ani grows up to be so bad?

Dark Lords of Sith
> www.method.org/sith
> Bios of favorite villains.

Darth Vader
> www.starwars.com/characters/darth_vader/
>> Official jumping-off site for the series' most imposing character.

David Prowse - All-Media Guide
> http://allmovie.com/cg/x.dll?UID=9:01:46|PM&p=avg&sql=B57960
>> Filmography & bio of Mr. Vader - David Prowse.

Duel of Darth Vader & Obi-wan Kenobi Video
> www.telecom.csuhayward.edu/~aleung/dv_ken.mov
>> Clip of Darth & ol' Ben wearing out batteries on their sabers.

Index of Multimedia Sounds.star.wars
> http://info.fuw.edu.pl/multimedia/sounds.star.wars/
>> Sound clips - mostly Darth Vader - from fuw university.

Injuries to Darth Vader
> www.theforce.net/swtc/injuries.html
>> Darth took a lot of physical punishment!

James Earl Jones - IMDb
> http://us.imdb.com/
>> Career database info on James Earl Jones.

Orin_J Kingdom
> www.qogs32.freeserve.co.uk/page1.htm
>> Does Darth like neon blues and greens!?

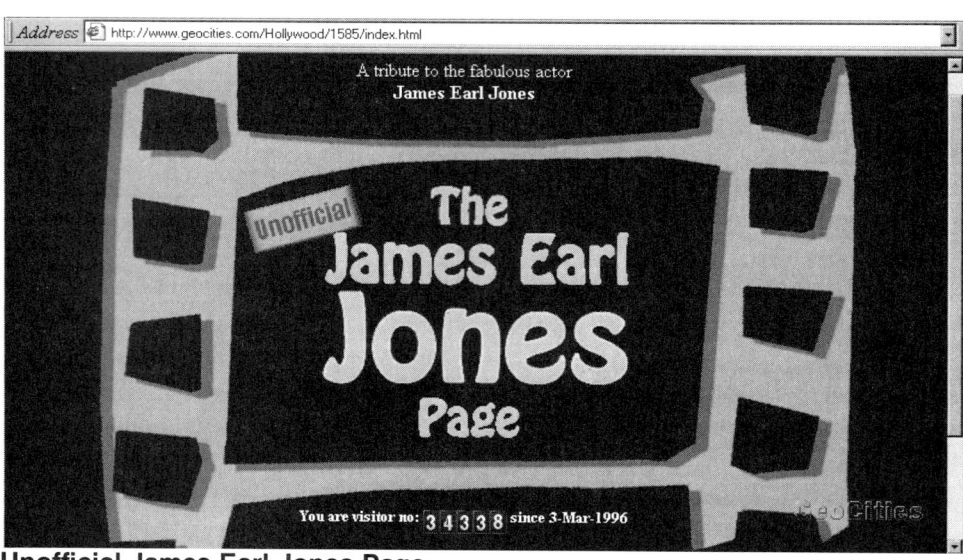

Unofficial James Earl Jones Page
> www.geocities.com/Hollywood/1585/index.html
>> Unofficial page, but some good James Earl Jones material!

Vader's Helmet Interior (museum piece)
> www.geocities.com/Area51/Vault/3227/smithsonian/9.htm
>> Vader's helmet on museum display.

What Does Vader's Chestplate Say?
> www.theforce.net/rouser/chestplate.shtml
>> There's a Hebrew message here!

Boba Fett -- Coolest of the Bounty Hunters

Boba has his own cult following and also his own section in this Incredible Internet Guide.

Boba Fett
http://members.aol.com/Fett15m/Fett.html
Almost everything you wanted to know about Boba Fett.

Boba Fett & Darth Vader Galleries
www.geocities.com/Area51/Shadowlands/4918/gallery.html
Picture gallery of villains Boba Fett & Darth Vader.

Boba Fett - Ultimate Star Wars Multimedia Page
www.geocities.com/Area51/Crater/3234/fett.html
16 Fett images, plus 2 quotes & animation of Slave 1.

Boba Fett at the Smithsonian
www.geocities.com/Area51/Vault/3227/smithsonian/1.htm
Wax-museum Boba Fett from the Smithsonian Exhibit.

Boba Fett Fan Club
www.bobafettfanclub.com
Everything else you wanted to know about Boba Fett.

Boba Fett's Awesome Homepage
www.geocities.com/Area51/Lair/2192/Home.html
Fett & bounty hunter eye-candy & commentary.

Boba Fett's Backyard
www.geocities.com/Area51/Stargate/9082/index.html
New site in the geocities Star Wars neighborhood.

Boba Fett's Home Sector
www.geocities.com/Hollywood/Set/5760/
A Boba Fett homepage on the geocities' net.

Boba Fett's Lair
www.geocities.com/Area51/Vault/3227/lair.htm
There's more to explore in this Lair.

Bond's Star Wars Page
http://home.tampabay.rr.com/bond/starwars.htm
Some unusual Pictures and an animated Boba Fett.

Britt's Boba Fett Site
www.geocities.com/Area51/Quadrant/2581/frmemain.html
Have a Fett-ish? You have to visit this Boba Site.

Dark Hunters
www.homestead.com/DarkHunters/index.html
Bounty Hunter mini-portal.

Fett Net
www.bobafett.net/page1.htm
Boba Fett news, views & more.

Han Solo Condemns Me to a Digestful Fate Video
www.telecom.csuhayward.edu/~aleung/fett.mov
Bye-bye Boba at the Sarlaac creature video.

Jason's Star Wars Page
http://http.tamu.edu:8000/~jpc6754/starwars.html
Slim pickings, but does have Boba Fett pix.

Lando Calrissian, Boba Fett, & Jabba The Hutt Books
www.geocities.com/Area51/Portal/7365/swpages/Lando.htm
Lando, Boba Fett & Jabba books - and links to others.

Pictures: Boba Fett & Others
http://pweb.netcom.com/~fragger/art.html
Pix of Boba Fett and - and - and - Muppets?

Quizzes from the Boba Fett Home Sector
www.geocities.com/Hollywood/Set/5760/
Trivia, arranged by Star Wars topics.

Skywalker's Star Wars Page
www.usmo.com/~starwars/index.html
Some pretty funny stuff, also serious image galleries.

Taz's Boba Fett Galleries
http://seconn4.yoda.com/~vader97/boba/boba.html
4 frames-worth of Boba Fett images!

Welcome to the Mandalorian Sector
www.geocities.com/Area51/Cavern/5723/index2.html
Early Fett site draws heavily from comic book information.

You Are Now a Prisoner in The Entertainment Cell
www.geocities.com/Hollywood/Set/1630/main.html
Your host: Boba Fett!

Zaphoids MS Plus Themes
http://synergy.foo.net/~zaphoid/starwars/ms_plus_themes/
Themes for MSPlus; one for each day o' the month.

Other Major & Minor Characters

Here are web sites that feature minor characters, such as Wedge and Porkins, or that list any or all Star Wars characters.

Blueharvest.net Star Wars Images
www.blueharvest.net/images
"It excels at it." - C-3PO. A "must see" image gallery.

Bossk's Homepage
www.geocities.com/Area51/Dimension/9216/
Info on bounty-hunter Bossk, also Star Wars images for wallpaper.

Characters of Star Wars Official Index
www.starwars.com/
Official subject directory of Star Wars characters - most of them.

Compendium, The
www.wcug.wwu.edu/~paradox/images/hyper/
Not the prettiest site, but one of the fullest!

Completely Unofficial Star Wars Encyclopedia 6th Edition
www.mindspring.com/~bobvitas/swenc.htm
Something about everyone - cast, crew, characters - all!

Delta Source
www.jedinet.com/delta/
Databases of events, characters, vehicles, weapons, more.

Don Post's Studios Star Wars Masks
www.nightmarefactory.com/starwars.html
Good selection of masks for fun, parties, or collecting.

Episode 1 Characters Addresses
www.geocities.com/Area51/Nebula/5101/main.html
Growing list of Episode 1 actors' addresses.

Hollywood Online Database
http://moviepeople.hollywood.com/
Good, quick way to find film & celebrity info!

Index (by Pablo Hildago) Hosted by Echo Station
http://index.echostation.com/
Indexes arranged by topic for ease of access.

Internet Movie Database (IMDb)
http://us.imdb.com/
Easy to use data on moviemakers, stars, & flix - bigger than the Empire.

Jedinet Pictures
www.jedinet.com/multimedia/pics/index.htm
Rates as the finest JPEG image gallery on this rock.

Knight Hammer
    www.geocities.com/Area51/Chamber/4182/index.html
        Good content for a site with an Imperial overcoat!

Main Characters (& Minor Characters) Prequel Spoilers
    http://meltingpot.fortunecity.com/greenwood/487/char/clist.html
        Get the skinny on the EP1 Characters here.

Masks - Star Wars
    www.anniescostumes.com/swmask.htm
        Trilogy character masks - most are full-head latex.

Movie Themes - WinFiles.com
    www.winfiles.com/apps/98/themes-movie.html
        Windows 95/98 Star Wars themes ala carte!

My Star Wars Experience
    http://seclab.cs.ucdavis.edu/~wetmore/camb/hope/
        What it's like to play a bit part in the Special Editions.

Nightmare Factory Star Wars Children's Costumes
    www.nightmarefactory.com/starwark.html
        Trilogy costumes for children - also links to adult & masks sites.

Now & Then
    www.usmo.com/~starwars/now&then/now&then.html
        Minor characters struggling in the world of entertainment.

Porkins Central
    http://web.gx.net/red6/Porkins/index.htm
        A fitting tribute to a true rebel & a so-so pilot.

Star Wars Accessories, Props, & Collectibles
    www.nightmarefactory.com/starwarz.html
        Collectibles from nightmarefactory: high-$$ down to economy.

Star Wars Fan Mail Addresses
    www.geocities.com/Area51/Nebula/5101/fanmail.html
        Addresses with autographed pix of Trilogy actors.

Star Wars Index to Characters
    http://index.echostation.com/char.html
        Information on ALL known characters & droids.

Stv1's Star Wars Characters
    http://members.tripod.com/~stv1/index-2.html
        Thumbnails of Star Wars characters.

Wedge Newgroup
    alt.fan.wedge

Why Wedge Rules
    www.silcom.com/~pruth/wedge.html
        Wedge, you really deserve more appreciation!

Star Wars in Ententertainment

Foremost in this Entertainment Chapter are the Star Wars web sites for the Star Wars movies. Star Wars is also big in the comic book world, and has had some presence on Television and Radio. You will also find sections for web sites that relate to movie and entertainment production generally, including sites dedicated to movers and shakers such as George Lucas.

The Films

Cast Lists & Cast Filmographies

Who was in the Star Wars films, and what other films/presentations were cast members in? The former is called cast lists; the latter are called filmographies.

Capeman's Prequel Homepage
http://members.aol.com/capeman69/index.html
A variety of Prequel news, peeks, & rumors.

Cast & Characters (Prequel)
http://members.aol.com/capeman69/cast.html
Early Prequel cast & characters roster.

Cast Lists - Knight Hammer
www.geocities.com/Area51/Chamber/4182/cast_tpm.html
Cast lists of "Imperial people" in each Star Wars movie.

Completely Unofficial Star Wars Encyclopedia 6th Edition
www.mindspring.com/~bobvitas/swenc.htm
Something about everyone - cast, crew, characters - all!

Dagobah
www.execpc.com/~zerob/Dagobah.html
Filmography of Prequel actors, also news, images.

Empire Strikes Back, The (1980)
http://us.imdb.com/Title?0080684
Film, cast, credits & links to almost everything you need for Empire.

Eye On Episode 1 - Cast & Crew
http://starwars.tierranet.com/episode1/frame4.html
Characters with actor's name. GIF pix of cast and crew

George Lucas - All Media Guide
http://allmovie.com/cg/x.dll?UID=9:01:46|PM&p=avg&sql=B100308
All-Media Guide all-out George Lucas info page!

George Walton Lucas Jr.
http://us.imdb.com/M/person-exact?Lucas%2C+George
Movie database info on Star Wars creator.

Internet Movie Database (IMDb)
http://us.imdb.com/
Easy to use data on moviemakers, stars, & flix - bigger than the Empire.

James Earl Jones - IMDb
http://us.imdb.com/
Career database info on James Earl Jones.

John Williams (II) - IMDb
http://us.imdb.com/M/person-exact?Williams%2C+John+(II)
All about the Greatest Composer on 12 systems.

Journal of the Whills Cast of the New Trilogy
www.geocities.com/Hollywood/Set/8008
Compare this old cast list with the real one.

Liam Neeson Appreciation Pages
www.geocities.com/Hollywood/Set/6510/index2.html
Neeson info, filmography. E-mail him a message, maybe.

Many Faces of Harrison Ford
www.geocities.com/Hollywood/Hills/2080/ford.html
Everything you should know about Harrison.

Natalie Portman Filmography
www.geocities.com/Hollywood/Lot/7181/filmography.html
Great Natalie filmography with pix from each movie.

New Star Wars, Episode 1
www.starwars.com/episode-i/features/intro/
Pre-release run-down; this could be a web site collectible later.

Prequel Crew
http://theforce.net/prequels/oldPreq/crew/crew.html
They made Episode 1.

Return of the Jedi (1983) - IMDb
http://us.imdb.com/Title?0086190
Facts & cast for Return of the Jedi from the Internet Movie Database.

Sci-fi Movie Clips
http://graffiti.u-bordeaux.fr/MAPBX/roussel/anim-e_03f.shtml
Big Sci-fi movie galleries from a French site.

Star Wars (1977) - IMDb
> http://us.imdb.com/Title?0076759
>> Facts about & great links to all involved in the 1977 movie.

STAR WARS - Welcome to the Official Site
> www.starwars.com
>> "Must see" official Lucasfilm Star Wars site.

Star Wars Database Prequel Cast
> www.swdatabase.com/prequels/cast.html
>> Early Prequel cast list database.

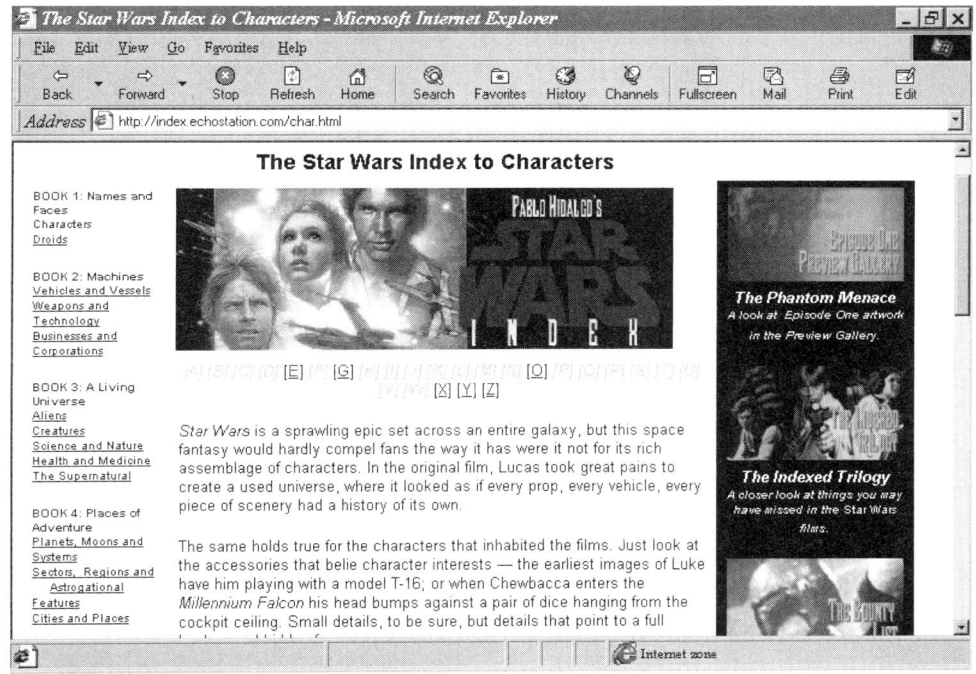

Star Wars Index to Characters
> http://index.echostation.com/char.html
>> Information on ALL known characters & droids.

Star Wars: Episode 1 - The Phantom Menace
> http://us.imdb.com/Title?0120915
>> Straightforward movie data on EP1 from Internet Movie db.

The Prequels

The Phantom Menace (Episode 1) & Prequels

Prequels is a term that was coined to describe the Star Wars movies that, in time frame, come before the original three Star Wars movies, known as the Trilogy (Episodes 4, 5, 6). So, even though the Prequels were made "after" the Star Wars Trilogy, the scenes take place before Star Wars, A New Hope (Episode 4). Each Prequel is numbered Episode 1, 2, or 3. Although most of the entries in this large section of web sites are for Episode 1, The Phantom Menace, you will also find web sites with information about Episodes 2 and 3.

Aaron's Star Wars Toy & Comic Price Guides Checklist
www.continet.com/aaronsmagic/pretoys/1Check.html
Checklist of new Kenner Prequel action figures.

All-Media Guide
http://allmovie.com/cg/x.dll?UID=9:01:46%7CPM&p=avg&sql=A179455
Read about it, connect to other good sites, vote in the survey.

Anakin's Hovel Set Plan
http://members.xoom.com/_XOOM/mb_starwars/anakin/index.htm
Blueprint of Anakin's house used for movie production.

Ask A Question - AllExperts.com
www.allexperts.com/tv/starwars.shtml
They provide the expert; you ask Prequel/Star Wars questions.

Capeman's Prequel Homepage
http://members.aol.com/capeman69/index.html
A variety of Prequel news, peeks, & rumors.

Capeman's Prequel Production Pictures
http://members.aol.com/CapeMan69/pic.html
Pix from the Prequel shooting locations.

Cast & Characters (Prequel)
http://members.aol.com/capeman69/cast.html
Early Prequel cast & characters roster.

Chewie's Web Site Pictures & Sounds
www.music.uh.edu/~chewie/ps.html
Phantom Menace sound clips, also South Park & Star Wars quotes.

Complete Star Wars Prequel Page
http://outland.cyberwar.com/~smad//Prequels.html
A rather good commentary, with good links, too

Dagobah
www.execpc.com/~zerob/Dagobah.html
Filmography of Prequel actors, also news, images.

Droopy McCool's Star Wars Page
www.geocities.com/SunsetStrip/Disco/1283/starwars.html
Phantom Menace action and main character pix.

Episode X
www.sevaan.com/starwars/
Multimedia page dedicated to the Prequels.

Episode 1 Characters Addresses
www.geocities.com/Area51/Nebula/5101/main.html
Growing list of Episode 1 actors' addresses.

Episode 1 Widevision Cards
www.sevaan.com/starwars/fanart/topps.htm
Collectible card images from Topps/Savaan Franks.

Episode 1: Phantom Menace Ship & Vehicle List
http://theforce.net/prequels/oldPreq/ships/ships.shtml
Prequel craft, vehicles, pix & specs.

Episode 1: The Phantom Menace
www.angelfire.com/sc/francis915/page2.html
Episode 1 characters and trailer pix.

Episode 2 at Sci-Fi Advance
http://scifi.simplenet.com/starwars/prequels/episode2.shtml
Episode 2 and 3 data is accumulating!

Evil Has a New Face - Darth Maul Galleries
www.dbmedia.org/maul/maultimedia/
It's intimidated just looking at this page; there's evil humor, too.

Eye On Episode 1
http://starwars.tierranet.com/episode1/frames.html
Co-op news and comments page by 2 Star Wars veterans.

Eye On Episode 1 - Cast & Crew
http://starwars.tierranet.com/episode1/frame4.html
Characters with actor's name. GIF pix of cast and crew

Eye On Episode 1 - News & Rumors
http://starwars.tierranet.com/episode1/frame3.html
News, rumors - plenty of details, foreign & domestic.

Graham's Star Wars & Homepage
www.angelfire.com/ga/glf/index.html
Prequel & box office info featured on this new multimedia page.

Hanger, The
www.jedinights.com/hanger
Brand new Prequel gaming site: TPM & Pods'R'us.

Images of Episode 1
http://plaza.harmonix.ne.jp/~m-falcon/Image_of_Episode1.html
Poster & image collection (will probably be updated often).

Institute For Impure Science - Star Wars
www.ifis.org.uk/p.cgi/multimedia/starwars/
UK site offers versions of Episode 1 & humor videos.

Jedi Paradise Episode 1
http://members.aol.com/bigeoz/JPhome.htm
Grab bag of Episode 1; news, products, galleries.

Journal of the Whills Cast of the New Trilogy
www.geocities.com/Hollywood/Set/8008
Compare this old cast list with the real one.

Journal of the Whills Star Wars Prequel Trilogy
www.geocities.com/Hollywood/Set/8008/prequels.html
Prequels 1, 2, 3, with cast, characters, effects & art

Land of The Prequels
www.the-mattman.com/starwars/
News, Galleries, characters for Episode 1.

Logic - The Whill Journal
www.geocities.com/Area51/Stargate/4465/logic.htm
Speculation on what we'll see in Prequels 2 & 3.

Main Characters (& Minor Characters) Prequel Spoilers
http://meltingpot.fortunecity.com/greenwood/487/char/clist.html
Get the skinny on the EP1 Characters here.

Martin Bond's Episode 1 Site
http://members.xoom.com/_XOOM/mb_starwars/index.html
Prequel videos, images, wallpaper, Anakin's House.

MaulNet.Com
www.maultnet.com
dbmedia's Darth Maul super site - evil, evil, evil (and recommended)

Marua Sector
www.marua.com/index2.html
New, developing semi-semi-mega all-purpose site.

Matt's Home Page
www.geocities.com/Area51/Rampart/6867/starwars.htm
Prequel text information (in development).

NaboOnline
www.naboonline.com
Wealth of information and variety of Prequel categories.

Phantom Menace - The Characters As We Know Them
www.allexperts.com/tv/swchar.shtml
Humorous run-down of Prequel characters.

Phantom Menace Mania
http://get.to/jedi/
Great variety of Episode 1 images, sounds, video.

Media — The Phantom Menace (Episode 1) & Prequels

Phantom Menace Mania Chat Room
http://pages.preferred.com/~whitesk/starwars/chatroom.html
Chat room for EP1 Phantom Menace comments.

Phantom Menace Site, The
www.users.wineasy.se/doot/starwars/index.html
Prequel site focusing mostly on main actors and Nat Portman.

Prequel Art Originals (the force.net)
www.theforce.net/museum/g_prequels/
Original Prequel art pix, posters, wallpaper.

Prequel Center
www.theprequelcenter.8m.com/
New site that's leaning toward Prequel multimedia.

Prequel Crew
http://theforce.net/prequels/oldPreq/crew/crew.html
They made Episode 1.

Prequel FAQ (Jedinet)
www.jedinet.com/prequels/faq/
Basic FAQs about the Prequel.

Prequel Images from Rancor Pit
www.sentex.net/~dah/prequel/images.html
Assortment of wide JPEG Prequel images.

Prequel Locations
http://theforce.net/prequels/oldPreq/locations/locations.shtml
Wonderful details and reports on Prequel locations.

Prequel Pics Page
http://outland.cyberwar.com/~smad//pics5.html
Well-organized and deep Prequel pix.

Prequel Rumors
http://members.aol.com/capeman69/rumors.html
Rumors, news, and facts surrounding the Prequels.

Prequel Spoilers
http://fly.to/prequel-spoilers
Before the movie was released, this spoiled it all!

Prequel Storyline, The (the force.net)
http://theforce.net/prequels/oldPreq/plot2.html
Prequel stories - generally - & birth order list.

Prequel Watch on Jedinet
www.jedinet.com/prequels/
Prequel news, calendar, discussions - lively & colorful.

Prequels UK
> http://members.tripod.com/Jona82/
>> Info on all 3 Prequels, plus pix, chat, forums, and more.

Prequels, The
> www.wavefront.com/~chad/starwars/prequel/index.htm
>> Clean Prequel site - hopefully it'll add more quality & quantity.

Prequels.com, The
> http://theprequels.com/main.htm
>> Lively, colorful Prequel site - mucho variety!

Rancor Pit, The
> http://fly.to/rancorpit
>> New high-energy site that hopes to do it all!

Roderick Vonhogen's Virtual Edition
> www.virtualedition.com/
>> Be treated to higher-end features on this great Netherland's site.

Second Prequel - What's Next
> www.allexperts.com/tv/swprequel1.shtml
>> They're guessing what'll be in the next Prequel. Oh, really?

Star Wars (Hollywood Liz)
> www.geocities.com/Hollywood/1165/starwars.html
>> Good Prequel pix and info, also reviews.

Star Wars - The Prequels
> www.nwlink.com/~gareth/starwars.htm
>> Variety of JPEG images - includes the Tunisia site map.

Star Wars Collectibles (tnc Universe)
> www.tncmagic.com/starwars/00masks.htm
>> Variety of collectibles, costumes, masks, CCG sets, & party gear.

Star Wars Database Interviews
> www.swdatabase.com/pages/interviews.html
>> Hot tip: Interviews let out secrets.

Star Wars Database Prequel Cast
> www.swdatabase.com/prequels/cast.html
>> Early Prequel cast list database.

Star Wars: Episode 1 - The Phantom Menace
> http://us.imdb.com/Title?0120915
>> Straightforward movie data on Episode 1 from Internet Movie Database.

Media　A New Hope (Episode 4)　　　37

Theed.net - City Beyond the Swamp
www.theed.net/
New site with news and tricks up its sleeve (more promised).

Timecruiser's Prequel Pictures
www.angelfire.com/co/Timecruiser/Menacepics.html
All types of images from the Prequel pre-release.

Trencher ALB's Episode 1: The Phantom Menace
http://members.tripod.com/trencheralb/index2.html
A steady, dependable Prequel news site.

Unofficial Episode 1 Homepage (Kentucky area)
http://come.to/tpmky/
News, comics, discussion with local Kentucky flavor.

Watto's Junkyard
www.wattosjunkyard.com/
Among our favorite-est Prequel sites - good variety & style.

Watto's Junkyard Downloads
www.wattosjunkyard.com/downloads.html
Good selection of QuickTime Prequel videos & game demos.

Whill Journal, The
www.geocities.com/Area51/Stargate/4465/
Looking ahead to the millenium Prequels.

Winse & Cameron's Episode 1 Pictures
www.geocities.com/TelevisionCity/Stage/5455/episode1.html
A good early Prequel photo site.

Winse & Cameron's Star Wars Section
www.geocities.com/TelevisionCity/Stage/5455/starwars.html
Prepared for the Phantom Menace.

A New Hope (Episode 4)

"A New Hope" is the official name for the incredible 1977 movie called simply "Star Wars," which introduced us to the Star Wars story.

A New Hope Video Clips
http://home.multiweb.nl/~bramenpim/staranh.htm
A New Hope AVI & QuickTime video clips.

A New Hope Wallpaper
www.jedinet.com/multimedia/windows/wallpaper/index.htm
Wallpaper selections for Star Wars A New Hope.

All-Media Guide Star Wars
http://allmovie.com/cg/x.dll?UID=9:01:46|PM&p=avg&sql=A46636
Obviously, the AMG people are big fans - good database.

Hello There Video of Obi-Wan Kenobi
http://users.why.net/radrock/sounds/hello.avi
It's a video of the first time we hear Obi-Wan speak.

Lost Scenes Compiled by Roderick VonHogen
    www.virtualedition.com/lost_scenes/index.html
        We're looking for "outtake images" here.

Sound America A New Hope
    http://soundamerica.com/sounds/movies/J-S/Star_Wars/A_New_Hope/
        Good WAV files from original Star Wars.

Star Wars (1977) - IMDb
    http://us.imdb.com/Title?0076759
        Facts about & great links to all involved in the 1977 movie.

Star Wars (A New Hope) MP3 Sounds
    www.psyc.canterbury.ac.nz/pgrad/carr/starwars.html
        MP3 Sound file quotes from the first movie.

Star Wars A New Hope Special Edition FAQ
    www.jax-inter.net/users/datalore/starwars/anhindex.htm
        Details on the new & changed scenes in Special Edition A New Hope.

Star Wars Final Draft by George Lucas
    www.geocities.com/Area51/Stargate/9082/Newhope.txt
        George Lucas' final draft for the original Star Wars.

Star Wars Trilogy Cards
    www.geocities.com/Area51/Corridor/4323/cards.html
        A New Hope storyline trading cards.

Star Wars, Adventures of Luke Starkiller
    www.geocities.com/Area51/Stargate/9082/swd3.txt
        Interesting third draft of Star Wars by George Lucas.

Stars Wars First Screenplay Draft
    www.geocities.com/Area51/Stargate/9082/swd1.txt
        5/74 Lucas rough draft.

Ted's Star Wars Pictures
    http://dvader.mit.edu/old/starwars.html
        Modest but neat collection of wide Star Wars action pix.

The Star Wars - Masthead: Adventures of The Starkiller
    www.geocities.com/Area51/Stargate/9082/swd2.txt
        Interesting variation of Lucas' original Star Wars, with name change.

Trilogy Blooper Guide
    www.egosystem.com/starwars/bloopers.html
        Trilogy nit-piks and bloopers by the dozens.

Empire Strikes Back (Episode 5)

Web sites that pay particular attention to the Episode 5, The Empire Strikes Back.

Empire Strikes Back Portfolio
    www.bantha-fodder.com/esbport/
        Original art by Ralph McQuarrie, top Star Wars artist.

Empire Strikes Back Special Edition FAQ
    www.jax-inter.net/users/datalore/starwars/esbindex.htm
        Commentaries on Special Edition scenes in Empire.

Empire Strikes Back Transcript
www.geocities.com/Area51/Stargate/9082/Empire.txt
Complete transcript of Star Wars' 2nd feature.

Empire Strikes Back Video Clips
http://home.multiweb.nl/~bramenpim/staresb.htm
Video clips & finds about the Empire Strikes Back.

Empire Strikes Back, The
www.starwars.com/episode-v/
Official Lucasfilms movie site, with the basic goodies.

Empire Strikes Back, The (1980)
http://us.imdb.com/Title?0080684
Film, cast, credits & links to almost everything you need for Empire.

Sound America Empire Strikes Back
http://soundamerica.com/sounds/movies/J-S/Star_Wars/Empire_Strikes_Back/
Many WAV sound files from Empire Strikes Back.

Trilogy Blooper Guide
www.egosystem.com/starwars/bloopers.html
Trilogy nit-piks and bloopers by the dozens.

Return of the Jedi (Episode 6)

Web sites that pay particular attention to the sixth & final episode: Return of the Jedi.

A-wing fighter
www.starwars.com/vehicles/a-wing/
A-wing fighters official Lucasfilms page.

B-wing Fighter
www.starwars.com/vehicles/b-wing/
Admiral Ackbar's contribution to the fleet at the Battle of Endor.

Bill's Dagobah Page
www.geocities.com/Area51/Dimension/6975/starwars.html
Sights & sounds of Return of the Jedi from a Dagobah site

Fierce Battle of Endor Video
www.telecom.csuhayward.edu/~aleung/fight.mov
Video of the Battle of Endor

Return of the Jedi
www.starwars.com/episode-vi/
Official movie site - its update could give us more info.

Return of the Jedi (1983) - IMDb
http://us.imdb.com/Title?0086190
Facts & cast for Return of the Jedi from the Internet Movie Database.

Return of the Jedi Special Edition FAQ
   www.jax-inter.net/users/datalore/starwars/rojindex.htm
      Commentaries on Special Edition scenes in Return of the Jedi.

Return of the Jedi Video Clips
   http://home.multiweb.nl/~bramenpim/starrotj.htm
      Return of the Jedi video clips collection.

Sound America Return of the Jedi
   http://soundamerica.com/sounds/movies/J-S/Star_Wars/Return_of_the_Jedi/
      Return of the Jedi WAV sound files by the dozens.

Speeder Bike Chase Video
   www.telecom.csuhayward.edu/~aleung/speeder.mov
      Video of speeder bike chase on the forest Moon of Endor.

Trilogy Blooper Guide
   www.egosystem.com/starwars/bloopers.html
      Trilogy nit-piks and bloopers by the dozens.

Trilogy Special Editions

"Special Editions" are the re-releases of the original Star Wars Trilogy films. These include new scenes and other changes, which are featured in some manner in the web sites that follow.

Bogus Star Wars Homepage
   www.cinenet.net/~agrapha/StarNet/SW.html
      Special effects & comments from Special Editions are featured.

E187vader's Special Edition Page
   www.geocities.com/Area51/Vault/6782/special.html
      Select pix from the Special Editions.

NetJunctions Movies
   www.netjunction.com/starwars/movies.htm
      12 QuickTime video movies; includes Trilogy Specials.

Special Edition Annotations
   www.theforce.net/swse/
      Paul Ens commentaries on Special Edition scenes.

Special Edition Screen Shots
   http://members.aol.com/T65Pilot/speced.html
      Screenshot GIFs of new Trilogy scenes.

Special Editions, The
   http://scifi.simplenet.com/starwars/special_edition/index.html
      Special edition galleries and reviews (closed 1/31/98)

Trilogy Special Edition FAQs
   www.jax-inter.net/users/datalore/starwars/sepage.htm
      Special Edition details, images, and explanations.

Flix -- Other Notable Films

Flix refers to "movies." Here you will find other notable movies featuring Star Wars main characters, also movies that have a relationship to Star Wars.

Air Force One
www.spe.sony.com/movies/airforceone/home_swf.html
Wasn't Harrison The Prez in this One?

American Graffiti
www.lucasfan.com/amgraf/index2.html
"Where were you in '62?" Lucas' 1st hit movie!

Cinescape Online
www.cinescape.com/
Rumors & spoilers on just about everything!

Ewok Adventure, The (1984)
http://uk.imdb.com/Title?0087225
Cast and specifics about the great Ewok Adventure movie.

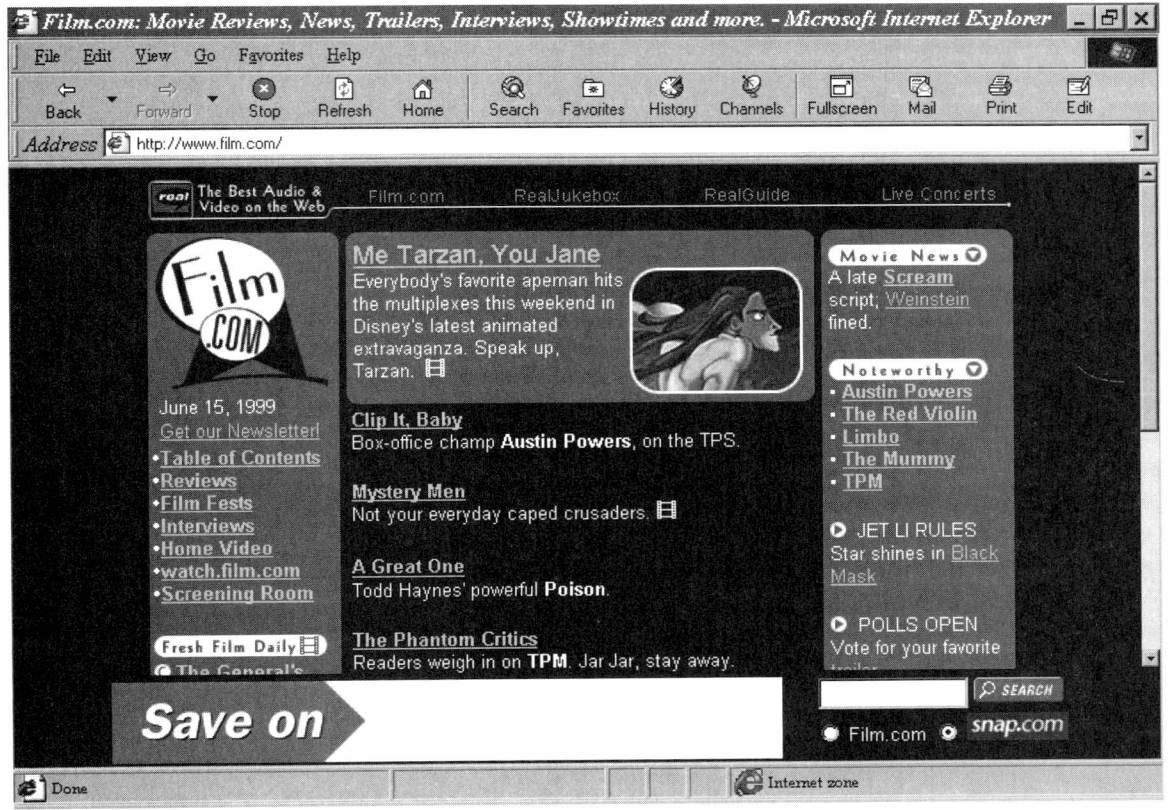

Film.com
www.film.com
It's gotta lot of film/movie/video stuff!

Hardware Wars - IMDb
http://us.imdb.com/Title?0077658
1st of the great Star Wars spoof videos. Here's the data.

Harrison Ford - A Web Guide to the Films
  www.smartlink.net/~deej7/harrison_ford.html
    Harrison - This ones for you! There is no "I" in "hero."

Movie References
  www.jedinet.com/multimedia/references/ref-movies.html
    Star Wars-isms that have made it into other movies.

Nocturne's Pulp Fiction
  www.skipnet.com/~nocturne/pulpfiction.html
    We had to include Samuel L. Jackson's breakout movie.

Phantom Menace Movie Poster
  http://ucaswww.mcm.uc.edu/english/hall/sw1.htm
    Need a real movie poster of Episode 1 or another movie?

Planet Indy - Home of the Fans
  http://indyjones.simplenet.com/
    Han, meet Indy. Mr. Jones, meet Mr. Solo.

Spaceballs - IMDb
  http://us.imdb.com/Title?0094012
    Lone Star, Dark Helmet, Barf (Chewie), Princess Vespa, etc.

Star Trek vs. Star Wars Newsgroup
  alt.startrek.vs.starwars

TROOPS - IMDb
  http://us.imdb.com/Title?0153301
    It's a kick in the afterburners - here's cast & production details.

Wing Commander Movie
  http://scifi.simplenet.com/wingcommander/index.html
    Wing Commander Movie facts, fun, models, pix.

The Mediums & The Media

Comics, First & Foremost!

Here are web sites dedicated to the comic books that feature Star Wars. Also in this list are editorial-page comics and comic strips. Some of these are also found in the Humor Section of the Star Wars Fun, Games, & Lifestyle Topics chapter.

Azeroth's Labrynth Comics Update
  www.otn.net/mypage/azeroth/comics.html
    Reviews of recent Star Wars comics.

Comic Book (Unnamed)
  www.geocities.com/Area51/Corridor/7410/pg1.html
    Homemade comics rule!

Media — Comics, First & Foremost! 43

Comics & Covers - Thrawn Art Gallery
http://empire.res.wabash.edu/art/comics/index.htm
Color cover images of comic books; click to open sub-pages.

Dark Horse Comics
www.dhorse.com/
The licensed comics - links directly from official Star Wars site.

Everything's Star Wars - the norm
www.thenorm.com/tfm/
Comic-drawing hero "the norm" is a great Star Wars humorist!

Ewoks - Star (Marvel) Comic Books Series
http://207.237.121.181/starwars/ewok01-06.html
15 Ewok Comic Book Covers in full color.

Jawa Force & Wampashit
www.lortaphanble.com/
Jawa Force Comic & Wampashit 'Zine. Required viewing.

Latest Star Wars Comics News
www.theforce.net/comics/
Lists, reviews, news on Dark Horse & Marvel comics.

Literature (LucasFan.com)
www.lucasfan.com/literature.html
Great resource for all types of reading media.

Scott & Kathi's Ultimate Pages of Comics
www.softcom.net/users/scottg/index.html
Check on other comics.

Scripts (Jedinet Collection)
www.jedinet.com/multimedia/scripts/index.htm
Offers a script for the Tales of the Jedi Comic Book CD-ROM edition.

Shadows of the Empire Pictures
www.jedinet.com/multimedia/pics/sote/index.html
Shadows of the Empire gallery at its best.

Star Park
www.jedinet.com/starpark/
South Park/Star Wars crossover fever spreads like a plague.

Star Wars Comics Price Lists
http://207.237.121.181/starwars/swcprices.html
Star Wars Comic Book prices currently.

Unofficial Episode 1 Ed Bain Comics Page
http://members.aye.net/~roncole/tpmky/comic.htm
Features cartoonist Ed Bain & his "Line Series."

Moviemakers, Executives, Studios, Movers & Shakers

Here are web sites that feature the bigger names connected with Star Wars movie production, also movie studios and pages that provide info about these movie people. Note that George Lucas has his own section, followed by a section for Production and FX (special effects).

20th Century Fox
www.20thcenturyfox.com/
Fox's big entertainment site for the 21st Century too.

Animatics: Moving Storyboards of Episode 1
www.starwars.com/episode-i/features/animatics/01/
Editing, cutting, and making it into a movie.

Ben Burtt: Sound Design of Episode 1
www.starwars.com/episode-i/features/burtt/
About Ben Burtt; movie sound design expert.

Creative Impulse, The
www.cwrl.utexas.edu/~daniel/309m/project4/christal/lucas.html
Essay on the value of Lucas' contribution to our world.

Dark Horizons
www.darkhorizons.com/index2.html
1-stop movie resource - news, trailers, facts.

Design Originals of Episode 1; Doug Chiang's Portfolio
www.starwars.com/episode-i/features/chiang/
Artist Doug Chiang talks/draws on this official site.

Frank Oz - IMDb
http://us.imdb.com/Name?Oz,+Frank
Frank Oz - Yoda's voice - his career from the IMDb

Gary Kurtz - All-Media Guide
http://allmovie.com/cg/x.dll?UID=9:01:46|PM&p=avg&sql=B98317
Searchable media database entry for Producer Gary Kurtz.

George Walton Lucas Jr.
http://us.imdb.com/M/person-exact?Lucas%2C+George
Movie database info on Star Wars creator.

Internet Movie Database (IMDb)
http://us.imdb.com/
Easy to use data on moviemakers, stars, & flix - bigger than the Empire.

John Williams (II) - IMDb
http://us.imdb.com/M/person-exact?Williams%2C+John+(II)
All about the Greatest Composer on 12 systems.

Lucas Companies
www.lucasfilm.com/companies_top.html
Employment ops with Lucas' companies.

Movies.Com
www.movies.com
Touchstone Pictures "Now Playing" & info page.

News Stand, The - CHUD (Cinematic Happenings Under Development)
www.chud.com/news.htm
CHUD - this movie info site isn't as bad as it sounds.

Prequel Crew
http://theforce.net/prequels/oldPreq/crew/crew.html
They made Episode 1.

George Lucas

Here are some of the databases and web sites that focus on George Lucas, the man who created Star Wars.

A Few Minutes with George Lucas
www.daforce.demon.nl/fightback/dfhw2.htm
George Lucas' "see it on the big screen" video.

Film 100: #32 George Lucas
www.film100.com/cgi/direct.cgi?v.luca
Lucas and other "gods of filmmaking" are here!

George Lucas (Lycos Network)
www.lycos.com/entertainment/celebrities/celebs/Lucas_George.html
Portal-like page for basic background on Star War's creator.

George Lucas - All Media Guide
http://allmovie.com/cg/x.dll?UID=9:01:46|PM&p=avg&sql=B100308
All-Media Guide all-out George Lucas info page!

Hollywood Online George Lucas
http://moviepeople.hollywood.com/people.asp?p_id=P100308
Lucas bio, films, awards from Hollywood Online's database.

Literature (LucasFan.com)
www.lucasfan.com/literature.html
Great resource for all types of reading media.

Lucasfan.com
www.lucasfan.com/
Lucas' media contributions documented. News & humor, too.

Prequel Trilogy & Special Edition Homepage
http://washington.xtn.net/~robf/sw.htm
This site is like a historic marker - 1996-97.

Productions & FX

Star Wars movies feature a barrage of special effects. Here are some selected web sites pertaining to special effects and to movie production in general. We've included sites that offer specific information about scenes, sets, sounds or the making of Star Wars media productions, both official and unofficial.

Anakin's Hovel Set Plan
http://members.xoom.com/_XOOM/mb_starwars/anakin/index.htm
Blueprint of Anakin's house used for movie production.

Behind The Magic of LucasArts Games Newsgroup
    alt.games.lucas-arts.star-wars,behind-magic

Bogus Star Wars Homepage
    www.cinenet.net/~agrapha/StarNet/SW.html
        Special effects & comments from Special Editions are featured.

Cg-Char Mailing List for 3D CG Character Animators
    www.cg-char.com/
        Resource for CG-character animators. 3D.

John Dykstra - All-Media Guide
    http://allmovie.com/cg/x.dll?UID=9:01:46|PM&p=avg&sql=B88556
        Special effects wizard's database page on the All-Media Guide.

Join the Campaign
    www.jax-inter.net/users/datalore/starwars/campaign.htm
        Lost scenes and technological mumbo-jumbo.

LucasArts Entertainment Company
    www.lucasarts.com/menu.html
        Double-recommended LucasArts game product site.

LucasArts Star Wars Games Newsgroup
    alt.games.lucas-arts.star-wars

Mastering 3D Graphics (M3G)
    www.mastering3dgraphics.com/
        3D artist galleries and tutorials for 3D graphics.

Millenium's End
    www.fadproductions.com/
        Video-documentary about the web, fans, & Star Wars.

Richard Edlund - All-Media Guide
    http://allmovie.com/cg/x.dll?UID=9:01:46|PM&p=avg&sql=B88665
        Special effects wizard and winner of 4 academy awards.

Roderick Vonhogen's Virtual Edition
    www.virtualedition.com/
        Treated to higher-end features on this great Netherland's site.

Skywalker Ranch Tour
    http://george.lucas.net/prologue.htm
        Online tour of George Lucas' Skywalker Ranch & outbuilding.

Star Wars Episode 1 - The Music
    http://members.es.tripod.de/Befan/Episode1music.html
        Who thought there wasn't much to Star Wars music? There sure is!

Media TV/Radio 47

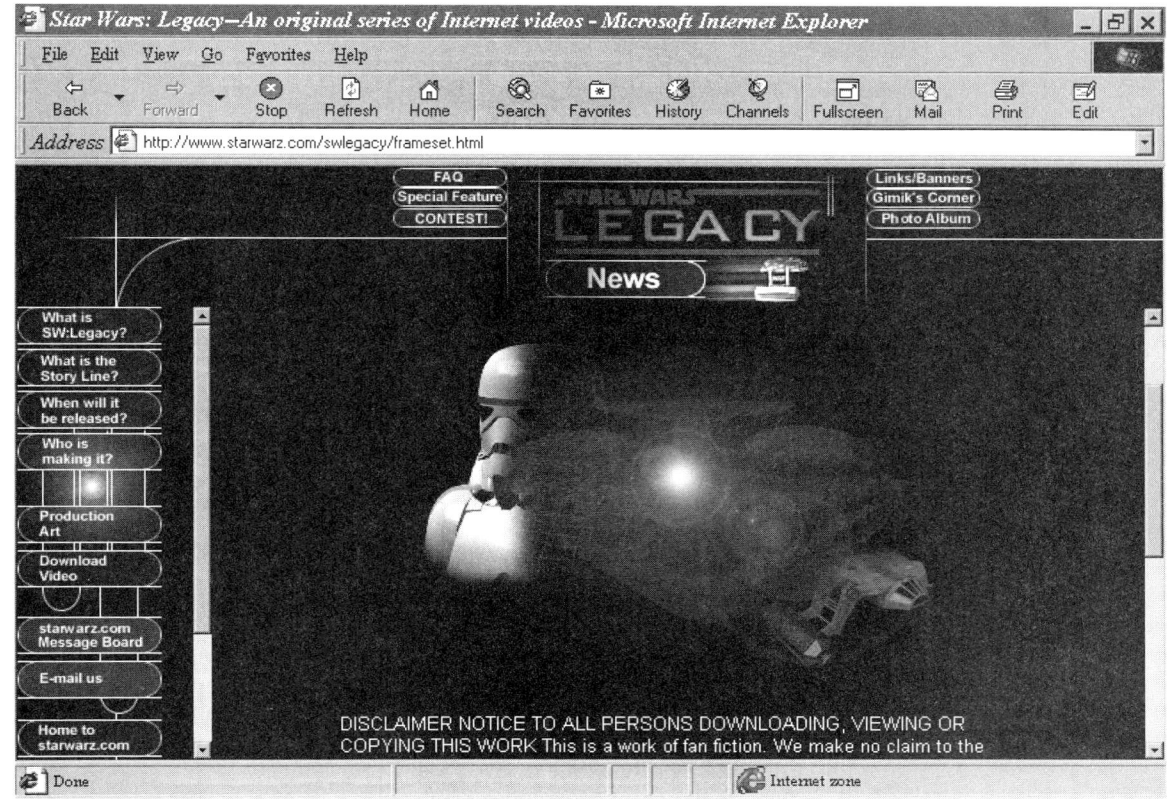

Star Wars Legacy
www.starwarz.com/swlegacy/frameset.html
Wildcat video project continues Star Wars 60 years hence.

Star Wars Sound Mix Comparison
www.jax-inter.net/users/datalore/starwars/soundfaq.htm
Lists sound & dialog changes, re-mastering. An earful.

THX
www.thx.com/main.html
Technological products & services.

Unofficial Industrial Light+Magic Web Site
www.ilmfan.com/index2.html
ILM unofficial page of info, news, downloads.

VFX HQ Archives (Visual Effects Headquarters)
www.vfxhq.com/
News & Reviews of Best Special Effects.

TV/Radio

Star Wars images, characters, and themes often make their way into radio or television productions. Here's web site listings for the broadcast media.

20th Century Fox
www.20thcenturyfox.com/
Fox's big entertainment site for the 21st Century too.

Cartoons - Droids & Ewoks
www.lucasfan.com/animated/animated.html
Droid & Ewok TV cartoons - pix, video, very nice!

Cinescape Online
www.cinescape.com/
Rumors & spoilers on just about everything!

Concerts - Star Wars Episode 1: The Music
http://members.es.tripod.de/Befan/Episode1music_Concerts.html
Star Wars music & John Williams performance schedules.

Ewoks [Star Wars: various titles] - TV Series 1985-87
http://us.imdb.com/Title?0088515
Tells us info about the Ewok TV series & its other titles.

Ewoks: The Battle For Endor (TV/Movie, 1985)
http://us.imdb.com/Title?0089110
Ewok TV movie that spawned the Ewok cartoons.

Guide to the Ewoks Cartoon Series
www.mvhs.srvusd.k12.ca.us/~ehall/ewoks.html
Ewok Cartoons listings: plots, author & date.

Star Wars As Seen On TV
www.lucasfan.com/swtv/index.html
Star Wars on the little screen collection.

Television References
www.jedinet.com/multimedia/references/ref-tv.html
Star Wars-isms make their way into TV - here's the list.

TV Now Entertainment - Stars on TV
www.tv-now.com/stars/stars.html
When will Star Wars people be on TV? Find out here!

Star Wars Discussion
Talk It Up, Fuzzball!

The Star Wars Universe would be a dull place if we couldn't talk to others about it! This chapter is dedicated to all the ways that you can communicate about Star Wars online, including web sites that feature quizzes, trivia, surveys and "your opinion."

Chat Rooms

In a chat room, you can expect to find others who have an interest in the topic. There are many "topic specific" Star Wars chat rooms, so finding the right one that has the people you want to chat with is the trick. In the list below, check the title and description to find the right chat room for you. With a proliferation of chat rooms now, you may encounter an empty chat room now and then.

A Feminine Perspective
http://members.aol.com/bananie42/index.html

Alan's Star Wars Page
www.geocities.com/SiliconValley/Pines/4928/index.html

Carrie Fisher Web Site
www.carriefisher.com/

Chat Server - Echo Station Interactive
www.echostation.com/chat/
Chat room with scheduled celebrities to interrogate!

Chewie's Web Page
www.music.uh.edu/~chewie/
Upbeat Chewie portal with sights, sounds, & fun.

Chico's Star Wars Video & Music
http://chico.simplenet.com/

Compendium, The
www.wcug.wwu.edu/~paradox/images/hyper/

Echo Station
www.echostation.com/
   Full Service Star Wars portal! A must see.

Han Soloists
www.geocities.com/Area51/Capsule/2324/

Hanger, The
www.jedinights.com/hanger

Harrison Ford (Lycos Network)
www.lycos.com/entertainment/celebrities/celebs/Ford_Harrison.html

HGWizard's Multimedia Archive
www.geocities.com/Hollywood/Hills/1792/opening.html

Imperial Executor
www.angelfire.com/ny/ImperialExecutor/index.html
   Find original animations here, also galleries, links to trivia, chat.

Jedi Academy
www.jediacademy.com/force.htm

Jedinet
www.jedinet.com/frame.htm
   By the Fans for the Fans - full-service super site.

Lucasfan.com
www.lucasfan.com/

LucasGames
www.lucasgames.com/

Marua Sector
www.marua.com/index2.html
   New, developing semi-semi-mega all-purpose site.

Mos Eisley Cantina Chat Room
www.angelfire.com/co/Timecruiser/StarChat.html
   We were afraid to go in - it's our fear of disintegration.

My Star Wars Web Site
www.geocities.com/Area51/Cavern/5033/
   Over 8 million visitors since '97.

Natalie's Mark Hamill Homepage
www.chez.com/jedinat/site1.html

Nintendo 64 Code Center
www.n64cc.com/MAIN.HTM

Phantom Menace Mania Chat Room
http://pages.preferred.com/~whitesk/starwars/chatroom.html
   Chat room for Episode 1 Phantom Menace comments.

Phantom Menace Site, The
www.users.wineasy.se/doot/starwars/index.html

Planet Indy - Home of the Fans
http://indyjones.simplenet.com/

Prequels UK
http://members.tripod.com/Jona82/
Info on all 3 Prequels, plus pix, chat, forums, and more.

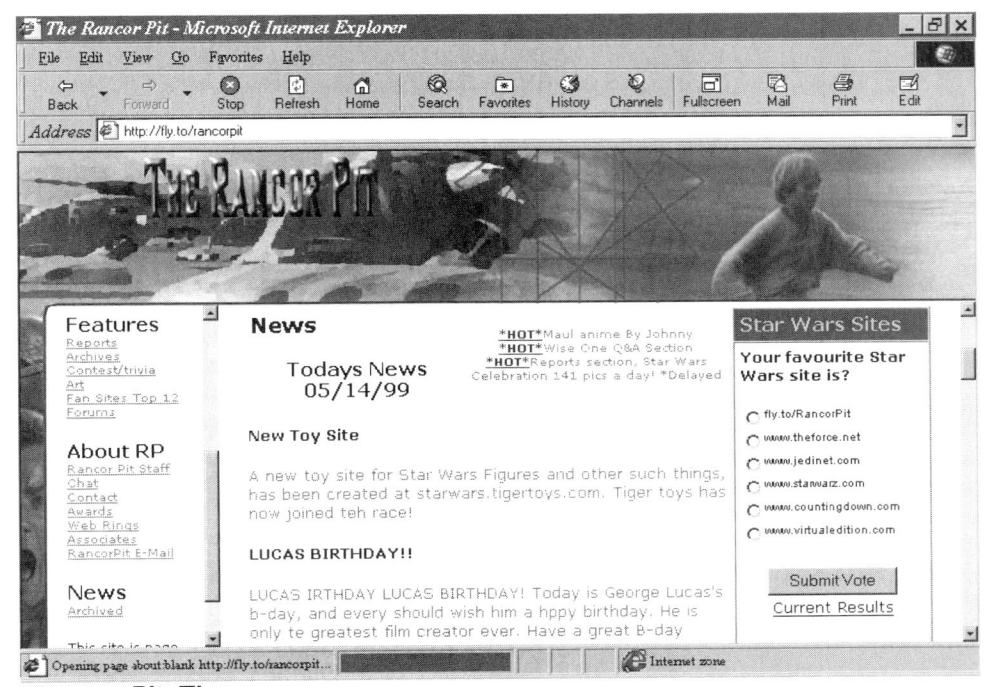

Rancor Pit, The
http://fly.to/rancorpit

Rebel Chat.com (toys/collectibles)
www.rebelchat.com/
Hey - a chat room for Star Wars toys/collectibles!

Rogue Squadron.Net
www.roguesquadron.net/

Sir Steve's Action Online Chat Room (Toys/Collectibles)
www.sirstevesguide.com/chatroom/chatroomg1.html
Toy/collectible chat room with an "ignore" feature.

Spynals Star Wars Site
http://members.xoom.com/Spynal/home.htm

Star Wars Cantina
http://members.tripod.com/~ss_star_wars/index.html
Sights, sounds, also chat, club links & a few games.

Star Wars Database
> www.swdatabase.com/
>> Features, features, features. A must see.

Startroop1 Star Wars Page
> http://members.xoom.com/Startroop1/

Stephen's TIE Fighter Page
> http://indigo.ie/~hanafin/starwars.html

Tantive 4 Chat Room
> www.talkcity.com/chat.htmpl?room=Tantive4
>> Talkcity chat room for Star Wars fans.

Timecruisers Star Wars Galaxy
> www.angelfire.com/co/Timecruiser/

Toy Box - Hydrospanner
> http://members.aol.com/MrkHmlRulz/HTB/
>> Toy news site that isn't totally fanatical.

Tripod's Pod Central Sci-fi Lounge
> www.tripod.com/pod_central/pods/sciencefiction/
>> Get involved - be heard! Entertainment & fun resource.

WebChat's Star Wars Cantina
> http://chat14.go.com/webchat3.so?cmd=cmd_doorway:Star_Wars

"Young Jedi surgeon" is not in Star Wars; it refers to John Carter on the TV Show ER.

Fan Clubs

The web has online versions of the old celebrity style "Fan Clubs." Traditionally, fan clubs are dedicated to one person or one theme, but the online fan club providers often mix a number of fan clubs under one banner. To find other fan clubs on the web not listed here, check the contents page for the section of the character you're looking for (in the Cast & Characters chapter). Often, that character's official web site, or a large tribute site, will have fan club-like types of information – appearance dates, collectibles, fan praise, posters, etc.

Boba Fett Fan Club
> www.bobafettfanclub.com

Clubs of Star Wars on Yahoo
> http://clubs.yahoo.com/Entertainment___Arts/Movies/Genres/Science_Fiction_and_Fantasy/Titles/Star_Wars_Series/index.html
>> Directory of Star Wars Clubs hosted by Yahoo.

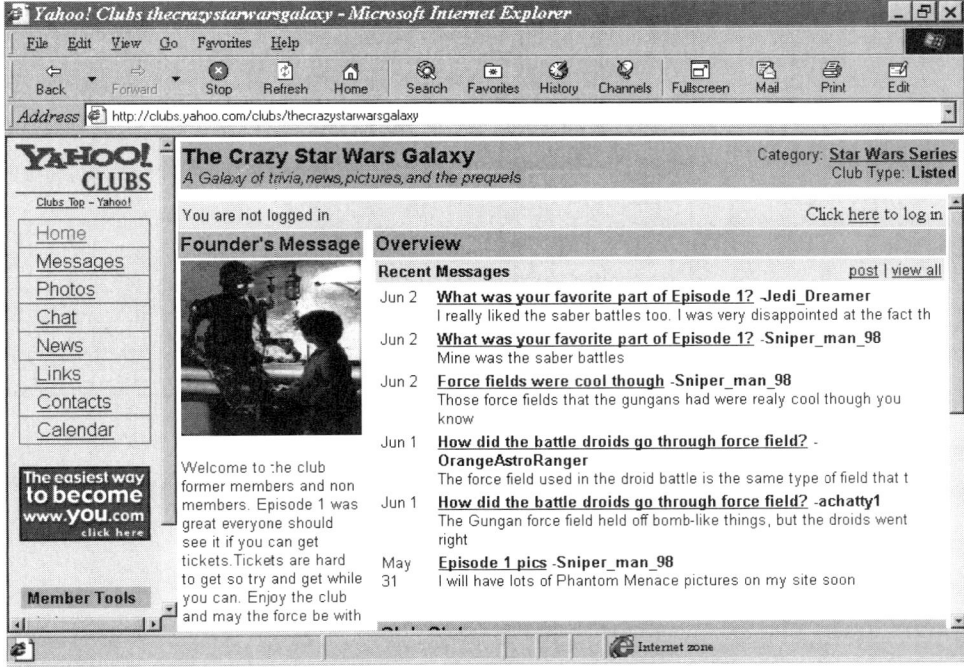

Discussion Forums & Message Boards

Crazy Star Wars Galaxy
> http://clubs.yahoo.com/clubs/thecrazystarwarsgalaxy
>> Member of Yahoo's Star Wars Club circuit.

Natalie Portman Fan Club
> www.natportman.com/fanclub/
>> New and booming Natalie Fan Club to join!

Official Dave Prowse Web Site
> www.daveprowse.com/
>> Dave Prowse DESERVES to win an academy award.

Forums & Message Boards

Some call them forums; others call them message boards. Join one and you're able to post messages and read them. Often, there is a moderator who makes certain the postings conform to the topic; these are usually the preferred message boards. However, un-moderated boards may allow you to expand the range of the topic.

20th Century Fox
> www.20thcenturyfox.com/

3D News
> www.3dnews.net/

Ain't-It-Cool-News Reviews
> www.aint-it-cool-news.com/section.cgi?type=Review
>> Alternative movie review site with forums, news.

Ask A Question - AllExperts.com
> www.allexperts.com/tv/starwars.shtml

Boba Fett's Page
http://members.tripod.com/~Rowlandc/
Searchable homepage for Star Wars links, with message boards.

Boober's Star Wars Galaxy
http://home.fuse.net/mckee/frames.htm

Celebrity Message Boards (Lycos Network)
http://boards.lycos.com/cgi-bin/WebX?13@32.1eteaz6maFa^2@.ee6b348
Celebrity message board index and search page from Lycos.

Clubs of Star Wars on Yahoo
http://clubs.yahoo.com/Entertainment___Arts/Movies/Genres/Science_Fiction_and_Fantasy/Titles/Star_Wars_Series/index.html
Directory of Star Wars Clubs hosted by Yahoo.

Compendium, The
www.wcug.wwu.edu/~paradox/images/hyper/
Not the prettiest site, but one of the fullest!

Countdown To Star Wars
http://starwars.countingdown.com/

Countingdown Star Wars Forum
http://countingdown.com/starwars/forum/
Very busy forums even before the Prequel opening.

Crazy Star Wars Galaxy
http://clubs.yahoo.com/clubs/thecrazystarwarsgalaxy
Member of Yahoo's Star Wars Club circuit.

Den, The
www.theden.com/
Light entertainment & Sci-fi news.

Droidshrine - Oh, Thank The Maker
http://members.aol.com/candyfish/droidshrine.htm

Echo Station
www.echostation.com/
Full Service Star Wars portal! A must see.

Ewan MacGregor
http://ucs.orst.edu/~harraha/

Fett Net
www.bobafett.net/page1.htm

FORCE.NET - Your Daily Dose of Star Wars
http://theforce.net/

Galactic Senate, The
http://starwarz.com/boards/
Be a galactic senator in this rhetorical forum.

Discussion — Forums & Message Boards

Hanger, The
www.jedinights.com/hanger
Brand new Prequel gaming site: TPM & Pods'R'us.

jawafortress.com
www.jawafortress.com/index2.html
Want to help build a good looking site? Check this…

Jedi Academy
www.jediacademy.com/force.htm

Jedi Domain
www.geocities.com/Area51/Shadowlands/3543/

Latest Scoop - Star Wars News from the Source
http://home1.gte.net/filter1/starwars/index.html

Liam Neeson Appreciation Pages
www.geocities.com/Hollywood/Set/6510/index2.html

LucasGames
www.lucasgames.com/

Mark Hamill Mailing List
www.chez.com/jedinat/list.html
Mailing list & message board dedicated to Hamill.

Marua Sector
www.marua.com/index2.html

Music Forums - Star Wars Episode 1: The Music
http://members.es.tripod.de/Befan/Episode1music_Forums.html
Multiple music forums for John Williams & Star Wars.

NaboOnline
www.naboonline.com

Natalie's Mark Hamill Homepage
www.chez.com/jedinat/site1.html

NatPortman.com
www.natportman.com/

Nintendo 64 Code Center
www.n64cc.com/MAIN.HTM

Planet Jedi
www.planetjedi.com/main.html

Power of the Force
http://welcome.to/star.warz
Multimedia site with message boards, spacecraft downloads.

Prequel Watch on Jedinet
www.jedinet.com/prequels/

Prequels UK
http://members.tripod.com/Jona82/
Info on all 3 Prequels, plus pix, chat, forums, and more.

Prequels.com, The
http://theprequels.com/main.htm

Rancor Pit, The
http://fly.to/rancorpit

RedFive85
www.geocities.com/Area51/Quadrant/4210/

Roderick Vonhogen's Virtual Edition
www.virtualedition.com/

Rogue 9's Star Wars Web Site
www.geocities.com/Baja/Mesa/4807/index2.html

Rogue Squadron.Net
www.roguesquadron.net/

Spynals Star Wars Site
http://members.xoom.com/Spynal/home.htm

Star Wars Collective
http://starwars.interspeed.net/index.shtml
Developing site - find excellent renderings in Fan Images section.

Star Wars Database
www.swdatabase.com/

Star Wars Database Message Boards
www.swdatabase.com:8080/~swdbase
Get mailings lists from topic-specific message board files.

Star Wars Episode 1 - The Music
http://members.es.tripod.de/Befan/Episode1music.html

Star Wars Fan Fiction
http://sw.simplenet.com/pages/fanfiction.html

Starwarz
www.starwarz.com/
Rates highly as an alternative fan site portal. Unique concept.

Stephen's TIE Fighter Page
http://indigo.ie/~hanafin/starwars.html

SWMA - Star Wars The 3D Modeling Alliance
www.swma.net/

Sylvia Christina's Special Thoughts for Mark Hamill A Very Special Person
www.yggdrasill.demon.nl/Serie01/MHHome2.htm

Theed.net - City Beyond the Swamp
www.theed.net/

Tripod's Pod Central Sci-fi Lounge
www.tripod.com/pod_central/pods/sciencefiction/
Get involved - be heard! Entertainment & fun resource.

Tusken Traders Trader Lists
http://yakface.com/hosted/tuskentrader/list.htm

Unofficial Episode 1 Homepage (Kentucky area)
http://come.to/tpmky/
News, comics, discussion with local Kentucky flavor.

Virtual Edition Forum
www.mvpforums.com/partners/virtualedition/
Air your Star Wars comments & questions (and read others).

Watto's Junkyard
www.wattosjunkyard.com/

Whill Journal, The
www.geocities.com/Area51/Stargate/4465/

Wookie Hooky
www.geocities.com/Hollywood/Studio/9203/
Get E-mail news updates & give/read tips for seeing Phantom Menace.

Mailing Lists

The purpose of mailing lists is to stay abreast of a topic and/or discuss it. When you subscribe to a mailing list, you automatically receive all messages sent to the subscribers of that list. Some lists are open, meaning that you can send a message to the list and all its subscribers receive a copy. Others are moderated closely, meaning that you only receive messages from the list, but cannot post any to it. Typically, the title of the list is indicative of the list's subject. For example, the topic of the "Mark Hamill Mailing List" is, you guessed it, Mark Hamill.

Address List from the Force.net
www.theforce.net/jedicouncil/addresses/
Alphabetized Star Wars people address list.

Cg-Char Mailing List for 3D CG Character Animators
www.cg-char.com/
Resource for CG-character animators. 3D.

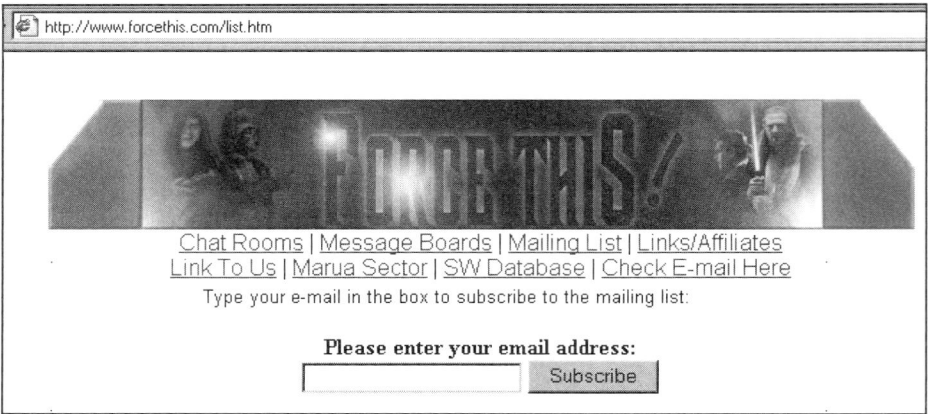

Forcethis Mailing List
>   www.forcethis.com/list.htm
>> Join this newer mailing list.

ICQ list; Star Wars (Echo Station Interactive)
>   www.echostation.com/icq/index.htm
>> ICQ mailing list - register & quickly join in chat, access sites, e-mail.

Mailing List Summary (Echo Station)
>   http://mail.novatech.net:81/guest/RemoteListSummary/SWML
>> Star Wars mailing list compiled by Echo Station.

Mark Hamill Mailing List
>   www.chez.com/jedinat/list.html
>> Mailing list & message board dedicated to Hamill.

NaboOnline
>   http://scifi.simplenet.com/starwars/prequels/index.html
>> Wealth of information and variety of Prequel categories.

Natalie Portman Fan Club
>   www.natportman.com/fanclub/
>> New and booming Natalie Fan Club to join!

Star Wars MUSH Mailing Lists
>   www.cae.wisc.edu/~steiner/mush/site/mailing.htm
>> Lists of MUSH players, dignitaries, officials, wizards.

SWMA - Star Wars 3D Modeling Alliance Member Directory
>   www.surfthe.net/swma/members/members.html
>> E-mail & WWWs for 3D modeling gurus.

Tusken Traders Trader Lists
>   http://yakface.com/hosted/tuskentrader/list.htm
>> Traders and their lists.

Newsgroups

By joining a newsgroup, you can offer news, or answer other's questions, or post your own questions. Star Wars newsgroups are many and cover diverse Star Wars topics. Some listed listed here are foreign. To access a newsgroup, your browser must be compatible. To determine the compatibility of your browser, input "news:" followed by a URL from this list. If a window pops up, chances are you are on your way to being "subscribed" to that newsgroup. AOL users should use Keyword Newsgroups.

alt.binaries.Star Wars Newsgroup
alt.binaries.starwars

Behind The Magic of LucasArts Games Newsgroup
alt.games.lucas-arts.star-wars.behind-magic

Chewy & Wookiees Newsgroup
alt.chewy.wookie.net

Collecting Star Wars Newgroup
rec.arts.sf.starwars.collecting

Customized Collecting Star Wars Newsgroup
rec.arts.sf.starwars.collecting.customizing

Dark Forces Game LucasArts Newsgroup
alt.games.lucas-arts.star-wars.dark-forces

Dark Forces Game Newsgroup
alt.games.dark-forces

Fans of Star Wars Newsgroup
alt.fan.starwars

Fantastyka Star Wars Newsgroup
pl.rec.fantastyka.starwars

fido. Star Wars
fido.starwars

Flight School LucasArts Newsgroup
alt.games.lucas-arts.star-wars.flight-school

Harrison Ford Newsgroup
alt.fan.harrison-ford

it.fan Star Wars
it.fan.starwars

Jedi Knight Game Newsgroup
alt.games.jedi-knight

Jedi Knight LucasArts Game Newsgroup
alt.games.lucas-arts.star-wars.jedi-knight

LucasArts Games Newsgroup
    alt.binaries.games.lucasarts

LucasArts Star Wars Games Newsgroup
    alt.games.lucas-arts.star-wars

Miscellaneous Star Wars Collecting Newsgroup
    rec.arts.sf.starwars.collecting.misc

Miscellaneous Star Wars Rec.arts Newsgroup
    rec.arts.sf.starwars.misc

Newsgroup: Star Wars Genre
    net.genre.sf.star-wars

Rec.Starwars
    tw.bbs.rec.starwars

Rogue Squadron LucasArts Game Newsgroup
    alt.games.lucas-arts.star-wars.rogue-squadron

RU Star Wars
    fido7.ru.star.wars

RU Star Wars Games
    fido7.ru.star.wars.games

Science Fiction - Star Wars Newsgroup
    de.rec.arts.sf.starwars

Science Fiction Fantasy Star Wars Newsgroup
    z-net.sf+fantasy.starwars.allgemein

Science Fiction Scale Models Newsgroup
    alt.sf.scale-models

Star Trek vs Star Wars Newsgroup
    alt.startrek.vs.starwars

Star Wars Information Newsgroup
    rec.arts.sf.starwars.info

Star Wars Rec.arts Games Newsgroup
    rec.arts.sf.starwars.games

Star Wars xvt Newsgroup
    alt.starwars.xvt

TIE Fighter Game Newsgroup
    alt.games.tie-fighter

Vintage Star Wars Collecting Newsgroup
`rec.arts.sf.starwars.collecting.vintage`

Wedge Newgroup
`alt.fan.wedge`

X-Wing Game Newsgroup
`alt.games.x-wing`

Quizzes, Trivia, & Knowledge Games

So, you think you know all there is to know about Star Wars? Test your knowledge using all the trivias, quizlets, and knowledge games that are found at these web sites:

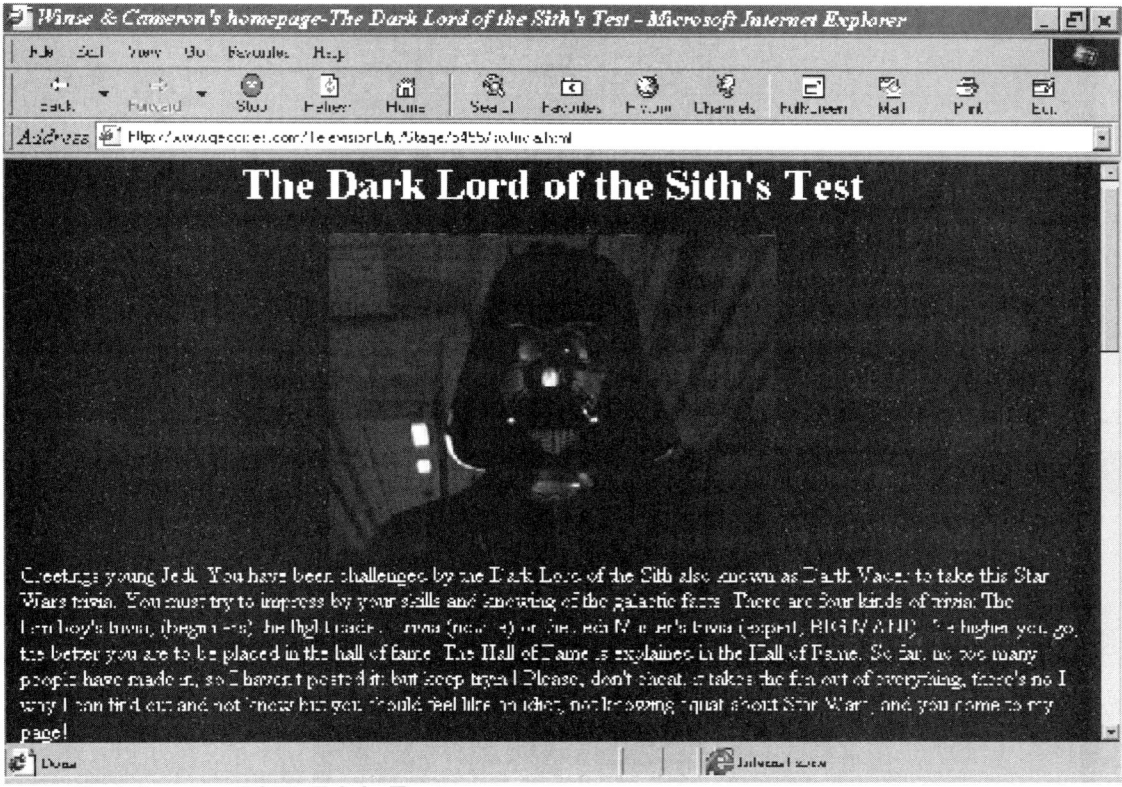

Dark Lords of Sith Trivia Test
`www.geocities.com/TelevisionCity/Stage/5455/swtrivia.html`
We like this 3-level trivia - beware of Sith mind tricks.

Hollywood Online - Star Wars The Phantom Menace
`www.hollywood.com/starwars/main.html`
Entertaining site has The Phantom Menace covered!

Jedi Trivia
`www.fortunecity.com/tattooine/lucas/66/jt-index.html`
Four levels of trivia to test your Trilogy knowledge.

Leia Quiz
    www.saunalahti.fi/~margot/quiz.htm
        So you think you know your Princess Leia trivia, do you?

Marua Sector
    www.marua.com/index2.html
        New, developing semi-semi-mega all-purpose site.

Question of the Month (Timecruiser's)
    www.angelfire.com/co/Timecruiser/StarQuiz.html
        Here's a question for you, big fan!

Rancor Pit, The
    http://fly.to/rancorpit
        New high-energy site that hopes to do it all!

Ryan's Star Wars Realm
    http://members.spree.com/sci-fi/swrealm
        Get involved through this multimedia page!

Ryan's Star Wars Trivia Page (Interactive)
    http://members.spree.com/sci-fi/swrealm/Trivia.htm
        Participate in a Trivia game for a weekly prize.

Sam Davatchi's Page
    http://perso.club-internet.fr/willow/Index.html
        Goodies you probably won't find elsewhere.

Besides the large studio in England, many segments of the Phantom Menace were filmed on location in Italy.

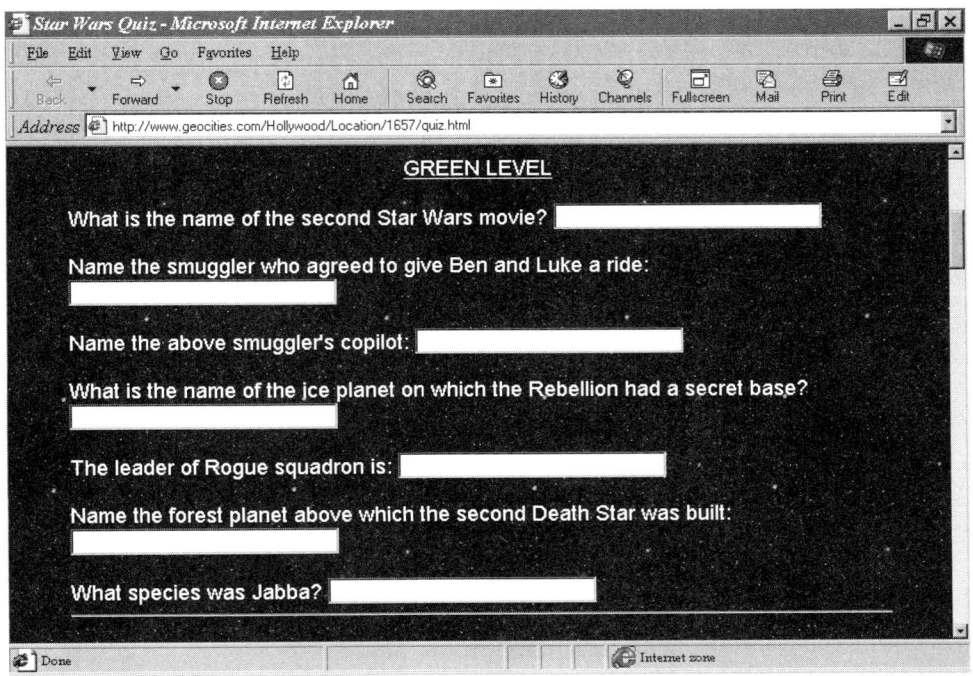

Discussion — Surveys, Polls, & Where Your Opinion Counts 63

Sith Lords Star Wars Quiz
www.geocities.com/Hollywood/Location/1657/quiz.html
You think you know your trivia? See what you know about bad guys.

Trivia - Jar Jar's on Jedinet
www.jedinet.com/multimedia/trivia/index.htm
Get 3 right you're doing good - there's 44 tough questions.

Trivia - LucasFan.com
www.lucasfan.com/humor/
Answer the questions, submit - how did you do?

Trivia - Star Wars Trivia on Echo Station
www.echostation.com/trivia/
Oooo! Star Wars Trivia online Sundays at 3 EST.

Trivial Side of the Force
www.theforce.net/jedicouncil/trivia/
Special trivia sections and a semi-daily trivia (w/ answers)

Surveys, Polls, & Where Your Opinion Counts

Your opinion does count! The sites below let you give that opinion. Often a poll or survey may have only one question, or it may offer a contest. We've tried to list sites that ask multiple questions. Look at the title and description of the site for clues about the subject of the survey.

A Feminine Perspective
http://members.aol.com/bananie42/index.html
Solid! None of that really mushy stuff.

Chewie's Web Page
www.music.uh.edu/~chewie/
Upbeat Chewie portal with sights, sounds, & fun.

Episode 1 News Archives
www.sevaan.com/starwars/news/archives/index.htm
News, editorials, surveys on Episode 1.

LeeboMan's New Star Wars Site
www.angelfire.com/co/LeeboMan/
Galleries, polls, fun, also chat and webring being developed.

Mfalcon's Star Wars Outpost
www.geocities.com/Area51/Zone/9049/
Collection of MIDI music, photos from 1st 3 episodes.

Our Generation - The Den
www.theden.com/den_ourgen/
What is this world coming to? Be amazed!

Senate Vote, The
www.theforce.net/jedicouncil/surveys/
You are a Senator - now vote! Read survey results, too.

Sith Lords Star Wars Quiz
www.geocities.com/Hollywood/Location/1657/quiz.html
You think you know your trivia? See what you know about bad guys.

Star Wars Episode 1 - The Music
http://members.es.tripod.de/Befan/Episode1music.html
Who thought there wasn't much to Star Wars music? There is!

Star Wars Geek Code
www.sevaan.com/starwars/news/archives/old_layout/news/code.htm
Create coded transmissions to attach to your E-mails.

Welcome to Endor
www.geocities.com/Area51/Cavern/9101/
MIDI music, survey, & a few good links, but no Endor!

World 'O Chewbacca
http://members.aol.com/andrewm675/chewbacca/chewie.html
Chewiee tribute site with videos, sounds, survey, & his bio

Star Wars Multimedia

"Multimedia" is a '90's computer buzzword. In this book, multimedia refers to web sites that either feature a large number of "multiple media" (see Multimedia Potpourri Section which follows) or specialize in videos or audio files. Specialized pages featuring a specific computer format are referred to as "galleries." (Visual Image galleries are found in the Images Chapter, after this Multimedia Chapter.)

A Multimedia Potpourri

Multimedia Potpourri includes all the sites that have a lot of variety to their content, but are not dominated by any one topic. A potpourri site may have any combination of images, sounds, videos, surveys, guestbooks, forums, chat rooms, news, opinions, odd ideas, tributes – anything. That's the fun of exploring multimedia sites: you really don't know exactly what's there until you explore it. A site named The Cantina may not have anything to do with the Cantina. A site may say "Star Wars," but could include personal info or other science fiction topics - or anything! Often, the "better galleries" that are found among Potpourri web sites are listed elsewhere in this book.

A Page of Undeniable Weirdness - Tribbles, Wookiees, & Ewoks
www.compusmart.ab.ca/macclan/Collpg1.htm
Sci-fi fan that's too off-the-wall - Trek, X-files, Star Wars.

A1's Star Wars Multimedia Page
http://members.aol.com/A1B2C369/index.html
Searchable "variety" collection, big on games, toys, also Pez.

Admiral's Star Wars Page
www.geocities.com/Area51/Hollow/2779/
Admiral has collected some very good Star Wars images and music.

Alan's Star Wars Page
www.geocities.com/SiliconValley/Pines/4928/index.html
Full fan site - worth the visit.

Anakin's Rebel Base
www.geocities.com/Area51/Labyrinth/8664/noframes.html
Father/son multimedia site; big on modeling.

Big Kourt's House of Star Wars, X-Files, Star Trek & Used Hubcaps
www.geocities.com/Area51/Lair/7558/
Won't find the hubcaps - will find unusual Star Wars phrases.

Bill's Star Wars Page
www.geocities.com/Area51/Dimension/6975/starwars.html
"Impressive." - Darth Vader. Good example of Star Wars multimedia site.

Boba Fett Fan Club
www.bobafettfanclub.com
Everything else you wanted to know about Boba Fett.

Boober's Star Wars Galaxy
http://home.fuse.net/mckee/frames.htm
Worth the visit. 625 multimedia files & a good games page.

Bossk's Homepage
www.geocities.com/Area51/Dimension/9216/
Info on bounty-hunter Bossk, also Star Wars images for wallpaper.

Bria's Retribution, Flagship of the Rebel Commander
www.geocities.com/Area51/Nebula/8247/sum.html
Explore more - a variety site.

Dagobah System, The
http://members.aol.com/Yoda328/index.html
Under construction - visit to find out what's new.

Dark Rising
http://home.sol.no/~mgrambo/index2.htm
Multimedia page with galleries of sights, sounds, action clips.

Dash Rendar's Star Wars Universe
www.angelfire.com/wi/SciFiPlace/

Dave's Star Wars HUB
http://empire.res.wabash.edu/
Wabash U. edu site's HUB has multimedia resources & Vader's Castle.

Echo Station
www.echostation.com/
Full Service Star Wars portal! A must see.

El Camino's Star Wars Page
www.geocities.com/Area51/Rampart/4264/ie4.htm
We liked it - interesting juxtaposition of pages.

Episode 1
www.sevaan.com/starwars/
A multimedia page dedicated to Episode 1.

Extreme Star Wars Site
www.angelfire.com/co/gavind/index.html
Good variety - includes some good text material.

FORCE.NET - Your Daily Dose of Star Wars
http://theforce.net/
Mega Star Wars Info Site - Mega!

Multimedia
A Multimedia Potpourri

Fort Tusken
>www.igw.clara.co.uk/index.html/
>>UK multimedia site with original art & Episode 1 pix.

Gothic Skywalker's Medieval to Mark Hamill Page
>www.geocities.com/TimesSquare/Dungeon/3913/
>>We've seen some strange sites beyond the norm.

Guerre Stellari
>http://users.iol.it/betv/gs.html
>>Italian index site - leads to good Cloud City, MPEG3s sites.

HGWizard's Multimedia Archive
>www.geocities.com/Hollywood/Hills/1792/opening.html
>>Movie clips are the strong point here.

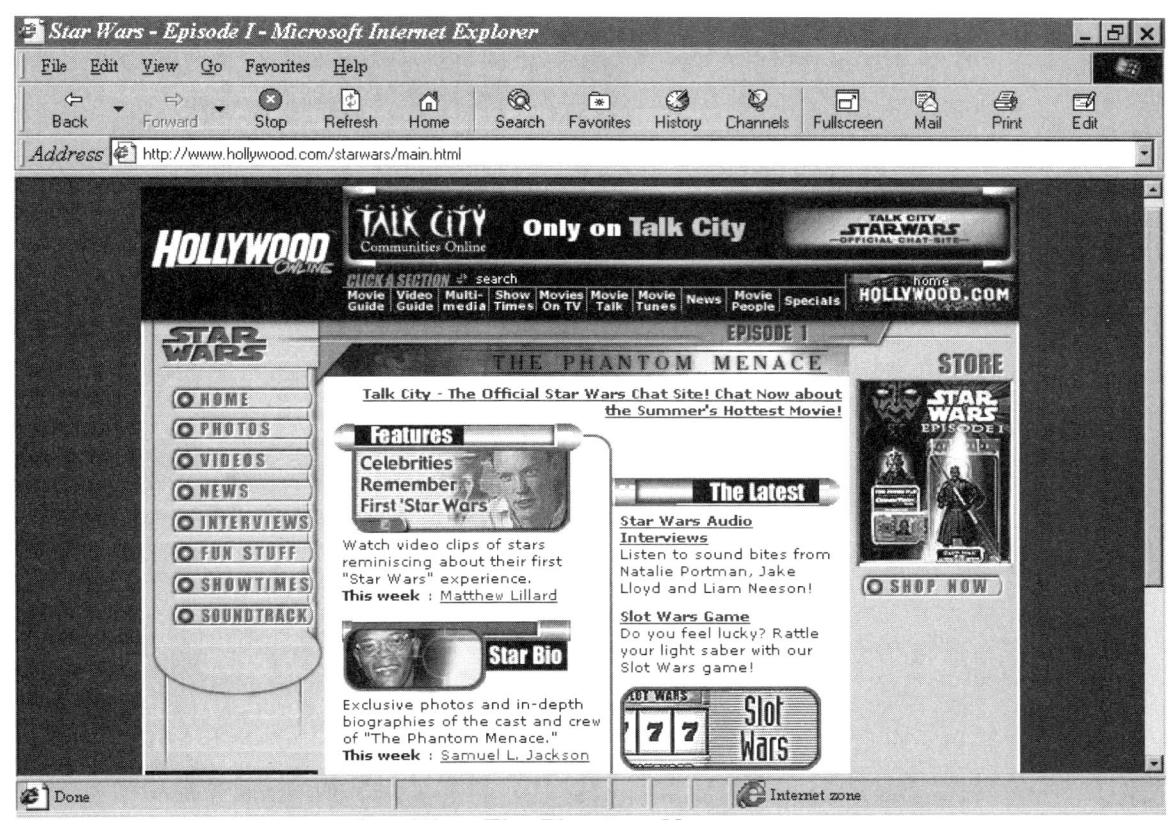

Hollywood Online - Star Wars The Phantom Menace
>www.hollywood.com/starwars/main.html
>>Entertaining site has The Phantom Menace covered!

Ian's Incredible Star Wars Page
>www.airnet.net/pcusers/ianspage/
>>Gets our seal of approval.

Imperial Executor
>www.angelfire.com/ny/ImperialExecutor/index.html
>>Find original animations here, also galleries, links to trivia, chat.

Imperial Outpost
>http://members.theglobe.com/bobafett66/
>>Stuff for your computer as well as a variety of pix, videos, and fun.

Imperial Spy Network
   www.angelfire.com/mo/StarWarsImages/
      Spies? Where? Here?
Imperial TIE Fighter Hangar Bay, The
   www.geocities.com/Area51/Shadowlands/4918/
      Multimedia from the Imperial perspective.
Jacen Solo's Homepage
   http://members.tripod.com/~jacenp/mainpage.html
      High content of non-movie Star Wars art - covers, illos, fantasy.
James' Star Wars Page
   http://webhome.idirect.com/~maguda/starwars.html
      Games & code info, with a Star Wars music gallery.
Jason's Star Wars Page
   http://http.tamu.edu:8000/~jpc6754/starwars.html
      Slim pickings, but does have Boba Fett pix.
Javval's Star Wars Page
   www.multiboard.com/~jhowarth/starwars.htm
      Javval the Hutt's story, also movie photos & MIDI sounds.
jawafortress.com
   www.jawafortress.com/index2.html
      Want to help build a good looking site? Check this...
Jedi Base
   www.bestweb.net/~fett/
      Didn't find specifics on Jedi here, just all-'round Star Wars fun!
Jedi Council Chamber, The
   www.geocities.com/Area51/Hollow/9125/
      We liked the audio files and the kisses.
Jedi Domain
   www.geocities.com/Area51/Shadowlands/3543/
      Multi-presentation site: Jedi flavor, Kenners, Jedi of the month.
Jim Butt's Star Wars Page
   http://members.accessus.net/~wbutts/
      Jukebox and good pix collection. What more do you need?
Juan's Star Wars Site
   www.civila.com/hispania/obi-juan/english.htm
      English and Spanish versions; good multimedia site!
Kessel Run
   www.kesselrun.com/
      Under construction - is it open now?
Knight Hammer
   www.geocities.com/Area51/Chamber/4182/index.html
      Good content for a site with an Imperial overcoat!
LeeboMan's New Star Wars Site
   www.angelfire.com/co/LeeboMan/
      Galleries, polls, fun, also chat and webring being developed.
Lord Vader's Lair
   www.geocities.com/Area51/Cavern/4897/vader.html
      Movie clips, sounds, computer themes ...

Multimedia | A Multimedia Potpourri | 69

MacCentral Online
www.maccentral.com/news/9903/mar17.shtml
Mac News & a download of versatile "Play It Cool" software.

Martinez Brothers Star Wars page
www.geocities.com/Area51/Dimension/5951/
Variety of sights, sounds, bios, also scripts.

MAW Installation
www.premier.net/~exar/MAW2.htm
More variety than most sites; includes bloopers, booklist, icons.

McLaurin's Center of Knowledge
http://members.xoom.com/maclaurin386/index1.htm
Star Wars, Star Trek, James Bond, and Emma sites all here.

McLaurin's Star Wars Site
http://members.xoom.com/maclaurin384/starwars/
Modern multimedia homepage index.

Mfalcon's Star Wars Outpost
www.geocities.com/Area51/Zone/9049/
Collection of MIDI music, photos from 1st 3 episodes.

Mike Gartley's Star Wars Page
www.ma.iup.edu/~tzqf/star/starwars.html
Posters, humor magazine covers, sights & sounds.

Mike's Star Wars Pages
www.ece.orst.edu/~volzmi/starwars/
Very good variety of sound, images, clips, computer stuff.

Monument Square Home Page
www.geocities.com/Area51/Lair/3373/home.html
Web site that we think will grow in size.

Mos Eisley Cantina
www.geocities.com/Hollywood/Set/7355/
Good multimedia, but forgot Mos Eisley Cantina stuff!

My Star Wars Web Site
www.geocities.com/Area51/Cavern/5033/
Over 8 million visitors since '97.

Nathan's Star Wars Page
http://members.aol.com/nathan224/starwars.html
Check for video of the week, info on novels, and more.

New Republic Multimedia
http://thenewrepublic.8m.com/cgi-bin/framed/2478/starwars2.html
Mixed media - true potpourri. Sounds, pix, computer do-dads.

Official Unofficial Star Wars Web Site
www.powerup.com.au/~crono/new_page_1.htm
A thin unapproved site, but does have a rare B'omarr monk pic.

Phantom Menace UK
www.thephantommenace.co.uk/naboo.htm
UK site with a lot of features & international Episode 1 news.

Power of the Force
http://welcome.to/star.warz
Multimedia site with message boards, spacecraft downloads.

Prequels UK
> http://members.tripod.com/Jona82/
> Info on all 3 Prequels, plus pix, chat, forums, and more.

Realm of the Dark Jedi
> http://members.tripod.com/~DarkJediCD/enter.html
> Mirrors Palace of the Raider King, with the author's poster added.

Rogue 9's Star Wars Website
> www.geocities.com/Baja/Mesa/4807/index2.html
> Grab-bag of multimedia goodies and webring connections.

Rouge Leader Star Wars Page
> http://members.tripod.com/rougeleader1/Starwars.html
> Didn't find Rouge Leader here; perhaps you can.

Ryan's Star Wars Realm
> http://members.spree.com/sci-fi/swrealm
> Get involved through this multimedia page!

Skywalker's Star Wars Page
> www.usmo.com/~starwars/index.html
> Some pretty funny stuff, also serious image galleries.

Space Depot 24
> www.geocities.com/Area51/Vault/4910/space.htm
> This sites been around awhile!

Spynals Star Wars Site
> http://members.xoom.com/Spynal/home.htm
> Good variety of content - easy to use.

Star Wars (Hollywood Liz)
> www.geocities.com/Hollywood/1165/starwars.html
> Good Prequel pix and info, also reviews.

Star Wars Cantina
> http://members.tripod.com/~ss_star_wars/index.html
> Sights, sounds, also chat, club links & a few games.

Star Wars Central
> www.geocities.com/Area51/Vault/3891/
> Get "toured" through to Imperial or rebel tech files.

Star Wars Database
> www.swdatabase.com/
> Features, features, features. A must see.

Star Wars Galaxy (a)
> www.geocities.com/Area51/Chamber/1458/frame1.htm

Star Wars Galaxy (b)
> www.geocities.com/Area51/Vault/6031/star_wars.html
> Best part: check in the "files" section.

Star Wars Multimedia Headquarters
> www.nerf-herder.com/swmhq/index.html
> 'been around awhile: light-hearted & fun.

Star Wars Spaceport
> www.geocities.com/TimesSquare/Corridor/1780/swars.html
> Hopefully this site is not still our example of an "empty" site.

Star Wars Trilogy, The
    www.linkline.be/users/duncan/starwars.html
        Sounds, scripts, photos of the 3 Trilogy movies.

Star Wars Wonderland
    http://wonder.simplenet.com/sww/home.html
        Wonderland - as in "I wonder what this was all about."

Startroop1 Star Wars Page
    http://members.xoom.com/Startroop1/
        Downloads, pix, sounds, and a flight simulator.

Stephen's Star Wars Den
    www.geocities.com/Area51/Labyrinth/1390/index.htm
        Some links are missing, but you'll find great color images.

Stephen's Star Wars Den Movies
    www.geocities.com/Area51/Labyrinth/1390/movie.htm
        Trilogy movie clips, also sound and picture files.

Stormtrooper Recruitment - The Replacements
    http://207.136.91.134/very/x-stream/
        Site reforming when we visited - new stuff should be stellar!

Stv1's Star Wars Page
    http://members.tripod.com/~stv1/index.html
        Multimedia site with a Kubrick feel to it.

Swammi's Star Wars Outpost
    http://members.xoom.com/kessel/outpost/
        Go there - gather the goodies for your own web site.

T'Bone Fenders Star Wars Universe
    www.starwarz.com/index.htm
        Among the best fan operated sites on the Net.

Take a Walk Through a Splinter of My Mind's Eye
    www.geocities.com/Area51/Corridor/7410/
        Unusual name - and not your typical web site!

Taz's Star Wars Page
    www.geocities.com/Area51/Corridor/4309/
        Access to character's pix archives. A variety of multimedia files.

Thomas Star Wars Home Page
    www.geocities.com/TimesSquare/4580/
        Mystery click-on: check to see if this site has been updated.

Timecruisers Star Wars Galaxy
    www.angelfire.com/co/Timecruiser/
        Found good early Prequel material, too.

Ultimate Star Wars Homepage
    http://members.aol.com/gio2003/frame.htm
        Sharp gallery of big rendered images is found here.

Ultimate Star Wars Multimedia Universe
    www.geocities.com/Area51/Lair/3724/
        Has a virtual reality page and beaucoups of computer goodies!

Welcome to Endor
    www.geocities.com/Area51/Cavern/9101/
        MIDI music, survey, & a few good links, but no Endor!

Willems Star Wars Homepage
www.tem.nhl.nl/~veen606/veen606.html
Icons, sounds, video game, choice of 2 languages.

Winse & Cameron's Star Wars Section
www.geocities.com/TelevisionCity/Stage/5455/starwars.html
Prepared for the Phantom Menace.

You Are Now a Prisoner in The Entertainment Cell
www.geocities.com/Hollywood/Set/1630/main.html
Your host: Boba Fett!

You People Should Know that My Loyalties Lie Very Firmly with the Empire
www.aaronklaassen.com/starwars/starwars.htm
Imperial fighter info and select pix, sounds, video.

Zaphoids Star Wars Multimedia Extravaganza
http://synergy.foo.net/~zaphoid/starwars/
More cool stuff for your computer, + fonts, GIFs.

A detailed 6 1/2 hour audio version of Star Wars for radio was produced & aired by National Public Radio. Mark Hamill performed as Luke.

Videos

Generally, online videos come in one of four formats: AVI, MPEG, QuickTime (MOV), or Real Video. Often the site has a link to a download of the software for playing the video, but this is not always the case.

Filez is a web site that offers shareware programs, including video players. If you need software to view your video files, visit www.filez.com *and search for the type of player you need, "AVI player" for example.*

AVIs

*AVI is a PC-based video format. Most Windows systems include the software to view these files. If you are a Windows user, try double-clicking on AVI files to view them. If that doesn't work, visit Shareware.Com (*www.shareware.com*) or Filez (*www.filez.com*) and search for "AVI Player" to find a program that will work for you.*

A Few Minutes with George Lucas
www.daforce.demon.nl/fightback/dfhw2.htm
George Lucas' "see it on the big screen" video.

A New Hope Video Clips
http://home.multiweb.nl/~bramenpim/staranh.htm
A New Hope AVI & QuickTime video clips.

Alan's Star Wars Page
www.geocities.com/SiliconValley/Pines/4928/index.html
Full fan site - worth the visit.

Anakin's Rebel Base
www.geocities.com/Area51/Labyrinth/8664/noframes.html
Father/son multimedia site; big on modeling.

Chico's Star Wars Video & Music
http://chico.simplenet.com/
Video clips a specialty.

Competely Phat Star Wars Site
www.perfekt.net/~snoopy/video/video.html
IMAX, Pepsi, Special & Prequel trailers - videos.

Dark Horizons Film Trailers
www.darkhorizons.com/trailers/index-n.htm
A whole trailer camp of current movies.

Darth Vader Song, The
http://198.70.186.7/enterhtml/live/Kidz/vader.html
Can you sing a song about Darth Vader? Here's one.

Empire Strikes Back Video Clips
http://home.multiweb.nl/~bramenpim/staresb.htm
Video clips & finds about the Empire Strikes Back.

Hello There Video of Obi-Wan Kenobi
http://users.why.net/radrock/sounds/hello.avi
It's a video of the first time we hear Obi-Wan speak.

Index of data/video/avi/Movie Trailers/Star Wars
www.burbclave.net/data/video/avi/Movie_Trailers/Star_Wars/
AVI format video files from the Trilogy.

Lord Vader's Lair Movie Clips
www.geocities.com/Area51/Cavern/4897/frmovie.html
MOV & AVI video clips at this Lair.

Masters of Teras Kasi
www.game-junkie.com/Reviews/Playstation/StarWars_Fight/SWMOTK.HTM
Review of this game, with video and image file samples.

McLaurin's Star Wars Movies
http://members.xoom.com/_XOOM/maclaurin384/starwars/movies/movies.html
AVI & MOV video gallery.

Mike's Star Wars Pages
www.ece.orst.edu/~volzmi/starwars/
Very good variety of sound, images, clips, computer stuff.

Movies - AVI & QuickTime
http://pweb.netcom.com/~fragger/movies.html
Collection of short movie clips from the Trilogy.

Movies: Star Wars Video
http://pweb.netcom.com/~fragger/movies.html
Video clips from Trilogy movies (may now have Prequel updates).

Parody Video: Episode 1 Trailer 'A' - Special Edition
> http://sabbeth.com/~menace/specialedition.htm
>> Spoof of the Trailer put together by fans for free.

Phantom Menace Mania
> http://get.to/jedi/
>> Great variety of Episode 1 images, sounds, video.

Return of the Jedi Video Clips
> http://home.multiweb.nl/~bramenpim/starrotj.htm
>> Return of the Jedi video clips collection.

Sci-fi Movie Clips
> http://graffiti.u-bordeaux.fr/MAPBX/roussel/anim-e_03f.shtml
>> Big Sci-fi movie galleries from a French site.

Star Wars (Videos)
> www.students.dsu.edu/hilleste/starwars.html
>> QuickTime & AVI Trilogy video clips.

Star Wars Legacy Download Videos
> www.starwarz.com/swlegacy/video.html
>> Trailers & Special Edition videos in various download formats.

Star Wars Movie Clips
> http://168.229.236.7/~cc/movie.html
>> 10 Trilogy AVI format video files.

Stephen's Star Wars Den Movies
> www.geocities.com/Area51/Labyrinth/1390/movie.htm
>> Trilogy movie clips, also sound and picture files.

Targeting Computer Quick Shot Video
http://users.why.net/radrock/sounds/trgcmptr.avi
Video of what Luke sees in his targeting computer.

Taz's Star Wars Movies
http://seconn4.yoda.com/~vader97/movies/movies.html
Over 50 AVI format video clips from the Trilogy.

Watch This - Video of Han & Leia in the Falcon
http://users.why.net/radrock/sounds/watchths.avi
"Watch This" says Han in this AVI video.

Yoda's Hut - Star Wars Movie Files
http://home.rogerswave.ca/gbarnes/swmovies.html
AVI and MOV video files of the Trilogy & Special Editions.

MPEGs

MPEG video - the next generation of video formatting - will eventually include more Star Wars pieces for our enjoyment. Below is a short list of what we have found.

Best of Meco
www.live-wire.com/record-reviews/frame/m/meco/best-of.html
Meco was the group that made the Star Wars Disco hit!

Cita Delle Nuvole (Cloud City)
www.geocities.com/Area51/Corridor/1431/
Italian Cloud City site with MP3 sounds & MPEG video, more!

Star Wars Driving/Steering Wheel Virtual System
http://iml.millersv.edu/html.stuff/wtkstuff/wheel.dir/wheel.html
3D resource page with MPEG videos & sounds files for VRML.

Star Wars Legacy Download Videos
www.starwarz.com/swlegacy/video.html
Trailers & Special Edition videos in various download formats.

WAV Central - Star Wars
www.godlike.org/frontpage/starwars/index.html
WAV sounds with text, also MPEG Episode 1 Trailer video.

QuickTime Movies (MOV Files)

QuickTime video format was originally created for the Macintosh. The software to view QuickTime files is standard on most Macintoshes as well as some PC systems. If you are a PC user and you have trouble opening a QuickTime file, visit Shareware.Com (www.shareware.com) or Filez (www.filez.com), and search for "QuickTime Player" to locate a program that you may download to view your QuickTime files.

A Few Minutes with George Lucas
www.daforce.demon.nl/fightback/dfhw2.htm
George Lucas' "see it on the big screen" video.

A New Hope Video Clips
　　http://home.multiweb.nl/~bramenpim/staranh.htm
　　　A New Hope AVI & QuickTime video clips.

Bill's Dagobah Page
　　www.geocities.com/Area51/Dimension/6975/starwars.html
　　　Sights & sounds of Return of the Jedi from a Dagobah site.

Blake's Ultimate Star Wars Site
　　www.geocities.com/Area51/Shadowlands/4351/index.html
　　　More variety than most multimedia sites.

Blueharvest.net Star Wars Videos
　　www.blueharvest.net/video/
　　　49 assorted QuickTime Videos - FX, trailers, spoofs, coms.

Carrie Videos (Unofficial Carrie Fisher Homepage)
　　www.offsoho.com/carrie/html/8video.html
　　　Fun MOV video clips featuring Carrie.

Competely Phat Star Wars Site
　　www.perfekt.net/~snoopy/video/video.html
　　　IMAX, Pepsi, Special & Prequel trailers - videos.

Daniel Feith's Star Wars Videos
　　www.germany.net/teilnehmer/101/78382/Star-Wars.html
　　　German site offers QuickTime videos.

Dark Horizons Film Trailers
　　www.darkhorizons.com/trailers/index-n.htm
　　　A whole trailer camp of current movies.

Design Originals of Episode 1; Doug Chiang's Portfolio
　　www.starwars.com/episode-i/features/chiang/
　　　Artist Doug Chiang talks/draws on this official site.

Duel of Darth Vader & Obi-wan Kenobi Video
　　www.telecom.csuhayward.edu/~aleung/dv_ken.mov
　　　Clip of Darth & ol' Ben wearing out batteries on their sabers.

Empire Strikes Back Video Clips
　　http://home.multiweb.nl/~bramenpim/staresb.htm
　　　Video clips & finds about the Empire Strikes Back.

HGWizard's Star Wars Movie Clips
　　www.geocities.com/Hollywood/Hills/1792/movie.html
　　　Various QuickTime action videos.

Interviews - Hollywood Online
　　www.hollywood.com/starwars/interview/interview.html
　　　Interviews in audio, video, or text formats.

Jedi Paradise Multimedia for Star Wars & Phantom Menace
　　http://members.aol.com/bigeoz/multimedia.html
　　　Sights, sounds, videos, humor videos all on 1 Prequel page.

Kave, The
　　www.educ.kent.edu/~kdevine/movies/
　　　Variety of QT videos, Trailers, MP3s, toys & Prequel fun.

Lake Washington Online
　　http://lwo.lkwash.wednet.edu/
　　　Prequel trailers in hi or low-res QuickTime / stereo.

Multimedia: QuickTime Movies (MOV Files)

Liquefy
http://grind.isca.uiowa.edu/
University resource of recent QuickTime video downloads.

Lord Vader's Lair Movie Clips
www.geocities.com/Area51/Cavern/4897/frmovie.html
MOV & AVI video clips at this Lair.

McLaurin's Star Wars Movies
http://members.xoom.com/_XOOM/maclaurin384/starwars/movies/movies.html
AVI & MOV video gallery.

Mike's Star Wars Pages
www.ece.orst.edu/~volzmi/starwars/
Very good variety of sound, images, clips, computer stuff.

Movies - A Feminine Perspective
http://members.aol.com/bananie42/movies.html
24 QuickTime Trilogy movies & trailers.

Movies - AVI & QuickTime
http://pweb.netcom.com/~fragger/movies.html
Collection of short movie clips from the Trilogy.

Movies.Com
www.movies.com
Touchstone Pictures "Now Playing" & info page.

Movies: Star Wars Video
http://pweb.netcom.com/~fragger/movies.html
Video clips from Trilogy movies (may now have Prequel updates).

My Quicktime Star Wars Video Library
http://weber.u.washington.edu/~sbode/starwars/clips.html
Trilogy QuickTime video selections.

NetJunctions Movies
www.netjunction.com/starwars/movies.htm
12 QuickTime video movies; includes Trilogy Specials.

Return of the Jedi Video Clips
http://home.multiweb.nl/~bramenpim/starrotj.htm
Return of the Jedi video clips collection.

Sci-fi Movie Clips
http://graffiti.u-bordeaux.fr/MAPBX/roussel/anim-e_03f.shtml
Big Sci-fi movie galleries from a French site.

Star Wars (Videos)
www.students.dsu.edu/hilleste/starwars.html
QuickTime & AVI Trilogy video clips.

Star Wars Sounds From --
www.pages.drexel.edu/undergrad/bzm22/starwars.html
WAVs, some choice AIFFs sounds, & QuickTime video files.

Stephen's Star Wars Den Movies
www.geocities.com/Area51/Labyrinth/1390/movie.htm
Trilogy movie clips, also sound and picture files.

Trailer Mirror Lists
http://sabbeth.com/starwars/mirrorlist.htm
Mirror lists of sites offering Star Wars Trailers.
TROOPS
www.theforce.net/troops/
Parody video of COPS-like stormtroopers - complete with sand.
Watto's Junkyard Downloads
www.wattosjunkyard.com/downloads.html
Good selection of QuickTime Prequel videos & game demos.
Yoda's Hut - Star Wars Movie Files
http://home.rogerswave.ca/gbarnes/swmovies.html
AVI and MOV video files of the Trilogy & Special Editions.

Real Video

The Real Video format is a good computer medium for somewhat longer files, interviews for example. A Real Player is available at www.realplayer.com.

Chico's Star Wars Video & Music
http://chico.simplenet.com/
Video clips a specialty.
Dark Horizons Film Trailers
www.darkhorizons.com/trailers/index-n.htm
A whole trailer camp of current movies.
Directory of multimedia/realvideo
www.lucasfan.com/multimedia/realvideo/
Small RAM RealVideo collection.

Jedi Paradise Multimedia for Star Wars & Phantom Menace
http://members.aol.com/bigeoz/multimedia.html
Sights, sounds, videos, humor videos all on 1 Prequel page.

Parody Video: Episode 1 Trailer 'A' - Special Edition
http://sabbeth.com/~menace/specialedition.htm
Spoof of the Trailer put together by fans for free.

RealVideo John Williams Interview
http://theforce.net/cgi-bin/tfn.cgi?action=getstory&storyID=2008
Launch RealVideo interview of John Williams here.

Star Wars Legacy Download Videos
www.starwarz.com/swlegacy/video.html
Trailers & Special Edition videos in various download formats.

Videos -- Miscellaneous

Sites here can offer videos in any combination of the four previous video formats. Also, many of the web sites listed under "Miscellaneous" may offer a single video, or they may be a resource tool that helps you find thousands of videos at other web sites. Also in this list are sites where you can "purchase" videos, or search for them.

A Feminine Perspective
http://members.aol.com/bananie42/index.html
Solid! None of that really mushy stuff.

AltaVista
www.altavista.com/
Good place to search for Star Wars images.

AV Photo & Media Finder
http://image.altavista.com/cgi-bin/avncgi
Random searching for Star Wars images, video, or audio files.

Bespin 2 Multimedia
www.marua.com/bespin/index3.htm
New, growing multimedia pages by resourceful Marua Sector.

Bill's Dagobah Page
www.geocities.com/Area51/Dimension/6975/starwars.html
Sights & sounds of Return of the Jedi from a Dagobah site.

Blake's Ultimate Star Wars Site
www.geocities.com/Area51/Shadowlands/4351/index.html
More variety than most multimedia sites.

Boba Fett's Awesome Homepage
www.geocities.com/Area51/Lair/2192/Home.html
Fett & bounty hunter eye-candy & commentary.

Boba Fett's Bungalow
www.geocities.com/Area51/Nebula/9901/bobafett.html
We trust your journey on Slave 1 was satisfactory.

Boober's Star Wars Galaxy
http://home.fuse.net/mckee/frames.htm
Worth the visit. 625 multimedia files & a good games page.

Britt's Boba Fett Site
www.geocities.com/Area51/Quadrant/2581/frmemain.html
Have a Fett-ish? You have to visit this Boba Site.

Carrie Videos (Unofficial Carrie Fisher Homepage)
www.offsoho.com/carrie/html/8video.html
Fun MOV video clips featuring Carrie.

Cartoons - Droids & Ewoks
www.lucasfan.com/animated/animated.html
Droid & Ewok TV cartoons - pix, video, very nice!

Chewbacca Homepage, The New
http://users.ids.net/~mtavares/chewie.html
Cool Java tricks onboard - high tech for a Wookiee super site.

Chewie's Web Site Pictures & Sounds
www.music.uh.edu/~chewie/ps.html
Episode 1 sound clips, also South Park & Star Wars quotes.

Chiv's Star Wars Page
http://highlander.cbnet.ns.ca/~bchivari/star/star.html
Multimedia page with trivia, transcripts, screensavers, & more.

Coruscant Project at Ord Mantell
www.geocities.com/Area51/Lair/8349/txindex.html
Coruscant - Welcome to the Sunny Shores of...

Dark Horizons
www.darkhorizons.com/index2.html
1-stop movie resource - news, trailers, facts.

Dark Rising
http://home.sol.no/~mgrambo/index2.htm
Multimedia page with galleries of sights, sounds, action clips.

Dark Side of Star Wars
www.geocities.com/Area51/Vault/2674/index2.html
Isn't really "Dark."

Dash's Star Wars Mania
http://members.tripod.com/~Dash88/index.html
Pix, movies, Prequel fluff, and page/links to movie goof-ups.

David Jansen's Star Wars Page
www.strw.leidenuniv.nl/~jansen/sw/
Multimedia site with fortune cookies (quotes), sounds & pix.

Den, The
www.theden.com/
Light entertainment & Sci-fi news.

E187vader's Star Wars Empire
www.geocities.com/Area51/Vault/6782/frames.html
Hard to find Darth Vader page.

El Camino's Star Wars Page
www.geocities.com/Area51/Rampart/4264/ie4.htm
We liked it - interesting juxtaposition of pages.

Electric GIFs
www.electricgifs.com/
Search tool that finds Star War GIFs - and other topics, too.

Episode 1 Multimedia (the force.net)
www.theforce.net/multimedia/epi.shtml
Episode 1 Sounds, Images, even some videos.

Multimedia — Videos -- Miscellaneous

Evil Has a New Face - Darth Maul Galleries
www.dbmedia.org/maul/maultimedia/
It's intimidated just looking at this page; there's evil humor, too.

Extreme Star Wars Site
www.angelfire.com/co/gavind/index.html
Good variety - includes some good text material.

Fighter Gets It In The Trench
www.telecom.csuhayward.edu/~aleung/trench.mov
Video of fighter in the Death Star Trench.

Film.com
www.film.com/
It's gotta lot of film/movie/video stuff!

FORCE.NET - Your Daily Dose of Star Wars
http://theforce.net/
Mega Star Wars Info Site - Mega!

FTP Echo Station
www.echostation.com/multimedia/
Join, then get FTP downloads of Star Wars humor videos.

Generic Star Wars Page, The
www.geocities.com/Area51/Corridor/9410/
Audio clips of interviews, plus links to other good, unusual sites.

Geocities Hollywood Studio
www.geocities.com/Hollywood/Studio/
Hosts plenty of Star Wars pages - a good place to search, too.

Harrison Ford - Viewing Room
www.smartlink.net/~deej7/pix.htm
Oh yeah - this is the place for Ford pix!

Hasbro Cool Stuff 3D VR Collectibles
www.hasbrotoys.com/coolstuf.html
Star Wars action figures in 3D in QuickTime videos.

HGWizard's Multimedia Archive
www.geocities.com/Hollywood/Hills/1792/opening.html
Movie clips are the strong point here.

Hollywood Online - Star Wars The Phantom Menace
www.hollywood.com/starwars/main.html
Entertaining site has The Phantom Menace covered!

Hydrospanner
www.hydrospanner.com/
Is a hydrospanner the most useful tool in space, or what?

Ian's Incredible Star Wars Page
www.airnet.net/pcusers/ianspage/
Gets our seal of approval.

Imperial Fleet Schleswig-Holstein
http://members.xoom.com/ADAM_IFSH/
Imperial-flavor in a German site. Do they belong together?

Imperial Outpost
http://members.theglobe.com/bobafett66/
Stuff for your computer as well as a variety of pix, videos, and fun.

Institute For Impure Science - Star Wars
   www.ifis.org.uk/p.cgi/multimedia/starwars/
      UK site offers versions of Episode 1 & humor videos.

Jabba's Palace Movie
   www.telecom.csuhayward.edu/~aleung/jabba's.mov
      QuickTime video of Jabba's Palace.

Jedi Council Chamber, The
   www.geocities.com/Area51/Hollow/9125/
      We liked the audio files and the kisses.

Jedinet
   www.jedinet.com/frame.htm
      By the Fans for the Fans - full-service super site.

Jedinet Software
   www.jedinet.com/software/
      Good coverage of software games news, screenshots.

Juan's Star Wars Site
   www.civila.com/hispania/obi-juan/english.htm
      English and Spanish versions; good multimedia site!

Lord Vader's Lair
   www.geocities.com/Area51/Cavern/4897/vader.html
      Movie clips, sounds, computer themes ...

Lucasfan.com
   www.lucasfan.com/
      Lucas' media contributions documented. News & humor, too.

MacCentral Online
   www.maccentral.com/news/9903/mar17.shtml
      Mac News & a download of versatile "Play It Cool" software.

Making of Episode 1
   www.starwars.com/making/
      Official "officials" clips from the making of Episode 1.

Martin Bond's Episode 1 Site
   http://members.xoom.com/_XOOM/mb_starwars/index.html
      Prequel videos, images, wallpaper, Anakin's House.

Martinez Brothers Star Wars page
   www.geocities.com/Area51/Dimension/5951/
      Variety of sights, sounds, bios, also scripts.

Marua Sector
   www.marua.com/index2.html
      New, developing semi-semi-mega all-purpose site.

MaulNet.Com
   www.maultnet.com
      dbmedia's Darth Maul super site - evil, evil, evil (and recommended)

MAW Installation
   www.premier.net/~exar/MAW2.htm
      More variety than most sites; includes bloopers, booklist, icons.

McLaurin's Center of Knowledge
   http://members.xoom.com/maclaurin386/index1.htm
      Star Wars, Star Trek, James Bond, and Emma sites all here.

Microsoft Flight Simulator 98 Star Wars Ships
http://members.xoom.com/Startroop1/Ships.html
Fly a TIE fighter, Interceptor or X-wing.

Monument Square Home Page
www.geocities.com/Area51/Lair/3373/home.html
Web site that we think will grow in size.

Mos Eisley Cantina
www.geocities.com/Hollywood/Set/7355/
Good multimedia, but forgot Mos Eisley Cantina stuff!

Nathan's Star Wars Page
http://members.aol.com/nathan224/starwars.html
Check for video of the week, info on novels, and more.

NatPortman.com
www.natportman.com/
All about Natalie Portman, plus images, video.

NetJunctions Star Wars Tribute
www.netjunction.com/starwars/
Memorable sounds, images, moves, and games pages.

New Republic Multimedia
http://thenewrepublic.8m.com/cgi-bin/framed/2478/starwars2.html
Mixed media - true potpourri. Sounds, pix, computer do-dads.

Nocturne's Pulp Fiction
www.skipnet.com/~nocturne/pulpfiction.html
We had to include Samuel L. Jackson's breakout movie.

Phantom Menace II Society
www.geocities.com/~noahklein/phantom.html
Hip-hop homeboy attitude applied to some Star Wars dialog.

Phantom Menace Site, The
www.users.wineasy.se/doot/starwars/index.html
Prequel site focusing mostly on main actors and Nat Portman.

Prequels.com, The
http://theprequels.com/main.htm
Lively, colorful Prequel site - mucho variety!

Roderick Vonhogen's Virtual Edition
www.virtualedition.com/
Treated to higher-end features on this great Netherland's site.

Rogue 9's Animations
www.geocities.com/Baja/Mesa/4807/index2.html
Animations of Imperial craft, also B-wings & more.

Rogue 9's Star Wars Website
www.geocities.com/Baja/Mesa/4807/index2.html
Grab-bag of multimedia goodies and webring connections.

S - Pete's Movie Page.com
www.petesmoviepage.com/s.html
S = Star Wars videos. Find QuickTime files here.

Simon Ray's Star Wars Files
www.fairfield.demon.co.uk/
Video & small sound collection from the United Kingdom.

Skystation Lounge
www.theforce.net/Skystation/
Skystation - it's a swanky place to catch CG animations.

Skywalker's MOVs & MPEGs
www.usmo.com/~starwars/mov&mpg.html
Short movie clips. Don't blink. Good variety.

Special Editions, The
http://scifi.simplenet.com/starwars/special_edition/index.html
Special edition galleries and reviews (closed 1/31/98)

Stakawaka's Natalie Portman Page
www.geocities.com/Hollywood/Lot/7181/natalie.html
Collection of Natalie info and poses over the years.

Star Wars As Seen On TV
www.lucasfan.com/swtv/index.html
Star Wars on the little screen collection.

Star Wars Cantina
http://members.tripod.com/~ss_star_wars/index.html
Sights, sounds, also chat, club links & a few games.

Star Wars Episode 1 - The Music
http://members.es.tripod.de/Befan/Episode1music.html
Who thought there wasn't much to Star Wars music? There sure is!

Star Wars Gamers
www.swgamers.com/
Hear about latest games; find downloads & demos.

Star Wars Legacy
www.starwarz.com/swlegacy/frameset.html
Wildcat video project continues Star Wars 60 years hence.

Star Wars Multimedia Headquarters
www.nerf-herder.com/swmhq/index.html
'been around awhile: light-hearted & fun.

Star Wars Virtual Reality System
http://zansiii.millersv.edu/work2/starwars.dir/
University Star Wars VRML sim project.

Starwarz
www.starwarz.com/
Rates highly as an alternative fan site portal. Unique concept.

Swammi's Star Wars Outpost
   http://members.xoom.com/kessel/outpost/
      Go there - gather the goodies for your own web site.

SWMA - Star Wars Modeling Alliance
   www.surfthe.net/swma/
      Great site - the force is definitely here.

T'Bone Fenders Star Wars Universe
   www.starwarz.com/index.htm
      Among the best fan operated sites on the 'Net.

Theatrical Trailers
   www.jedinet.com/multimedia/movies/index.htm
      Unzip and view these Trilogy & Special Edition videos and promos.

Trailer Mirror Lists
   http://sabbeth.com/starwars/mirrorlist.htm
      Mirror lists of sites offering Star Wars Trailers.

Troops - IMDb
   http://us.imdb.com/Title?0153301
      It's a kick in the afterburners - here's cast & production details.

Unofficial Carrie Fisher Homepage
   www.offsoho.com/carrie/html/86home.html
      It's Unofficial but it's very stellar. Big Carrie pix sections.

Watto's Junkyard
   www.wattosjunkyard.com/
      Among our favorite-est Prequel sites - good variety & style.

World 'O Chewbacca
   http://members.aol.com/andrewm675/chewbacca/chewie.html
      Chewiee tribute site with videos, sounds, survey, & his bio.

X-Wing Attack Video Preview
   www.hollywood.com/multimedia/movies/starwars/video/mmindex.html
      X-Wing Attack video preview in AVI, MOV, & Mac formats.

Surprisingly, actor Liam Neeson is the same age as Mark Hamill, who played Luke Skywalker.

Audio

It takes ears – and an audio player on your computer – to hear the audio files found on our list of audio web sites. Sounds files are listed under 4 format types: MIDI (music, generally), MP3s (most require an FTP utility), Real Audio (somewhat longer files), and WAVs (usually short quotes and sounds).

MIDIs

MIDI files usually contain music. Web sites often collect their MIDIs together, placing them on one page, then arranging them by category on that page. Other sites may list MIDIs with other sound formats, usually WAVs.

Alan's Star Wars MIDI Page
www.geocities.com/SiliconValley/Pines/4928/midi2.htm
Good list of MIDI sound clips.

Anakin14's Star Wars Home Page
www.geocities.com/Area51/Chamber/6138/frames.html
Fairly solid site; the focus is on sounds files.

Ben's Awesome Star Wars Page
www.geocities.com/Area51/Zone/7153/
"Had a slight weapons malfunction, everything under control now."

Big Kourt's House of Star Wars, X-Files, Star Trek & Used Hubcaps
www.geocities.com/Area51/Lair/7558/
Won't find the hubcaps - will find unusual Star Wars phrases.

Bill's Dagobah Page
www.geocities.com/Area51/Dimension/6975/starwars.html
Sights & sounds of Return of the Jedi from a Dagobah site.

Blake's Ultimate Star Wars Site
www.geocities.com/Area51/Shadowlands/4351/index.html
More variety than most multimedia sites.

Danny's Super Star Wars Page
www.geocities.com/Area51/Comet/3947/index.html
Photos & sounds are served up hot here.

Deak's Den
http://frodo.hiof.no/~deak/audio/miniwav.html
MP3s, WAVs, MIDIs, and Sun Audio Sound Files.

Jedi Base Audio Files
www.bestweb.net/~fett/audiomain.htm
WAVs and MIDI sounds files from the Trilogy.

Luke & Leia Musical Piece
www.thenorm.com/tfm/
Mixes Star Wars music & Peanuts piano themes.

MIDI Files (Jedinet)
www.jedinet.com/multimedia/midi/index.htm
MIDI music Trilogy themes for your ears.

MIDI Music by Scott M Leonard
>www.geocities.com/TheTropics/Shores/5972/midimusic.html
>>Arrangements and Star Wars-related original MIDI music.

Mike's Star Wars Pages
>www.ece.orst.edu/~volzmi/starwars/
>>Very good variety of sound, images, clips, computer stuff.

Monument Square Sound Collection
>www.geocities.com/Area51/Lair/3373/sounds.html
>>Mostly quotes like "You may fire when ready."

Rogue 8's Media Vault
>http://members.xoom.com/rogue88/mediavault.htm
>>Well-arranged Trilogy sound files, font collection; vault is open!

Sounds - Jedi Council Chamber
>www.geocities.com/Area51/Hollow/9125/Audioi.htm
>>Many character quotes & sounds. Some common, some rare.

Sounds; Star Wars - from Entertainment Cell
>http://pweb.netcom.com/~fragger/media.html
>>Selection of music themes and sound phrases.

Space Depot 24
>www.geocities.com/Area51/Vault/4910/space.htm
>>This site has been around awhile!

Star Wars MIDI Music
>www.geocities.com/Area51/9394/
>>Yes, music/sounds from movies & games!

Star Wars Multimedia HQ Sounds
>http://nerf-herder.com/swmhq/sounds.html
>>"Never tell me the odds" and other memorable quotes & music.

Star Wars Sound Page
>www.xs4all.nl/~meelberg/index.html
>>Lots o' quotes and music in WAV and MIDI formats.

Star Wars Sounds (Clemson .edu)
>http://people.clemson.edu/~jvalice/starS.htm
>>Quotes and MIDI music from the Trilogy.

Stv1's Star Wars MIDI Clips
>http://members.tripod.com/~stv1/index-5.html
>>Trilogy music clips in MIDI format.

Swammi's Star Wars MIDIs (music)
>http://members.xoom.com/kessel/outpost/midi.html
>>Music that might fit nicely on your web page.

Ultimate Star Wars Midi's Page
>www.geocities.com/Area51/Lair/3724/midis.html
>>It's simple to hear music here.

MP3s

MP3s are the latest technology in quality sound reproduction, and are suitable for exacting sound duplication. Due to their size, most MP3 files are only accessible using an FTP utility.

bkf-star wars episode 1 the phantom menace soundtrack
ftp://mp3:mp3@150.140.186.78:500/uploadz
Episode 1 soundtrack MP3 pieces (check if open).

Cita Delle Nuvole (Cloud City)
www.geocities.com/Area51/Corridor/1431/
Italian Cloud City site with MP3 sounds & MPEG video, more!

Deak's Den
http://frodo.hiof.no/~deak/audio/miniwav.html
MP3s, WAVs, MIDIs, and Sun Audio Sound Files.

Disco Mix Star Wars MP3
ftp://mp3:mp3@24.64.91.138:8145/pub/mp3s
Find the Star Wars Disco Remix in MP3 FTP format.

Imperial March MP3
ftp://mp3:mp3@193.10.244.68:2000/Unsorted%20MP3z/(Star_Wars)_Imperial_March.mp3
Daht, Daht, Daht, tawh daht. Imperial March MP3.

Imperial March.mp3
ftp://mp3:mp3@24.64.98.51/Star%20Wars%20-%20Imperial%20March.mp3
Feel the power of the Imperial March.

Jedi Paradise Multimedia for Star Wars & Phantom Menace
http://members.aol.com/bigeoz/multimedia.html
Sights, sounds, videos, humor videos all on 1 Prequel page.

Kave, The
www.educ.kent.edu/~kdevine/movies/
Variety of QT videos, Trailers, MP3s, toys & Prequel fun.

Parody Song: Star Wars Cantina.mp3 (to tune of Copa Cabana)
ftp://comedy:archives@24.65.86.38/Song%20Parodies/
Downloadable MP3 Cantina parody FTP file.

Star Wars (A New Hope) MP3 Sounds
www.psyc.canterbury.ac.nz/pgrad/carr/starwars.html
MP3 sound file quotes from the first movie.

Star Wars - Mega Mix
ftp://mp3:mp3@parlea.dynip.com:21/c:/ftp/music-mp3z/techno/star wars - megamix.mp3
FTP downloadable MP3 Mega Mix.

Star Wars - Remix mp3
ftp://mp3:mp3@206.140.159.75:21/c:/WINDOWS/Web/Webpage/MP3/
Big MP3 collection featuring 2 Star Wars versions.

Star Wars Episode One Trailer.mp3 (John Williams)
ftp://mp3:mp3@195.34.154.136/music4/entertaining
Episode 1 MP3 music.

Star Wars Imperial March (Metallica) mp3
ftp://mp3z:mp3z@24.65.109.81:21/RealMP3's/Misc/
Metallica's Imperial March in MP3 FTP.

Star Wars Main Theme (Skywalker Symphony) mp3
ftp://mp3:mp3@parlea.dynip.com:21/c:/ftp/music-mp3z/classical/
FTP download of MP3 Skywalker Theme.

Star Wars MP3 Audio Tracks
http://168.229.236.7/~cc/mp3.html
Empire & Return of the Jedi MP3 music files.

Theme - Star Wars.mp3
ftp://mp3:mp3@24.64.98.51/Theme%20-%20Star%20Wars.mp3
Star Wars Theme in downloadable MP3 format.

Themes - Star Wars
ftp://mp3:mp3@24.64.169.207:555/MP3
Star Wars & other movie themes.

Thrawn Art Gallery Music Collection
http://empire.res.wabash.edu/art/music/index.htm
Download zipped MP3 audio files from the Trilogy & Special Editions.

Real Audio

Real Audio (.ra or .au) format sound files are a suitable format for interviews or longer audio episodes. A Real Player is available at www.realplayer.com.

Admiral's Star Wars Page
www.geocities.com/Area51/Hollow/2779/
Admiral has collected some very good Star Wars images and music.

Anakin14's Star Wars Home Page
www.geocities.com/Area51/Chamber/6138/frames.html
Fairly solid site; the focus is on sounds files.

Audio Booth, The
www.smartlink.net/~deej7/audio.htm
Harrison sound clips in Real Audio. Player downloads, too.

Ben & Grovers Media Archives
www.bmartin.u-net.com/media.htm
Large, categorized collection of Real Audio Sound files.

E187vader's Favorite WAV & AU Sounds
www.geocities.com/Area51/Vault/6782/wavs.html
Quote clips from Vader, Han Yoda, & Leia.

Generic Star Wars Page, The
www.geocities.com/Area51/Corridor/9410/
Audio clips of interviews, plus links to other good, unusual sites.

Index of Multimedia Sounds.star.wars
http://info.fuw.edu.pl/multimedia/sounds.star.wars/
Sound clips - mostly Darth Vader - from fuw university.

Interviews - Hollywood Online
www.hollywood.com/starwars/interview/interview.html
Interviews in audio, video, or text formats.

Real Audio (Jedinet)
www.jedinet.com/multimedia/realaudio/index.htm
Real Audio sound clips downloads gallery.

WAVs

WAVs are the most common sound format for the computer. Usually, WAV format is used for quotes downloaded from other media such as videos. WAV format is also a good medium for delivering sounds on web sites.

A1's Star Wars Sounds
http://members.aol.com/XxKypxX/sound.html
Rebels & Imperial phrases, sounds.

Anakin14's Star Wars Home Page
www.geocities.com/Area51/Chamber/6138/frames.html
Fairly solid site; the focus is on sounds files.

Artwork & Symbols
www.wcug.wwu.edu/~paradox/art.html
Surprising large & varied collection of images.

Audio Recordings (Knight Hammer)
www.geocities.com/Hollywood/Bungalow/3606/
WAV audio file from the Imperial Knight Hammer.

Ben's Awesome Star Wars Page
www.geocities.com/Area51/Zone/7153/
"Had a slight weapons malfunction, everything under control now."

Big Kourt's House of Star Wars, X-Files, Star Trek & Used Hubcaps
www.geocities.com/Area51/Lair/7558/
Won't find the hubcaps - will find unusual Star Wars phrases.

Bill's Dagobah Page
www.geocities.com/Area51/Dimension/6975/starwars.html
Sights & sounds of Return of the Jedi from a Dagobah site.

Blake's Ultimate Star Wars Site
www.geocities.com/Area51/Shadowlands/4351/index.html
More variety than most multimedia sites.

Chewie's Web Site Pictures & Sounds
www.music.uh.edu/~chewie/ps.html
Episode 1 sound clips, also South Park & Star Wars quotes.

Deak's Den
http://frodo.hiof.no/~deak/audio/miniwav.html
MP3s, WAVs, MIDIs, and Sun Audio Sound Files.

Debo's House of Star Wars WAV Site
http://houseofdebo.simplenet.com/wavhouse/starwars.html
One of the bigger collections of Star Wars A New Hope sounds.

Multimedia — WAVs

E187vader's Favorite WAV & AU Sounds
www.geocities.com/Area51/Vault/6782/wavs.html
Quote clips from Vader, Han Yoda, & Leia.

EarthStation1's Movie Sounds Showcase: Star Wars WAVs
http://earthstation1.simplenet.com/starwars.html
Movie Sounds Showcase Trilogy WAV sound bites.

Hear Mark
www.chez.com/jedinat/sounds.html
Mark speaks! WAV sound files of his quotes.

Index of Waves/Star Wars
www.ug.cs.sunysb.edu/~bouzakij/waves/Star_Wars/
University resource of WAV sound files.

Jedi Base Audio Files
www.bestweb.net/~fett/audiomain.htm
WAVs and MIDI sounds files from the Trilogy.

Jon's Fly-By-Night Sci-fi Image Gallery & Sound Archive
http://web.wt.net/~jquick/archive.html
Variety of WAV sound files, but limited pix. A modern Sci-fi site.

Massassi Order
www.hta.nl/php/Jan.Jacob.Mosselaar/swring.htm
Very useful site once you delve into it!

Netjunctions Sounds Page
www.netjunction.com/starwars/sounds.htm
Variety of sound clips in WAV format.

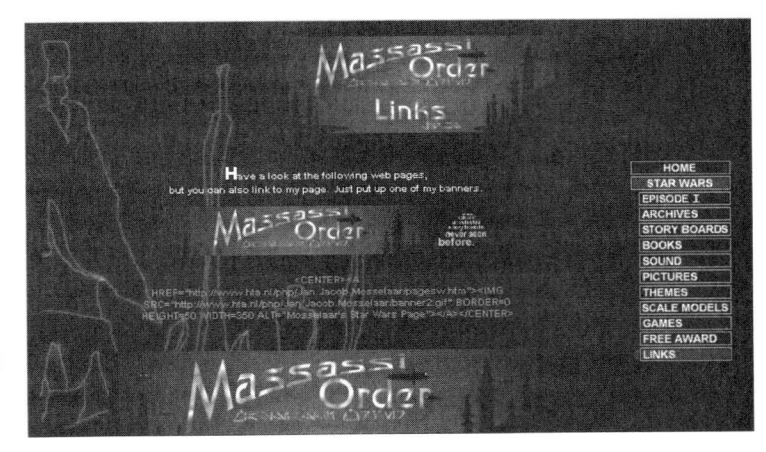

Phantom Menace Mania
http://get.to/jedi/
Great variety of Episode 1 images, sounds, video.

Rogue 8's Media Vault
http://members.xoom.com/rogue88/mediavault.htm
Well-arranged Trilogy sound files, font collection; vault is open!

Sound America A New Hope
http://soundamerica.com/sounds/movies/J-S/Star_Wars/A_New_Hope/
Good WAV files from original Star Wars.

Sound America Empire Strikes Back
http://soundamerica.com/sounds/movies/J-S/Star_Wars/Empire_Strikes_Back/
Many WAV sound files from Empire Strikes Back.

Sound America Return of the Jedi
   http://soundamerica.com/sounds/movies/J-S/Star_Wars/Return_of_the_Jedi/
   Return of the Jedi WAV sound files by the dozens.

Sounds - Jedi Council Chamber
   www.geocities.com/Area51/Hollow/9125/Audioi.htm
   Many character quotes & sounds. Some common, some rare.

Sounds - Spynals Star Wars Site
   http://members.xoom.com/Spynal/sounds.htm
   WAV sound files arranged by character.

Sounds; Star Wars - from Entertainment Cell
   http://pweb.netcom.com/~fragger/media.html
   Selection of music themes and sound phrases.

Space Depot 24
   www.geocities.com/Area51/Vault/4910/space.htm
   This sites been around awhile!

Star Wars Multimedia HQ Sounds
   http://nerf-herder.com/swmhq/sounds.html
   "Never tell me the odds" and other memorable quotes & music.

Star Wars Sound Page
   www.xs4all.nl/~meelberg/index.html
   Lots o' quotes and music in WAV and MIDI formats.

Star Wars Sounds
   www.strw.leidenuniv.nl/~jansen/sw/sound.html
   "We don't serve their kind here" - quotes too good to forget.

Star Wars Sounds (Clemson .edu)
   http://people.clemson.edu/~jvalice/starS.htm
   Quotes and MIDI music from the Trilogy.

Star Wars Sounds (Imperial)
   www.aaronklaassen.com/starwars/swwavs.htm
   Quotes from villains/Imperials in WAV sound format.

Star Wars Sounds From --
   www.pages.drexel.edu/undergrad/bzm22/starwars.html
   WAVs, some choice AIFFs sounds, & QuickTime video files.

Star Wars WAV Files
   http://168.229.236.7/~cc/wav.html
   Audio WAV files of memorable Trilogy quotes & R2.

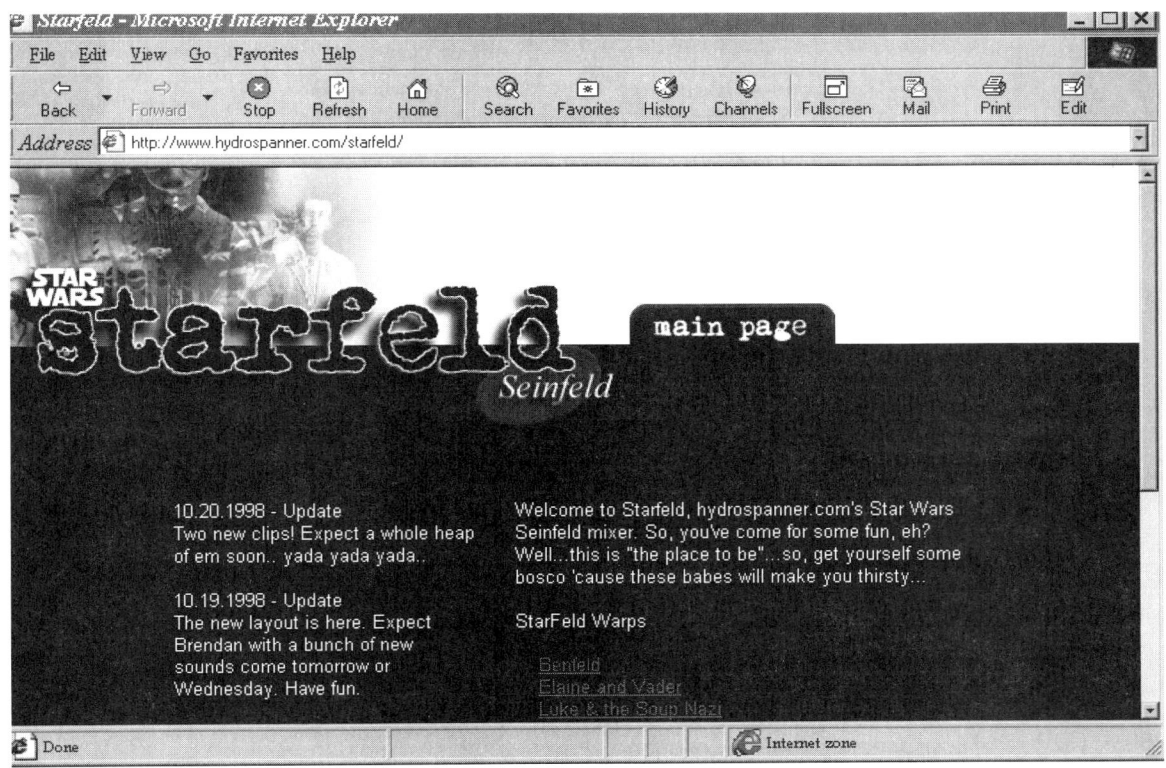

Starfeld
www.hydrospanner.com/starfeld/
Yada yada yada Star Wars/Seinfeld mixers.

Stephen's Star Wars Den Movies
www.geocities.com/Area51/Labyrinth/1390/movie.htm
Trilogy movie clips, also sound and picture files.

SW Wav Archive - Well, You Wanted Sounds, You Got em'
http://swwa.webjump.com/
200+ sounds and quotes, arranged by character.

WAV Archive - RPG at Echo Station
http://rpg.echostation.com/wav/wav.html
WAV sounds & music for roleplaying and other fun.

WAV Central - Star Wars
www.godlike.org/frontpage/starwars/index.html
WAV sounds with text, also MPEG Episode 1 Trailer video.

WAV Files
www.jedinet.com/multimedia/sounds/wav.htm
WAV sound clips arranged by Trilogy characters.

Wave Central Star Wars
www.wavcentral.com/starwars.htm
70+ WAV sound files arranged by movie.

Welcome to Death Star III
www.pitt.edu/~rsest4/starwars.html
WAV sound files arranged by character or topic.

Welcome to my page of Star Wars WAV files
http://members.tripod.com/~Satan15/SWars.html
Satan15's collection of WAV Trilogy sound files.

World's Best Star Wars Web Site Sounds
www.geocities.com/Area51/Nebula/4247/
WAV sound files - go fishing for your favorites.

Audio -- Miscellaneous

Here are audio files that may contain a combination of file formats, or, they may be a page that features but one clip. A few are found in AIFF format. We've included some audio search engines as well.

A Feminine Perspective
http://members.aol.com/bananie42/index.html
Solid! None of that really mushy stuff.

A Page of Undeniable Weirdness - Tribbles, Wookiees, & Ewoks
www.compusmart.ab.ca/macclan/Collpg1.htm
Sci-fi fan that's too off-the-wall - Trek, X-files, Star Wars.

A1's Star Wars Multimedia Page
http://members.aol.com/A1B2C369/index.html
Searchable "variety" collection, big on games, toys, also Pez.

Alan's Star Wars Page
www.geocities.com/SiliconValley/Pines/4928/index.html
Full fan site - worth the visit.

Alien Vocalizations
http://buteo.colorado.edu/~yosh/psi/system2/sounds/
A few alien AIFFs - but we need more!

Avanzada Rebeldo
www.ing.puc.cl/~bsg/
Chilian Star Wars mixed-media site (Spanish)

Bespin 2 Multimedia
www.marua.com/bespin/index3.htm
New, growing multimedia pages by resourceful Marua Sector.

Best of Meco
www.live-wire.com/record-reviews/frame/m/meco/best-of.html
Meco was the group that made the Star Wars Disco hit!

Bill's Star Wars Page
www.geocities.com/Area51/Dimension/6975/starwars.html
"Impressive." - Darth Vader. Good example of Star Wars multimedia site.

Boba Fett - Ultimate Star Wars Multimedia Page
www.geocities.com/Area51/Crater/3234/fett.html
16 Fett images, plus 2 quotes & animation of Slave 1.

Boba Fett's Bungalow
www.geocities.com/Area51/Nebula/9901/bobafett.html
We trust your journey on Slave 1 was satisfactory.

Multimedia — Audio -- Miscellaneous

Boober's Star Wars Galaxy
> http://home.fuse.net/mckee/frames.htm
>> Worth the visit. 625 multimedia files & a good games page.

Cantina, The
> www.the-cantina.com/
>> Award-winning site of Star Wars favorite watering hole.

Cartoons - Droids & Ewoks
> www.lucasfan.com/animated/animated.html
>> Droid & Ewok TV cartoons - pix, video, very nice!

Chewbacca Homepage, The New
> http://users.ids.net/~mtavares/chewie.html
>> Cool Java tricks onboard - high tech for a Wookiee super site.

Chewie's Web Page
> www.music.uh.edu/~chewie/
>> Upbeat Chewie portal with sights, sounds, & fun.

Chico's Star Wars Video & Music
> http://chico.simplenet.com/
>> Video clips a specialty.

Chiv's Star Wars Page
> http://highlander.cbnet.ns.ca/~bchivari/star/star.html
>> Multimedia page with trivia, transcripts, screensavers, & more.

Compendium, The
> www.wcug.wwu.edu/~paradox/images/hyper/
>> Not the prettiest site, but one of the fullest!

Dark Rising
> http://home.sol.no/~mgrambo/index2.htm
>> Multimedia page with galleries of sights, sounds, action clips.

Dark Side of Star Wars
> www.geocities.com/Area51/Vault/2674/index2.html
>> Isn't really "Dark."

Darth Vader Song, The
http://198.70.186.7/enterhtml/live/Kidz/vader.html
   Can you sing a song about Darth Vader? Here's one.

Dash Rendar's Star Wars Universe
www.angelfire.com/wi/SciFiPlace/

Dash's Star Wars Mania
http://members.tripod.com/~Dash88/index.html
   Pix, movies, Prequel fluff, and page/links to movie goof-ups.

David Jansen's Star Wars Page
www.strw.leidenuniv.nl/~jansen/sw/
   Multimedia site with fortune cookies (quotes), sounds & pix.

DJ Rhythm's Dance Music Database
www.djrhythms.com/db/
   Star Wars disco and a whole galaxy more of dance music.

E187vader's Star Wars Empire
www.geocities.com/Area51/Vault/6782/frames.html
   Hard to find Darth Vader page.

Echo Station
www.echostation.com/
   Full Service Star Wars portal! A must see.

El Camino's Star Wars Page
www.geocities.com/Area51/Rampart/4264/ie4.htm
   We liked it - interesting juxtaposition of pages.

Episode 1 Multimedia (the force.net)
www.theforce.net/multimedia/epi.shtml
   Episode 1 Sounds, Images, even some videos.

Extreme Star Wars Site
www.angelfire.com/co/gavind/index.html
   Good variety - includes some good text material.

FORCE.NET - Your Daily Dose of Star Wars
http://theforce.net/
   Mega Star Wars Info Site - Mega!

Frangisco's Star Wars PC Themes
http://coyote.accessnv.com/fasalvo/sw/theme.html
   Themes & goodies that make a computer into a Star Wars machine.

Free Resources from Dave Labbett
http://users.netmatters.co.uk/davelabbett/free/resinfo.html
   AIFF sounds and some plain Star Wars background screens

Geocities Hollywood Studio
www.geocities.com/Hollywood/Studio/
   Hosts plenty of Star Wars pages - a good place to search, too.

Gonkite's Groovy Grotto & Glossary
http://members.aol.com/gonkite/index.htm
   A get-you-acquainted glossary and Gonk info pages.

Graham's Star Wars & Homepage
www.angelfire.com/ga/glf/index.html
   Prequel & box office info featured on this new multimedia page.

Multimedia Audio -- Miscellaneous

Harrison Ford - A Web Guide to the Films
www.smartlink.net/~deej7/harrison_ford.html
Harrison - This ones for you! There is no "I" in "hero."

Harrison Ford - Viewing Room
www.smartlink.net/~deej7/pix.htm
Oh yeah - this is the place for Ford pix!

HGWizard's Multimedia Archive
www.geocities.com/Hollywood/Hills/1792/opening.html
Movie clips are the strong point here.

Hollywood Online - Star Wars The Phantom Menace
www.hollywood.com/starwars/main.html
Entertaining site has The Phantom Menace covered!

Hydrospanner
www.hydrospanner.com/
Is a hydrospanner the most useful tool in space, or what?

Ian's Incredible Star Wars Page
www.airnet.net/pcusers/ianspage/
Gets our seal of approval.

ICQ Soundpack, Irc Script Pack, New Star Wars Font
www.jedinet.com/multimedia/windows/misc/index.htm
Computer accessories you probably hadn't thought of!

Imperial Outpost
http://members.theglobe.com/bobafett66/
Stuff for your computer as well as a variety of pix, videos, and fun.

Imperial Spy Network
www.angelfire.com/mo/StarWarsImages/
Spies? Where? Here?

Imperial TIE Fighter Hangar Bay, The
www.geocities.com/Area51/Shadowlands/4918/
Multimedia from the Imperial perspective.

Jabba's Palace - Outer-Rim Multimedia
http://outer-rim.net/multimedia/sounds/Palace
"I will not give up my favorite decoration...Han Solo!" - Jabba.

Jason's Star Wars Page
http://http.tamu.edu:8000/~jpc6754/starwars.html
Slim pickings, but does have Boba Fett pix.

Javval's Star Wars Page
www.multiboard.com/~jhowarth/starwars.htm
Javval the Hutt's story, also movie photos & MIDI sounds.

Jedi Base
www.bestweb.net/~fett/
Didn't find specifics on Jedi here, just all-'round Star Wars fun!

Jedi Council Chamber, The
www.geocities.com/Area51/Hollow/9125/
We liked the audio files and the kisses.

Jedinet
www.jedinet.com/frame.htm
By the Fans for the Fans - full-service super site.

Jim Butt's Star Wars Page
http://members.accessus.net/~wbutts/
Jukebox and good pix collection. What more do you need?

Juan's Star Wars Site
www.civila.com/hispania/obi-juan/english.htm
English and Spanish versions; good multimedia site!

Knight Hammer
www.geocities.com/Area51/Chamber/4182/index.html
Good content for a site with an Imperial overcoat!

LeeboMan's New Star Wars Site
www.angelfire.com/co/LeeboMan/
Galleries, polls, fun, also Chat and webring being developed.

LeeboMan's Star Wars Sound Page
www.angelfire.com/co/LeeboSounds/index.html
Contains rare sound clips.

Lord Vader's Lair
www.geocities.com/Area51/Cavern/4897/vader.html
Movie clips, sounds, computer themes ...

MacCentral Online
www.maccentral.com/news/9903/mar17.shtml
Mac News & a download of versatile "Play It Cool" software.

Martinez Brothers Star Wars page
www.geocities.com/Area51/Dimension/5951/
Variety of sights, sounds, bios, also scripts.

Marua Sector
www.marua.com/index2.html
New, developing semi-semi-mega all-purpose site.

MaulNet.Com
www.maultnet.com
dbmedia's Darth Maul super site - evil, evil, evil (and recommended)

MAW Installation
www.premier.net/~exar/MAW2.htm
More variety than most sites; includes bloopers, booklist, icons.

McLaurin's Center of Knowledge
http://members.xoom.com/maclaurin386/index1.htm
Star Wars, Star Trek, James Bond, and Emma sites all here.

Mfalcon's Star Wars Outpost
www.geocities.com/Area51/Zone/9049/
Collection of MIDI music, photos from 1st 3 episodes

Mike Gartley's Star Wars Page
www.ma.iup.edu/~tzgf/star/starwars.html
Posters, humor magazine covers, sights & sounds.

Monument Square Home Page
www.geocities.com/Area51/Lair/3373/home.html
Web site that we think will grow in size.

Mos Eisley Cantina
www.geocities.com/Hollywood/Set/7355/
Good multimedia, but forgot Mos Eisley Cantina stuff!

My Star Wars Web Site
www.geocities.com/Area51/Cavern/5033/
Over 8 million visitors since '97.

Nathan's Star Wars Page
http://members.aol.com/nathan224/starwars.html
Check for video of the week, info on novels, and more.

NetJunctions Star Wars Tribute
www.netjunction.com/starwars/
Memorable sounds, images, moves, and games pages.

New Republic Multimedia
http://thenewrepublic.8m.com/cgi-bin/framed/2478/starwars2.html
Mixed media - true potpourri. Sounds, pix, computer do-dads.

Nocturne's Pulp Fiction
www.skipnet.com/~nocturne/pulpfiction.html
We had to include Samuel L. Jackson's breakout movie.

Orin_J Kingdom
www.gogs32.freeserve.co.uk/page1.htm
Does Darth like neon blues and greens!?

Rogue 9's Star Wars Web Site
www.geocities.com/Baja/Mesa/4807/index2.html
Grab-bag of multimedia goodies and webring connections.

Salacious Crumb Homepage
www.madbbs.com/~salaciouscrumb/INDEX.HTM
Salacious Crumb - a character, a band, a Sword of Chaos gamer, a legend!

Simon Ray's Star Wars Files
www.fairfield.demon.co.uk/
Video & small sounds collection from the United Kingdom.

Spynals Star Wars Site
http://members.xoom.com/Spynal/home.htm
Good variety of content - easy to use.

Star Wars Cantina
http://members.tripod.com/~ss_star_wars/index.html
Sights, sounds, also chat, club links & a few games.

Star Wars Driving/Steering Wheel Virtual System
http://iml.millersv.edu/html.stuff/wtkstuff/wheel.dir/wheel.html
3D resource page with MPEG videos & sounds files for VRML.

Star Wars Episode 1 - The Music
http://members.es.tripod.de/Befan/Episode1music.html
Who thought there wasn't much to Star Wars music? There sure is!

Star Wars Multimedia Headquarters
www.nerf-herder.com/swmhq/index.html
'been around awhile: light-hearted & fun.

Star Wars Trilogy, The
www.linkline.be/users/duncan/starwars.html
Sounds, scripts, photos of the 3 Trilogy movies.

Star Wars Virtual Reality System
http://zansiii.millersv.edu/work2/starwars.dir/
University Star Wars VRML sim project.

Startroop1 Star Wars Page
http://members.xoom.com/Startroop1/
Downloads, pix, sounds, and a flight simulator.

Stv1's Star Wars Page
http://members.tripod.com/~stv1/index.html
Multimedia site with a Kubrick feel to it.

Swammi's Star Wars Outpost
http://members.xoom.com/kessel/outpost/
Go there - gather the goodies for your own web site.

T'Bone Fenders Star Wars Universe
www.starwarz.com/index.htm
Among the best fan operated sites on the Net.

Thomas Star Wars Home Page
www.geocities.com/TimesSquare/4580/
Mystery click-on: check to see if this site has been updated.

Ultimate Star Wars Multimedia Universe
www.geocities.com/Area51/Lair/3724/
Has a virtual reality page and beaucoups of computer goodies!

Unofficial Carrie Fisher Homepage
www.offsoho.com/carrie/html/86home.html
It's unofficial but it's very stellar. Big Carrie pix sections.

Virtual McGregor
www.enter.net/~cybernut/articles.htm
Ewan has some of the best fan web sites. Visit this one.

Welcome to Endor
www.geocities.com/Area51/Cavern/9101/
MIDI music, survey, a few good links, Hanson punch, but no Endor!

Welcome to the Mandalorian Sector
www.geocities.com/Area51/Cavern/5723/index2.html
Early Fett site draws heavy from comic book information.

Willems Star Wars Homepage
www.tem.nhl.nl/~veen606/veen606.html
Icons, sounds, video game, choice of 2 languages.

World 'O Chewbacca
http://members.aol.com/andrewm675/chewbacca/chewie.html
Chewiee tribute site with videos, sounds, survey, & his bio.

World's Best Star Wars Web Page
www.geocities.com/Area51/Nebula/5101/
Mailing addresses of actors, pix, sounds, computer goodies.

Star Wars Image Galleries

One of the most common features found on Star Wars-related web sites. Galleries are places on web sites where you can view, print and download images. The sites included in this chapter contain images on the page listed here or through links on the main page. Look for buttons or text links such as "Pictures," "Gallery" or "Images."

Almost all images found online are "downloadable" -- that is, you can save the image to your computer for viewing later, or for use in artwork or what not. However, not all web site owners want you to download the "pix" they offer. Usually, in these cases, the webmaster will say "nay" somewhere on the site. Images from the Star Wars movies are owned by Lucasfilms Ltd, which is the production company of George Lucas (you know him -- he invented Star Wars!). It is not a good idea to download "their" stuff and use it in a distasteful or commercial manner -- or any manner that would not be approved of in this galaxy or the next.

3D Images & Stereovision

Three-dimensional imaging is currently a hot topic on the web. 3D and stereovision have been around for awhile, but only in recent years have they become common on the Web. Here are some of our favorite Star Wars 3Ds as well as sites that offer 3D resources or information.

3D Fan Art - Marua Sector
www.marua.com/banners/3d/
50 3D pix; most are suitable for wallpaper.

3D Palette
www.3dpalette.com/
3D resource and mega-site.

3D Stereovision Star Wars Pix
   http://seconn4.yoda.com/~vader97/3d/3d.html
      Stereovision pix - stare at them 'til the image pops out.

Berlin's Network
   www.geocities.com/SouthBeach/Lights/5679/index.html
      Active 3D homepage with games, info, originals.

Hasbro Cool Stuff 3D VR Collectibles
   www.hasbrotoys.com/coolstuf.html
      Star Wars action figures in 3D in QuickTime videos.

Mastering 3D Graphics (M3G)
   www.mastering3dgraphics.com/
      3D artist galleries and tutorials for 3D graphics.

Star Wars 3D Gallery
   www.ipr.nl/sw-3d/
      Cool example of an early 3D modeling site from Holland.

Star Wars Fan & CG Art
   http://empire.res.wabash.edu/art/cg/index.htm
      "Must see" CG images. Spacecraft, magic eye pix, props.

SWMA - Star Wars 3D Modeling Alliance Archives
   www.surfthe.net/swma/archives/archives.html
      Storehouse of 3D that takes light years to see all of.

SWMA - Star Wars Modeling Alliance
   www.surfthe.net/swma/
      Great site - the force is definitely here.

Taz's Collection of Star Wars 3D Renderings
   www.chez.com/lordvader/3drender.html
      3D renderings files of spacecraft, vehicles, droids, Darth.

trueSpace 3dGraphics webring Sites List
   www.webring.org/cgi-bin/webring?ring=truespace;index
      tS Webring member list devoted to superb 3D Graphics.

Jedi's use "the force."
The evil emperor and
his warriors use Sith Powers.

Animations -- Images That Move

Animations – those rather small images that appear as short movie clips or banners that seem like "garnish" on web sites – are usually complex GIF images strung together to produce a short action sequence. We've included some of the better sites for finding animations, also places to download them.

A Lot More Star Wars Animations
http://seconn4.yoda.com/~vader97/animated/animated.html
A great place to catch some animations.

Animated GIFs Collection
www.geocities.com/Area51/Cavern/3129/
Good place to quick pick some Star Wars action files.

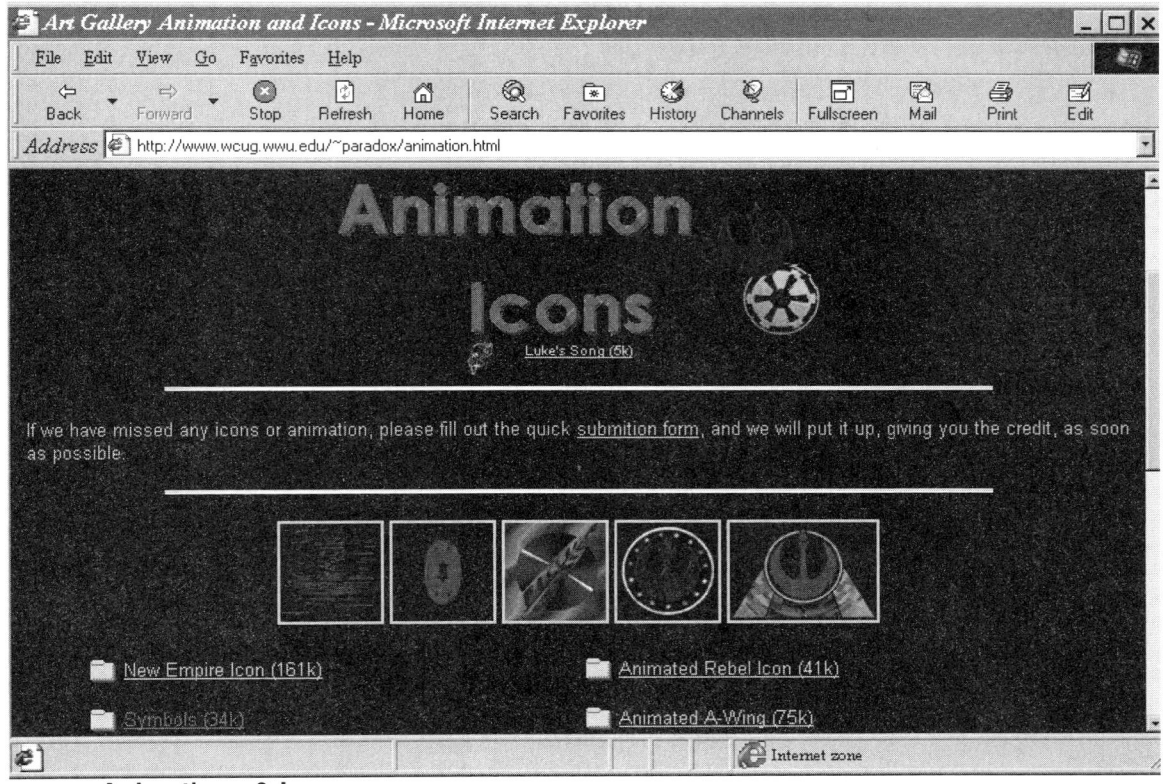

Animations & Icons
www.wcug.wwu.edu/~paradox/animation.html
Animated GIF logos and spacecraft.

Banners of other Star Wars Sites (Swammi collection)
http://members.xoom.com/kessel/outpost/thumbnail.html
Banners - those cool titles that make Star Wars pages hot.

Cartoons - Droids & Ewoks
www.lucasfan.com/animated/animated.html
Droid & Ewok TV cartoons - pix, video, very nice!

Electric GIFs
www.electricgifs.com/
Search tool that finds Star War GIFs - and other topics, too.

Holocron, The
>www.infinet.com/~schieltz/
>>A great GIF site once upon a time.

Imperial Executor
>www.angelfire.com/ny/ImperialExecutor/index.html
>>Find original animations here, also galleries, links to trivia, chat.

Jedi Mark's Place
>www.geocities.com/Area51/Hollow/9125/
>>No sissy stuff here! Han Solo would love this.

Rogue 9's Animations
>www.geocities.com/Baja/Mesa/4807/index2.html
>>Animations of Imperial craft, also B-wings & more.

Skystation Lounge
>www.theforce.net/Skystation/
>>Skystation - it's a swanky place to catch CG animations.

Skywalker's MOV's & MPG's
>www.usmo.com/~starwars/mov&mpg.html
>>Short movie clips. Don't blink. Good variety.

Star Wars Graphic Magic
>www.geocities.com/Hollywood/Theater/3518/
>>More animation magic may be on the way.

Star Wars JPEGs & GIFs Image Files
>www.geocities.com/Area51/Corridor/1086/swimages.html
>>The many pix here are rated for quality by the site author.

Startroop1 Star Wars Page
>http://members.xoom.com/Startroop1/
>>Downloads, pix, sounds, and a flight simulator.

Swammi's Star Wars Animated GIFs
>http://members.xoom.com/kessel/outpost/anim.html
>>Animations for web sites.

SWMA - Star Wars 3D Modeling Alliance
>www.swma.net
>>Great site - the force is definitely here.

Taz's Star Wars Animations
>www.geocities.com/Area51/Corridor/4307/starwarsani.html
>>Animations for your computer or web site.

Zaphoid's Animated GIFs
>http://synergy.foo.net/~zaphoid/starwars/animated_gifs/
>>Good GIFs action collection!

Cover Images

Covers for Star Wars books, comics, videos, and other products are quite visually pleasing, so we have collected sites together that specialize in galleries of covers.

Blueharvest.net Star Wars Images
www.blueharvest.net/images
"It excels at it." - C-3PO. A "must see" image gallery.

Comics & Covers - Thrawn Art Gallery
http://empire.res.wabash.edu/art/comics/index.htm
Color cover images of comic books; click to open sub-pages.

Covers to Star Wars Products
http://members.xoom.com/kessel/outpost/cover.html
Covers for the Star Wars video transporters.

Dagobah - or - Yoda, The Jedi Master
http://207.79.146.3/employees/jamieb/art.htm
Superb collection of name artists, covers & posters.

Ewan McGregor Gallery
www.geocities.com/~ewanmcgregor/gallery/
More Ewan images than your eyes can stand.

Ewoks - Star (Marvel) Comic Books Series
http://207.237.121.181/starwars/ewok01-06.html
15 Ewok Comic Book Covers in full color.

Novels of Star Wars (Thrawn Art Gallery)
http://empire.res.wabash.edu/art/novels/yjk.htm
Cover art for books by famous Star Wars fiction writers.

GIFs

GIF is often the visual format used for capturing images directly from video, but GIF is also a useful format for making animations and art come to life on the computer screen. See also "Animations" for more GIF pages, or see JPEG for more images and image galleries.

A Lot More Star Wars Animations
http://seconn4.yoda.com/~vader97/animated/animated.html
A great place to catch some animations.

Animated GIFs Collection
www.geocities.com/Area51/Cavern/3129/
Good place to quick pick some Star Wars action files.

Artwork & Symbols
www.wcug.wwu.edu/~paradox/art.html
Surprising large & varied collection of images.

Banners of other Star Wars Sites (Swammi collection)
http://members.xoom.com/kessel/outpost/thumbnail.html
Banners - those cool titles that make Star Wars pages hot.

Covers to Star Wars Products
http://members.xoom.com/kessel/outpost/cover.html
Covers for the Star Wars video transporters.

David Jansen's Star Wars Page
www.strw.leidenuniv.nl/~jansen/sw/
Multimedia site with fortune cookies (quotes), sounds & pix.

Droopy McCool's Star Wars Page
www.geocities.com/SunsetStrip/Disco/1283/starwars.html
Episode 1 action and main character pix.

E187vader's Special Edition Page
www.geocities.com/Area51/Vault/6782/special.html
Select pix from the Special Editions.

Electric GIFs
www.electricgifs.com/
Search tool that finds Star War GIFs - and other topics, too.

Eye On Episode 1 - Cast & Crew
http://starwars.tierranet.com/episode1/frame4.html
Characters with actor's name. GIF pix of cast and crew.

Holocron, The
www.infinet.com/~schieltz/
A great GIF site once upon a time.

Palace of the Raider King
http://members.tripod.com/~KingOfTheRaiders/Frames.html
Icons, also themes, screen saver, and GIF pix gallery.

Schematics Collection (Taz's)
http://seconn4.yoda.com/~vader97/Schematics/schematics.html
Schematics by the dozens, presented as GIF images.

Screenshots.net
www.screenshots.net/
Pictures from new Prequel games in GIF format.

Ships in the Star Wars Universe
http://members.xoom.com/kessel/outpost/ships.html
GIF & JPEG images of favorite spacecraft.

Special Edition Screen Shots
http://members.aol.com/T65Pilot/speced.html
Screenshot GIFs of new Trilogy scenes.

Star Backgrounds (Swammi Collection)
http://members.xoom.com/kessel/outpost/background.html
Starry, starry night backgrounds.

Star Wars Archives by SWKID
www.paulshome.cjb.net/swa
Galleries of JPEG & GIFs (some animated) to view/download.

Star Wars Force Graphics
http://plaza.harmonix.ne.jp/~m-falcon/
Stellar Japanese graphics site; most pix are posters.

Star Wars Gear
www.gogs32.freeserve.co.uk/gear.htm
Imperial craft animations, lightsaber lore. Different.

Star Wars Graphic Magic
    www.geocities.com/Hollywood/Theater/3518/
        More animation magic may be on the way.

Star Wars JPEGs & GIFs Image Files
    www.geocities.com/Area51/Corridor/1086/swimages.html
        The many pix here are rated for quality by the site author.

Star Wars Multimedia HQ Still Pictures
    http://nerf-herder.com/swmhq/pics.html
        Color & B&W galleries of characters, ships, more.

Star Wars Pictures (Clemson .edu)
    http://people.clemson.edu/~jvalice/starS.htm
        Plenty of action; also pix from the Special Editions.

Swammi's Characters in the Star Wars Universe
    http://members.xoom.com/kessel/outpost/char.html
        Can I get images for my web site? Affirmative!

Swammi's Knicknacks & Other Assorted Images
    http://members.xoom.com/kessel/outpost/kniknak.html
        Some hard-2-find Star Wars GIFs for web site publishers.

Swammi's Star Wars Animated GIFs
    http://members.xoom.com/kessel/outpost/anim.html
        Animations for web sites.

Swammi's Star Wars Logos
    http://members.xoom.com/kessel/outpost/logo.html
        Logos! Get yer Star Wars logos here!

Swedish University Network SUNET Star Wars
    ftp://ftp.sunet.se/pub/pictures/tv.film/Star_Wars/
        Swedish Star Wars and movie pix resource.

Taz's Star Wars Animations
    www.geocities.com/Area51/Corridor/4307/starwarsani.html
        Animations for your computer or web site.

Zaphoid's Animated GIFs
    http://synergy.foo.net/~zaphoid/starwars/animated_gifs/
        Good GIFs action collection!

*How many planets can be found in the original Star Wars Trilogy?
Eight planets & the Forest Moon of Endor.*

JPEGs

JPEG is perhaps the most common format for reproducing images – pictures, photos, art – on the computer. Included in the following list are web sites offering JPEG image galleries. These galleries are often presented on their own individual page or pages, and further separated into categories. We have included some web sites offering JPEG images on topics other than the movies – card galleries, publicity photos, and out-takes, to name a few.

Artwork & Symbols
www.wcug.wwu.edu/~paradox/art.html
Surprisingly large & varied collection of images.

Banners of other Star Wars Sites (Swammi collection)
http://members.xoom.com/kessel/outpost/thumbnail.html
Banners - those cool titles that make Star Wars pages hot.

Boba Fett - Ultimate Star Wars Multimedia Page
www.geocities.com/Area51/Crater/3234/fett.html
16 Fett images, plus 2 quotes and an animation of Slave 1.

Boba Fett's Awesome Homepage
www.geocities.com/Area51/Lair/2192/Home.html
Fett & bounty hunter eye-candy & commentary.

Bogus Star Wars Homepage
www.cinenet.net/~agrapha/StarNet/SW.html
Special effects & comments from Special Editions are featured.

Capeman's Prequel Production Pictures
http://members.aol.com/CapeMan69/pic.html
Pix from the Prequel shooting locations.

Cards (Jedinet)
www.jedinet.com/multimedia/pics/cards/index.htm
Best card/image file on 12 systems.

Chewbacca Galleries (Taz's)
http://seconn4.yoda.com/~vader97/chewie/chewie.html
Chewie in glorious Wookiee-color!

Chewbacca Homepage, The New
http://users.ids.net/~mtavares/chewie.html
Cool Java tricks onboard - high tech for a Wookiee super site.

Christmas Pictures
www.jedinet.com/multimedia/pics/xmas/index.html
6 Star Wars Christmas images.

Collecting (the force.net)
www.theforce.net/collecting/
You'll see a lot of big corporate promos here; Pepsi cans.

Images | JPEGs

Covers to Star Wars Products
http://members.xoom.com/kessel/outpost/cover.html
Covers for the Star Wars video transporters.

Dagobah - or - Yoda, The Jedi Master
http://207.79.146.3/employees/jamieb/art.htm
Superb collection of name artists, covers & posters.

Darth Vader Galleries (Taz's)
http://seconn4.yoda.com/~vader97/darth/darth.html
3 image galleries featuring Darth's hand-picked favorites!

Design Originals of Episode 1; Doug Chiang's Portfolio
www.starwars.com/episode-i/features/chiang/
Artist Doug Chiang talks/draws on this official site.

Dr. Itos Star Wars Images
http://www1.iastate.edu/~dritos/pix.html
JPEG images - some are very BIG.

E187vader's Special Edition Page
www.geocities.com/Area51/Vault/6782/special.html
Select pix from the Special Editions.

Emperor Palpatine Archive
http://seconn4.yoda.com/~vader97/emperor/emperor.html
Emperor Palpatine in all his living (or deathly) color.

Episode 1 Widevision Cards
www.sevaan.com/starwars/fanart/topps.htm
Collectible card images from Topps/Savaan Franks.

Ewan McGregor Gallery
www.geocities.com/~ewanmcgregor/gallery/
More Ewan images than your eyes can stand.

Ewoks Photo Archive
www.geocities.com/Area51/Corridor/4307/ewoks.html
Small but colorful JPEG image gallery of Ewoks.

GH Moose Star Wars Pictures
www.dsu.edu/~denholmr/StarWars.html
JPEG gallery of spacecraft in action.

Han Solo Archive
http://seconn4.yoda.com/~vader97/han/han.html
Han (Harrison Ford) in five gallery files - in living color.

Han Soloists
www.geocities.com/Area51/Capsule/2324/
In love with Han Solo, or would you rather kiss a Wookiee?

Harrison Ford - Viewing Room
www.smartlink.net/~deej7/pix.htm
Oh yeah - this is the place for Ford pix!

Hi-Impact Photo Gallery - Star Wars
www.armory.com/~paladin/gallery/starwars/starwars-c.html
Home grown Star Wars settings, costumes, and fun.

How to Build a Stormtrooper Costume
www.studiocreations.com/stormtrooper/
Wanna build your own stormtrooper uniform? Here's how.

Images of EP1
http://plaza.harmonix.ne.jp/~m-falcon/Image_of_Episode1.html
  Poster & image collection (will probably be updated often).

Imperial Officers
www.geocities.com/Area51/Corridor/8727/imperial_officers.html
  Big pix of big villains.

Imperial Pictures
www.geocities.com/Area51/Corridor/4312/imperial.html
  Big JPEG pictures of Darth, basically.

Jabba The Hutt Archives
http://seconn4.yoda.com/~vader97/jabba/jabba.html
  Pictures, pictures & more pictures of Jabba

Jedi Paradise Multimedia for Star Wars & Phantom Menace
http://members.aol.com/bigeoz/multimedia.html
  Sights, sounds, videos, humor videos all on 1 Prequel page.

Jedinet Pictures
www.jedinet.com/multimedia/pics/index.htm
  Rates as the finest JPEG image galleries on this rock.

Lando's Star Wars Galaxy
www.geocities.com/Area51/Chamber/5094/index.html
  A solid Lando fan site that is worth exploring.

Lars Family, The
http://seconn4.yoda.com/~vader97/lars/lars.html
  The Lars family met an unfortunate end.

Lesser Known Rebels
www.geocities.com/Area51/Corridor/8737/rebels.html
  JPEG images (some BIG) of rebels in action.

Lightsaber Pictures
www.jedinet.com/multimedia/pics/sabers/index.html
  Lightsabers featured in their own picture gallery.

Locations: Prequel Planets
http://meltingpot.fortunecity.com/greenwood/487/places/planets.html
  Info & pix of the 3 major Prequel planets.

Lost Scenes Compiled by Roderick VonHogen
www.virtualedition.com/lost_scenes/index.html
  We're looking for "outtake images" here.

Luke Skywalker Galleries (Taz's)
http://seconn4.yoda.com/~vader97/luke/luke.html
  Luke pix galleries arranged by movie.

MaulNet.Com: Maultimedia
www.maultnet.com/maultimedia
  dbmedia's Darth Maul super site - evil, evil, evil (and recommended)

Massassi Order Pictures
www.hta.nl/php/Jan.Jacob.Mosselaar/mmpict.htm
  520 Trilogy & Special Edition JPEG images categorized.

Masters of Teras Kasi
www.game-junkie.com/Reviews/Playstation/StarWars_Fight/SWMOTK.HTM
Review of this game, with video and image file samples.

Millenium Falcon Pictures
www.jedinet.com/multimedia/pics/falcon/index.html
100+ Falcon images!

Natalie Portman Photo Gallery
www.geocities.com/Hollywood/Lot/7181/natpics.html
100+ photos of Natalie.

Natalie Portman's Hang Out
http://ucsu.colorado.edu/~vuong/Natalie.html
Biographical info on Natalie & youthful images of her.

Orionsaint Presents Images from Episode 1
www.angelfire.com/ok2/orionsaint/
Nice collection of large wide Episode 1 pix.

Phantom Menace Mania
http://get.to/jedi/
Great variety of Episode 1 images, sounds, video.

Phantom Menace RPG Screens
www.planetjedi.com/hangar/TPM/screens.html
What you'll see in The Phantom Menace RPG computer game.

Phantom Menace UK Images
www.thephantommenace.co.uk/pics.htm
TPM-UK collections of Prequel images.

Pod Racer Screens
www.planetjedi.com/hangar/PR/screens.html
Thumbnail color scenes from Pod Racer the Game.

Prequel Images from Rancor Pit
www.sentex.net/~dah/prequel/images.html
Assortment of wide JPEG Prequel images.

Prequel Pics Page
http://outland.cyberwar.com/~smad//pics5.html
Well-organized and deep Phantom Menace pix.

Raith's Page of Star Wars Art
http://www2.cybernex.net/~flip1/images1.htm
Largest collection of Star Wars meshes done by 1 man on the Net.

Rogue Squadron Screenshots
www.roguesquadron.net/screenshots.html
Test view screen images from Rogue Squadron game.

Ryan's Star Wars Pictures
http://members.spree.com/sci-fi/swrealm/Pictures.htm
Pix in all shapes, sizes, & sorts - cruise on through!

Screenshots (Jedinet Software Pages)
www.jedinet.com/software/screenshots/index.htm
Want to see scenes from Star Wars games before buying them?

Shadows of the Empire Pictures
    www.jedinet.com/multimedia/pics/sote/index.html
        Shadows of the Empire gallery at its best.

Ships in the Star Wars Universe
    http://members.xoom.com/kessel/outpost/ships.html
        GIF & JPEG images of favorite spacecraft.

Skystation Lounge
    www.theforce.net/Skystation/
        Skystation - it's a swanky place to catch CG animations.

Special Editions, The
    http://scifi.simplenet.com/starwars/special_edition/index.html
        Special edition galleries and reviews (closed 1/31/98)

Spynals Star Wars Site
    http://members.xoom.com/Spynal/home.htm
        Good variety of content - easy to use.

Star Backgrounds (Swammi Collection)
    http://members.xoom.com/kessel/outpost/background.html
        Starry, starry night backgrounds.

Star Wars - The Prequels
    www.nwlink.com/~gareth/starwars.htm
        Variety of JPEG images - includes the Tunisia site map.

Star Wars Archives by SWKID
    www.paulshome.cjb.net/swa
        Galleries of JPEG & GIFs (some animated) to view/download.

Star Wars Fan & CG Art
    http://empire.res.wabash.edu/art/cg/index.htm
        "Must see" CG images. Spacecraft, magic eye pix, props.

Star Wars Force Graphics
    http://plaza.harmonix.ne.jp/~m-falcon/
        Stellar Japanese graphics site; most pix are posters.

Star Wars Galaxy (a) Pictures
    www.geocities.com/Area51/Chamber/1458/pics.htm
        A galaxy of popular characters.

Star Wars JPEGs & GIFs Image Files
    www.geocities.com/Area51/Corridor/1086/swimages.html
        The many pix here are rated for quality by the site author.

Star Wars Movie Art
    http://empire.res.wabash.edu/art/movies/index.htm
        Paintings & pix used for movie production.

Star Wars Multimedia HQ Still Pictures
    http://nerf-herder.com/swmhq/pics.html
        Color & B&W galleries of characters, ships, more.

Star Wars Pictures (Clemson .edu)
    http://people.clemson.edu/~jvalice/starS.htm
        Plenty of action; also pix from the Special Editions.

Starbase Rickover - Computer Graphics Archives
    http://cs.heritage.edu/student/newton/archives/starwars/index.html
        Educational computer graphic JPEG image gallery.

Stormtrooper HQ
www.ausnet.net.au/~jaseod/stormtrooper/stormtrooper.htm
Stormtrooper gear JPEG images.

Swedish University Network SUNET Star Wars
ftp://ftp.sunet.se/pub/pictures/tv.film/Star_Wars/
Swedish Star Wars and movie pix resource.

Symbols from Star Wars
www.geocities.com/Area51/Corridor/4323/symbols.html
Big, colorful JPEG logo images.

Taz's Yoda Archives
http://seconn4.yoda.com/~vader97/yoda/yoda.html
Yoda JPEG image archive.

Technical Pictures
www.jedinet.com/multimedia/pics/tech/index.html
Technical drawings of craft, Deathstar, even C-3PO.

ThBeNDdS Clone Vat
www.swdatabase.com/thbends/
Models and images of Prequel Characters.

Thrawn Art Gallery - Videos, Toys & Others
http://empire.res.wabash.edu/art/others/index.htm
Star Wars art - it gets around. Thrawn art gallery collection.

Timecruiser's Prequel Pictures
www.angelfire.com/co/Timecruiser/Menacepics.html
All types of images from the Prequel pre-release.

Timecruiser's The Picture Gallery
www.angelfire.com/co/Timecruiser/StarPicture.html
Photo collection of some of the most memorable pix.

Welcome To The Cantina (Gallery)
www.geocities.com/Area51/Corridor/8540/cantina.html
Wow! Cantina pix - various, big & risque out-takes.

Winse & Cameron's Episode 1 Pictures
www.geocities.com/TelevisionCity/Stage/5455/episode1.html
A good early Prequel photo site.

World's Best Star Wars Web Site Pics
www.geocities.com/Area51/Nebula/6259/
Assorted JPEG pix, with 14 of Leia.

XXX Pictures
http://members.aol.com/gio2003/pictures.htm
Fabulous renderings along with standard Star Wars pix.

Yoda's Swamp
http://www2.netdoor.com/~broberts/yodapg.html
Tribute to Yoda; his favorite sayings and pix.

Logo Images

Our selection of logo web pages includes Star Wars-related logos for web sites as well as logos and insignia on movie character uniforms.

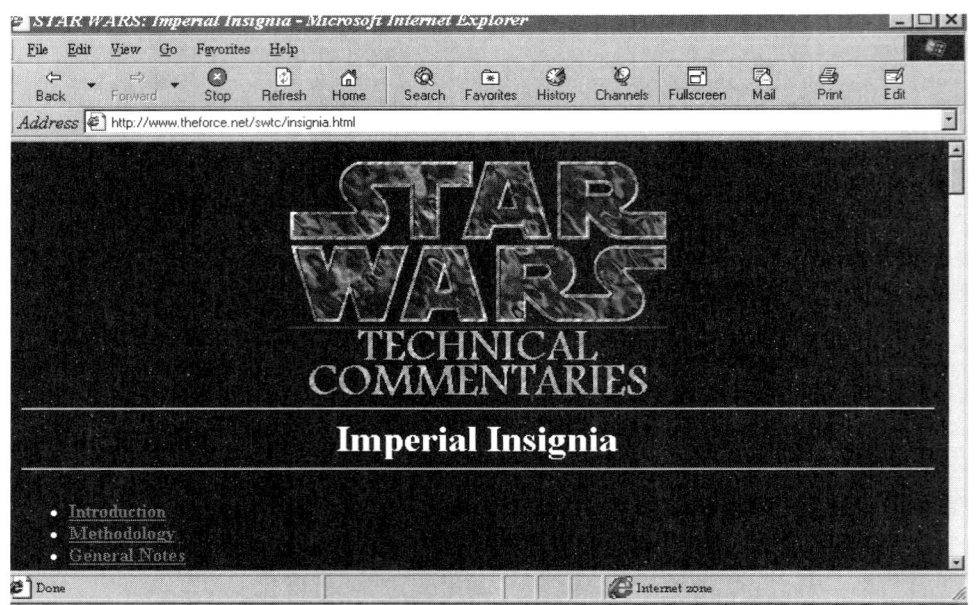

Imperials Uniforms, Insignia, Logos, Technical Commentary
www.theforce.net/swtc/insignia.html
Who wears what in the Evil Empire.

Insignias
www.jedinet.com/multimedia/pics/insignia/index.html
Imperial, Rebel Alliance, bounty hunter - show your allegiance.

Logos (Jedinet)
www.jedinet.com/multimedia/pics/swlogo/index.html
Variety of logos for Trilogy, Lucasfilms, Fox, & Far, far away.

Rebel Alliance Insignia
www.theforce.net/swtc/domino.html
Insignia and logos of the rebel military.

Rogue 8's Media Vault
http://members.xoom.com/rogue88/mediavault.htm
Great logos to download.

Symbols from Star Wars
www.geocities.com/Area51/Corridor/4323/symbols.html
Big, colorful JPEG logo images.

Targeting Computer (Rogue 8's)
http://members.xoom.com/rogue888/computer.htm
Startup screens featuring Star Wars logos.

Original Artwork, Paintings, Sketches, Renderings, CG, & ASCII

These are web pages featuring original artworks that were created by fans or graphics people. Original pictures are usually found in JPEG format. However, ASCII art is best if it is downloaded as a complete file, since the artwork relies of the width of the page and keyboard language. As you would expect, elaborate and sometimes very large computer generated graphics (Cg or CG) may take some time to download. After this section of original art, you will find the photographic arts – photos by amateurs and professionals.

Amara's Cantina
www.flyingarmadillo.com/cantina/index.html
Artist galleries, humor, cartoon, song lyrics! Must See!

Art (Jedinet)
www.jedinet.com/multimedia/pics/art/index.htm
We don't need Picasso's or Dali's - these are great enough!

Art (Rancor Pit)
www.sentex.net/~dah/art/
Original Prequel sketches and posters of four web artists.

ASCII Star Wars Images
www.civila.com/hispania/obi-juan/swascii.txt
What is ASCII Star Wars art? You'll see!

BCR (Scott Thompson) Saga of the Wind Image Archives
www.flash.net/~draegos/Archives.html
Developing a gallery of Star Wars game/scenario art.

Boba Fett at the Smithsonian
www.geocities.com/Area51/Vault/3227/smithsonian/1.htm
Wax-museum Boba Fett from the Smithsonian Exhibit.

Bria's Retribution, Flagship of the Rebel Commander
www.geocities.com/Area51/Nebula/8247/sum.html
Explore more - a variety site.

Computer Generated Artwork (the force.net)
www.theforce.net/Skystation/artscrn.html
Cool computer generated art works!

Dagobah - or - Yoda, The Jedi Master
http://207.79.146.3/employees/jamieb/art.htm
Superb collection of name artists, covers & posters.

Dioramas at Louis Inman's Fett's Place
http://members.aol.com/lfett/custom/diorama.htm
Good linklist to works of diorama artists.

Dioramas at Moff Peter's Dominion
http://members.aol.com/moffpeter/www/diorama.html
Before CG there was dioramas - here's about 50 of them.

Dioramas Maintained by Gus Lopez
www.toysrgus.com/images-displays.html
Dioramas put toys & models into real looking scenic creations.

Droidcentric Art & Fan Fiction
http://members.aol.com/candyfish/gateway.htm
Fan fiction & pix in honor of 2 droids who've been 'round the block.

Empire Strikes Back Portfolio
www.bantha-fodder.com/esbport/
Original art by Ralph McQuarrie, top Star Wars artist.

Everything's Star Wars - the norm
www.thenorm.com/tfm/
Comic-drawing hero "the norm" is a great Star Wars humorist!

Fan Art Museum (the force.net)
www.theforce.net/museum/
Galleries of original Star Wars art collected by theforce.net.

Fan Created Art (Echo Station Interactive)
www.echostation.com/art/index.htm
One of our very favorite original art galleries.

Fort Tusken
www.igw.clara.co.uk/index.html/
UK multimedia site with original art & Episode 1 pix.

House of Skywalker Luke & Leia Paper Dolls
www.flyingarmadillo.com/cantina/fashion/leia/leia.htm
Cut out Luke, Leia, clothes, then dress 'em to impress.

Imperial Fleet Schleswig-Holstein
http://members.xoom.com/ADAM_IFSH/
Imperial-flavor in a German site. Do they belong together?

Jedi Base Galleries
www.bestweb.net/~fett/davemain.htm
Fine McQuarrie & Dorman art works.

Kaya Cloud's Star Wars Clip Art
http://members.tripod.com/~KayaCloud/
Line drawings of R2D2, X-wing, AT-AT, and a blaster.

Literature (LucasFan.com)
www.lucasfan.com/literature.html
Great resource for all types of reading media.

Lithographs - Limited Edition
www.tncmagic.com/starwars/00litho.htm
12 collector lithographs for the serious art collector.

Matt Busch Original Art (the force.net)
www.theforce.net/museum/g_mattb/
Colorful originals are among the best on the Web.

Mike Gartley's Miscellaneous Page
www.ma.iup.edu/~tzqf/star/misc.html
Cereal Boxes? Yes. Also, magazine covers.

NetJunctions Pictures Pages
www.netjunction.com/starwars/gallery.htm
Black & whites, posters, sketches, poses.

Original Art by Me & Mine
www.geocities.com/Area51/Corridor/7410/art.html
Originals, for sure!

PC & Miniature Galleries
http://rpg.echostation.com/gallery/gallery.html
Roleplaying and modeling resources - sketches, mini's, scenery.

Prequel Art Originals (the force.net)
www.theforce.net/museum/g_prequels/
Original Prequel art pix, posters, wallpaper.

Production Paintings, Star Wars
www.cadvision.com/geoff/swimg.html
Collection of paintings from all four films.

Randy Martinex Star Wars Gallery
www.citcomputers.com/randy/starwars.html
We're talking art here.

Ray Traced (Jedi Planet)
http://members.xoom.com/jediplanet/page3.html
Ray Traced art works - spendide! (Italian site)

Scott O'Hair's Hyperspace
http://members.iquest.net/~sohair/hyperspace/menup.html
Model dioramas of famous Trilogy places; Cantina, Jabba's Palace.

Smithsonian Museum Exhibit - Star Wars: The Magic of Myth
www.geocities.com/Area51/Vault/3227/smithsonian/index.htm
Private photos from the Smithsonian Star Wars exhibit, 1/98

Star Wars ASCII Art Collection
www.1stock.demon.nl/swlaunch2.html
Impressive collection of computer keyboard-created art.

Star Wars Collective
http://starwars.interspeed.net/index.shtml
Developing site - find excellent renderings in Fan Images section.

Star Wars Customs.com
http://members.aol.com/awyant3477/index.htm
Make toys come alive in realistic-as-possible dioramas.

Star Wars Drawings
www.geocities.com/SoHo/Gallery/9741/STARWARSPage.htm
Drawings gallery that features some excellent pieces.

SWMA - Star Wars Modeling Alliance
www.surfthe.net/swma/
Great site - the force is definitely here.

Take a Walk Through a Splinter of My Mind's Eye
www.geocities.com/Area51/Corridor/7410/
Unusual name - and not your typical web site!

Taz's Star Wars Art Galleries
http://seconn4.yoda.com/~vader97/art/art.html
10 galleries with 20 original pix in each.

Watto's Junkyard Archive
www.wattosjunkyard.com/fanart.html
Prequel posters, software & lots of color JPEG images.

XXX Pictures
http://members.aol.com/gio2003/pictures.htm
Fabulous renderings along with standard Star Wars pix.

Photos & Photography

If a camera was required and the image was once on film, then it may be found on a web page using this list of sites. You may also search for photos in other Image gallery sites listed in this book. We recommend looking among the JPEG images.

Artwork & Symbols
www.wcug.wwu.edu/~paradox/art.html
Surprising large & varied collection of images.

AV Photo & Media Finder
http://image.altavista.com/cgi-bin/avncgi
Random searching for Star Wars images, video, or audio files.

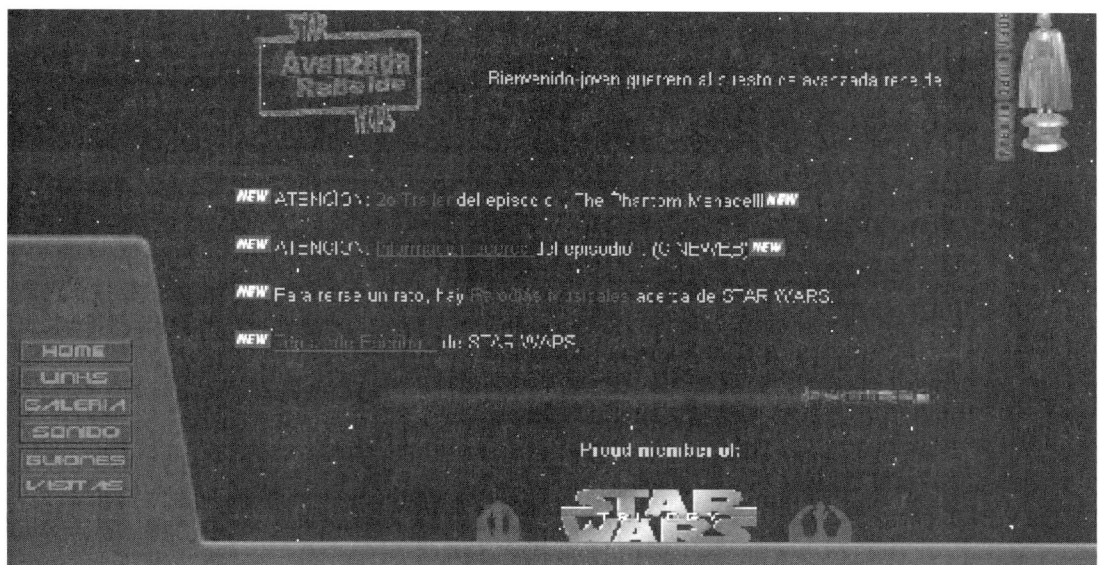

Avanzada Rebeldo
> www.ing.puc.cl/~bsg/
> Chilian Star Wars mixed-media site (Spanish)

Boba Fett & Darth Vader Galleries
> www.geocities.com/Area51/Shadowlands/4918/gallery.html
> Picture gallery of villains Boba Fett & Darth Vader.

Bond's Star Wars Page
> http://home.tampabay.rr.com/bond/starwars.htm
> Some unusual Pictures and an animated Boba Fett.

Bounty Hunters
> http://people.a2000.nl/tvdbrink/
> Searchable Bounty Hunter collection with pix.

Carrie Photographs (Unofficial Carrie Fisher Homepage)
> www.offsoho.com/carrie/html/8photographs.html
> Unofficial Carrie photo pix collection.

Chewbacca the Wookiee
> www.starwars.com/characters/chewbacca/
> Official Chewbacca Lucasfilm page.

Dagobah System, The
> http://members.aol.com/Yoda328/index.html
> Under construction - visit to find out what's new.

Danny's Super Star Wars Page
> www.geocities.com/Area51/Comet/3947/index.html
> Photos & sounds are served up hot here.

Dash's Star Wars Mania
> http://members.tripod.com/~Dash88/index.html
> Pix, movies, Prequel fluff, and page/links to movie goof-ups.

David Jansen's Star Wars Page
> www.strw.leidenuniv.nl/~jansen/sw/
> Multimedia site with fortune cookies (quotes), sounds & pix.

El Camino's Star Wars Pictures
www.geocities.com/Area51/Rampart/4264/pics.htm
  80+ character photos from the Trilogy.

Electric GIFs
www.electricgifs.com/
  Search tool that finds Star War GIFs - and other topics, too.

Ewan McGregor Gallery
www.geocities.com/~ewanmcgregor/gallery/
  More Ewan images than your eyes can stand.

Fort Tusken
www.igw.clara.co.uk/index.html/
  UK multimedia site with original art & Episode 1 pix.

FTP Directory / Star Wars
ftp://ftp.sunet.se/pub/pictures/tv.film/Star_Wars/
  Directory of Star Wars images available from a Swedish edu site.

FTP Directory Bladerunner
ftp://ftp.sunet.se/pub/pictures/tv.film/Bladerunner/
  Harrison in Bladerunner pix - by the dozens.

Imperial Spy Network
www.angelfire.com/mo/StarWarsImages/
  Spies? Where? Here?

Jon's Fly-By-Night Sci-fi Image Gallery & Sound Archive
http://web.wt.net/~jquick/archive.html
  Variety of WAV sound files, but limited pix. A modern Sci-fi site.

Kyle's Star Wars Web Site
www.angelfire.com/ca2/starwarslover/
  Photo gallery on a stellar background.

License Plates
www.theforce.net/tfnnews/
  License plate collection from Jedi to Jar-Jar.

Mark Hamill Rare Images (Gothic Skywalker's)
www.geocities.com/TimesSquare/Dungeon/3913/mark.html
  Mark Hamill wonder years? Are they authentic?

Massassi Order Schale Models
www.hta.nl/php/Jan.Jacob.Mosselaar/swmodel.htm
  Spacecraft & vehicle models are artistically presented.

Millenium Falcon - Ship of Riddles
www.synicon.com.au/sw/mf/falcon.htm
  Just how big is it? Just about everything you should know.

Mos Eisley Photo Gallery
www.geocities.com/Hollywood/Set/7355/photo.html
  Some items you're likely to find in Mos Eisley Cantina.

Mysterious Characters
www.fortunecity.com/tattooine/lucas/66/bio-index.html
  Background info on aliens - and Boba Fett.

Natalie Portman Image Gallery
www.natportman.com/images/
  Literally hundreds of Natalie pix!

NetJunctions Pictures Pages
  www.netjunction.com/starwars/gallery.htm
    Black & whites, posters, sketches, poses.

Palace of the Raider King
  http://members.tripod.com/~KingOfTheRaiders/Frames.html
    Icons, also themes, screen saver, and GIF pix gallery.

Phantom Menace Site, The
  www.users.wineasy.se/doot/starwars/index.html
    Prequel site focusing mostly on main actors and Nat Portman.

Phantom Menace UK Images
  www.thephantommenace.co.uk/pics.htm
    TPM-UK collections of Prequel images.

Pictures: Boba Fett & Others
  http://pweb.netcom.com/~fragger/art.html
    Pix of Boba Fett and - and - and - muppets?

Ryan's Star Wars Pictures
  http://members.spree.com/sci-fi/swrealm/Pictures.htm
    Pix in all shapes, sizes, & sorts - cruise on through!

Star Wars Galaxy (a) Pictures
  www.geocities.com/Area51/Chamber/1458/pics.htm
    A galaxy of popular characters.

Star Wars Multimedia HQ Still Pictures
  http://nerf-herder.com/swmhq/pics.html
    Color & black & white galleries of characters, ships, more.

Star Wars Trilogy Gallery
  www.linkline.be/users/duncan/sw-pictures.html
    Photos of character scenes arranged by movie title.

Star Wars Unnamed Site
  www.angelfire.com/ak/jskywalker/starwars.html
    Picture gallery collection.

Swedish University Network SUNET Star Wars
  ftp://ftp.sunet.se/pub/pictures/tv.film/Star_Wars/
    Swedish Star Wars and movie pix resource.

SWMA - Star Wars 3D Modeling Alliance Archives
  www.surfthe.net/swma/archives/archives.html
    Storehouse of 3D that takes light years to see all of.

SWMA - Star Wars Modeling Alliance
  www.surfthe.net/swma/
    Great site - the force is definitely here.

Taz's Boba Fett Galleries
  http://seconn4.yoda.com/~vader97/boba/boba.html
    4 frames-worth of Boba Fett images!

Ted's Star Wars Pictures
  http://dvader.mit.edu/old/starwars.html
    Modest but neat collection of wide Star Wars action pix.

Timecruiser's The Picture Gallery
  www.angelfire.com/co/Timecruiser/StarPicture.html
    Photo collection of some of the most memorable pix.

Welcome to the Mandalorian Sector
www.geocities.com/Area51/Cavern/5723/index2.html
Early Fett site draws heavy from comic book information.

Poster Images

Poster images are usually composites or derivative works that are meant to promote a Star Wars movie. We've included non-advertising posters and parody posters web sites as well.

A1's Star Wars Poster Page
http://members.aol.com/A1B2C369/posters.html
A few good posters available here.

Aaron's Star Wars Multimedia page
www.geocities.com/Area51/Stargate/3350/
New site with posters as its very best feature.

Dagobah - or - Yoda, The Jedi Master
http://207.79.146.3/employees/jamieb/art.htm
Superb collection of name artists, covers & posters.

Episode 1 Humor Pages
www.theforce.net/humor/episodei/
Remember: It's only jokes.

Images of EP1
http://plaza.harmonix.ne.jp/~m-falcon/Image_of_Episode1.html
Poster & image collection (will probably be updated often).

Jedinet Pictures
www.jedinet.com/multimedia/pics/index.htm
Rates as the finest JPEG image gallery on this rock.

Mario's Star Wars Page
http://andrix.biophysics.mcw.edu/mariusz/mario/starwars/starmain.htm
2 Special Edition movie posters, Yoda lyrics, & Trilogy scripts.

Mike Gartley's Poster Page
www.ma.iup.edu/~tzqf/star/poster.html
Collection of posters; many are rare.

Phantom Menace Movie Poster
http://ucaswww.mcm.uc.edu/english/hall/sw1.htm
Need a real movie poster of Phantom Menace or another movie?

Poster Pictures, Star Wars
http://empire.res.wabash.edu/art/posters/index.htm
Good number collected from the Trilogy, hither, and yon.

Star Wars Force Graphics Posters
http://plaza.harmonix.ne.jp/~m-falcon/poster_art1_boba.html
Limited number, but very high quality.

Watto's Junkyard Archive
www.wattosjunkyard.com/fanart.html
Prequel posters, software & lots of color JPEG images.

STAR WARS Fun, Games, & Lifestyle Topics

Acknowledge your Star Wars allegiance in your everyday life! In this part of the Star Wars Galaxy, you'll find web sites offering news, humor, involvement activities like modeling, gaming, collecting – and most of all – Star Wars merchandise. Beside Collectibles, this merchandise section includes electronic gear for your entertainment pleasure, and of course, lists of online stores for purchasing Star Wars products.

Merchandise

Collectibles

Do you have a collection of "something" Star Wars? Many people do. This Collectible Section will enlighten you as to what's going on in the world of Star Wars collecting. Following Collectibles, you will find the Toys and Trading Cards sections.

Andrew Gruner's Custom Star Wars Projects
www.mesastate.edu/~agruner/sw/custom/
Figurines, costuming, dioramas & modeling.

Collecting (the force.net)
www.theforce.net/collecting/
You'll see a lot of big corporate promos here; Pepsi cans.

Collecting Star Wars Newgroup
rec.arts.sf.starwars.collecting

Clicket.com Star Wars Gallery
www.clicket.com/clicket/swgal/swgal.html
Costume & collectible company is easy to shop at.

Customized Collecting Star Wars Newsgroup
rec.arts.sf.starwars.collecting.customizing

Episode 1 Widevision Cards
www.sevaan.com/starwars/fanart/topps.htm
Collectible card images from Topps/Savaan Franks.

ForceCollectors.Com
www.forcecollectors.com
Search to find the droids you're looking for - or sell.

Lord Vader's Australian Collectibles
www.corplink.com.au/~hatten/lord.htm
Star Wars collectibles from the land down under.

Masks - Star Wars
www.anniescostumes.com/swmask.htm
Trilogy character masks - most are full-head latex.

MaulNet.Com
www.maultnet.com
dbmedia's Darth Maul super site - evil, evil, evil (and recommended)

Miscellaneous Star Wars Collecting Newsgroup
rec.arts.sf.starwars.collecting.misc

On The Mark
www.geocities.com/Hollywood/Set/7029/otm.html
Offers free lists of Star Wars and Mark Hamill collectibles.

Power of the Force 2 Action Figures
http://oneclick.ucr.edu/chamber/aflist/swlist01.htm
Action figures

Rebel Chat.com (toys/collectibles)
www.rebelchat.com/
Hey - a chat room for Star Wars toys/collectibles!

Rebel Scum.com Up To Date News (Collectibles)
www.rebelscum.com/
Oh yeah - this is a great place for toys/collectibles.

Sir Steve's Action Online Chat Room (Toys/Collectibles)
www.sirstevesguide.com/chatroom/chatroomgl.html
Toy/collectible chat room with an "ignore" feature.

Sir Steve's Star Wars (Collectibles) Guide
www.sirstevesguide.com/
Toy/collectible mega-site - irresistible & kid friendly.

Star Wars Accessories, Props, & Collectibles
www.nightmarefactory.com/starwarz.html
Collectibles from nightmarefactory: high-$$ down to economy.

Star Wars Collectibles (tnc Universe)
www.tncmagic.com/starwars/00masks.htm
Variety of collectibles, costumes, masks, CCG sets, & party gear.

Tally Ho! Movie Prop Replicas - Star Wars
www.dsctoys.com/swcl.html
Prop replicas & collectibles subject to availability.

Tally Ho! Star Wars Collectors
www.dsctoys.com/warsc.html
Potpourri of Star Wars items - click thru alphabetized-categories.

Tazos & Pogs
www.starwarscards.net/pogs.htm
Worldwide info on pogs, tazos, stickers & small collectibles.

Toy Box - Hydrospanner
http://members.aol.com/MrkHmlRulz/HTB/
Toy news site that isn't totally fanatical.

Toys, Gifts, Collectibles - Mos Espa Marketplace
http://mosespa.starwars.com/products/
Official Star Wars marketplace arranged by category.

Trading Tips
http://yakface.com/hosted/tuskentrader/tips.htm
Etiquette & protocol for trading - you don't need a droid.

Tusken Traders Trader Lists
http://yakface.com/hosted/tuskentrader/list.htm
Traders and their lists.

Vintage Star Wars Collecting Newsgroup
rec.arts.sf.starwars.collecting.vintage

Yakface's Realm
www.yakface.com/
Toys, collectibles, and added special features.

Toys

Figurines, playsets, and all sorts of Star Wars toys – even Luke & Leia paper dolls – are found on the web sites in this toy section. You'll find that many of the toy sites also offer chat rooms, so it's easy to find toy information online. See also the Collectibles and Trading Cards sections. For "game" web sites, see Games, Video Games, & Simulators of all Types.

A1's Star Wars Toys
http://members.aol.com/sonofskywr/toys.html
Not big, but might have what you're looking for.

Aaron's Star Wars Toy & Comic Price Guides Checklist
www.continet.com/aaronsmagic/pretoys/1Check.html
Checklist of new Kenner Prequel action figures.

Aaron's Star Wars Toys & Comics
www.swdatabase.com/collectables/
Toys, collectibles, news, reviews, guides.

eBay Listings: Star Wars Toys
http://listings.ebay.com/aw/listings/list/category751/index.html
eBay = big auctions - hundreds of pages!

Fandom Menace
www.fandommenace.com/
News & views about new toys & merchandise.

Hasbro - Making The World Smile
www.hasbro.com/
This is a big one for toys.

Hasbro Cool Stuff 3D VR Collectibles
www.hasbrotoys.com/coolstuf.html
Star Wars action figures in 3D in QuickTime videos.

House of Skywalker Luke & Leia Paper Dolls
www.flyingarmadillo.com/cantina/fashion/leia/leia.htm
Cut out Luke, Leia, clothes, then dress 'em to impress.

Jedi Domain
www.geocities.com/Area51/Shadowlands/3543/
Multi-presentation site: Jedi flavor, Kenners, Jedi of the month.

MaulRats.com
www.maulrats.com/
Action figures and toys - like a "mall."

Naboo Temple Ruins Playset
www.fandommenace.com/toys/e1mmplaynabootemple.jpg
Naboo planet playset toy

Phantom Menace Action Figures
www.continet.com/aaronsmagic/pretoys/phantom.htm
Prequel Kenner toy site and guide.

Power of the Force 2 Action Figures
http://oneclick.ucr.edu/chamber/aflist/swlist01.htm
Action figures -- it figures.

Rebel Chat.com (toys/collectibles)
www.rebelchat.com/
Hey - a chat room for Star Wars toys/collectibles!

Rebel Scum.com Up To Date News (Collectibles)
www.rebelscum.com/
Oh yeah - this is a great place for toys/collectibles.

Sir Steve's Action Online Chat Room (Toys/Collectibles)
www.sirstevesguide.com/chatroom/chatroomgl.html
Toy/collectible chat room with an "ignore" feature.

Sir Steve's Star Wars (Collectibles) Guide
www.sirstevesguide.com/
Toy/collectible mega-site - irresistible & kid friendly.

Star Toys Online
www.startoysonline.com/
Under construction. We're waiting, Mr. Toy Site Man.

Toy Box - Hydrospanner
http://members.aol.com/MrkHmlRulz/HTB/
Toy news site that isn't totally fanatical.

Toys, Gifts, Collectibles - Mos Espa Marketplace
http://mosespa.starwars.com/products/
Official Star Wars marketplace arranged by category.

Yakface's Realm
www.yakface.com/
Toys, collectibles, and added special features.

Trading Cards

Here is a small list of Trading Cards web sites, but it's got it where it counts, kid! Look for CCGs in the Games Section later in this chapter.

Cards (Jedinet)
www.jedinet.com/multimedia/pics/cards/index.htm
Best card/image file on 12 systems.

Episode 1 Widevision Cards
www.sevaan.com/starwars/fanart/topps.htm
Collectible card images from Topps/Savaan Franks.

Fett Net
www.bobafett.net/page1.htm
Boba Fett news, views & more.

Gamesa Cards (Starwarscards.net)
www.starwarscards.net/gamesa.htm
Rare trading cards once distributed in Mexico.

Tally Ho! Star Wars Collectors
www.dsctoys.com/warsc.html
Potpourri of Star Wars items - click thru alphabetized-categories.

Electronic Gear for Your Home & Entertainment Pleasure

Some of us are not satisfied with Star Wars movies on puny 25 inch TV screens, or listening to non-THX blow-you-away sound systems, or playing on little itsy-bitsy kid video game systems. Here's a few web sites to check out for the big sound systems and big video games.

Amusement Enterprises
www.aeigames.com/
Some free downloads - online games & gaming resources.

Home THX Product Database
www.thx.com/consumer_products/av_equip.html
THX home theatre products database.

THX Consumer Products
www.thx.com/consumer_products/index.html
Info about THX home entertainment systems.

Stores Online

A lot of web sites for toys, collectibles or other Star Wars merchandise have their own stores right on their pages. However, here are some of the big merchandiser sites on the web where you can purchase a wider range of Star Wars goodies, such as books (see also the Text Chapter). See the other sections of this chapter for Collectibles, Toys, Games, etc.

eBay
www.ebay.com/
Auction site - type in Star Wars, "search" and see!

emerchandise
http://www2.emerchandise.com/consumer/
Shop for Star Wars needs by category.

Mos Espa Marketplace
http://mosespa.starwars.com/books/
Official Star Wars Book site; reviews and store.

Star Wars: Episode 1 Merchandise
http://scifistore.lycos.com/
Lycos Episode 1 merchandise find-it center.

Lifestyle

The sections that follow have web sites that keep you up to date with Star Wars' "happening things," starting with web sites with the latest news:

News

All the Star Wars news that is fit to publish on the web – and even some that isn't! The site titles and descriptions should clue you in as to what the main "news" focus is.

Azeroth's Labyrinth
www.otn.net/mypage/azeroth/default.htm
Reviews and infrequent news about Star Wars & games.

Boober's Star Wars Galaxy
http://home.fuse.net/mckee/frames.htm
Worth the visit. 625 multimedia files & a good games page.

Books - the force.net Expanded Universe
www.theforce.net/books/
Great resource for all varieties of Star Wars books & reviews.

Comlink, The
http://homepages.tig.com.au/~echo3/
Pic hits of the month for best site and best audio clip.

Countdown To Star Wars
http://starwars.countingdown.com/
What it was like waiting for the EP1 opening.

Dark Horizons
www.darkhorizons.com/index2.html
1-stop movie resource - news, trailers, facts.

Dark Rising
http://home.sol.no/~mgrambo/index2.htm
Multimedia page with galleries of sights, sounds, action clips.

Crystals make lightsabers work. Ilum and Adegan crystals were preferred by the ancient lightsaber makers.

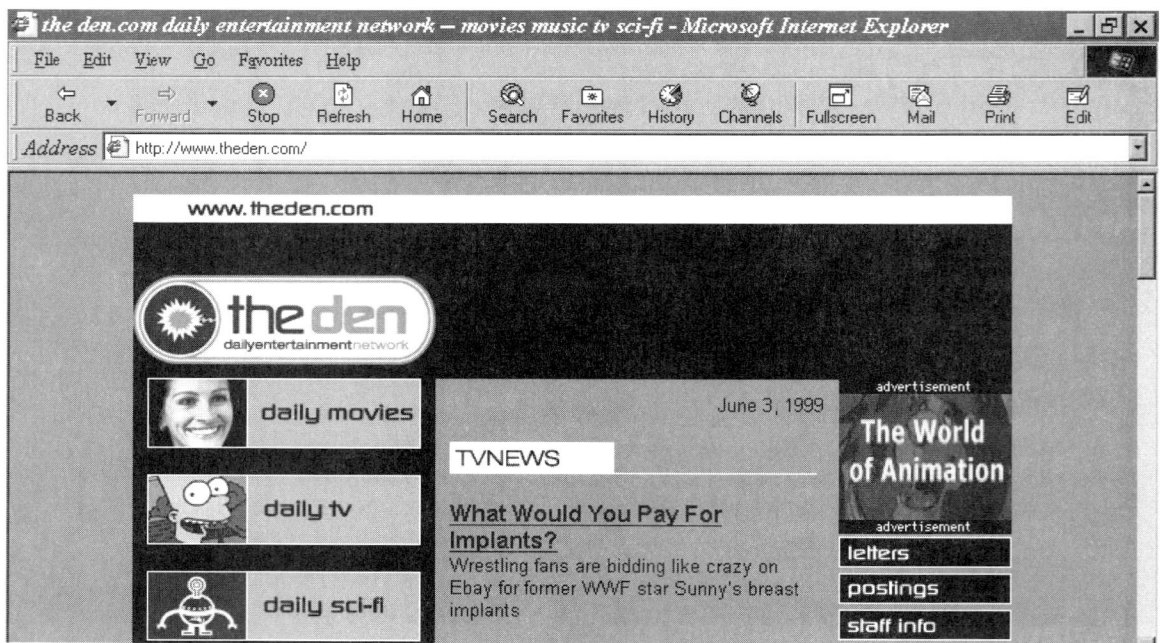

Den, The
> www.theden.com/
> Light entertainment & Sci-fi news.

Episode 1
> www.sevaan.com/starwars/
> Multimedia page dedicated to Episode 1.

Episode 1 News Archives
> www.sevaan.com/starwars/news/archives/index.htm
> News, editorials, surveys on Episode 1.

Episode 1: The Phantom Menace News Page
> www.angelfire.com/sc/francis915/news.html
> News site that reports items you may not find elsewhere.

Episode 2 at Sci-FI Advance
> http://scifi.simplenet.com/starwars/prequels/episode2.shtml
> Episode 2 and 3 data is accumulating!

Eye On Episode 1
> http://starwars.tierranet.com/episode1/frames.html
> Co-op news and comments page by 2 Star Wars veterans.

Eye On Episode 1 - News & Rumors
> http://starwars.tierranet.com/episode1/frame3.html
> News, rumors - plenty of details, foreign & domestic.

Film.com
> www.film.com/
> It's gotta lot of film/movie/video stuff!

FORCE.NET - Your Daily Dose of Star Wars
> http://theforce.net/
> Mega Star Wars Info Site - Mega!

Games - the force.net Expanded Universe
`www.theforce.net/games/`
News, pix, archives of Star Wars games & guides.

Get Ready for Star Wars
`www.excite.com/events/star_wars`
Excite's Star Wars page informs & links to some great sites.

Hollywood Online - Star Wars The Phantom Menace
`www.hollywood.com/starwars/main.html`
Entertaining site has The Phantom Menace covered!

Holonet (the force.net)
`www.theforce.net/holonet/`
Fan contributions of news, videos, audio, interviews.

Hydrospanner
`www.hydrospanner.com/`
Is a hydrospanner the most useful tool in space, or what?

Jedi Paradise Episode 1
`http://members.aol.com/bigeoz/JPhome.htm`
Grab bag of Episode 1; news, products, galleries.

JediKnight.net
`www.jediknight.net/`
Jedi's on the gaming circuits! Game resources & news.

Jedinet
`www.jedinet.com/frame.htm`
By the Fans for the Fans - full-service super site.

Jedinet Software
`www.jedinet.com/software/`
Good coverage of software games news, screenshots.

Land of The Prequels
`www.the-mattman.com/starwars/`
News, galleries, characters for Episode 1.

Latest Scoop - Star Wars News from the Source
`http://home1.gte.net/filter1/starwars/index.html`
Organized memorial for Steven Curnow - killed at Columbine HS.

LucasGames
`www.lucasgames.com/`
Gaming news, features. Connect to 4 major game sites.

MaulNet.Com
`www.maultnet.com`
dbmedia's Darth Maul super site - evil, evil, evil (and recommended)

MSN Star Wars Web Guide
`www.musiccentral.msn.com/movies/StarWars/StarWars.asp`
Some say it's a bit predictable & commercial - you decide.

NaboOnline
`www.naboonline.com`
Wealth of information and variety of Prequel categories.

News Stand, The - CHUD (Cinematic Happenings Under Development)
`www.chud.com/news.htm`
CHUD - this movie info site isn't as bad as it sounds.

Newsdroid
www.newsdroid.com/
Latest news arranged by lifestyle category.

Phantom Menace UK
www.thephantommenace.co.uk/naboo.htm
UK site with a lot of features & international EP1 news.

Planet Jedi
www.planetjedi.com/main.html
New gaming site has news, store, & excellent resources.

Pod Race Reporter Homepage
http://podracereporter.listbot.com/
Current Star Wars news items are a couple clicks away.

Prequel Crew
http://theforce.net/prequels/oldPreq/crew/crew.html
They made Episode 1.

Prequel News
www.execpc.com/~zerob/Jediside.html
Prequel articles listed with the publications they appear in.

Prequel Watch on Jedinet
www.jedinet.com/prequels/
Prequel news, calendar, discussions - lively & colorful.

Prequels.com, The
http://theprequels.com/main.htm
Lively, colorful Prequel site - mucho variety!

Rancor Pit, The
http://fly.to/rancorpit
New high-energy site that hopes to do it all!

Rebel Scum.com Up To Date News (Collectibles)
www.rebelscum.com/
Oh yeah - this is a great place for toys/collectibles.

Sir Steve's Star Wars (Collectibles) Guide
www.sirstevesguide.com/
Toy/collectible mega-site - irresistible & kid friendly.

Star Wars Database
www.swdatabase.com/
Features, features, features. A must see.

Star Wars Episode 1 - The Music
http://members.es.tripod.de/Befan/Episode1music.html
Who thought there wasn't much to Star Wars music? There sure is!

Star Wars Gamers
www.swgamers.com/
Hear about latest games; find downloads & demos.

Star Wars Prequels
www.execpc.com/~zerob/Dataside.html
Prequel news listed by the date it happened.

Theed.net - City Beyond the Swamp
www.theed.net/
New site with news and tricks up its sleeve (more promised).

Trencher ALB's Episode 1: The Phantom Menace
    http://members.tripod.com/trencheralb/index2.html
        A steady, dependable Prequel news site.

Unofficial Episode 1 Homepage (Kentucky area)
    http://come.to/tpmky/
        News, comics, discussion with local Kentucky flavor.

Unofficial Industrial Light+Magic Web Site
    www.ilmfan.com/index2.html
        ILM unofficial page of info, news, downloads.

Watto's Junkyard
    www.wattosjunkyard.com/
        Among our favorite-est Prequel sites - good variety & style.

Wookie Hooky
    www.geocities.com/Hollywood/Studio/9203/
        Get E-mail news updates & give/read tips for seeing Episode 1.

Yakface's Realm
    www.yakface.com/
        Toys, collectibles, and added special features.

Events & Schedules

Details, details, details! Is there a Star Wars Event coming your way? Would you like to meet other Star Wars fans in person, or know appearance schedules? Do you need as excuse to see the Phantom Menace again?

1999 Prequel Calendar
    www.jedinet.com/prequels/TPM/fandom.htm
        Prequel calendar that you wish you had months ago!

Christmas Pictures
    www.jedinet.com/multimedia/pics/xmas/index.html
        6 Star Wars Christmas images.

Concerts - Star Wars Episode 1: The Music
    http://members.es.tripod.de/Befan/Episode1music_Concerts.html
        Star Wars music & John Williams performance schedules.

Conventions (the force.net)
    http://theforce.net/main/cons.shtml
        If it's scheduled, it's likely to be here.

Echo Station Event Guide
    www.echostation.com/events/index.htm
        The skinny on upcoming Star Wars con-fabs.

Holonet (the force.net)
    www.theforce.net/holonet/
        Fan contributions of news, videos, audio, interviews.

Rassmcon
    www.shavenwookie.com/rassmcon/
        Star Wars Usenet conventions/meeting schedules.

Wookie Hooky
www.geocities.com/Hollywood/Studio/9203/
Get E-mail news updates & give/read tips for seeing Episode 1.

Humor -- The Light & The Dark Side

One thing is for sure about Star Wars fans: they have a sense of humor – that or they like to poke fun. Here are dozens of sites where you might get a laugh, or insulted, or see the lighter side of the dark side.

10 of the Weirdest Star Wars Sites - Music Central
www.musiccentral.msn.com/movies/StarWars/StarWars5.asp
Variety of whacky, weird sites found by MSN.

An Appeal to the Tolerance-Challenged
http://members.aol.com/candyfish/appeal.htm
Droids are our friends. Droids are our friends.

Bad Guide to Star Wars
www.geocities.com/Area51/Vault/6031/bgsw53.txt
Details of bloopers, cinematography, and oddities.

Big Kourt's House of Star Wars, X-Files, Star Trek & Used Hubcaps
www.geocities.com/Area51/Lair/7558/
Won't find the hubcaps - will find unusual Star Wars phrases.

Bloopers (Jedinet)
www.jedinet.com/multimedia/blooper/index.htm
Call it nitpiks, call it bloopers, call it sloppy scenework.

Blueharvest.net Star Wars Images
www.blueharvest.net/images
"It excels at it." - C-3PO. A "must see" image gallery.

Cracked Mags EP1 Line Waiting Rules
www.jedinet.com/prequels/news/cracked/line.jpg
Cracked Magazine's cheap shot at Star Wars fans.

Crossover Universe
http://pages.prodigy.com/crossover/
Crossover "what ifs" & gee-whiz's for SW, Sci-fi & pop productions.

Dash's Star Wars Mania Nitpicks Page
http://members.tripod.com/~Dash88/nodead.html
Did you ever notice these mistakes in Star Wars?

Disgruntled Ewok & Malcontent Jawas Page
http://netdial.caribe.net/~orinoco/jae.html
Is life (& Star Wars browsing) too serious? While away time here.

Droidstuff
http://members.aol.com/fishdroid/Droidstuff.htm
Worth a quick look and quick laugh.

Emag - Echo Station
http://emag.echostation.com/
Free online variety magazine of Star Wars topics.

Episode 1 Humor Pages
    www.theforce.net/humor/episodei/
        Remember: It's only jokes.

Everything I Know I Learned From Star Wars
    www.geocities.com/Hollywood/Set/5760/
        Always let the Wookie Win and other essential tips.

Everything's Star Wars - the norm
    www.thenorm.com/tfm/
        Comic-drawing hero "the norm" is a great Star Wars humorist!

Ewoks Stink - What Ought to Happen to Ewoks
    www.silcom.com/~pruth/ewok.html
        Ewoks don't stink - do they? Whiner complains about Ewoks.

Freak7's Star Wars Realm
    www.geocities.com/Area51/Zone/2365/
        May improve during Summer '99.

FTP Echo Station
    www.echostation.com/multimedia/
        Join, then get FTP downloads of Star Wars humor videos.

Gammy's Altar
    www.toshistation.com/gammy.htm
        Pig, Gammy, Mork icons, sick humor. Twisted, Bent.

Hardware Wars - IMDb
    http://us.imdb.com/Title?0077658
        1st of the great Star Wars spoof videos. Here's the data.

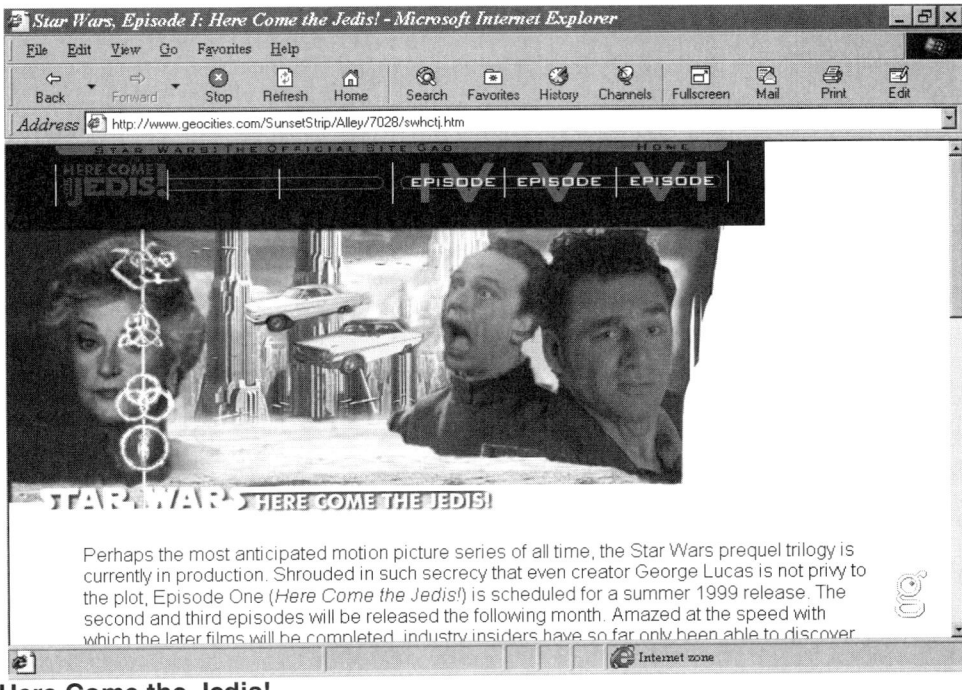

Here Come the Jedis!
    www.geocities.com/SunsetStrip/Alley/7028/swhctj.htm
        Humorous Prequel parody renamed "Here Come the Jedis!"

Humor; Entertainment Cell (Boba Fett)
    `http://pweb.netcom.com/~fragger/load_humor.html`
        Humor from a Boba Fett perspective. This site is changing.

Hydrospanner
    `www.hydrospanner.com/`
        Is a hydrospanner the most useful tool in space, or what?

Imperial Funnies
    `www.flyingarmadillo.com/cantina/starfun/starfun.html`
        Darth's day job (at CNN of course!) and other cartoons.

Imperial Rhapsody, The
    `www.geocities.com/Hollywood/Set/5760/`
        You guessed it: new words for Queen's Bohemian Rhapsody.

Institute for Impure Science - Star Wars
    `www.ifis.org.uk/p.cgi/multimedia/starwars/`
        UK site offers versions of Episode 1 & humor videos.

Jawa Force & Wampashit
    `www.lortaphanble.com/`
        Jawa Force Comic & Wampashit 'Zine. Required viewing.

Lando Calrissian - The Suavest Man In Space
    `www.geocities.com/Area51/3642/lando.htm`
        Lando tribute page with an obvious humor slant!

late night with you kung fu colt daddy L Silky
    `www.toshistation.com/lizard.htm`
        Oh Baby (as said by Barry White)

License Plates
    `www.theforce.net/tfnnews/`
        License plate collection from Jedi 2 Jar-Jar.

Lyrics to YODA (by Weird Al)
    `www.geocities.com/Hollywood/Set/5760/`
        Tribute to Yoda using the tune of the Kink's Lola.

Monument Square Humor Page
    `www.geocities.com/Area51/Lair/3373/humor.html`
        Song parodies and other lol gems.

More Comebacks To Another Stupids List
    `www.geocities.com/Hollywood/Set/5760/`
        Weak Trekkie putdowns of Star Wars are easily lambasted here.

More Star Wars Humor
    `http://rpg.echostation.com/humor/swjokes.html`
        Humor from various newsgroups over FIDOnet & Usenet.

Mos Eisley Humor Page
    `www.geocities.com/Hollywood/Set/7355/hah.html`
        Star Trek lambasted with a vengeance.

MST3K Version of "A Galaxy Not So Far Away"
    `www.geocities.com/Hollywood/Set/5760/`
        See if you can translate this - for some yuks.

Now & Then
    `www.usmo.com/~starwars/now&then/now&then.html`
        Minor characters struggling in the world of entertainment.

Pants of the Mind's Eye
www.powerup.com.au/~jdc/pants.htm
"I find your lack of pants disturbing."

Parody Video: Episode 1 Trailer 'A' - Special Edition
http://sabbeth.com/~menace/specialedition.htm
Spoof of the Trailer put together by fans for free.

Phantom Menace - The Characters As We Know Them
www.allexperts.com/tv/swchar.shtml
Humorous run-down of Prequel characters.

Phantom Menace II Society
www.geocities.com/~noahklein/phantom.html
Hip-hop homeboy attitude applied to some Star Wars dialog.

Second Prequel - What's Next
www.allexperts.com/tv/swprequel1.shtml
They're guessing what'll be in the next Prequel. Oh, really?

Shaven Wookie LTD
www.shavenwookie.com/
You haven't shaved until you've shaved a Wookie.

Signs That You May Be A Complete Star Wars Addict
www.geocities.com/Hollywood/Set/5760/
You may need some "help." Here's how to tell.

Skywalker's Star Wars Page
www.usmo.com/~starwars/index.html
Some pretty funny stuff, also serious image galleries.

Spaceballs - IMDb
http://us.imdb.com/Title?0094012
Lone Star, Dark Helmet, Barf (Chewie), Princess Vespa, etc.

Star Park
www.jedinet.com/starpark/
South Park/Star Wars crossover fever spreads like a plague.

Star Trek (*what's that*?) & Star Wars Jokes
www.geocities.com/Hollywood/4256/jtrek6.html
Includes Malaysia/Singapore jokes, if you're into that.

Star Wars Drinking Game, The
www.geocities.com/Hollywood/Set/5760/
Start with a good stock on hand.

Star Wars Humor
www.geocities.com/Hollywood/Set/5760/
Humorous pieces brought together at Boba Fett/geocities.

Star Wars Sight Gag Site
www.geocities.com/SunsetStrip/Alley/7028/swosg.htm
Yes, it's a parody gateway site!

Star Wars The Phantom Menace
www.allexperts.com/tv/swplot.shtml
Read the mucked-up version of the plot.

Star Wars Versus Titanic
www.geocities.com/Hollywood/Theater/5049/
It's no contest - and it's not fair, either.

Starfeld
www.hydrospanner.com/starfeld/
Yada yada yada Star Wars/Seinfeld mixers.

Third Prequel Movie: You Slice Me, I Slice You
www.allexperts.com/tv/swprequel2.shtml
Humor about the plot of the 3rd Prequel.

Top 10 Lists
http://members.xoom.com/_XOOM/maclaurin384/starwars/jokes/jokes.htm
Witty and also only semi-witty Top 10 humor lists.

Top Ten Reasons Why Star Wars Is Better Than Star Trek
www.geocities.com/Hollywood/Set/5760/
Sorry Trekkies - here's what some Star Wars fans think of Star Trek.

Toshi Station
www.toshistation.com/jedi.htm
We had to recommend this site - it's bad to the bone.

Trilogy Blooper Guide
www.egosystem.com/starwars/bloopers.html
Trilogy nit-piks and bloopers by the dozens.

TROOPS
www.theforce.net/troops/
Parody video of COPS-like stormtroopers - complete with sand.

Troops - IMDb
http://us.imdb.com/Title?0153301
It's a kick in the afterburners - here's cast & production details.

Unofficial Episode 1 Ed Bain Comics Page
http://members.aye.net/~roncole/tpmky/comic.htm
Features cartoonist Ed Bain & his "Line Series"

Various Beers from the Star Wars Universe
> http://rpg.echostation.com/humor/SWBEER.TXT
>> Yes, it's true. Not recommended, but it's true.

Watto's Junkyard Downloads
> www.wattosjunkyard.com/downloads.html
>> Good selection of QuickTime Prequel videos & game demos.

Why Luke Stinks
> www.silcom.com/~pruth/luke.html
>> Downside of Luke - what little there is to berate.

Why Wedge Rules
> www.silcom.com/~pruth/wedge.html
>> Wedge, you really deserve more appreciation!

Yoda's Hooked On Phonics, Help You It Can
> http://pweb.netcom.com/~fragger/Phonics.html
>> Why don't we all talk like Yoda?

You Are Now a Prisoner in The Entertainment Cell
> www.geocities.com/Hollywood/Set/1630/main.html
>> Your host: Boba Fett!

You're Not A Star Wars Junkie Until
> www.geocities.com/Hollywood/Set/5760/
>> You MAY need a twelve step program.

Parties -- Where to Find Masks, Costumes, Novelties, & Gear

One of the great things about Star Wars is the excellent costuming in the movies, so, for a Wars party to be a success – get the right gear!

Britt's Boba Fett Site
> www.geocities.com/Area51/Quadrant/2581/frmemain.html
>> Have a Fett-ish? You have to visit this Boba Site.

Clicket.com Star Wars Gallery
> www.clicket.com/clicket/swgal/swgal.html
>> Costume & collectible company is easy to shop at.

Cultural Abstractions Index
> http://index.echostation.com/cult.html
>> Etiquette & protocol - advice for attending events, also slang.

DJ Rhythm's Dance Music Database
> www.djrhythms.com/db/
>> Star Wars disco and a whole galaxy more of dance music.

Don Post's Studios Star Wars Masks
> www.nightmarefactory.com/starwars.html
>> Good selection of masks for fun, parties, or collecting.

emerchandise
> http://www2.emerchandise.com/consumer/
>> Shop for Star Wars needs by category.

Hi-Impact Photo Gallery - Star Wars
> www.armory.com/~paladin/gallery/starwars/starwars-c.html
>> Home grown Star Wars settings, costumes, and fun.

How to Build a Stormtrooper Costume
> www.studiocreations.com/stormtrooper/
>> Wanna build your own stormtrooper uniform? Here's how.

Insignias
> www.jedinet.com/multimedia/pics/insignia/index.html
>> Imperial, Rebel Alliance, bounty hunter - show your allegiance.

Masks - Star Wars
> www.anniescostumes.com/swmask.htm
>> Trilogy character masks - most are full-head latex.

Nightmare Factory Star Wars Children's Costumes
> www.nightmarefactory.com/starwark.html
>> Trilogy costumes for children - also links to adult & masks sites.

Pants of the Mind's Eye
> www.powerup.com.au/~jdc/pants.htm
>> "I find your lack of pants disturbing."

Star Wars Accessories, Props, & Collectibles
> www.nightmarefactory.com/starwarz.html
>> Collectibles from nightmarefactory: high-$$ down to economy.

Star Wars Classic Costumes (Annie's Costumes)
> www.anniescostumes.com/starkids.htm
>> Trilogy & Prequel costumes & some accessories.

Star Wars Collectibles (tnc Universe)
> www.tncmagic.com/starwars/00masks.htm
>> Variety of collectibles, costumes, masks, CCG sets, & party gear.

Star Wars Drinking Game, The
> www.geocities.com/Hollywood/Set/5760/
>> Start with a good stock on hand.

Tally Ho! Movie Prop Replicas - Star Wars
> www.dsctoys.com/swcl.html
>> Prop replicas & collectibles subject to availability.

Wig Outlet
> www.wigs.com/plist.html
>> Find a Princess Leia wig - or wig for almost any occasion.

Games, Video Games, & Simulators of All Types

Everything from board games to the most advanced 3D video games – and don't forget the CD-ROM version of Star Wars Monopoly!

3D News
> www.3dnews.net/
>> 3D news & links to best resources & hardware.

Aaron Allston's Home Site
www.io.com/~allston/
Authors and game creators have the best sites!

Alan's Star Wars Page
www.geocities.com/SiliconValley/Pines/4928/index.html
Full fan site - worth the visit.

All About Episode 1 Racer
www.next-generation.com/jsmid/news/6205.html
How the Phantom Menace Pod Race turns into games for PC & Nintendo 64.

Amusement Enterprises
www.aeigames.com/
Some free downloads - online games & gaming resources.

Azeroth's Labyrinth
www.otn.net/mypage/azeroth/default.htm
Reviews and infrequent news about Star Wars & games.

Behind The Magic of LucasArts Games Newsgroup
alt.games.lucas-arts.star-wars,behind-magic

Berlin's Network
www.geocities.com/SouthBeach/Lights/5679/index.html
Active 3D homepage with games, info, originals.

Blake's Ultimate Star Wars Site
www.geocities.com/Area51/Shadowlands/4351/index.html
More variety than most multimedia sites.

Boober's Star Wars Galaxy
http://home.fuse.net/mckee/frames.htm
Worth the visit. 625 multimedia files & a good games page.

Bria's Retribution, Flagship of the Rebel Commander
www.geocities.com/Area51/Nebula/8247/sum.html
Explore more - a variety site.

Continuum, The
www.the-continuum.com/
Quake & flight simulators - check for new Star Wars.

Dark Forces Game LucasArts Newsgroup
alt.games.lucas-arts.star-wars.dark-forces

Dark Forces Game Newsgroup
alt.games.dark-forces

Dark Lords of Sith Trivia Test
www.geocities.com/TelevisionCity/Stage/5455/swtrivia.html
We like this 3-level trivia - beware of Sith mind tricks.

Episode 1 Racer
www.gamespot.com/features/sw_racer/
Pod Racer Game review in Gamespot.

Flight School LucasArts Newsgroup
alt.games.lucas-arts.star-wars.flight-school

Freak7's Star Wars Realm
>   www.geocities.com/Area51/Zone/2365/
>   May improve during Summer '99.

Galaxy Software
>   www.nwlink.com/~gareth/
>   Scroll & view selections of computer game software.

Games & Sport Index (Echostation)
>   http://index.echostation.com/games.html
>   Star Wars universe games & sports explained.

Games - the force.net Expanded Universe
>   www.theforce.net/games/
>   News, pix, archives of Star Wars games & guides.

Hanger, The
>   www.jedinights.com/hanger
>   Brand new Prequel gaming site: the Phantom Menace & Pods'R'us.

Heat.net Online Gaming
>   www.heat.net/
>   Log in to any of 100 different online games. News, Events.

Imperial Outpost
>   http://members.theglobe.com/bobafett66/
>   Stuff for your computer as well as a variety of pix, videos, and fun.

James' Star Wars Page
>   http://webhome.idirect.com/~maguda/starwars.html
>   Games & code info, with a Star Wars music gallery.

Jedi Academy at Yavin IV
>   www.nerf-herder.com/jedi/
>   Page through and find scenarios and fun.

Jedi Knight Clan Legacy
>   www.starwarz.com/swlegacy/clan/frameset.html
>   Jedi Clan plays games & makes videos.

Jedi Knight Game Newsgroup
>   alt.games.jedi-knight

Jedi Knight LucasArts Game Newsgroup
    `alt.games.lucas-arts.star-wars.jedi-knight`

JediKnight.net
    `www.jediknight.net/`
        Jedi's on the gaming circuits! Game resources & news.

LucasArts Entertainment Company
    `www.lucasarts.com/menu.html`
        Double-recommended LucasArts game product site.

LucasArts Games Newsgroup
    `alt.binaries.games.lucasarts`

LucasArts Press Room
    `www.lucasarts.com/pages/IndexAnnouncement.main.html`
        Learn about new LucasArt game releases.

LucasArts Star Wars Games Newsgroup
    `alt.games.lucas-arts.star-wars`

LucasGames
    `www.lucasgames.com/`
        Gaming news, features. Connect to 4 major game sites.

Masters of Teras Kasi
    `www.game-junkie.com/Reviews/Playstation/StarWars_Fight/SWMOTK.HTM`
        Review of this game, with video and image file samples.

Microsoft Flight Simulator 98 Star Wars Ships
    `http://members.xoom.com/Startroop1/Ships.html`
        Fly a TIE fighter, interceptor or X-wing.

Monopoly Star Wars CD Win95
    `www.shopper.com/prdct/955/561.html`
        Comparison shop for the Star Wars Monopoly game CD.

NetJunction Games
    `www.netjunction.com/starwars/games.htm`
        5 games including X-Wing, Tie Fighter, & Yoda Stories.

New Republic, The
    `http://thenewrepublic.8m.com/`
        Add-ons for Jedi Knights, plus a multimedia section.

Nintendo 64 Code Center
    `www.n64cc.com/MAIN.HTM`
        Updates, codes, and all the Nintendo 64 universe.

NSX Digital Gaming Site
    `www.digitalnsx.com/`
        Check for X-wing demo and selected NSX gaming news.

Online Gaming - Kalidor Squadron
    `http://kalidor.echostation.com/`
        Go to the Bridge and get onboard this online game.

Pants of the Mind's Eye
    `www.powerup.com.au/~jdc/pants.htm`
        "I find your lack of pants disturbing."

Path Not Taken, The
> www.flash.net/~draegos/path/main1.html
> A fiction? - A game? - An internet development?

Phantom Menace RPG Screens
> www.planetjedi.com/hangar/TPM/screens.html
> What you'll see in The Phantom Menace RPG computer game.

Phantom Menace UK
> www.thephantommenace.co.uk/naboo.htm
> UK site with a lot of features & international EP1 news.

Planet Jedi
> www.planetjedi.com/main.html
> New gaming site has news, store, & excellent resources.

Pod Racer Screens
> www.planetjedi.com/hangar/PR/screens.html
> Thumbnail color scenes from Pod Racer the Game.

Quizzes from the Boba Fett Home Sector
> www.geocities.com/Hollywood/Set/5760/
> Trivia, arranged by Star Wars topics.

Rogue Squadron LucasArts Game Newsgroup
> alt.games.lucas-arts.star-wars.rogue-squadron

Rogue Squadron Screenshots
> www.roguesquadron.net/screenshots.html
> Test view screen images from Rogue Squadron game.

Rogue Squadron.Net
> www.roguesquadron.net/
> Live the life of the Rogue Squadron game player.

Roleplaying in a Star Wars MUSH
> www.cae.wisc.edu/~steiner/mush/site/rp/roleplay.htm
> Basic instructions for MUSH roleplaying.

RU Star Wars Games for Newsgroups
> fido7.ru.star.wars.games

Ryan's Star Wars Trivia Page (Interactive)
> http://members.spree.com/sci-fi/swrealm/Trivia.htm
> Participate in a Trivia game for a weekly prize.

Salacious Crumb Homepage
> www.madbbs.com/~salaciouscrumb/INDEX.HTM
> Salacious Crumb - a character, a band, a Sword of Chaos gamer, a legend!

Screenshots (Jedinet Software Pages)
> www.jedinet.com/software/screenshots/index.htm
> Want to see scenes from Star Wars games before buying them?

Screenshots.net
> www.screenshots.net/
> Pictures from new Prequel games in GIF format.

Star Wars Drinking Game, The
> www.geocities.com/Hollywood/Set/5760/
> Start with a good stock on hand.

Star Wars Episode 1 - The Phantom Menace Game
www.gamespot.com/features/sw_phantom/
  Reviews the PC & Playstation Phantom Menace Game.

Star Wars Gamers
www.swgamers.com/
  Hear about latest games; find downloads & demos.

Star Wars Games Cheat Codes
http://rpg.echostation.com/cheat/swgame.html
  Cheats, codes, FAQs and hints for various Star Wars games.

Star Wars MIDI Music
www.geocities.com/Area51/9394/
  Yes, music/sounds from movies & games!

Star Wars MUD & MUSHes
www.radeleff.de/swmudlist/
  MUSHes, MOOs, Muds, Muxes - Roleplaying sites lists.

Star Wars Multimedia HQ Games
http://nerf-herder.com/swmhq/games.html
  Selection of downloadable games for young and old.

Star Wars Rec.arts Games Newsgroup
rec.arts.sf.starwars.games

Star Wars The Game
www.tem.nhl.nl/~veen606/egame.htm
  Star Wars arcade game of young'uns to learn on.

Star Wars Trilogy Cards
www.geocities.com/Area51/Corridor/4323/cards.html
  A New Hope storyline trading cards.

Star Wars - a game written in Java
www.ktb.net/~rrobb/karim/stapplet/StarWarsApplet.html
  Too difficult for adults - probably great for kids.

Stephen's TIE Fighter Page
http://indigo.ie/~hanafin/starwars.html
  TIE Fighter (the game) resources, info, discussion, & fun!

Stronghold Academy
http://mama.indstate.edu/rpg/games/weg/starwars/index.html
  RPG games and resources from indstate.edu.

SW:RPG - Star Wars Roleplaying Game Site
http://members.tripod.com/KSantos/swrpg/index.html/
  Experienced or not, this RPG site has info you may need.

Targeting Computer (Rogue 8's)
http://members.xoom.com/rogue888/computer.htm
  Computer goodies - logos, software - great collection of fonts.

Thrawn Art Gallery - Videos, Toys & Others
http://empire.res.wabash.edu/art/others/index.htm
  Star Wars art - it gets around. Thrawn art gallery collection.

TIE Fighter Game Newsgroup
alt.games.tie-fighter

TIE Fighters Free Downloads
> http://indigo.ie/~hanafin/download.html
>> TIE fighter resource for gaming / scenarios.

Tips & Tricks - Gamestats
> www.gamestats.com/tips/List/All/
>> Tips, tricks & cheats for computer games, games, games.

Totally Games
> www.totallygames.com/
>> Flight combat game developer of X-wing & TIE Fighters games.

Trivia - Star Wars Trivia on Echo Station
> www.echostation.com/trivia/
>> Oooo! Star Wars Trivia online Sundays at 3 EST.

Voodoo Extreme Games
> www.voodooextreme.com/
>> May have Star Wars - mostly, it's extreme computer game stuff.

WarCraft II Sg-1 SAGA
> www.geocities.com/Area51/Vault/4910/sg1.html
>> Help in the development of a Sci-fi roleplaying game.

Watto's Junkyard Downloads
> www.wattosjunkyard.com/downloads.html
>> Good selection of QuickTime Prequel videos & game demos.

Wing Commander Movie
> http://scifi.simplenet.com/wingcommander/index.html
>> Wing Commander Movie facts, fun, models, pix.

Wing Commander Prophecy
> www.wingcommanderprophecy.com/
>> Wing Commander the Game demo/intro page.

Word Finds
> www.geocities.com/Area51/Chamber/4182/hunts.html
>> Several Word Search puzzles to solve.

X-Wing Attack Video Preview
> www.hollywood.com/multimedia/movies/starwars/video/mmindex.html
>> X-Wing Attack video preview in AVI, MOV, & Mac formats.

X-Wing Game Newsgroup
> alt.games.x-wing

X-Wing vs TIE Fighter Webring
> www.webring.org/cgi-bin/webring?ring=xvt1997;index
>> List of 17 TIE & X-wing Fighter web sites.

X-word Squadron Online Edition
> www.echostation.com/crossword/
>> 9 Star Wars online crossword puzzles.

Collectible Card Games (CCGs)

Whether you know them as Collectible Card Games or as Customizable Card Games, here is our list of CCG web sites. See also the Trading Cards section earlier in this chapter.

CCG: The Imperial Domination Sites List
www.webring.org/cgi-bin/webring?index&ring=empire
47 CCG/game sites in a link list.

Latest Scoop - Star Wars News from the Source
http://home1.gte.net/filter1/starwars/index.html
Organized memorial for Steven Curnow - killed at Columbine HS.

Let The Wookie Win
www.shavenwookie.com/ccg/
From a Wookiee perspective.

Newsdroid
www.newsdroid.com/
Latest news arranged by lifestyle category.

Star Wars Collectibles (tnc Universe)
www.tncmagic.com/starwars/00masks.htm
Variety of collectibles, costumes, masks, CCG sets, & party gear.

SW:CCG Webring
www.geocities.com/Area51/5657/ring.html
CCG web sites web ring.

Electronic Greeting Cards

Have a Star Wars Greeting Card sent by e-mail to someone special. Most of these electronic greeting card sites will let you customize the message.

Cards - A Prequel Message
http://thephantommenace.co.uk/postcard/
Prequel customizable electronic greeting cards.

Ewan McGregor Greeting Cards
www.ewanspotting.com/multimedia/postcards.html
Send a Ewan McGregor greeting card (non-Star Wars)

Holocards
http://outer-rim.net/card.html
Big selection of customizable Star Wars greeting cards.

Stakawaka's Natalie Portman Page
www.geocities.com/Hollywood/Lot/7181/natalie.html
Collection of Natalie info and poses over the years.

Sci-Fi Fandom

Generally, these are Star Wars sites that mix a lot of other science fiction into their content.

Area 51
www.geocities.com/Area51/Cavern/
Geocities Sci-fi web page searchable directory.

Area 51 Dimension - Geocities
www.geocities.com/Area51/Dimension/
Develop a web page or explore for Sci-fi pages.

Conduit 9
www.conduit.utah.edu/program.html
Education site that sponsors Sci-fi events, games.

Den, The
www.theden.com/
Light entertainment & Sci-fi news.

Dreams of Space: Space Art in Children's Books
http://sun3.lib.uci.edu/~jsisson/john.htm
Space in children's literature helps creativity.

Jon's Fly-By-Night Sci-fi Image Gallery & Sound Archive
http://web.wt.net/~jquick/archive.html
Variety of WAV sound files, but limited pix. A modern Sci-fi site.

Newsgroup: Star Wars Genre
net.genre.sf.star-wars

Prequels.com, The
http://theprequels.com/main.htm
Lively, colorful Prequel site - mucho variety!

Sci-fi Movie Clips
http://graffiti.u-bordeaux.fr/MAPBX/roussel/anim-e_03f.shtml
Big Sci-fi movie galleries from a French site.

Science Fiction - Star Wars Newsgroup
de.rec.arts.sf.starwars

Science Fiction Fantasy Star Wars Newsgroup
z-net.sf+fantasy.starwars.allgemein

Science Fiction Scale Models Newsgroup
alt.sf.scale-models

Sci-Fi Advance
http://scifi.simplenet.com/
Sci-fi resource featuring 3 Star Wars database collections.

Tripod's Pod Central Sci-fi Lounge
www.tripod.com/pod_central/pods/sciencefiction/
Get involved - be heard! Entertainment & fun resource.

Modeling

Some fans are excellent at creating Star Wars models – real-looking 3D models on the computer, and real live scale models in real life 3D! Dioramas are listed separately. For other 3D special effects, see the Productions & FX Section of the Films chapter.

3-D Modeling Alliance Forum
http://apps.vantagenet.com/aforums/thread.asp?old=Y&id=199851010212
3-D Modeling Alliance Discussion zone.

3D Palette
www.3dpalette.com/
3D resource and mega-site.

Andrew Gruner's Custom Star Wars Projects
www.mesastate.edu/~agruner/sw/custom/
Figurines, costuming, dioramas & modeling.

Deck Plans (for Star Wars)
www.geocities.com/Area51/Labyrinth/6246/DP.html
Deck plan specs for light freighters, pods, scout craft.

Dioramas at Louis Inman's Fett's Place
http://members.aol.com/lfett/custom/diorama.htm
Good link list to works of diorama artists.

Dioramas at Moff Peter's Dominion
http://members.aol.com/moffpeter/www/diorama.html
Before CG there was dioramas - here's about 50 of them.

Dioramas Maintained by Gus Lopez
www.toysrgus.com/images-displays.html
Dioramas put toys & models into real looking scenic creations.

How to Build a Stormtrooper Costume
www.studiocreations.com/stormtrooper/
Wanna build your own stormtrooper uniform? Here's how.

Massassi Order Scale Models
www.hta.nl/php/Jan.Jacob.Mosselaar/swmodel.htm
Spacecraft & vehicle models are artistically presented.

Mos Eisley Cantina Diorama
http://members.iquest.net/~sohair/hyperspace/cantina/page0.html
Cantina diorama - say, do large insects like this model?

PC & Miniature Galleries
http://rpg.echostation.com/gallery/gallery.html
Roleplaying resources - sketches, mini's, scenery.

Powerflicker's Model Page
www.geocities.com/Area51/Labyrinth/8664/models.html
Model and display pictures.

Schematics Collection (Taz's)
http://seconn4.yoda.com/~vader97/Schematics/schematics.html
Schematics by the dozens, presented as GIF/Corel images.

Scott O'Hair's Hyperspace
http://members.iquest.net/~sohair/hyperspace/menup.html
Model dioramas of famous Trilogy places; Cantina, Jabba's palace.

Star Wars 3D Gallery
>   www.ipr.nl/sw-3d/
>   Cool example of an early 3D modeling site from Holland.

Star Wars Customs.com
>   http://members.aol.com/awyant3477/index.htm
>   Make toys come alive in realistic-as-possible dioramas.

Star Wars Force Graphics
>   http://plaza.harmonix.ne.jp/~m-falcon/
>   Stellar Japanese graphics site; most pix are posters.

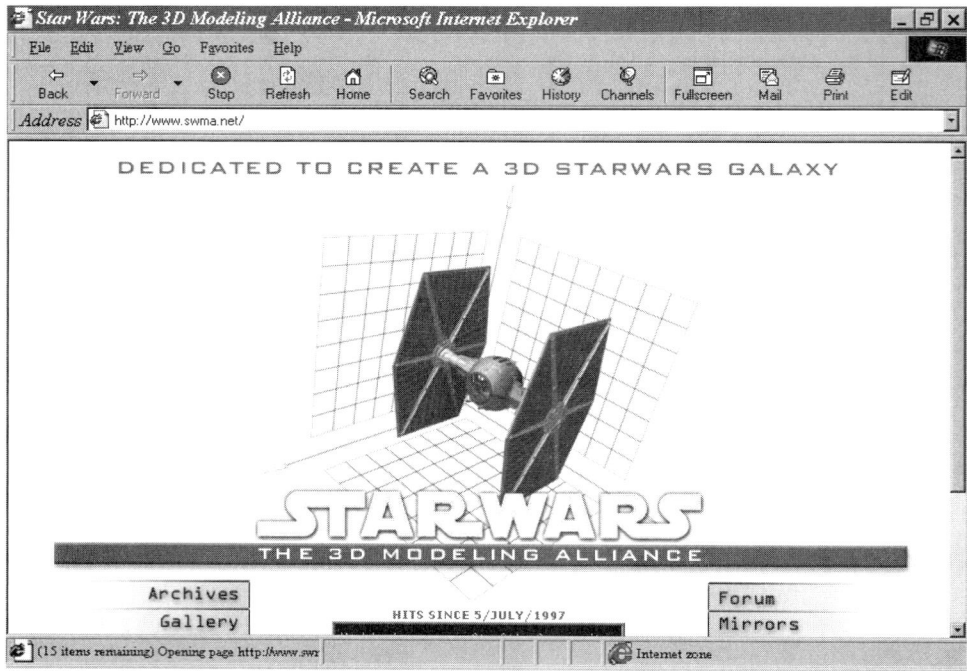

SWMA - Star Wars 3D Modeling Alliance
>   www.surfthe.net/swma/

SWMA - Star Wars 3D Modeling Alliance Archives
>   www.surfthe.net/swma/archives/archives.html
>   Storehouse of 3D that takes light years to see all of.

Technical Repository
>   www.cae.wisc.edu/~steiner/swsatellite/technic/
>   Specifications, text, and images of craft & weapons.

ThBeNDdS Clone Vat
>   www.swdatabase.com/thbends/
>   Models and images of Prequel Characters.

Wing Commander Movie
>   http://scifi.simplenet.com/wingcommander/index.html
>   Wing Commander Movie facts, fun, models, pix.

| Fun | Dioramas | 151 |

Dioramas

Try to make a life-like scene for showing off your Star Wars character figures. These web sites have a done a very good job of it!

Andrew Gruner's Custom Star Wars Projects
www.mesastate.edu/~agruner/sw/custom/
Figurines, costuming, dioramas & modeling.

Dioramas at Louis Inman's Fett's Place
http://members.aol.com/lfett/custom/diorama.htm
Good linklist to works of diorama artists.

Dioramas at Moff Peter's Dominion
http://members.aol.com/moffpeter/www/diorama.html
Before CG there was dioramas - here's about 50 of them.

Dioramas Maintained by Gus Lopez
www.toysrgus.com/images-displays.html
Dioramas put toys & models into real looking scenic creations.

Mos Eisley Cantina Diorama
http://members.iquest.net/~sohair/hyperspace/cantina/page0.html
Cantina diorama - say, do large insects like this model?

Scott O'Hair's Hyperspace
http://members.iquest.net/~sohair/hyperspace/menup.html
Model dioramas of famous Trilogy places; Cantina, Jabba's palace.

Star Wars Customs.com
http://members.aol.com/awyant3477/index.htm
Make toys come alive in realistic-as-possible dioramas.

Educational Material

We can learn a lot from Star Wars – here are web sites with a focus on education and learning. Included are glossaries, finder directories, and LucasLearning web pages.

Conduit 9
www.conduit.utah.edu/program.html
Education site that sponsors Sci-fi events, games.

Criminal Organizations in Star Wars, The Index to
http://index.echostation.com/crime.html
What & who to watch out for in the Star Wars underworld.

Cultural Abstractions Index
http://index.echostation.com/cult.html
Etiquette & protocol - advice for attending events, also slang.

Dreams of Space: Space Art in Children's Books
http://sun3.lib.uci.edu/~jsisson/john.htm
Space in children's literature helps creativity.

Ewoks Story
www.foxhome.com/animated/html/ewstory.htm
Childrens story & activity book online - Fun with Ewoks.

Games & Sport Index (Echostation)
>http://index.echostation.com/games.html
>>Star Wars universe games & sports explained.

Gonkite's Groovy Grotto & Glossary
>http://members.aol.com/gonkite/index.htm
>>A get-you-acquainted glossary and Gonk info pages.

Governments & Institutions Index
>http://index.echostation.com/gov.html
>>Governing bodies good & bad found in the Star Wars Universe.

HTML Files of Interest to Educators
>http://users.hub.ofthe.net/~mtalkmit/VRMLsearching.htm
>>VRML resources that all experts should have.

Kevin's Angle On Things - Why . . . Be a Jedi Knight
>http://orion.it.luc.edu/~kriorda/angle.html
>>All Jedi need to check Kevin's 6th & final paragraph.

Letterman Digital Center at the Presidio
>www.lucasfilm.com/presidio/
>>Lucas' new educational/training resource center project.

Lucas Learning
>www.lucaslearning.com/
>>Doing, exploring, creating - Star Wars teaching resource & products.

Myth in Star Wars - What Makes Star Wars Special?
>www.synicon.com.au/sw/myth/myth.htm
>>It's special for a lot of reasons - many of them are here.

New Mythology - the Star Wars Trilogy
>www.dom.net/wrd/new/ref/sw/
>>Why myths & the Star Wars stories work for us.

Religion, Star Wars The
>http://hamp.hampshire.edu/~elwF94/planet/test.html
>>14 religion-like lessons for Jedi or anyone.

Science & Nature
>http://index.echostation.com/ysci.html
>>Index of scientific and natural things in Star Wars.

Star Wars Index to Health & Medicine
>http://index.echostation.com/med.html
>>Alphabetical Health Care index of Star Wars.

Star Wars Index to the Supernatural
>http://index.echostation.com/super.html
>>Supernatural things of Star Wars listed alphabetically.

Jabba is a Hutt; that's his species. Did you know that Hutts are originally from the planet Varl?

Roleplaying

Roleplaying Games (RPGs) on the virtual world of the computer has been a great way to be creative and show your "Star Wars" moxie. In roleplaying, you are kinda acting, kinda playing, as you follow the rules for participation.

MUSH

MUSH is the acronym for "Multi User Shared Hallucination." A MUSH is a virtual world on the Internet, a lot like a "let's pretend" chat room. Following are all types of web sites for MUSHes.

Gothic Skywalker's MUSH Page
www.geocities.com/TimesSquare/Dungeon/3913/mush.html
Roleplaying site anchored in "Gothic" Wisconsin.

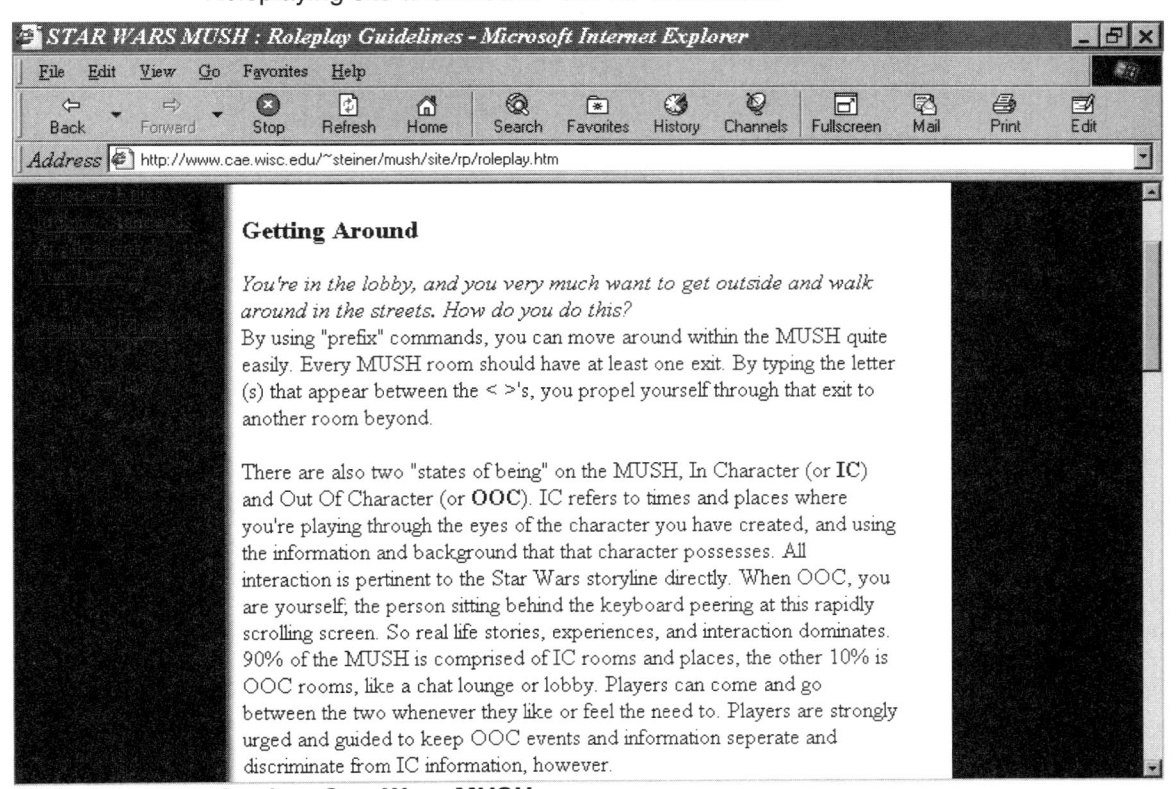

Roleplaying in a Star Wars MUSH
www.cae.wisc.edu/~steiner/mush/site/rp/roleplay.htm
Basic instructions for MUSH roleplaying.

Star Wars MUD & MUSHes
www.radeleff.de/swmudlist/
MUSHes, MOOs, Muds, Muxes - Roleplaying sites lists.

Star Wars MUSH
www.cae.wisc.edu/~steiner/mush/site/index.html

Star Wars MUSH Mailing Lists
www.cae.wisc.edu/~steiner/mush/site/mailing.htm
Lists of MUSH players, dignitaries, officials, wizards.

Resources

For good roleplaying, the participant should know what they're doing, and what they're talking about. These RPG "Resource" sites help you get acquainted, and fill you in on the details "of many things."

2nd Empire - The Emperor's Wrath
http://members.tripod.com/~Dolmyn/empire.htm
Imperial database and mission statement at its worst.

B Squared's Star Wars Stuff
www.synicon.com.au/sw/
Can't get enough spacecraft & lightsaber info? Come hither!

Battles & Events
http://members.tripod.com/Tiger887/EmpireBattles.html
Texts about battles and losses - Imperial site.

Captain Needa's Star Destroyer
www.geocities.com/Area51/Rampart/5559/
Star Destroyer info for role playing and for the curious.

Classified Military Plan - Secret (Example)
www.geocities.com/Area51/Corridor/4309/secret.html
Secret communication about a stardestroyer.

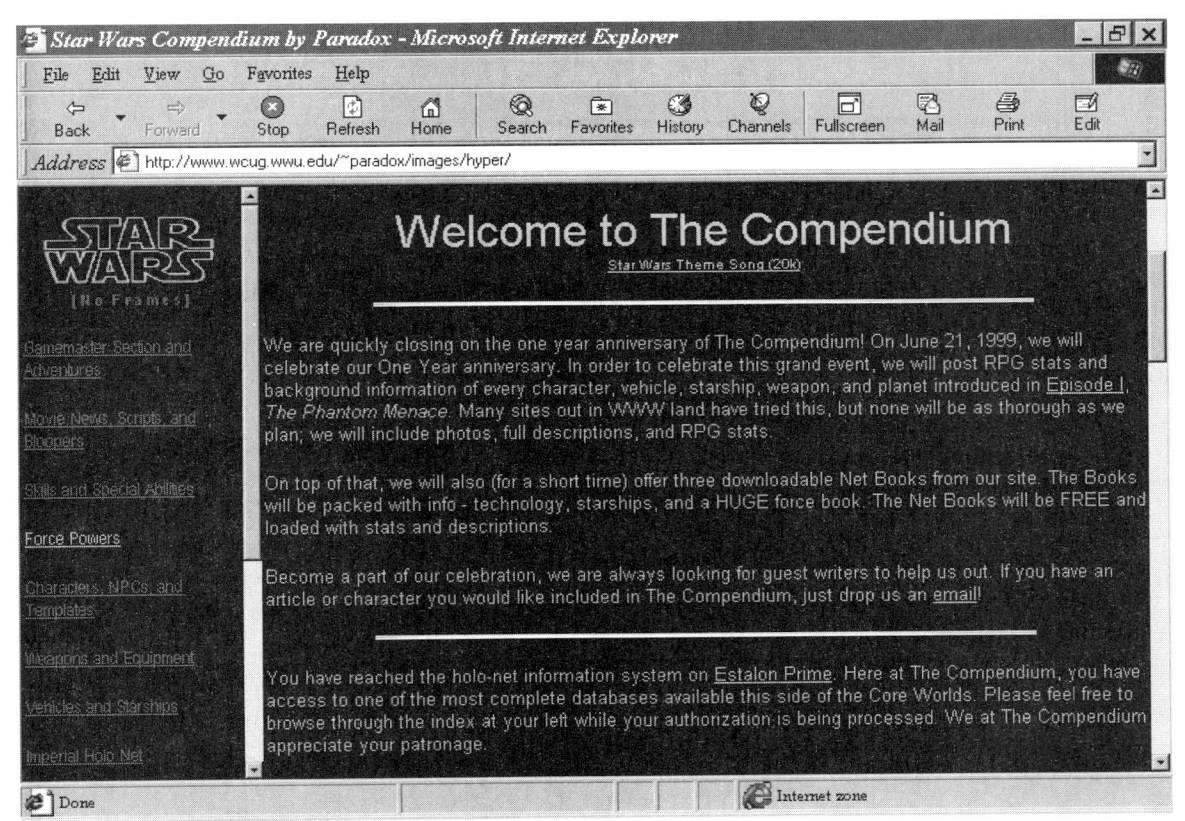

Compendium, The
>   www.wcug.wwu.edu/~paradox/images/hyper/
>   Not the prettiest site, but one of the fullest!

Criminal Organizations in Star Wars, The Index to
>   http://index.echostation.com/crime.html
>   What & who to watch out for in the Star Wars underworld.

Cultural Abstractions Index
>   http://index.echostation.com/cult.html
>   Etiquette & protocol - advice for attending events, also slang.

Dark Lords of Sith
>   www.geocities.com/Hollywood/Location/1657/darthandexar.html
>   Feel the dark side. Webring site and Lords of Sith mini-portal.

Deck Plans (for Star Wars)
>   www.geocities.com/Area51/Labyrinth/6246/DP.html
>   Deck plan specs for light freighters, pods, scout craft.

Galactic Empire Data Bank
>   www.iaw.on.ca/~btaylor1/index.html
>   Imperial, rebel, bounty hunter & "other" vessels.

Games & Sport Index (Echostation)
>   http://index.echostation.com/games.html
>   Star Wars universe games & sports explained.

Governments & Institutions Index
>   http://index.echostation.com/gov.html
>   Governing bodies good & bad found in the Star Wars Universe.

Imperial Intelligence Agency
www.angelfire.com/ab/ewok/starwarsframe1.html

Internet Role Playing Society
http://irps.engr.ucf.edu/
Roleplaying site - resources, E-zine, scenarios.

IRC RPG Resource; Star Wars (Echo Station)
http://rpg.echostation.com/
RPG - take that droid to Anchorhead to have its memory erased.

Jedi Academy
www.jediacademy.com/force.htm
Jedi training and info site for the serious Jedi.

Jedi Academy at Yavin IV
www.nerf-herder.com/jedi/
Page through and find scenarios and fun.

Mandalorian Portfolio
http://scifi.simplenet.com/starwars/prequels/portfolio/mand/mand.html
Like an spreading cancerous evil - these Mandalorians!

Palpatine Portfolio
http://scifi.simplenet.com/starwars/prequels/portfolio/pal/palpatine.html
Watch out for this fellow - there's no end to evil!

Prequel Vehicles
http://meltingpot.fortunecity.com/greenwood/487/vehic/vlist.html
Sith Speeders & pod racers to big Federation Battleships.

Role Play: Mind's Eye (Echo Station Emag)
http://emag.echostation.com/roleplay/rpg1009.htm
Article about Star Wars Roleplaying - State-o-the-game.

RPG Revised & Expanded Rules - Star Wars
http://rpg.echostation.com/updates/updates.html
Downloads of updates of rules of Star Wars RPGs.

Saber Combat (Jedi Academy)
www.jediacademy.com/saber.htm
Care, feeding, & handling of lightsabers, with lessons.

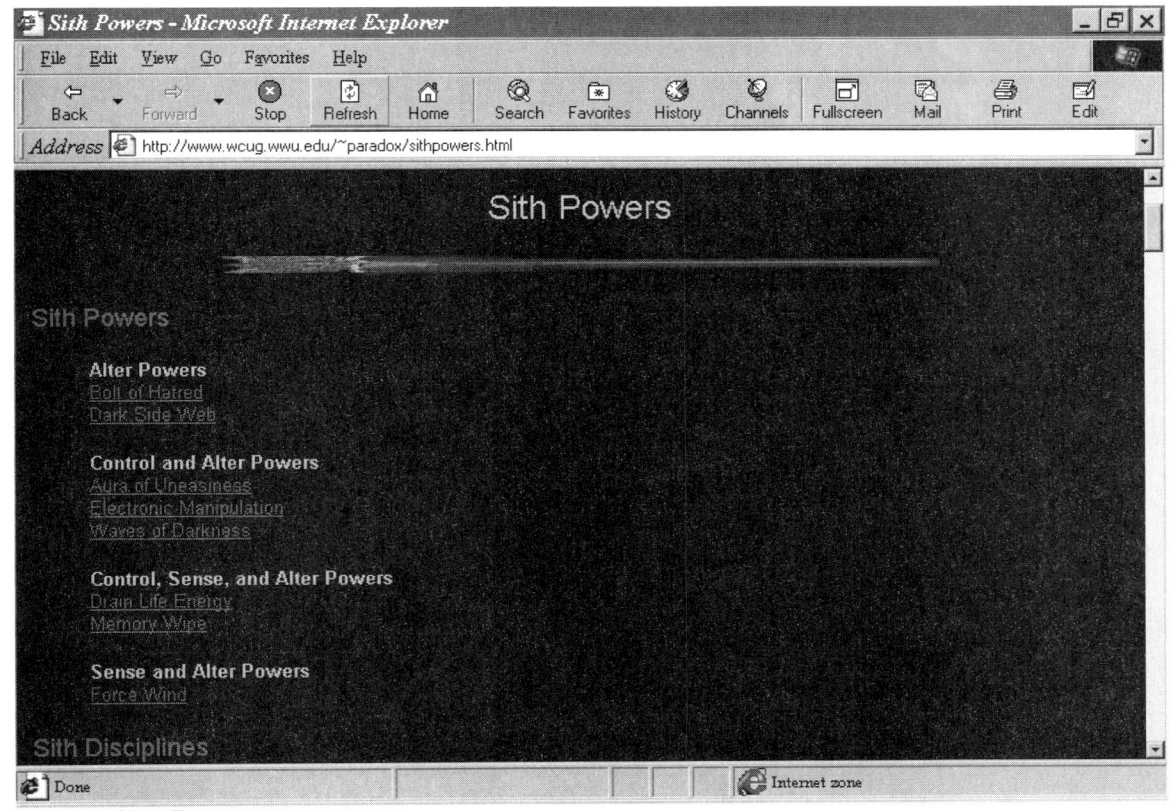

Sith Powers
www.wcug.wwu.edu/~paradox/sithpowers.html
Villains should at least know what they're doing.

Star Wars Index to Characters
http://index.echostation.com/char.html
Information on ALL known characters & droids.

Star Wars Index to the Supernatural
http://index.echostation.com/super.html
Supernatural things of Star Wars listed alphabetically.

Starfighters
http://frankg.dgne.com/swsv/starfighters.html
Specifications & info on smaller Star Wars craft.

Stormtrooper Recruitment - The Replacements
http://207.136.91.134/very/x-stream/
Site reforming when we visited - new stuff should be stellar!

SW:RPG - Star Wars Roleplaying Game Site
http://members.tripod.com/KSantos/swrpg/index.html/
Experienced or not, this RPG site has info you may need.

The Core
> www.geocities.com/Area51/Rampart/2117/
>> Imperial destinations and gaming/roleplaying site.

TIE Fighters Technical Commentaries
> www.theforce.net/swtc/tie.html
>> From technical aspects to the broader TIE issues.

Time Tours - Roderick Vonhogen's Virtual Edition
> www.virtualedition.com/timetours/timetours_splash.htm
>> Time Tour "Timespeeder" adventure scenario.

Various Beers from the Star Wars Universe
> http://rpg.echostation.com/humor/SWBEER.TXT
>> Yes, it's true. Not recommended, but it's true.

WAV Archive - RPG at Echo Station
> http://rpg.echostation.com/wav/wav.html

Reference | Databases | 159

Star Wars
Reference Points

Finding Tip: Don't forget that you can use your browser's "search" feature to find a word or phrase on a web page – Control + F.

Databases

Databases collect information on their pages, making it easier to find. There are databases for toys, media, events, comics – even listing for current movies, where they're playing, and the times.

2nd Empire - The Emperor's Wrath
http://members.tripod.com/~Dolmyn/empire.htm
Imperial database and mission statement at its worst.

Aaron's Star Wars Toy & Comic Price Guides Checklist
www.continet.com/aaronsmagic/pretoys/1Check.html
Checklist of new Kenner Prequel action figures.

All-Media Guide
http://allmovie.com/cg/x.dll?UID=9:01:46%7CPM&p=avg&sql=A179455
Read about it, connect to other good sites, vote in the survey.

All-Media Guide Star Wars
http://allmovie.com/cg/x.dll?UID=9:01:46|PM&p=avg&sql=A46636
Obviously, the AMG people are big fans - good database.

Battles & Events
http://members.tripod.com/Tiger887/EmpireBattles.html
Texts about battles and losses - Imperial site.

Complete Star Wars Timeline
www.swdatabase.com/pages/time.html
What happened "when" in the Star Wars universe.

Completely Unofficial Star Wars Encyclopedia 6th Edition
www.mindspring.com/~bobvitas/swenc.htm
Something about everyone - cast, crew, characters - all!

Delta Source
www.jedinet.com/delta/
Databases of events, characters, vehicles, weapons, more.

DJ Rhythm's Dance Music Database
www.djrhythms.com/db/
Star Wars disco and a whole galaxy more of dance music.

Hollywood Online Database
http://moviepeople.hollywood.com/
Good, quick way to find film & celebrity info!

Index (by Pablo Hildago) Hosted by Echo Station
http://index.echostation.com/
Indexes arranged by topic for ease of access.

Internet Movie Database (IMDb)
http://us.imdb.com/
Easy to use data on moviemakers, stars, & flix - bigger than the Empire.

Latest Star Wars Comics News
www.theforce.net/comics/
Lists, reviews, news on Dark Horse & Marvel comics.

Movielink
www.movielink.com/
Search for movies currently playing: place, time, dates

Sci-Fi Advance
http://scifi.simplenet.com/
Sci-fi resource featuring 3 Star Wars database collections.

Star Wars Database
www.swdatabase.com/
Features, features, features. A must see.

SWMA - Star Wars 3D Modeling Alliance Archives
www.surfthe.net/swma/archives/archives.html
Storehouse of 3D that takes light years to see all of.

Directories

Directories are lists of web sites. Usually, by clicking on a site name or URL, you are linked to the new site. Often, a directory will break its list into categories, making it easier to find what you're looking for.

AltaVista
www.altavista.com/
Good place to search for Star Wars images.

Area 51
www.geocities.com/Area51/Cavern/
Geocities Sci-fi web page searchable directory.

Characters of Star Wars Official Index
www.starwars.com/
Official subject directory of Star Wars characters - most of them.

Reference FAQs   161

direct search
>   http://gwis2.circ.gwu.edu/~gprice/direct.htm
>   Great starting place for finding real-life technology & ideas.

Emag - Echo Station
>   http://emag.echostation.com/
>   Free online variety magazine of Star Wars topics.

Geocities Hollywood Studio
>   www.geocities.com/Hollywood/Studio/
>   Hosts plenty of Star Wars pages - a good place to search, too.

Links to the Star Wars Galaxy
>   www.shavenwookie.com/swlinks.html
>   Search Star Wars subject directories by Web site name.

Star Wars As Seen On TV
>   www.lucasfan.com/swtv/index.html
>   Star Wars on the little screen collection.

Star Wars MUD & MUSHes
>   www.radeleff.de/swmudlist/
>   MUSHes, MOOs, Muds, Muxes - Roleplaying sites lists.

Tripod's Star Wars Fan Pages
>   www.tripod.com/explore/entertainment/wire/wire_969531_71102_best_1.html
>   Directory of all the Tripod-hosted Star Wars pages. Search!

Yahoo!: News & Media: Television
>   http://dir.yahoo.com/News_and_Media/Television/
>   This is where you'll find Star Trek stuff 'cause TV is free.

FAQs

FAQ stands for "frequently asked questions." Technically, a FAQ page offers a bunch of questions that you're likely to ask, followed by the answers. We've also included pages that focus on presenting Star Wars "facts." You may also wish to see the Commentaries section of the Written in the Stars chapter.

Empire Strikes Back Special Edition FAQ
>   www.jax-inter.net/users/datalore/starwars/esbindex.htm
>   Commentaries on Special Edition scenes in Empire.

Empire Strikes Back, The
>   www.starwars.com/episode-v/
>   Official Lucasfilms movie site, with the basic goodies.

Etcetera (Virtual McGregor)
>   www.enter.net/~cybernut/ewanlinx.htm
>   The truth about Ewan - don't worry, it's good.

Forum FAQ
>   http://jedicouncil.net/forum/faq.html
>   Learn about Forums and how to participate in them.

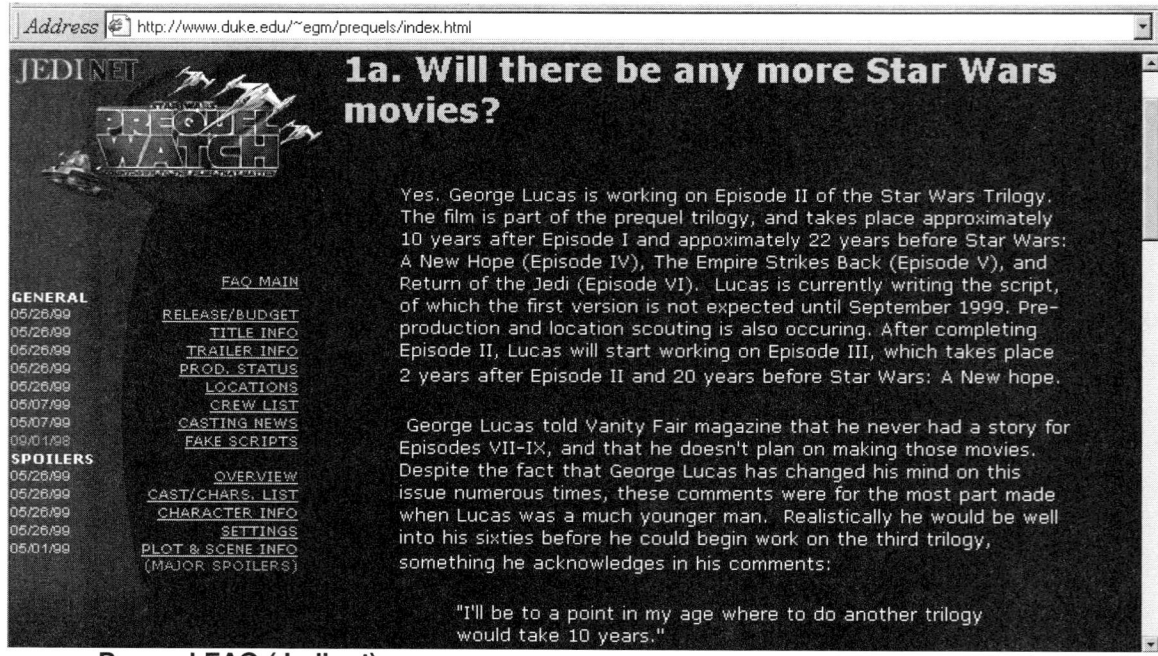

Prequel FAQ (Jedinet)
> www.jedinet.com/prequels/faq/
> Basic FAQs about the Prequel.

Return of the Jedi
> www.starwars.com/episode-vi/
> Official movie site that we hoped would have just a little more info.

STAR WARS - Welcome to the Official Site
> www.starwars.com
> "Must see" official Lucasfilm Star Wars site.

Star Wars A New Hope Special Edition FAQ
> www.jax-inter.net/users/datalore/starwars/anhindex.htm
> Details on the new & changed scenes in Special Edition ANH.

Star Wars Games Cheat Codes
> http://rpg.echostation.com/cheat/swgame.html
> Cheats, codes, FAQs and hints for various Star Wars games.

Star Wars Information Newsgroup
> rec.arts.sf.starwars.info

SWMA - 3D Modeling Information
> www.surfthe.net/swma/information/information.html
> Everything you want to know about Star Wars 3D modeling.

Theed.net - City Beyond the Swamp
> www.theed.net/
> New site with news and tricks up its sleeve (more promised).

Link Lists

Link Lists on a web page are lists of other, separate web sites. Usually, these "linked sites" have been approved by the person putting up the link list, and you will automatically open the "linked" site when you click on it. Most Star Wars sites offer some sort of link list. The sites below are exceptionally good or relate to a specific topic, or they list the sites in a webring.

3D Modeling Alliance Link Page
www.surfthe.net/swma/links/links.html
Link list with linked site logos. "Impressive" - Vader.

Boba Fett's Page
http://members.tripod.com/~Rowlandc/
Searchable homepage for Star Wars links, with message boards.

CCG: The Imperial Domination Sites List
www.webring.org/cgi-bin/webring?index&ring=empire
47 CCG/game sites in a link list.

Coruscant Webring Sites List
www.webring.org/cgi-bin/webring?ring=corusring;list
19 recent sites and growing. It could be a great ring.

Elite Star Wars Webring: The Best in the Galaxy
www.shavenwookie.com/elitering.html
Sites selected for quality of content and Star Wars lifestyle.

Full Force Webring Sites List
www.webring.org/cgi-bin/webring?ring=fullforce&list
How many of 253 member sites can you visit?

Geographic Links - Shaven Wookie
www.shavenwookie.com/swlinkslocate.html
Lists of sites by Star Wars location (place names).

Guide to the Star Wars Universe
http://bobafett.metrolink.net.au/guide/
Not a big alphabetized list, but the sites are rated.

Han Solo Webring Sites List
www.webring.org/cgi-bin/webring?ring=6827;list
30 sites of the Han Solo Webring.

Ivor's Star Wars Webring Sites List
www.webring.org/cgi-bin/webring?ring=ivor;list
48 sites collected over the years.

Jedi Archives
http://listen.to/thejedi/
A short, viewed (person-approved) link list.

Jedi Ring Site Index
www.webring.org/cgi-bin/webring?ring=Star_Wars&index
62 various Star Wars sites in a common ring/bond.

Jedi Society
http://members.aol.com/Myau84/society.html
Links to Star Wars sites that display cool new banners.

Journeyman Protector's Elite Star Wars Webring Sites List
www.webring.org/cgi-bin/webring?ring=capjas;list
The 30 sites found here are like a family of coolness.

Links to the Star Wars Galaxy
www.shavenwookie.com/swlinks.html
Search Star Wars subject directories by Web site name.

Phantom Menace.com, The
www.the-phantommenace.com/
Links arranged by title/subject, also find toy pix, wallpaper.

Pod Race Reporter Homepage
http://podracereporter.listbot.com/
Current Star Wars news items are a couple clicks away.

Rebels vs. The Empire Webring Sites List
www.webring.org/cgi-bin/webring?ring=rvse&list
113 web sites - but Death Star Bathroom was gone.

Rogue 8's Forceful Webring
www.webring.org/cgi-bin/webring?ring=forceful;list
30 Star Wars webrings found in Rogue 8's collection.

Shaven Wookie LTD
www.shavenwookie.com/
You haven't shaved until you've shaved a Wookie.

Star Seeker: Star Wars Episode 1
www.starseeker.com/films/1999film/starwars.htm
Search engine generated resource link lists.

Star Wars - Arts et Culture: Cinema et Video: Films
http://recherche.toile.qc.ca/quebec/qcart_ci_films_starwars.htm
List of Star Wars web sites in French.

Star Wars Fans Confederation Sites List
www.webring.org/cgi-bin/webring?ring=jedibase&list
207 glorious sites in this ring.

Star Wars Link Engine
www.project-m31.com/prequels.shtml
Link lists for each of the four movies.

Star Wars Multimedia
www.cadvision.com/geoff/sw.html
Multimedia linked sites collected by Geoff Holmes.

Star Wars Top 100 Sites List
http://coolsurfin.net/starwars/index.html
We saw only 55 sites listed, but they are okay ones.

Star Wars Universe Webring Sites List
www.webring.org/cgi-bin/webring?ring=swuniverse&list
343 web sites in this 3-year old ring.

Star Wars Web Ring Special Edition Site List
www.webring.org/cgi-bin/webring?ring=1starwars&list
666 (!!) sites. It has quite a few foreign pages.

Trailer Mirror Lists
http://sabbeth.com/starwars/mirrorlist.htm
Mirror lists of sites offering Star Wars Trailers.

Reference | Portals

Webring Javigator Purple Pages
www.javigate.com/Webring/PurplePages/ent/scifi_starwars.html
Enter a query and get a list of 20+ webrings on your topic.

Webring of the Jedi of Yavin 4 Sites List
www.webring.org/cgi-bin/webring?ring=santillies;list
132 sites linked by Samantha the Jedi Goddess.

Portals

Portals are larger sites that, once you are there, let you get to a wide range of other web sites quickly. Often, a portal will have a "search feature" that lets you quickly search the site for other pages.

AV Photo & Media Finder
http://image.altavista.com/cgi-bin/avncgi
Random searching for Star Wars images, video, or audio files.

Echo Station
www.echostation.com/
Full Service Star Wars portal! A must see.

FORCE.NET - Your Daily Dose of Star Wars
http://theforce.net/
Mega Star Wars Info Site - Mega!

Geocities Hollywood Studio
www.geocities.com/Hollywood/Studio/
Hosts plenty of Star Wars pages - a good place to search, too.

Geocities Neighborhoods: Hollywood
www.geocities.com/Hollywood/Set/
Search for geocities "Hollywood-related" web sites.

Get Ready for Star Wars
www.excite.com/events/star_wars
Excite's Star Wars page informs & links to some great sites.

Jedinet
www.jedinet.com/frame.htm
By the Fans for the Fans - full-service super site.

Lycos Star Wars Mini-Guide
www.lycos.com/entertainment/scifi/miniguide/starwars.html
Search engine's Entertainment portal for Star Wars.

Marua Sector
www.marua.com/index2.html
New, developing semi-semi-mega all-purpose site.

MSN Star Wars Web Guide
www.musiccentral.msn.com/movies/StarWars/StarWars.asp
Some say the film's a bit predictable & commercial - you decide.

Shaven Wookie LTD
www.shavenwookie.com/
You haven't shaved until you've shaved a Wookie.

STAR WARS - Welcome to the Official Site
www.starwars.com
"Must see" official Lucasfilm Star Wars site.

Starwarz
www.starwarz.com/
Rates highly as an alternative fan site portal. Unique concept.

T'Bone Fenders Star Wars Universe
www.starwarz.com/index.htm
Among the best fan operated sites on the Net.

Tripod's Pod Central Sci-fi Lounge
www.tripod.com/pod_central/pods/sciencefiction/
Get involved - be heard! Entertainment & fun resource.

Search Engines & Finders

Need to find something on the Internet? Here are our favorite (and best) search tools. We recommend that you use the advanced features (where available) on these search engines, especially AltaVista and Hotbot.

AltaVista
http://www.altavista.com/
Good place to search for Star Wars images.

Ask Jeeves
http://www.askjeeves.com/
Ask a Star Wars question - or ANY question.

HotBot
http://www.hotbot.com/
Get 100 results at once on Star Wars searches!

Search Engines (Knight Hammer)
http://www.geocities.com/Area51/Chamber/4182/search.html
Search by search engine, geocities, or a big link list.

Spider's Apprentice
www.monash.com/spidap.html
This site will help you explore Star Wars on the Internet.

Yahoo!: News & Media: Television
http://dir.yahoo.com/News_and_Media/Television/
This is where you'll find stuff 'cause TV is free.

Timelines & Chronologies

What happened when in Star Wars? That's what timelines and chronologies are all about.

Jim's Star Wars Chronology
www.gis.net/~mcfadden/jmm/swhome.html
Useful knowledge and an invaluable calendar!

Steve's Star Wars Timeline
www.echostation.com/
Our favorite timeline site for clicking and going!

Timeline (Jedinet)
www.jedinet.com/multimedia/timeline/index.htm
List of when events occur, but the sources are not quoted.

Timeline - Knight Hammer
www.geocities.com/Area51/Chamber/4182/timeline.html
A fair if not too-sophisticated sequence of events.

Webrings

Webrings are a group of sites organized in a "ring-like" fashion, meaning that by clicking on the "Next" and "Previous" buttons of a webring's logo, you can travel around to the sites that are part of that ring. When you reach the end, the ring automatically takes you back to the first site. Therefore, ring travel forms an endless loop or "ring." Some webring logos also offer the opportunity to view all the sites in the ring by clicking on "List Sites." The link lists for some of the webrings listed here can be accessed using the URLs listed in the Link Lists section earlier in this chapter.

Anakin14's Ring of the Jedi
www.geocities.com/Area51/Chamber/6138/ringofjedi.html
Jedi's & others are invited to join - and view - the ring.

Bantha Tracks Webring
www.angelfire.com/fl/VELARDE/webring.html
A ring for "serious" Star Wars fans.

Bespin - Cite des Nuages Webring
www.chez.com/quibs/webring/
French Language Webring; good links to other French sites.

Coruscant Webring
www.angelfire.com/md/ultstarwars/index.html
Virtually new when we visited!

Dark Jedi Webring
www.geocities.com/Area51/Dimension/4634/

Death Star Ring
www.swdvader.com/wrmain.htm

Elite Star Wars Webring: The Best in the Galaxy
www.shavenwookie.com/elitering.html
Sites selected for quality of content and Star Wars lifestyle.

Empire Star Wars CCG Webring
www.geocities.com/Area51/4132/empire.html
The webring to see for CCG.

Galactic Web Connection Ring, The
www.geocities.com/SouthBeach/Surf/2144/galactic.html

Han Solo Webring Join Up Page
www.geocities.com/Area51/Vault/2750/myring.htm
Find Lando's, Han's and others web pages in this ring.

Imperial & Federation Database Ring
www.geocities.com/Area51/Nebula/3657/

Imperial Power Web Ring
www.geocities.com/Area51/Dunes/3630/IPWR.html
Save the emperor above all others!

Imperial Stormtroopers Webring
www.geocities.com/Area51/Zone/5881/
No, you do not need a stormtrooper helmet.

Italiano di Gerre Stellari Webring
www.geocities.com/Area51/Corridor/1431/logoring.html
Italian language webring - we assume English sites are okay.

Ivor's Star Wars Webring
www.geocities.com/Area51/Zone/5641/mywebring.html
We don't know who Ivor is, but his ring had 48 sites in line.

Jabba's Palace Webring
www.geocities.com/SiliconValley/Pines/4928/jabbaring.htm
Is this webring as big as Jabba? Not exactly. You can join!

Jedi Master's Webring
www.angelfire.com/ky/devindamrell/ring.html
A newer cleaner webring - 8 sites & growing when we visited.

Jedi Praxeum Webring
www.geocities.com/Area51/Vault/2220/Force.html
An older webring with older sites - just like the Falcon.

Jedi Ring
www.geocities.com/Area51/Cavern/5798/ring.html
A "Luke Skywalker" leads this webring.

JediLinks - Science Fiction Webring
www.geocities.com/Area51/Zone/4283/jedilink.html

JediLinks Webring
www.geocities.com/Area51/Zone/4283/jedilink.html
Sci-fi web sites, mostly Star Trek & Star Wars.

Journeyman Protector's Elite Star Wars Webring
www.geocities.com/Area51/Chamber/8256/jpr.html
Journeyman protectors are bounty-hunters for the Empire.

Luke Skywalker Ring of Dreams
www.webring.org/cgi-bin/webring?ring=lukefans;index
Basicly, this is the "We Love Luke" webring.

Luke Skywalker Webring
www.geocities.com/Area51/Lair/8709/webring.html

Official Rassm Webring
www.shavenwookie.com/rassmring.html
Usenet group outlet - membership re-opened 6/99.

Outrider Webring
www.geocities.com/Hollywood/Set/5206/webring.html
Strictly Star Wars Web Sites - and no questions asked.

Prince Xizor's Black Sun Webring Sites List
www.webring.org/cgi-bin/webring?ring=tbarte;list
16 sites but most are newer generation Star Wars pages.

Rebels vs. The Empire Webring
www.geocities.com/Area51/Lair/5677/index.htm
Older - and folksier - Star Wars generic webring.

Ring of the Wookiees
www.geocities.com/Area51/Vault/5841/wookrng.html
Now, what kind of a ring could Wookiees put together?

Rogue 8's Forceful Webring
www.webring.org/cgi-bin/webring?ring=forceful;list
30 Star Wars webrings found in Rogue 8's collection.

Sci-Fi Connections Webring
www.geocities.com/Area51/1499/sciring.html

Sci-Fi Galaxy Ring, The
www.cyberstreet.com/users/petei/ring.htm

Sci-Fi/Fantasy Ring
www.geocities.com/Area51/Vault/4639/scififantasyring.html
Expand your horizons - put your Star Wars site on this Sci-fi ring.

Science Fiction Fandom Webring
http://fanac.org/sffandom/

Science Fiction on TV Ring
www.geocities.com/TelevisionCity/Set/2327/Ring.html
Find Sci-fi sites that relate to TV - mostly Trek, but some Star Wars.

Science Fiction TV Series Ring
www.geocities.com/TelevisionCity/Stage/1125/Home.html
Sites that are interested in Star Trek on TV - also Star Wars sites.

Shaven Wookie LTD
www.shavenwookie.com/
You haven't shaved until you've shaved a Wookie.

Star Wars Cantina Club Webring
http://nav.webring.com/cgi-bin/navcgi?ring=ringfriends;list

Star Wars Collective Webring
http://starwars.interspeed.net/swring.html
Small, but growing. Join and you could rule!

Star Wars Fans Confederation Webring
www.bestweb.net/~fett/join.htm
Sites are asked to have multimedia, Prequel, humor sections.

Star Wars Galaxy Webring
www.webring.org/cgi-bin/webring?ring=tswg;list
Webring start-up point.

Star Wars Information Ring
www.geocities.com/Area51/Nebula/8023/
A new webring? With new sites? Get 'em while they're young!

Star Wars Internet Webring
http://members.aol.com/GOLF4US/join.html

Star Wars Jedi Webring
http://members.tripod.com/CatarinaKerr/jedi_webring.html

Star Wars RPG Webring
www.angelfire.com/fl/Nakata/webring.html

Star Wars Squadron Webring
www.geocities.com/Area51/Corridor/4625/squads.html
Appears to be open to any fan with Star Wars on their page.

Star Wars the Webring
www.geocities.com/Area51/Rampart/2720/starwarsthewebring.html

Star Wars Trilogy Webring
www.freedave.com/starwars.htm
Sites that relate primarily to the Trilogy.

Star Wars Universe Role Play Confederation Webring
http://geocities.com/Area51/Station/8305/Webring/

Star Wars Universe Webring
www.geocities.com/Hollywood/Boulevard/6983/index.html
Join the SWU webring - it is your destiny says Darth.

Star Wars Web Ring Special Edition
    `www.algonet.se/~paolsson/ring/`
        Special Edition era webring.

Superior Star Wars Webring
    `www.geocities.com/Area51/Corridor/1978/`
        Obi-wan on one side - Darth on the other.

SW:CCG Webring
    `www.geocities.com/Area51/5657/ring.html`
        CCG web sites web ring.

SWDN Star Wars Database Network Webring
    `http://members.xoom.com/schnoor/starwars/webrings.html`
        Open to all types of web sites.

SyFy World Webring
    `www.geocities.com/Area51/Hollow/9416/webadmin.html`

The Crossroads Webring
    `www.geocities.com/Area51/Vault/2088/crossroads.html`
        Variety! some foreign. Qualifications are: just be Star Wars.

The Han Solo-ists
    `www.geocities.com/Area51/Capsule/2324/thering.htm`
        Do they go solo-ing with Han?

The Holoring
    `www.geocities.com/Area51/Dimension/7335/ring.html`

Top Star Wars (Webring)
    `http://coolsurfin.net/starwars/newbie.html`
        Squeeky-clean webring with a un-webring-like format.

trueSpace Webring
    `www.logicbit.com/webring/`
        200 fabulous 3D artist sites/pages (a few are Star Wars)

Ultimate Star Wars Webring
    `http://pages.prodigy.net/robertrihn/ring.htm`

Webring of the Jedi of Yavin 4 Official Site
    `www.angelfire.com/md/jedigoddess/webring.html`
        Rule 4 of this wondrous webring includes: do not complain.

World of Science Fiction Webring, The
www.geocities.com/TelevisionCity/1701/world.html

XVT (X-wing vs. TIE Fighter) Webring Site
www.hydra.com.au/neelix/xvt1997.htm
Dedicated to X-wing & TIE Fighters.

Yoda's Star Wars Webring
www.geocities.com/Area51/Cavern/1783/webring.htm
Yoda's Webring actually has great sites!

Star Wars Software

The Web is full of Star Wars sites that let you download "stuff" so that you can make your computer "Star Wars friendly." This includes things to help your computer run better as well as cursors, screensavers, and computer do-dads, even some things that let you communicate, like free e-mail systems.

Accessories

Most of the computer accessories found at the following web sites are downloadable to your own computer, and will help you in the Star Wars Universe as well as your own. See also the separate sections for Icons & Cursors, Fonts, Themes, and Wallpaper.

Frontpage - Your Internet Start Point
www.godlike.org/frontpage/starwars/index.html
Zero-in on downloadable computer accessories.

ICQ Soundpack, Irc Script Pack, New Star Wars Font
www.jedinet.com/multimedia/windows/misc/index.htm
Computer accessories you probably hadn't thought of!

Macromedia
www.macromedia.com/
Web page accessories & sitebuilding resources.

Shell & Desktop Tools
www.winfiles.com/apps/98/shelldesk.html
The right tools to make your computer happy.

SHOW-URL
htt://netvigator.com/~godfreyk/showurl/
Print & manage your Star Wars bookmarks!

Startup/Shutdown Screens
www.jedinet.com/multimedia/windows/screens/index.htm
See Star Wars every time your computer starts & shuts down.

Ultimate Star Wars Cursors Page
www.geocities.com/Area51/Lair/3724/cursors.html
More computer cursors than you can imagine.

Ultimate Star Wars Multimedia Universe
www.geocities.com/Area51/Lair/3724/
Has a virtual reality page and Beaucoup of computer goodies!

Fonts

"Fonts" are typestyles. So, if you want to imitate Star Wars or science fiction graphics, then download and use the typestyles from any of the following sites. These Fonts are also useful to web site builders.

Add-ons, from Jedi Council Chamber
www.geocities.com/Area51/Hollow/9125/addons.htm
Wallpaper, icons and other Star Wars goodies for your computer.

Boba Fonts
http://starwars.fans.net/bobafonts/
Newer fonts, cursors, fan-fiction, and calendars.

Desktop - Star Wars: A Feminine Perspective
http://members.aol.com/bananie42/desktop.html
Could your computer use these icons, cursors & fonts?

Fonts From All Over the Place
www.homeusers.prestel.co.uk/mania/fonts2.html
Sci-fi & other odd, cool fonts for your computer.

ICQ Soundpack, Irc Script Pack, New Star Wars Font
www.jedinet.com/multimedia/windows/misc/index.htm
Computer accessories you probably hadn't thought of!

Rogue 8's Media Vault
http://members.xoom.com/rogue88/mediavault.htm
Great fonts for download.

Rogue 9's Star Wars Web Site
www.geocities.com/Baja/Mesa/4807/index2.html
Grab-bag of multimedia goodies and webring connections.

Star Wars Fonts
http://members.xoom.com/scriptkeeper/fonts.htm
8 Star Wars fonts for your graphic & web site use.

Targeting Computer (Rogue 8's)
http://members.xoom.com/rogue888/computer.htm
Computer goodies - logos, software - great collection of fonts.

Tommy of Escondido's Alien Fonts Page
www.geocities.com/TimesSquare/4965/

Trilogy Font
http://yakface.com/hosted/tuskentrader/font.htm
Trilogy font for Mac (optional-site for PC)

Zaphoids Star Wars Fonts
http://synergy.foo.net/~zaphoid/starwars/fonts/
2 Star Wars fonts (typefaces) in zip format.

Free E-Mail Systems

If you must have e-mail, why not have a free e-mail through a Star Wars-related web site? We've included a few generic e-mail sites, too.

Free E-mail (Imagine Games Network)
www.ignmail.com/

Free E-mail (The Rancor Pit)
www.sentex.net/~dah/mail.html
Free and quick e-mail for you!

Naboo Mail
www.brbpub.com/iig/starwars
Click on Naboo Mail to get a free @naboo.zzn.com e-mail address.

New Republic, The
http://thenewrepublic.8m.com/
Add-ons for Jedi Knights, plus a multimedia section.

Star Wars Database
www.swdatabase.com/
Features, features, features. A must see.

StarWarsRealm Mail
http://starwarsrealm.zzn.com/email/login/login.asp
Get a Star Wars Realm e-mail address from ZZN.

Icons & Cursors

Those little things for a computer screen that turn it into a Star Wars computer.

Add-ons, from Jedi Council Chamber
www.geocities.com/Area51/Hollow/9125/addons.htm
Wallpaper, icons and other Star Wars goodies for your computer.

Cursors & Icons
www.jedinet.com/multimedia/windows/cursors/index.htm
Imperial Vehicle icons, also standard Star Wars icon sorts.

Desktop - Star Wars: A Feminine Perspective
http://members.aol.com/bananie42/desktop.html
Could your computer use these icons, cursors & font?

Gammy's Altar
www.toshistation.com/gammy.htm
Pig, Gammy, Mork icons, sick humor. Twisted, Bent.

Icon Collection - Star Wars
www.airnet.net/pcusers/ianspage/SWicons.zip
Hundreds of Star Wars icons for your computer.

Orin_J Kingdom
www.gogs32.freeserve.co.uk/page1.htm
Does Darth like neon blues and greens!?

Palace of the Raider King
http://members.tripod.com/~KingOfTheRaiders/Frames.html
Icons, also themes, screen saver, and GIF pix gallery.

Shell & Desktop Tools
www.winfiles.com/apps/98/shelldesk.html
The right tools to make your computer happy.

Space Depot 24
www.geocities.com/Area51/Vault/4910/space.htm
This great site has been around awhile!

Star Wars Icons
www.tem.nhl.nl/~veen606/eicon.htm
Icons from Star Wars games to download to your computer.

Star Wars Multimedia Database
http://members.aol.com/am54g/sw/index.html
Click Windows section to find icons, wallpapers, and S-savers.

Star Wars Multimedia HQ Still Pictures
http://nerf-herder.com/swmhq/pics.html
Color & B&W galleries of characters, ships, more.

Swammi's Star Wars Bullets
http://members.xoom.com/kessel/outpost/bullet.html
Icons for your web site or computer - some animated.

Ultimate Star Wars Cursors Page
www.geocities.com/Area51/Lair/3724/cursors.html
More computer cursors than you can imagine.

Ultimate Star Wars Icons
www.geocities.com/Area51/Lair/3724/icons.html
We couldn't count all the Star Wars icons here.

Zaphoid's Star Wars Cursors
http://synergy.foo.net/~zaphoid/starwars/cursors/
Cursors galore! Why have a dull computer?

Zaphoid's Star Wars Icons
http://synergy.foo.net/~zaphoid/starwars/icons/
15 files of icons to choose from. Too much input!

Screensavers

We wouldn't want you to burn out your computer monitor because you didn't have a screensaver! Here are sites with excellent Star Wars screensavers.

Chiv's Star Wars Page
http://highlander.cbnet.ns.ca/~bchivari/star/star.html
Multimedia page with trivia, transcripts, screensavers, & more.

Screen Savers
www.jedinet.com/multimedia/windows/savers/index.htm
Replace that dumb screensaver with a cool Star Wars one.

Screensaver Plaza, Star Wars
www.dukus.com/swsp/index.html
Offering deluxe screensavers: Trilogy, Prequel, & humorous.

Shell & Desktop Tools
www.winfiles.com/apps/98/shelldesk.html
The right tools to make your computer happy.

Space Depot 24
www.geocities.com/Area51/Vault/4910/space.htm
This great site has been around awhile!

Star Wars Multimedia Database
http://members.aol.com/am54g/sw/index.html
Click Windows section to find icons, wallpapers, and S-savers.

Zaphoids Star Wars Screensavers
http://synergy.foo.net/~zaphoid/starwars/screensavers/
Screensaver Star Wars posters, ships, characters.

Themes

"Themes" are packages for your Windows computer system that include sounds, images, and other items for your computer's desktop environment. Change your themes often to avoid boredom. Our list has plenty to choose from.

Chiv's Star Wars Page
http://highlander.cbnet.ns.ca/~bchivari/star/star.html
Multimedia page with trivia, transcripts, screensavers, & more.

Desktop Starships: Sci-Fi Themes
www.desktopstarships.com/themes.html

Frangisco's Star Wars PC Themes
http://coyote.accessnv.com/fasalvo/sw/theme.html
Themes & goodies that make a computer into a Star Wars machine.

Lord Vader's Lair Computer Stuff
www.geocities.com/Area51/Cavern/4897/misc.html
Miscellaneous stuff for loading on your computer.

Luke Skywalker Movie Theme
www.winfiles.com/apps/98/themes-movie-q.html
Luke Skywalker "Theme" for your computer with Windows.

Massassi Order
www.hta.nl/php/Jan.Jacob.Mosselaar/swring.htm
Very useful site once you delve into it!

Movie Themes - WinFiles.com
www.winfiles.com/apps/98/themes-movie.html
Windows 95/98 Star Wars themes ala carte!

Rogue Squadron.Net
www.roguesquadron.net/
Live the life of the Rogue Squadron game player.

Targeting Computer (Rogue 8's)
http://members.xoom.com/rogue888/computer.htm
Computer goodies - logos, software - great collection of fonts.

Zaphoids MS Plus Themes
http://synergy.foo.net/~zaphoid/starwars/ms_plus_themes/
Themes for MSPlus; one for each day o' the month.

Wallpaper

No, not the wallpaper in the dining room – we mean the wallpaper on your computer! Wallpaper is the term used to describe an image that is shown on the desktop or "background" of your computer screen (in other words, the main screen where all of your icons are). Remember, too, that by using your right mouse button, your browser allows you to select and automatically "Set Image as Wallpaper." But, keep in mind, the images plucked from web sites are usually too small to cover the entire screen, and are instead presented as tiles.

A New Hope Wallpaper
www.jedinet.com/multimedia/windows/wallpaper/index.htm
Wallpaper selections for Star Wars A New Hope.

Add-ons, from Jedi Council Chamber
www.geocities.com/Area51/Hollow/9125/addons.htm
Wallpaper, icons and other Star Wars goodies for your computer.

Bossk's Homepage
www.geocities.com/Area51/Dimension/9216/
Info on bounty-hunter Bossk, also Star Wars images for wallpaper.

Digital Blasphemy
www.digitalblasphemy.com/
Space and other cosmic scenery for your cyber-vehicle.

Freeware Web: Desktop Management
http://freewareweb.hypermart.net/deskman1.html

Jedi's Planet
http://members.xoom.com/jediplanet/
Gallery of Ray Traced artworks here - spendide!

K7 Graphics
www.k7group.com
3-D, space, & modern images

Martin Bond's Episode 1 Site
http://members.xoom.com/_XOOM/mb_starwars/index.html
Prequel videos, images, wallpaper, Anakin's House.

Mike Bonnell's Computer Wallpaper
www.mikebonnell.com/
Unique background & wallpaper source for Windows.

Phantom Menace.com Wallpaper
www.the-phantommenace.com/wallpaper.html
Phantom Menace Wallpapers for your computer.

Shell & Desktop Tools
www.winfiles.com/apps/98/shelldesk.html
The right tools to make your computer happy.

Skystation Lounge
www.theforce.net/Skystation/
Skystation - it's a swanky place to catch CG animations.

Star Backgrounds (Swammi Collection)
   http://members.xoom.com/kessel/outpost/background.html
   Starry, starry night backgrounds.

Star Wars Multimedia Database
   http://members.aol.com/am54g/sw/index.html
   Click Windows section to find icons, wallpapers, and S-savers.

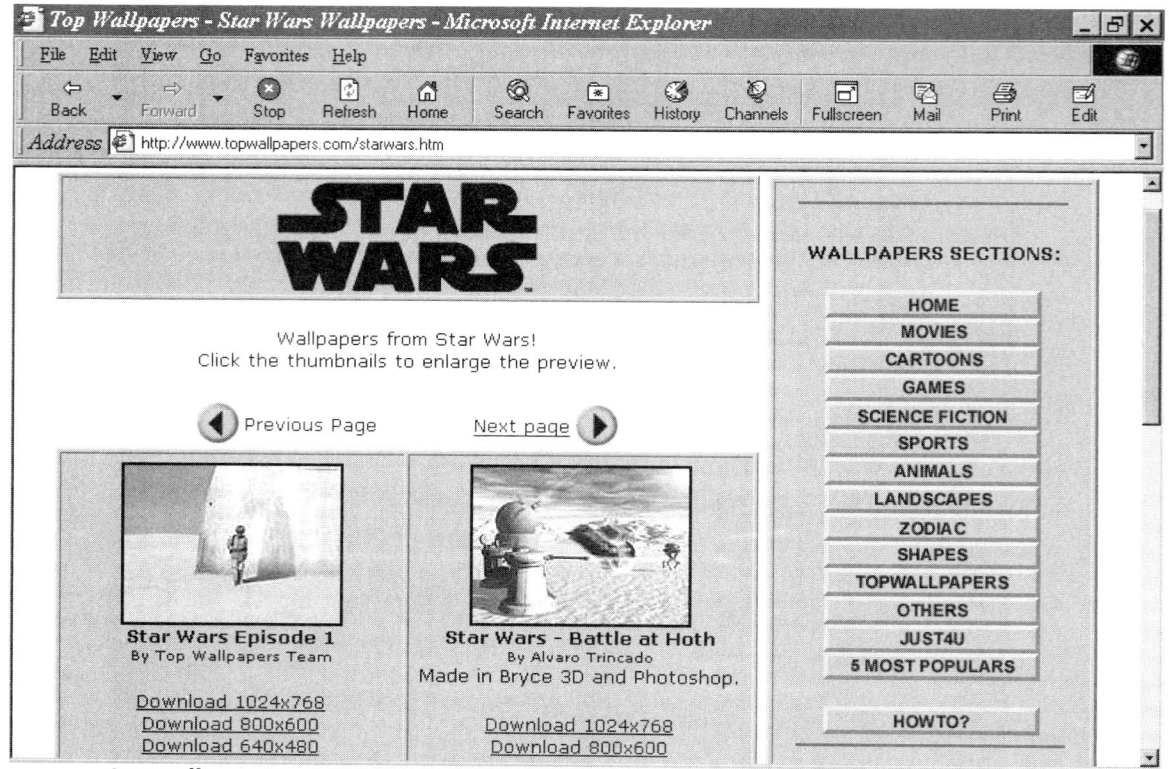

topwallpapers.com: Star Wars
   www.topwallpapers.com/starwars.htm
   Star Wars Wallpapers from topwallpapers.com.

Watto's Junkyard Archive
   www.wattosjunkyard.com/fanart.html
   Prequel posters, software & lots of color JPEG images.

Written in the Stars

A lot has been written about Star Wars – on the Web and in books, magazines, newspapers – everywhere! In this chapter we explore everything written about Star Wars, including the many scripts.

Scripts & Storylines

Here are sites with scripts and text about the movie stories – also sites with story analysis or a humorous slant. See the Commentary & Essays section for further comments and insights about the Star Wars Universe.

Ben's Awesome Star Wars Page
www.geocities.com/Area51/Zone/7153/
"Had a slight weapons malfunction, everything under control now."

Empire Strikes Back Transcript
www.geocities.com/Area51/Stargate/9082/Empire.txt
Complete transcript of Star Wars' 2nd feature.

I Don't Get It
http://outland.cyberwar.com/~smad//getit2.html
"How comes" and "what was that all abouts?" Incongruities.

Logic - The Whill Journal
www.geocities.com/Area51/Stargate/4465/logic.htm
Speculation on what we'll see in Prequels 2 & 3.

MST3K Version of "A Galaxy Not So Far Away"
www.geocities.com/Hollywood/Set/5760/
See if you can translate this - for some yuks.

Prequel Storyline, The (the force.net)
http://theforce.net/prequels/oldPreq/plot2.html
Prequel stories - generally - and birth order list.

Return of the Jedi Script
www.geocities.com/Area51/Stargate/9082/Return.txt
Complete script for Episode 6.

Rogue 8's Media Vault
http://members.xoom.com/rogue88/mediavault.htm
Well-arranged Trilogy sound files, font collection; vault is open!

Scripts (Jedinet Collection)
www.jedinet.com/multimedia/scripts/index.htm
Script collection (including 5 versions of A New Hope) downloadable at Jedinet.

Scripts - Star Wars
http://members.xoom.com/scriptkeeper/scripts.htm
10 scripts collected - but the Episode 3 text may not be real.

Star Wars Final Draft by George Lucas
www.geocities.com/Area51/Stargate/9082/Newhope.txt
George Lucas' final draft for the original Star Wars.

Star Wars III, Fall of the Republic
www.geocities.com/Hollywood/Lot/6700/fallofr.txt
Episode 3 Fan Fiction.

Star Wars The Musical
www.geocities.com/Hollywood/Lot/6700/swm-scr.txt
Yes, it's true - here's the transcript to prove it.

Star Wars, Adventures of Luke Starkiller
www.geocities.com/Area51/Stargate/9082/swd3.txt
Interesting third draft of Star Wars by George Lucas.

Starkiller - The Jedi Bendu Script Page
http://starwarz.com/starkiller/frame.htm
Jedi Bendu wish to preserve & collect historic documents.

Stars Wars First Screenplay Draft
www.geocities.com/Area51/Stargate/9082/swd1.txt
5/74 Lucas rough draft.

The Star Wars - Masthead: Adventures of The Starkiller
www.geocities.com/Area51/Stargate/9082/swd2.txt
Interesting variation of Lucas' original Star Wars, with name change.

Willems Star Wars Homepage
www.tem.nhl.nl/~veen606/veen606.html
Icons, sounds, video game, choice of 2 languages.

Commentary & Essays

"What makes Star Wars Special" and other written works that "explain" things about Star Wars are found in this Commentary & Essays section. To get personally involved in the commenting, see the Discussion Chapters earlier in this book. See also the Reviews and Articles sections elsewhere in this chapter.

Bad Guide to Star Wars
www.geocities.com/Area51/Vault/6031/bgsw53.txt
Details of bloopers, cinematography, and oddities.

Bogus Star Wars Homepage
www.cinenet.net/~agrapha/StarNet/SW.html
   Special effects & comments from Special Editions are featured.

Compendium, The
www.wcug.wwu.edu/~paradox/images/hyper/
   Not the prettiest site, but one of the fullest!

Creative Impulse, The
www.cwrl.utexas.edu/~daniel/309m/project4/christal/lucas.html
   Essay on the value of Lucas' contribution to our world.

Crossover Universe
http://pages.prodigy.com/crossover/
   Crossover "what ifs" & gee-whiz's for Star Wars, Sci-fi & pop productions.

Dark Side, The - Jedi Academy Lesson
www.jediacademy.com/dark.htm
   Know thy enemy. Be good not evil. Here's why.

Empire Strikes Back Special Edition FAQ
www.jax-inter.net/users/datalore/starwars/esbindex.htm
   Commentaries on Special Edition scenes in Empire.

Imperials Uniforms, Insignia, Logos, Technical Commentary
www.theforce.net/swtc/insignia.html
   Who wears what in the Evil Empire.

Myth in Star Wars - What Makes Star Wars Special?
www.synicon.com.au/sw/myth/myth.htm
   It's special for a lot of reasons - many of them are here.

Prequel Spoilers: Questions
http://meltingpot.fortunecity.com/greenwood/487/questions/answers.html
   Answers to some Prequel "burning questions."

Rebel Alliance Insignia
www.theforce.net/swtc/domino.html
   Insignia and logos of the rebel military.

Return of the Jedi Special Edition FAQ
www.jax-inter.net/users/datalore/starwars/rojindex.htm
   Commentaries on Special Edition scenes in Return of the Jedi.

Sam Davatchi's Page
http://perso.club-internet.fr/willow/Index.html
   Goodies you probably won't find elsewhere. We're for Fans Rights!

Special Edition Annotations
www.theforce.net/swse/
   Paul Ens commentaries on Special Edition scenes.

Speculation
http://outland.cyberwar.com/~smad//spec55.html
   As the story goes - comments and analysis.

Star Wars A New Hope Special Edition FAQ
www.jax-inter.net/users/datalore/starwars/anhindex.htm
   Details on the new & changed scenes in Special Edition A New Hope.

Star Wars Sound Mix Comparison
> www.jax-inter.net/users/datalore/starwars/soundfaq.htm
> Lists sound & dialog changes, re-mastering. An earful.

T'Bone Fenders Star Wars Universe
> www.starwarz.com/index.htm
> Among the best fan operated sites on the Net.

Technical Commentaries
> www.theforce.net/swtc/
> Could you explain it again for me?

Trilogy Special Edition FAQs
> www.jax-inter.net/users/datalore/starwars/sepage.htm
> Special Edition details, images, and explanations.

Whill Journal, The
> www.geocities.com/Area51/Stargate/4465/
> Looking ahead to the millenium Prequels.

Quotes

Web sites that offer collections of quotes from Star Wars are featured here. Are you looking for a favorite quote or favorite characters? You can also look in the Cast & Characters chapter for individual character sections, which may contain their quotes. Sound clips of quotes are usually found in the Multimedia chapter's audio sections.

Da Quotes
> www.geocities.com/Area51/Chamber/4182/quotes.html
> Quotes by characters, and comments about themes in Star Wars.

David Jansen's Star Wars Page
> www.strw.leidenuniv.nl/~jansen/sw/
> Multimedia site with fortune cookies (quotes), sounds & pix.

Mark Hamill Quotes
> www.chez.com/jedinat/quotes.html
> Collection of Luke Quotes from everywhere.

Star Wars Quote Generator
> www.surfnet.fi/~zargon/swchan/quote2.html
> Press the "generate button" then read a quote.

Yoda's Swamp
> http://www2.netdoor.com/~broberts/yodapg.html
> Tribute to Yoda; his favorite sayings and pix.

Reviews

Reviews by professional reviewers are supposed to list the "aspects" - qualities and content - of a presentation. Here are some Star Wars reviews from over the past 25 years, including those for movies, books, and games. See also the Editorials section later in this chapter.

Aaron's Star Wars Multimedia page
www.geocities.com/Area51/Stargate/3350/
New site with posters as its very best feature; also has reviews.

Ain't-It-Cool-News Reviews
www.aint-it-cool-news.com/section.cgi?type=Review
Alternative movie review site with forums, news.

Books Section of Hydrospanner
www.hydrospanner.com/books/
All about Star Wars books - submit your own reviews, too.

Dark Horizons
www.darkhorizons.com/index2.html
1-stop movie resource - news, trailers, facts, reviews.

Episode 1 Racer
www.gamespot.com/features/sw_racer/
Pod Racer Game review in Gamespot.

Essential Guide To Droids - Review
http://theforce.net/books/reviews/guidedroids.shtml
Online review of Essential Guide to Droids book.

Fett Files, The
www.geocities.com/Area51/Vault/3227/index.html
2 topics: Boba Fett bounty hunter details; reviews of publications.

Film.com
www.film.com/
It's gotta lot of film/movie/video stuff!

Jedinet Software
www.jedinet.com/software/
Good coverage of software games news, reviews, screenshots.

Liz's Book Reviews
www.geocities.com/Hollywood/1165/books.html
Reviews & ratings of recent Star Wars books.

Masters of Teras Kasi
www.game-junkie.com/Reviews/Playstation/StarWars_Fight/SWMOTK.HTM
Review of this game, with video and image file samples.

Movie Review Query Engine (MRQE): Star Wars Episode 1
www.mrqe.com/lookup?^Star+Wars:+Episode+I+(1999)
Finding movie reviews is "like dustin' crops, boy."

New York Times Flashback Review (on countingdown.com)
http://sabbeth.com/~menace/nytreview.htm
When Star Wars opened, this is what the Times said.

Review of NPR's Dramatization of Star Wars
http://members.xoom.com/kessel/outpost/nprreview.html
Review of NPRs Star Wars Original Radio Drama.

Star Wars Book Reviews
> http://people.clemson.edu/~jvalice/starb.htm
> Description & reviews of novels.

Star Wars Episode 1 - The Phantom Menace Game
> www.gamespot.com/features/sw_phantom/
> Reviews the PC & Playstation Episode 1 Phantom Menace Game.

Articles

Here are articles from publications and online sources about a variety of Star Wars topics. The list would take up this whole book if it were complete; we trust you'll find something of interest among the variety of articles presented here.

Animatics: Moving Storyboards of Episode 1
> www.starwars.com/episode-i/features/animatics/01/
> Editing, cutting, and making it into a movie.

Ben Burtt: Sound Design of Episode 1
> www.starwars.com/episode-i/features/burtt/
> About Ben Burtt; movie sound design expert.

Design Originals of Episode 1; Doug Chiang's Portfolio
> www.starwars.com/episode-i/features/chiang/
> Artist Doug Chiang talks/draws on this official site.

The last of the three Prequels is scheduled to be released in 2003.

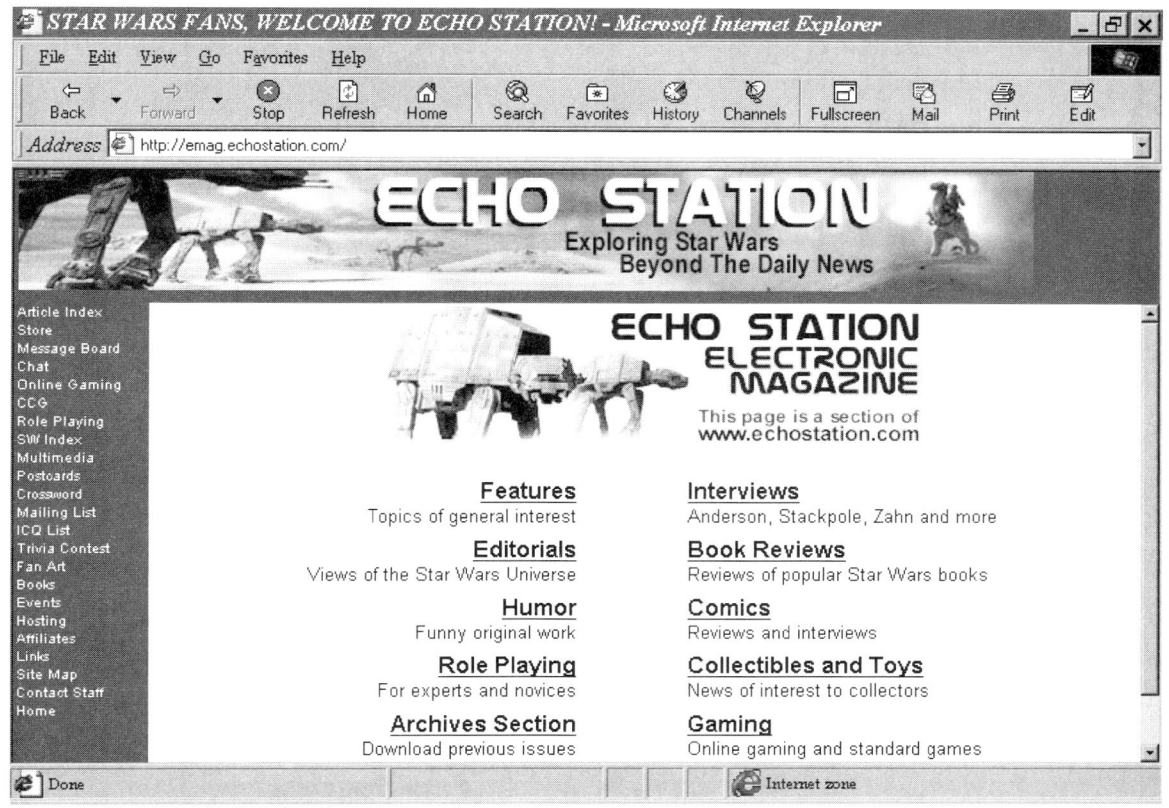

Emag - Echo Station
> http://emag.echostation.com/
>> Free online variety magazine of Star Wars topics.

Entertainment Weekly's Top 25 Actors of the 90s - Samuel L Jackson
> http://cgi.pathfinder.com/ew/features/minisite/90s_actors/0,2566,16-16,jackson.html
>> Biographical material on Jackson from an Entertainment Weekly write-up

Gungan Din - Article EW Daily News
> http://cgi.pathfinder.com/ew/daily/0,2514,1308,insidelookatmore.html
>> Article with more pieces for "future" trivia games.

Logic - The Whill Journal
> www.geocities.com/Area51/Stargate/4465/logic.htm
>> Speculation on what we'll see in Prequels 2 & 3.

LucasArts Press Room
> www.lucasarts.com/pages/IndexAnnouncement.main.html
>> Learn about new LucasArt game releases.

Pod Race Reporter Homepage
> http://podracereporter.listbot.com/
>> Current Star Wars news items are a couple clicks away.

Prequel News
> www.execpc.com/~zerob/Jediside.html
>> Prequel articles listed with the publications they appear in.

Remembering The Past: Early Drafts of Star Wars
http://theforce.net/prequels/oldPreq/anhvsepi.htm
   Evolution of Star Wars.

Sci-Tech: The Net Feels The Force (BBC)
http://news.bbc.co.uk/hi/english/sci/tech/newsid_217000/217090.stm
   BBC's early article about fantastic crowds for the new Star Wars.

Starkiller - The Jedi Bendu Script Page
http://starwarz.com/starkiller/frame.htm
   Jedi Bendu wish to preserve & collect historic documents.

Watto's Junkyard Archive
www.wattosjunkyard.com/fanart.html
   Prequel posters, software, text & lots of color JPEG images.

Ways of the Sith, The
www.geocities.com/Hollywood/Location/1657/sith.html
   Monthly online magazine featuring the dark side's perspective.

What Does Vader's Chestplate Say?
www.theforce.net/rouser/chestplate.shtml
   There's a Hebrew message here!

Editorials & Editorializing

Unlike "reviewing," editorializing lets the author sound off. Editorials can be anywhere from soap-box shouting, book-thumping, butt-ripping, to waxing prophetic or outright guessing.

Ask A Question - AllExperts.com
www.allexperts.com/tv/starwars.shtml
   They provide the expert; you ask Prequel/Star Wars questions.

Dark Side Rumors
http://sw.simplenet.com/darkside/
   Whery Inta-westing! What can you contribute?

Editorials - Echo Station Emag
http://emag.echostation.com/editorials/index.htm
   Echo Station yip-sters give their views of the Star Wars universe.

Episode 1 News Archives
www.sevaan.com/starwars/news/archives/index.htm
   News, editorials, surveys on Episode 1.

Episode 1 Script Review
www.sevaan.com/starwars/news/archives/old_layout/news/scriptreview.htm
   Pre- Prequel editorial with Episode 1 insights.

Liam, Liam, Liam!!!!
http://members.tripod.com/~BASKERTON/Liam.html
   So, you wanted to see a celebrity "un-tribute" web site?

Prequel Editorials
www.jedinet.com/prequels/senate/editoriala/index.htm
   We've heard things.

Rancor Pit, The
   http://fly.to/rancorpit
      New high-energy site that hopes to do it all!

Shaven Wookie LTD
   www.shavenwookie.com/
      You haven't shaved until you've shaved a Wookie.

Interviews

Straight from the protocol droid's mouth! These are texts of what people have said. However, we cannot guarantee the authenticity. Also see the Articles Section and the Cast & Characters Chapter for more information about Star Wars people.

Emag - Echo Station
   http://emag.echostation.com/
      Free online variety magazine of Star Wars topics.

Face to Face with the Masters
   www.theforce.net/jedicouncil/interview/
      Interviews collected from Star Wars players, creators, & experts.

Generic Star Wars Page, The
   www.geocities.com/Area51/Corridor/9410/
      Audio clips of interviews, plus links to other good, unusual sites.

Holonet (the force.net)
   www.theforce.net/holonet/
      Fan contributions of news, videos, audio, interviews.

Interviews (with authors & obscure characters)
   www.lucasfan.com/interviews/
      In-person interviews you won't find anywhere else.

Interviews - Hollywood Online
   www.hollywood.com/starwars/interview/interview.html
      Interviews in audio, video, or text formats.

Prequel Trilogy & Special Edition Homepage
   http://washington.xtn.net/~robf/sw.htm
      This site is like a historic marker - 1996-97.

Star Wars Database Interviews
   www.swdatabase.com/pages/interviews.html
      Hot tip: Interviews let out secrets.

Books

Not many Star Wars books are presented in their entirety on the Web, but there are many sites that offer information about what you'll find in Star Wars books.

Aaron Allston's Home Site
   www.io.com/~allston/
      Authors and game creator's have the best sites!

amazon.com
www.amazon.com
Books, videos, music - a galaxy-sized discount store!

Barnes & Noble.com
www.barnesandnoble.com/
Universe-sized searchable bookstore and more!

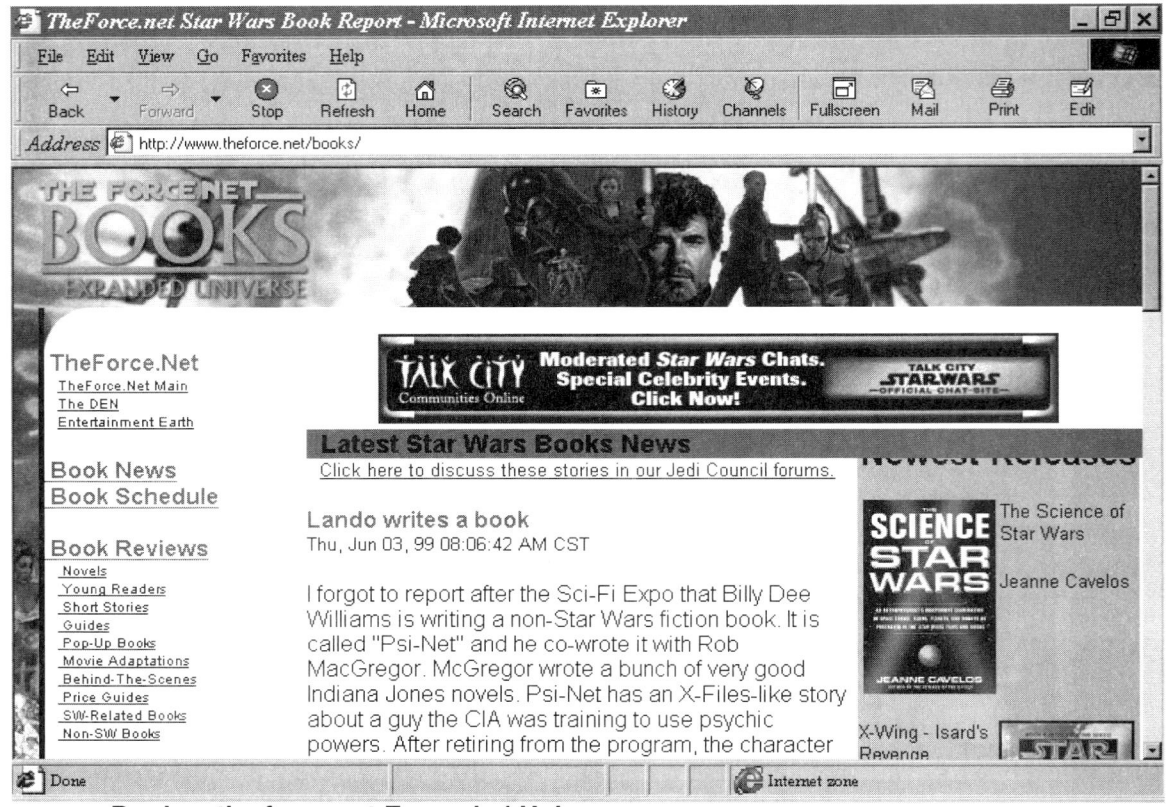

Books - the force.net Expanded Universe
www.theforce.net/books/
Great resource for all varieties of Star Wars books & reviews.

Books Section of Hydrospanner
www.hydrospanner.com/books/
All about Star Wars books - submit your own reviews, too.

Carrie Books
www.saunalahti.fi/~margot/books.htm
Pix of Carrie's book covers along with comments.

Completely Unofficial Star Wars Encyclopedia 6th Edition
www.mindspring.com/~bobvitas/swenc.htm
Something about everyone - cast, crew, characters - all!

Edis Krad's Online Bookshop
http://george.lucas.net/edis.htm
Find and get official Lucas books at a discount online.

Ewoks Story
www.foxhome.com/animated/html/ewstory.htm
Children's story & activity book online - Fun with Ewoks.

Garindan's Book Reviews
www.geocities.com/Area51/Shadowlands/4918/bookrev.html
Star Wars books reviewed by Garindan...

Heir to the Empire
http://books.echostation.com/heir.html
Author Timothy Zahn's Postquel fiction.

Incredible Internet Guide to Star Wars
www.brbpub.com/iig/starwars
The home page for this book! Order online and find out about future editions.

Incredible Internet Guide Series
www.brbpub.com/iig
Home page for Incredible Internet Guide Series. Check out the other titles!

Lando Calrissian Adventures
www.ozemail.com.au/~alkenned/starwars/swlcst.htm
Lando & Han adventure books are linked here.

Lando Calrissian, Boba Fett, & Jabba The Hutt Books
www.geocities.com/Area51/Portal/7365/swpages/Lando.htm
Lando, Boba Fett & Jabba books - and links to others.

Literature (LucasFan.com)
www.lucasfan.com/literature.html
Great resource for all types of reading media.

Massassi Order
www.hta.nl/php/Jan.Jacob.Mosselaar/swring.htm
Very useful site once you delve into it!

Mos Espa Marketplace
http://mosespa.starwars.com/books/
Official Star Wars Book site; reviews and store.

Novels of Star Wars (Thrawn Art Gallery)
http://empire.res.wabash.edu/art/novels/yjk.htm
Cover art for books by famous Star Wars fiction writers.

Printed References
www.jedinet.com/multimedia/references/ref-books.html
Selected references to Star Wars in pop author's works.

Production - Echo Station Interactive Store
www.echostation.com/shop/amazproduct.htm
Books about production, "making of" and art of Star Wars.

RPG Revised & Expanded Rules - Star Wars
http://rpg.echostation.com/updates/updates.html
Downloads of updates of rules of Star Wars RPGs.

Sector 827 (Mystery Site!)
http://swwa.webjump.com/books/book.html
Judge a book by its cover.

Fiction & Fan Fiction

Unlike books, fan fiction stories are not, usually, published in print. Generally, they are found in full or part on a web site, either alone, or more commonly, as part of a collection. We hope you'll enjoy reading these wonderful stories created by Star Wars fans.

A Feminine Perspective
http://members.aol.com/bananie42/index.html
Solid! None of that really mushy stuff.

Boba Fonts
http://starwars.fans.net/bobafonts/
Newer fonts, cursors, fan-fiction, and calendars.

Books - the force.net Expanded Universe
www.theforce.net/books/
Great resource for all varieties of Star Wars books & reviews.

Droidcentric Art & Fan Fiction
http://members.aol.com/candyfish/gateway.htm
Fan fiction & pix in honor of 2 droids who've been 'round the block.

Fan Fiction by Brendon Wahlberg
www.theforce.net/fanfiction/
Fan fiction for you to read!

Javval's Star Wars Page
www.multiboard.com/~jhowarth/starwars.htm
Javval the Hutt's story, also movie photos & MIDI sounds.

Knight Hammer
www.geocities.com/Area51/Chamber/4182/index.html
Good content for a site with an Imperial overcoat!

NaboOnline
www.naboonline.com
Wealth of information and variety of Prequel categories.

New Mythology - the Star Wars Trilogy
www.dom.net/wrd/new/ref/sw/
Why myths & the Star Wars stories work for us.

New Star Wars, Episode 1
www.starwars.com/episode-i/features/intro/
Pre-release run-down; this could be a web site collectible later.

Novels of Star Wars (Thrawn Art Gallery)
http://empire.res.wabash.edu/art/novels/yjk.htm
Cover art for books by famous Star Wars fiction writers.

Novels' Timelines
www.geocities.com/Area51/Zone/9015/books.html
List of novels arranged by time period.

Path Not Taken, The
www.flash.net/~draegos/path/main1.html
A fiction? - A game? - An internet development?

Prologue to the Imperial Trilogy
www.geocities.com/Hollywood/Location/1657/harkov.html
Prologue of a dark-side novel based on the game TIE Fighters.

Rancor Pit, The
    http://fly.to/rancorpit
        New high-energy site that hopes to do it all!

Royal Library - Star Wars Fan Fiction
    www.geocities.com/Area51/Shadowlands/4918/fanfic.html
        Fan Fiction from a bit of an Imperial slant.

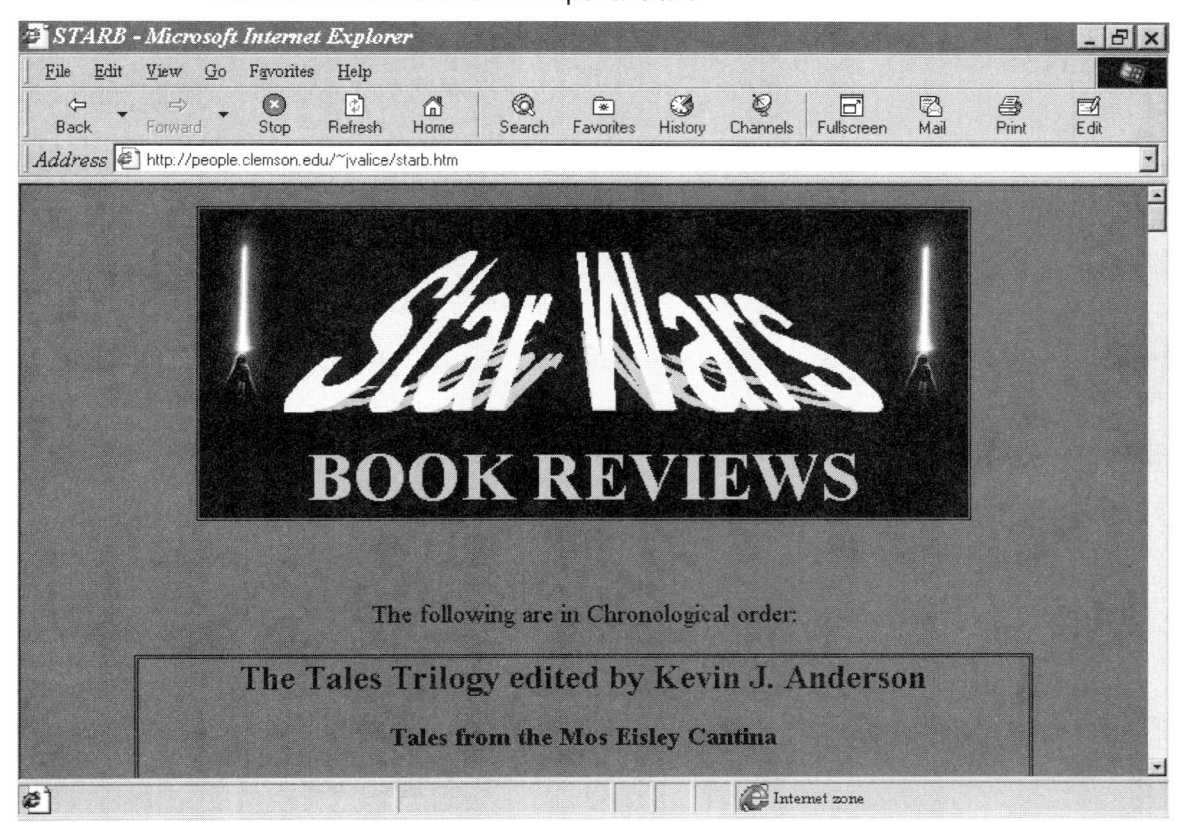

Star Wars Book Reviews
    http://people.clemson.edu/~jvalice/starb.htm
        Description & reviews of novels.

Star Wars Fan Fiction
    http://sw.simplenet.com/pages/fanfiction.html
        Got a story? Show it off, or read others.

Star Wars 3, Fall of the Republic
    www.geocities.com/Hollywood/Lot/6700/fallofr.txt
        Episode 3 fan fiction.

Stories by Fans
    http://members.xoom.com/scriptkeeper/fanstories.htm
        Rare Fan fiction stories to read, or submit your own.

Whill Journal, The
    www.geocities.com/Area51/Stargate/4465/
        Looking ahead to the millenium Prequels.

Song Lyrics

Not the music, just the words to Star Wars songs. Some songs listed on the web sites here are honest to goodness tunes; others are parodies and for humor.

Disgruntled Ewok & Malcontent Jawas Page
http://netdial.caribe.net/~orinoco/jae.html
Is life (& Star Wars browsing) too serious? While away time here.

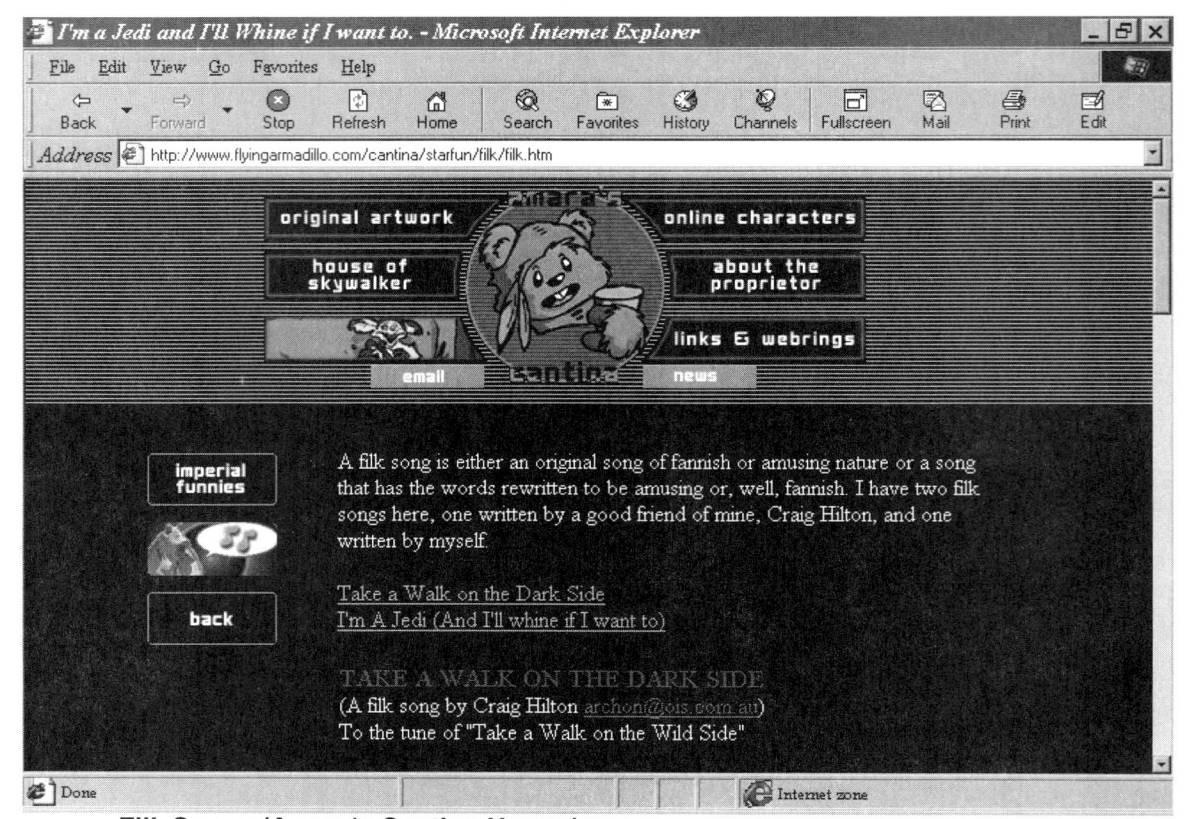

Filk Songs (Amara's Cantina Humor)
www.flyingarmadillo.com/cantina/starfun/filk/filk.htm
Humorous lyrics for new Star Wars songs.

Imperial Rhapsody, The
www.geocities.com/Hollywood/Set/5760/
You guessed it: new words for Queen's Bohemian Rhapsody.

Lyrics to YODA (by Weird Al)
www.geocities.com/Hollywood/Set/5760/
Tribute to Yoda using the tune of the Kink's Lola.

More Star Wars Humor
http://rpg.echostation.com/humor/swjokes.html
Humor from various newsgroups over FIDOnet & Usenet.

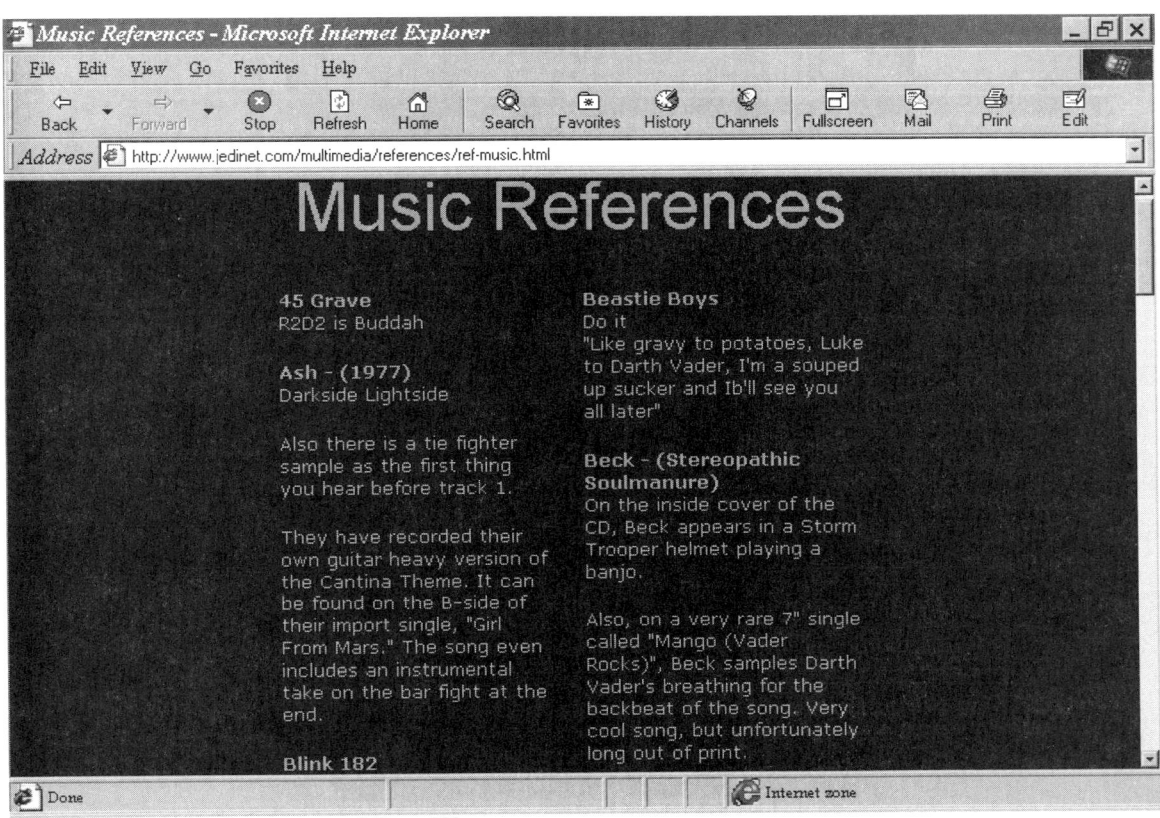

Music References of Star Wars
www.jedinet.com/multimedia/references/ref-music.html
Star Wars gets mentioned in the music world a lot.

Star Wars The Musical
www.geocities.com/Hollywood/Lot/6700/swm-scr.txt
Yes, it's true - here's the transcript to prove it.

Themes - Star Wars Episode 1 - The Music
http://members.es.tripod.de/Befan/Episode1music_Themes.html
Music themes for Episode 1 with commentaries, times, etc.

Rumors

Rumors are all over the Internet. We didn't believe that one that had Leann Rimes singing in the Phantom Menace, though. We rank these web sites in the rumor-mill category.

Cinescape Online
www.cinescape.com/
Rumors & spoilers on just about everything!

Dark Side Rumors
http://sw.simplenet.com/darkside/
Whery Inta-westing! What can you contribute?

Filmthreat Online
> www.filmthreat.com/Welcome.htm
> Their newsletter revealed the plot synopsis for Episode 2.

Prequel Rumors
> http://members.aol.com/capeman69/rumors.html
> Rumors, news, and facts surrounding the Prequels.

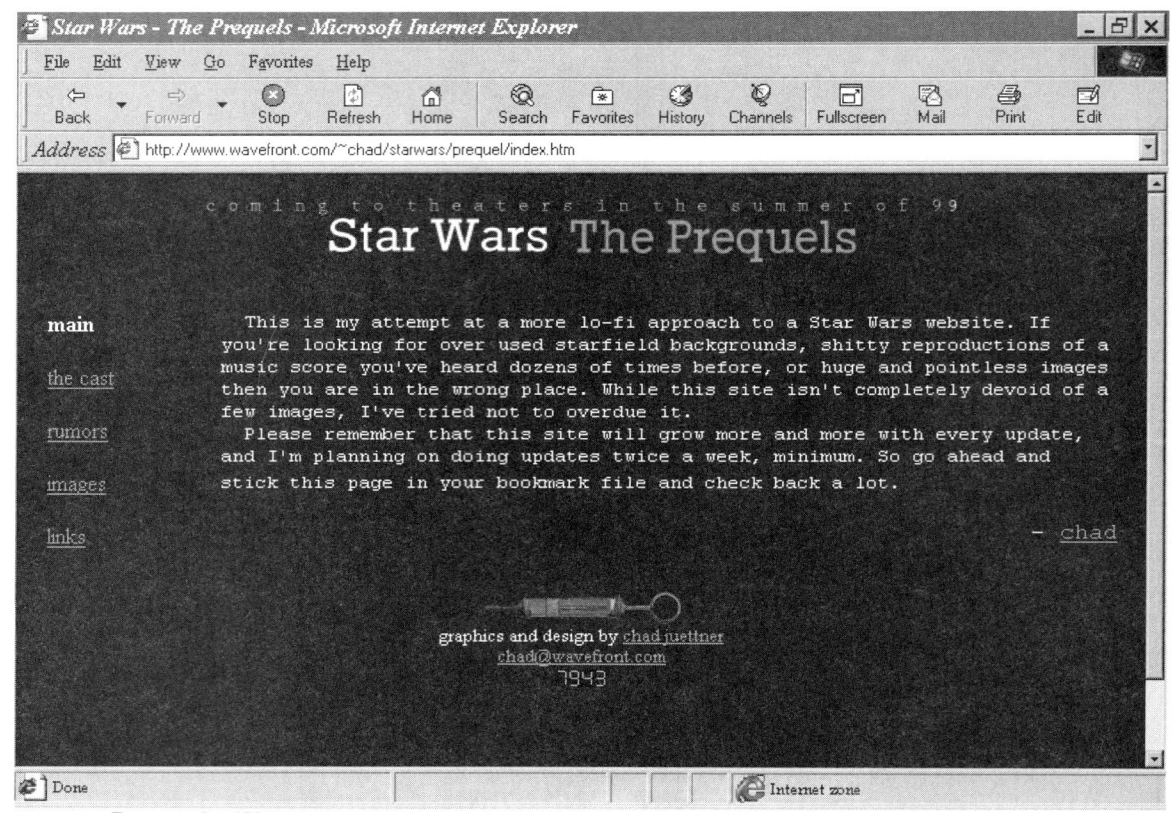

Prequels, The
> www.wavefront.com/~chad/starwars/prequel/index.htm
> Clean Prequel site - hopefully it'll add more quality & quantity.

RedFive85 Rumors
> www.geocities.com/Area51/Quadrant/4210/rumors.htm
> Rumor: Leann Rimes was to sing in Episode 1!? Give us a break.

All in the Family? Ewan MacGregor's uncle played Wedge Antilles in the original Star Wars.

STAR WARS Locations, Spacecraft, & Hardware

Star Wars would not be complete without its eclectic collection of well-thought out spacecraft, locations, and hardware, such as weapons like the lightsaber. Could you imagine Star Wars without lightsabers?

Locations & Places in the Star Wars Universe

The Cantina

Lots of sites found on the web say "Cantina," but only a few sites are exclusively "Cantina."

Cantina, The
www.the-cantina.com/
Award-winning site of Star Wars favorite watering hole.

Mos Eisley Cantina Diorama
http://members.iquest.net/~sohair/hyperspace/cantina/page0.html
Cantina diorama - say, do large insects like this model?

Welcome To the Cantina (Gallery)
www.geocities.com/Area51/Corridor/8540/cantina.html
Wow! Cantina pix - various, big & risque out-takes.

Planets, generally Bespin, Dagobah, or Naboo

Magical places! These are the fictional planets where Star Wars action takes place, when we are not flying around in space! The planets Hoth, Bespin, Dagobah, and Naboo are found in this section, but you will find that Coruscant, Tatooine, and the Forest Moon of Endor each have their own sections.

Bespin
www.starwars.com/locations/bespin/
A planet like Venus and/or Jupiter.

Cita Delle Nuvole (Cloud City)
www.geocities.com/Area51/Corridor/1431/
Italian Cloud City site with MP3 sounds & MPEG video, more!

Cloud City
www.starwars.com/locations/cloud_city/
Afloat above Planet Bespin.

Dagobah Official Site
www.starwars.com/locations/dagobah/
This swamp really isn't that bad; official site.

Delta Source
www.jedinet.com/delta/
Databases of events, characters, vehicles, weapons, more.

Endor
www.starwars.com/locations/endor/
A Moon, actually. Official Star Wars page.

Geographic Links - Shaven Wookie
www.shavenwookie.com/swlinkslocate.html
Lists of sites by Star Wars location (place names).

Guerre Stellari
http://users.iol.it/bety/gs.html
Italian index site - leads to good Cloud City, MPEGs sites.

Hoth
www.starwars.com/locations/hoth/index.html
An Official Lucasfilms location page.

Jedinet Pictures
www.jedinet.com/multimedia/pics/index.htm
Rates as the finest JPEG image gallery on this rock.

Locations: Prequel Planets
http://meltingpot.fortunecity.com/greenwood/487/places/planets.html
Info & pix of the 3 major Prequel planets.

Naboo Temple Ruins Playset
www.fandommenace.com/toys/e1mmplaynabootemple.jpg
Naboo planet Playset toy

Planets (of Star Wars) Technical Commentaries
  www.theforce.net/swtc/orbs.html
    Analysis of Star Wars Planets - to the nth!

Prequel Locations
  http://theforce.net/prequels/oldPreq/locations/locations.shtml
    Wonderful details and reports on Prequel locations.

Star Wars Movie Art
  http://empire.res.wabash.edu/art/movies/index.htm
    Paintings & pix used for movie production.

Tatooine -- Mos Eisley, Jundland Wastes, The Pit

The Cantina at Mos Eisley Spaceport has its own section at the start of this chapter. However, you will find other Mos Eisley web sites, also web sites relating to all the great desert locations on Planet Tatooine, below.

Dune Sea
  www.starwars.com/locations/dune_sea/
    Where banthas roam.

Han Solo Condemns Me to a Digestful Fate Video
  www.telecom.csuhayward.edu/~aleung/fett.mov
    Bye-bye Boba at the Sarlaac creature video.

Jabba The Hutt
  www.starwars.com/characters/jabba_the_hutt/
    Not a perfect date.

Jabba's Palace
  www.starwars.com/locations/jabbas_palace/
    A very unpleasant place; did you squirm in your theatre seat?

Jabba's Palace Movie
  www.telecom.csuhayward.edu/~aleung/jabba's.mov
    QuickTime video of Jabba's Palace.

Jundland Wastes
  www.starwars.com/locations/jundland_wastes/1_bg.html
    Tatooine's badlands.

Mos Eisley Spaceport
  www.starwars.com/locations/mos_eisley/
    Wretched hive of scum and villainy.

Pit of Carkoon
  www.starwars.com/locations/pit_of_carkoon/
    Don't go there.

Prequel Locations
  http://theforce.net/prequels/oldPreq/locations/locations.shtml
    Wonderful details and reports on Prequel locations.

Sand People
  www.starwars.com/aliens/sandpeople/
    Easily scared, but annoying!

Tatooine
www.starwars.com/locations/tatooine-vi/
A key Star Wars location.

Tatooine Text
www.angelfire.com/co/gavind/tatooine.html
Text on a famous place far from the galactic center.

Endor -- Actually, the Forest Moon of Endor

Forested home of the Ewoks! For more web sites featuring Ewoks, see their section near the end of the Cast & Characters chapter.

Daisy Hill Village
www.angelfire.com/fl/yubcantina/daisyhill.html
Ewok village that's forming in England.

Endor
www.starwars.com/locations/endor/
A Moon, actually. Official Star Wars page.

Ewok Warrior Headquarters
www.angelfire.com/al/cybertrees/dwf.html
Ewok version of World News & War Report.

Zaphoids MS Plus Themes
http://synergy.foo.net/~zaphoid/starwars/ms_plus_themes/
Themes for MSPlus; one for each day o' the month.

Coruscant -- The Imperial City

Planet Coruscant is the cultural and governmental center of the Star Wars Universe -- also home to the Jedi Council. But, could they please clean up that traffic mess?

Coruscant Project at Ord Mantell
www.geocities.com/Area51/Lair/8349/txindex.html
Coruscant - Welcome to the Sunny Shores of...

Journal of the Whills - Miscellaneous: Imperial City
www.geocities.com/Hollywood/Set/8008/misc.html
Concept art used to create Coruscant; McQuarrie images too.

Locations: Prequel Planets
http://meltingpot.fortunecity.com/greenwood/487/places/planets.html
Info & pix of the 3 major Prequel planets.

Prequel Locations
http://theforce.net/prequels/oldPreq/locations/locations.shtml
Wonderful details and reports on Prequel locations.

Spacecraft

Alliance Spacecraft

Alliance Spacecraft are those used by the good guys. The Millenium Falcon and some Alliance Spacecraft that are "fighters" may also be found in their own sections, following this one.

A-wing fighter
www.starwars.com/vehicles/a-wing/
A-wing fighters official Lucasfilms page.

B-wing Fighter
www.starwars.com/vehicles/b-wing/
Admiral Ackbar's contribution to the fleet at the Battle of Endor.

Description About Star Wars' Vessels
www.civila.com/hispania/obi-juan/ship.txt
Specifics about warcraft in Spanish or English.

Episode 1: Phantom Menace Ship & Vehicle List
http://theforce.net/prequels/oldPreq/ships/ships.shtml
Prequel craft, vehicles, pix & specs.

Galactic Empire Data Bank
www.iaw.on.ca/~btaylor1/index.html
Imperial, rebel, bounty hunter & "other" vessels.

Rebel Fleet
www.starwars.com/locations/rebel_fleet/
Official Lucasfilms site, but lean on specifics.

Ships in the Star Wars Universe
http://members.xoom.com/kessel/outpost/ships.html
GIF & JPEG images of favorite spacecraft.

Star Wars Central
www.geocities.com/Area51/Vault/3891/
Get "toured" through to Imperial or rebel tech files.

Warships of the Mon Calamari, Technical Commentaries
www.theforce.net/swtc/mcc.html
Federation or rebel alliance large spacecraft.

X-Wing Fighter
www.starwars.com/vehicles/x-wing/
X-wing Fighters - Centerstage on the official Lucasfilms site.

X-Wing Game Newsgroup
alt.games.x-wing

Y-wing Fighters
www.starwars.com/vehicles/y-wing/
Avoid flying Y-wings unless you have a deathwish.

Millenium Falcon

Millenium Falcon information can be found on the following web sites. See also Star Fighters and Alliance Spacecraft for sites that contain partial information on the Falcon as well as other "friendly" spacecraft.

Millenium Falcom - Ship of Riddles
www.synicon.com.au/sw/mf/falcon.htm
Just how big is it? Just about everything you should know.

Millenium Falcon
www.starwars.com/vehicles/millennium_falcon/
Official Millenium Falcon site.

Millenium Falcon (museum piece)
www.geocities.com/Area51/Vault/3227/index.html
Museum version of Millenium Falcon.

Millenium Falcon Pictures
www.jedinet.com/multimedia/pics/falcon/index.html
100+ Falcon images!

Millenium Falcon Text
www.angelfire.com/oh/gavinda/falcon.html
About the Falcon - not your standard YT1300 cargo vessel!

Watch This - Video of Han & Leia in the Falcon
http://users.why.net/radrock/sounds/watchths.avi
"Watch This" says Han in this AVI video.

Yoda is the oldest of the Star Wars characters, but it surprises many to know that Chewbacca the Wookiee is the second oldest.

Star Fighters

Here are sites that specialize in fighter spacecraft from all sides of the conflict.

A-wing fighter
www.starwars.com/vehicles/a-wing/
A-wing fighters official Lucasfilms page.

B-wing Fighter
www.starwars.com/vehicles/b-wing/
Admiral Ackbar's contribution to the fleet at the Battle of Endor.

Fighter Gets It In The Trench
www.telecom.csuhayward.edu/~aleung/trench.mov
Video of fighter in the Death Star Trench.

Imperial Shipyards
http://members.tripod.com/~Dolmyn/shipyard.htm
Facts & pix on Imperial spacecraft.

Rebel Fleet
www.starwars.com/locations/rebel_fleet/
Official Lucasfilms site, but lean on specifics.

Rogue 9's Animations
www.geocities.com/Baja/Mesa/4807/index2.html
Animations of Imperial craft, also B-wings & more.

Starfighters
http://frankg.dgne.com/swsv/starfighters.html
Specifications & info on smaller Star Wars craft.

Startup/Shutdown Screens
www.jedinet.com/multimedia/windows/screens/index.htm
See Star Wars every time your computer starts & shuts down.

TIE Fighters Free Downloads
http://indigo.ie/~hanafin/download.html
TIE fighter resource for gaming / scenarios.

X-Wing Attack Video Preview
www.hollywood.com/multimedia/movies/starwars/video/mmindex.html
X-Wing Attack video preview in AVI, MOV, & Mac formats.

X-Wing Fighter
www.starwars.com/vehicles/x-wing/
X-wing Fighters - Centerstage on the official Lucasfilms site.

X-Wing vs TIE Fighter Webring
www.webring.org/cgi-bin/webring?ring=xvt1997;index
List of 17 TIE & X-wing Fighter web sites.

Y-wing Fighters
www.starwars.com/vehicles/y-wing/
Avoid flying Y-wings unless you have a deathwish.

TIE Fighters

TIEs are the small nasty fighter spacecraft used by the Imperial Empire. You will find sites for and about them below, as well as sites for the game TIE Fighter.

Darth Vader's TIE Fighter
www.starwars.com/vehicles/vaders_tie_fighter/
Lucasfilms put Darth Vader in his own special celestial-chariot.

Imperial Navy Technical Database
www.geocities.com/Area51/Shadowlands/4918/tech.html
Details, details, details!

Powerflicker's Model Page
www.geocities.com/Area51/Labyrinth/8664/models.html
Model and display pictures.

Stephen's TIE Fighter Page
http://indigo.ie/~hanafin/starwars.html
TIE Fighter (the game) resources, info, discussion, & fun!

Stormtrooper Recruitment - The Replacements
http://207.136.91.134/very/x-stream/
Site reforming when we visited - new stuff should be stellar!

TIE Fighter Game Newsgroup
alt.games.tie-fighter

TIE Fighter Mailing List
http://indigo.ie/~hanafin/maillist.html
Get listed with others who share a Starfighter interest.

TIE Fighters
www.starwars.com/vehicles/tie_fighter/
Official page for the Imperial Forces most-numerous fighter craft.

TIE Fighters Technical Commentaries
www.theforce.net/swtc/tie.html
From technical aspects to the broader TIE issues.

TIE Interceptor
www.starwars.com/vehicles/tie_interceptor/
Lucasfilms' page on the latest generation of TIE Fighter craft.

You People Should Know that My Loyalties Lie Very Firmly with the Empire
www.aaronklaassen.com/starwars/starwars.htm
Imperial fighter info and select pix, sounds, video.

Paintings that were used for creating scenes and sets the Star Wars Trilogy were by artist Ralph McQuarrie.

Imperial Spacecraft

All sorts of information can be found about the Imperial Spacecraft on the web sites below. The Death Stars are given their own section, which follows this one. Also, find information about TIE Fighters and Star Fighters on the previous pages.

Captain Needa's Star Destroyer
www.geocities.com/Area51/Rampart/5559/
Star Destroyer info for role playing and for the curious.

Classified Military Plan - Secret (Example)
www.geocities.com/Area51/Corridor/4309/secret.html
Secret communication about a stardestroyer.

Description About Star Wars' Vessels
www.civila.com/hispania/obi-juan/ship.txt
Specifics about warcraft in spanish or english.

Episode 1: Phantom Menace Ship & Vehicle List
http://theforce.net/prequels/oldPreq/ships/ships.shtml
Prequel craft, vehicles, pix & specs.

Galactic Empire Data Bank
www.iaw.on.ca/~btaylor1/index.html
Imperial, rebel, bounty hunter & "other" vessels.

Imperial Fleet Schleswig-Holstein
http://members.xoom.com/ADAM_IFSH/
Imperial-flavor in a German site. Do they belong together?

Imperial Shipyards
http://members.tripod.com/~Dolmyn/shipyard.htm
Facts & pix on Imperial spacecraft.

Ships in the Star Wars Universe
http://members.xoom.com/kessel/outpost/ships.html
GIF & JPEG images of favorite spacecraft.

Star Destroyer
www.starwars.com/vehicles/star_destroyer/
"Heavyweights of the Imperial fleet" says this Official page.

Star Wars Central
www.geocities.com/Area51/Vault/3891/
Get "toured" through to Imperial or rebel tech files.

Technical Repository
www.cae.wisc.edu/~steiner/swsatellite/technic/
Specifications, text, and images of craft & weapons.

Warships of the Empire, Technical Commentaries
www.theforce.net/swtc/warships.html
Wow - if the rebels got a hold of all this!

The Death Stars

Two Death Stars have to be destroyed in the Star Wars Trilogy. You will find detailed information about these awesome menaces at the following web pages:

Death Star I
www.starwars.com/locations/deathstar/
Official Death Star page, with some unusual official pix.

Death Star II
www.starwars.com/locations/deathstar_ii/index.html
Mean machine that never did get to its grand opening.

Death Stars, Technical Commentaries
www.theforce.net/swtc/ds.html
Gee whiz commentaries on a truly big spacecraft.

Fighter Gets It In The Trench
www.telecom.csuhayward.edu/~aleung/trench.mov
Video of fighter in the Death Star Trench.

Rogue 9's Animations
www.geocities.com/Baja/Mesa/4807/index2.html
Animations of Imperial craft, also B-wings & more.

Star Wars Driving/Steering Wheel Virtual System
http://iml.millersv.edu/html.stuff/wtkstuff/wheel.dir/wheel.html
3D resource page with MPEG videos & sounds files for VRML.

Specs, Diagrams, & Secret Information

A number of web sites are created about Star Wars Spacecraft for gaming, modeling, and roleplaying purposes. The following sites are high in technical data, and many have diagrams and other hard-to-find information about spacecraft.

Capital Ships
http://frankq.dgne.com/swsv/capital-ships.html
Info about big ships, ships, and more ships.

Death Stars, Technical Commentaries
www.theforce.net/swtc/ds.html
Gee whiz commentaries on a truly big spacecraft.

Deck Plans (for Star Wars)
www.geocities.com/Area51/Labyrinth/6246/DP.html
Deck plan specs for light freighters, pods, scout craft.

Description About Star Wars' Vessels
www.civila.com/hispania/obi-juan/ship.txt
Specifics about warcraft in Spanish or English.

Millenium Falcon Text
www.angelfire.com/oh/gavinda/falcon.html
About the Falcon - not your standard YT1300 cargo vessel!

Star Wars Central
www.geocities.com/Area51/Vault/3891/
Get "toured" through to Imperial or rebel tech files.

Starfighters
http://frankq.dgne.com/swsv/starfighters.html
Specifications & info on smaller Star Wars craft.

Technical Repository
www.cae.wisc.edu/~steiner/swsatellite/technic/
Specifications, text, and images of craft & weapons.

Warships of the Empire, Technical Commentaries
www.theforce.net/swtc/warships.html
Wow - if the rebels got a hold of all this!

Warships of the Mon Calamari, Technical Commentaries
www.theforce.net/swtc/mcc.html
Federation or rebel alliance large spacecraft.

Hardware

Equipment Found in the Star Wars Universe

Whether you want to throw a party with authentic Star Wars gear, or you want information on the devices and "things" in the movies, you are likely to find that information among the web sites listed here. Weapons & Lightsabers are listed in their own section, as are Star Wars Vehicles, later..

- **Jedinet Pictures**
  www.jedinet.com/multimedia/pics/index.htm
  Rates as the finest JPEG image gallery on this rock.

- **Technology (Official Star Wars Site)**
  www.starwars.com/technology/
  Official scoop on some Wars high-tech.

- **Vader's Helmet Interior (museum piece)**
  www.geocities.com/Area51/Vault/3227/index.html
  Vader's helmet on museum display.

- **Weapons & Equipment (The Compendium)**
  www.wcug.wwu.edu/~paradox/weapons.html
  Details on equipment & weapons for gaming or for curiosity.

Weapons & Lightsabers

There are many web sites with information on the "elegant weapon of the Jedi – the Lightsaber." You will also find sites with information about other weapons here.

- **AT-AT**
  www.starwars.com/vehicles/at-at/
  Official page for the long-legged Imperial walking weapon.

- **Delta Source**
  www.jedinet.com/delta/
  Databases of events, characters, vehicles, weapons, more.

- **Droids-Weapons (Star Wars Force Graphics)**
  http://plaza.harmonix.ne.jp/~m-falcon/c-3po.html
  Graphic poster images of weapons & droids.

- **Jedinet Pictures**
  www.jedinet.com/multimedia/pics/index.htm
  Rates as the finest JPEG image gallery on this rock.

- **Lightsaber Pictures**
  www.jedinet.com/multimedia/pics/sabers/index.html

- **Lightsaber Technology**
  www.wcug.wwu.edu/~paradox/forcelight.html
  Lightsaber facts for enlightened & unenlightened alike.

Lightsabers - Jedi Knights
   http://members.aol.com/Myau84/sabers.html
      Diagram and background of this handy little weapon.

Lightsabers Text
   www.angelfire.com/oh/gavinda/lightsaber.html
      What everyone should know about lightsabers!

Official Weapons
   www.starwars.com/weapons/
      Subject directory weapons list from official Star Wars pages.

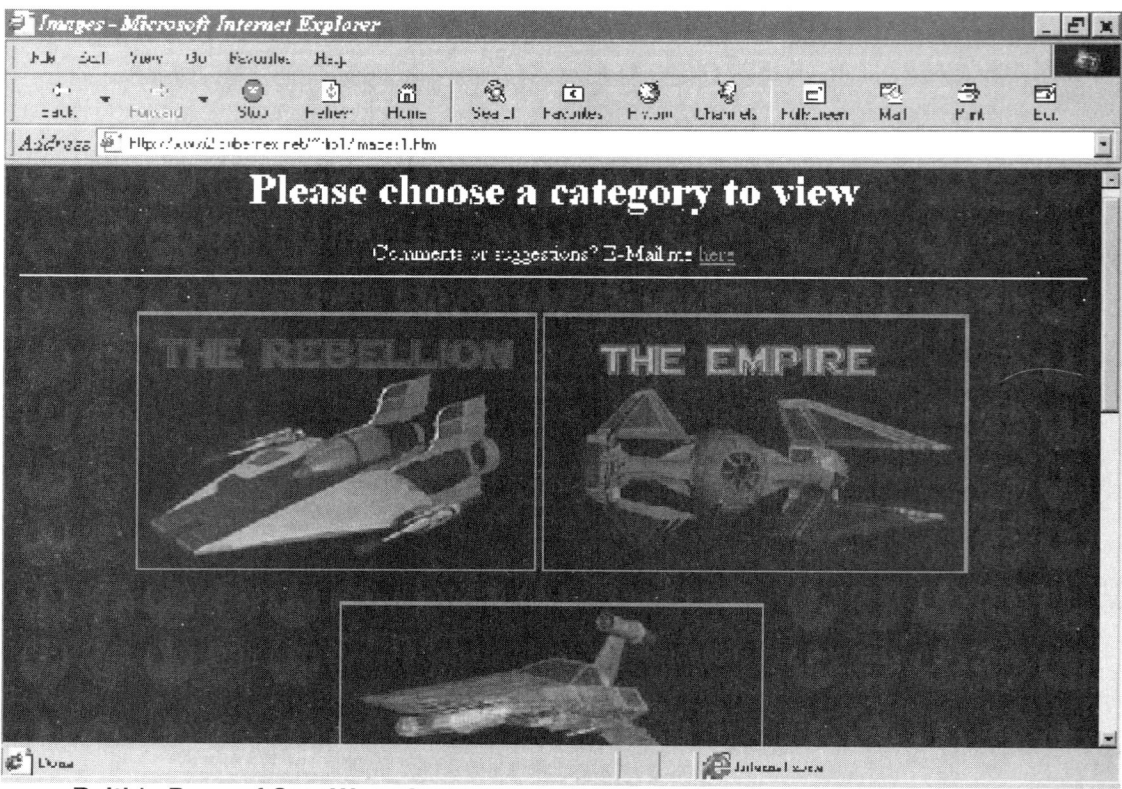

Raith's Page of Star Wars Art
   http://www2.cybernex.net/~flip1/images1.htm
      Largest collection of Star Wars meshes done by 1 man on the Net.

Saber Combat (Jedi Academy)
   www.jediacademy.com/saber.htm
      Care, feeding, & handling of lightsabers, with lessons.

Sabers Plus
   http://meltingpot.cfortunecity.com/brodie/286/index.html
      Deddicated to creating custom and replica lightsabers!

Star Wars Gear
   www.gogs32.freeserve.co.uk/gear.htm
      Imperial craft animations, lightsaber lore. Different.

Turbolaser Commentaries
www.snowhill.com/~by/
Turbo-lasers, ion cannons, blasters, lightsabers unplugged!

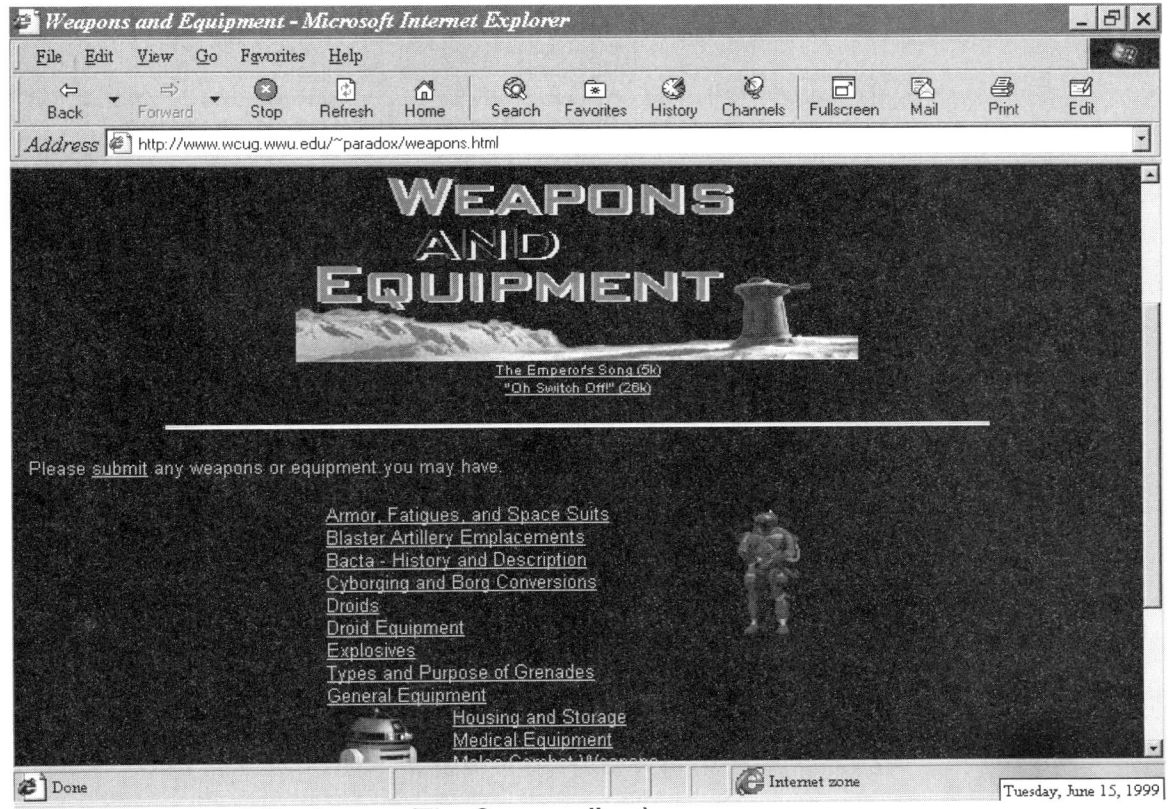

Weapons & Equipment (The Compendium)
www.wcug.wwu.edu/~paradox/weapons.html
Details on equipment & weapons for gaming or for curiosity.

Weapons of Episode 1
www.starwars.com/episode-i/features/weapons/
Episode 1 pix of weapons, with comments.

Vehicles (Excluding Spacecraft)

Since Star Wars' creator George Lucas was into auto racing before filmmaking, it's not surprising to find a variety of unique vehicles in his movies. Below are the sites with information about vehicles like speeders, pod racers, and more as well as pictures and models of them.

All About Episode 1 Racer
www.next-generation.com/jsmid/news/6205.html
How Episode 1 Pod Race turns into games for PC & Nintendo 64.

AT-AT
www.starwars.com/vehicles/at-at/
Official page for the long-legged Imperial walking weapon.

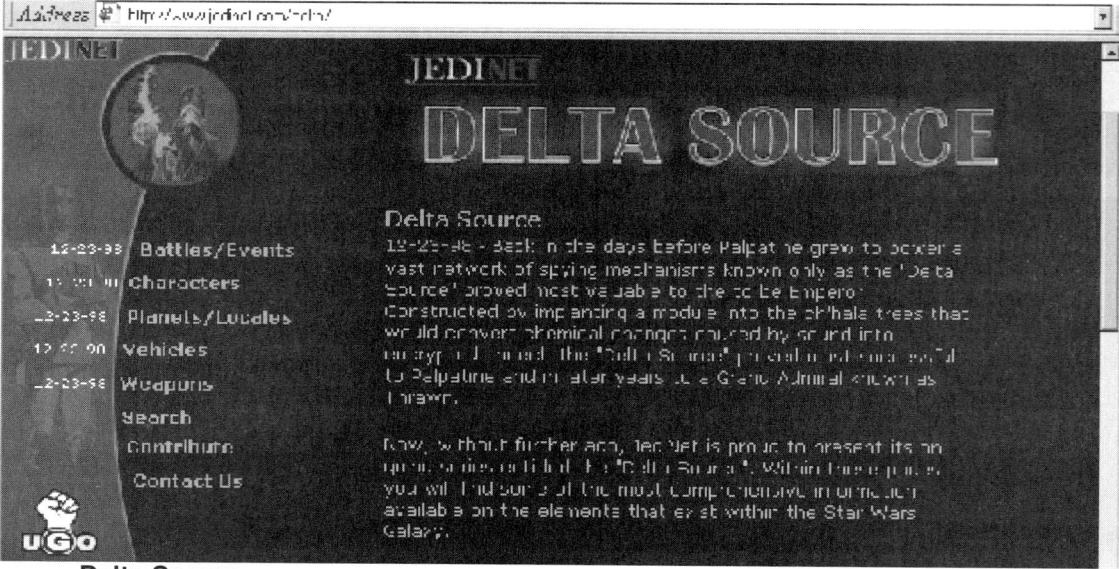

Delta Source
www.jedinet.com/delta/
Databases of events, characters, vehicles, weapons, more.

Episode 1: Phantom Menace Ship & Vehicle List
http://theforce.net/prequels/oldPreq/ships/ships.shtml
Prequel craft, vehicles, pix & specs.

Powerflicker's Model Page
www.geocities.com/Area51/Labyrinth/8664/models.html
Model and display pictures.

Prequel Vehicles
http://meltingpot.fortunecity.com/greenwood/487/vehic/vlist.html
Sith Speeders & pod racers to big Federation Battleships.

Star Wars Site Profiles

Not sure where you want to start? Here you will find full descriptions of most of the web pages that appear in this book. Along with the description, you will see various icons that are designed to help you size up the sites before you visit them. For instance, sites that are considered "must see" material are marked with an 👁 icon. By browsing here before you go online, you can find out if these sites have content of any interest to you.

10 of the Weirdest Star Wars Sites - Music Central
www.musiccentral.msn.com/movies/StarWars/StarWars5.asp
Here's a list of 10 small humor sites that aren't listed separately in this book - they're on MSN Music Central humor page as "10 weird pics." We visited and found stick figures, Mr T vs. Darth, Bubba Fett, and, especially, "I can hold it - Porkins Central."

1999 Prequel Calendar 👁
www.jedinet.com/prequels/TPM/fandom.htm
Here's a printable 1999 color calendar by Davide Canavo that appears in the Jedinet Prequel section. The JPEG collages on each calendar page are especially pleasing. Also, check the excellent Prequel news section linked here.

20th Century Fox ⬇ $ 🔍
www.20thcenturyfox.com
In case you you didn't know, Fox is big in the entertainment biz. In addition to distributing Star Wars and movies, their site lets you in on Fox news, TV, sports, home entertainment, studios, schedules. There's sections for kids, interaction, a store, pressroom, forums & "Ask Fox."

2nd Empire - The Emperor's Wrath 🖼
http://members.tripod.com/~Dolmyn/empire.htm
Senator Tamthas Velykk's (P. Marchand) site is a fiction that is also a database of Imperial info, ships, intelligence (how can that be?), laws, and a mission statement bent on world domination. Definitely a site to avoid, unless ---.

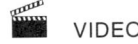

🖼 IMAGES   🎬 VIDEO   📢 AUDIO
👁 MUST SEE! $ SELLS STUFF   ⬛ ADULT CONTENT   🔍 SEARCHABLE
💬 CHAT ROOMS   ⬇ MESSAGE BOARDS   📬 MAILING LISTS

3D Fan Art - Marua Sector
www.marua.com/banners/3d
"Impressive." About 50 pieces of JPEG 3D fan art has been collected at this Marua Sector gallery site. Submissions are welcomed. Many of these make excellent 3D wallpaper for your computer.

3D Modeling Alliance Forum
http://apps.vantagenet.com/aforums/thread.asp?old=Y&id=199851010212
SWMA fully censored forum for discussion of Star Wars 3D modeling issues. Threaded and a good place for postings about 3D and 3D news.

3D Modeling Alliance Link Page
www.surfthe.net/swma/links/links.html
To be on this link list, you have to have a super logo - super logos lead you to super sites!

3D News
www.3dnews.net
Want to get on the 3D bandwagon but you don't know what you need to do to get your old 512K or Commodore 64 up to speed? Well forget about 512Ks and Commodore 64s - you'll need a lot more juice than that! Find out about 3D, upgrades, demos, products, news, and a newsletter here.

3D Palette
www.3dpalette.com
Not a Star Wars site (you may find some Star Wars 3D's, though) this is a 3D modeling/fan site, rich in resources, news, downloads, tutorials. Also, 2D, galleries, site hosting, frag network, survey, job listings and news archives.

3D Stereovision Star Wars Pix
http://seconn4.yoda.com/~vader97/3d/3d.html
You know those 3D images where you relax your eyes and the image jumps out in 3D? Here are 5 of them: Boba Fett, B-wing, X-wing, Imperial Royal Guard, and Planet Yavin, courtesy ot Taz's site.

A Feminine Perspective
http://members.aol.com/bananie42/index.html
Annie Darlington's SWF site's biggest feature is the excellent tribute to Leia, but it also hosts good image and sound files, software downloads, fan fiction, chat, humor, trivia and the guestbook, links, webrings. Who's better: Han, Luke, or Jabba? You vote. (Hint: Jabba doesn't win).

A Few Minutes with George Lucas
www.daforce.demon.nl/fightback/dfhw2.htm
Video: George Lucas discusses the importance of seeing Star Wars on the big screen. QuickTime and AVI format.

A Lot More Star Wars Animations
http://seconn4.yoda.com/~vader97/animated/animated.html
"A Lot More Animations" because this is the second big file offered by Taz on his web page (see alternate URL). Animations here are high quality, many with backgrounds (not just spinning models in space). Includes lightsabers, symbols, characters, spacecraft, e-mail, even Han acting arrogant after capturing stormtroopers.

A New Hope Video Clips
http://home.multiweb.nl/~bramenpim/staranh.htm
> Downloads of AVI or QuickTime format video clips from A New Hope and its Special Edition. Includes the IMAX version of the opening, the missing Biggs scene, the Bith Band, and a whole slew more. Also links back to the other 2 Trilogy movies. (Some files may be down)

A New Hope Wallpaper
www.jedinet.com/multimedia/windows/wallpaper/index.htm
> Two collages of the original Star Wars that you can quickly transfer to your computer for use as wallpaper (screen backgrounds). From this site you can also find Empire Strikes Back and Return of the Jedi collages.

A Page of Undeniable Weirdness - Tribbles, Wookiees, & Ewoks
www.compusmart.ab.ca/macclan/Collpg1.htm
> We never did figure out exactly what IS here, except that there's Star Wars, Star Trek, X-Files, a guestbook, home page references, links, and a variety of fun files. We just were looking for Ewoks.

A-wing fighter
www.starwars.com/vehicles/a-wing
> Official Lucasfilm page describing the Rebel Fleet's A-wing fighter. This is the company-line on the tough, fast fighter seen in Return of the Jedi. Background text, but few details. The site has easy links to other official sites.

A1's Star Wars Multimedia Page
http://members.aol.com/A1B2C369/index.html
> Lots of Links to vehicles, creatures, posters, toys, Prequel news, and interviews (occasionally). Is searchable. Collections of sounds and a section for "food" which is largely Star Wars Pez collectibles.

A1's Star Wars Poster Page
http://members.aol.com/A1B2C369/posters.html
> Linked to A1's multimedia site, this poster page promises more than the few posters that we found here. It's worth checking for recent additions to this page.

A1's Star Wars Sounds
http://members.aol.com/XxKypxX/sound.html
> Nice collection of sounds and phrases from the movies, divided into Rebels and Imperial sections.

A1's Star Wars Toys $
http://members.aol.com/sonofskywr/toys.html
> Offers 3 1/2 inch figures, 3 packs, Hong Kong exclusives, 12 inch dolls and mailaways.

Aaron Allston's Home Site
www.io.com/~allston
> Have you ever wondered, "What does author Aaron Allston have that's good on his web page?" or "I'd like to know some of his secrets about creating Star Wars games." Go to his site; it's full of information, and you can learn all about Aaron's Star Wars world..

IMAGES   VIDEO   AUDIO
MUST SEE! $ SELLS STUFF   ADULT CONTENT   SEARCHABLE
CHAT ROOMS   MESSAGE BOARDS   MAILING LISTS

Aaron's Star Wars Multimedia page
www.geocities.com/Area51/Stargate/3350
   Under construction, this site hopes to offer autographs of characters/cast. Nearly 20 posters and reviews of novels.

Aaron's Star Wars Toy & Comic Price Guides Checklist
www.continet.com/aaronsmagic/pretoys/1Check.html
   Do you want to get a complete collection of Phantom Menace 3 3/4 Action Figures because you're still smarting for not getting all the Star Wars figures 20 years ago? If so, use this checklist to track Phantom Menace pieces.

Aaron's Star Wars Toys & Comics $
www.swdatabase.com/collectables
   And price guides. Aaron actually has a staff helping to compile news (fans go wild over Furbie Yoda!), reviews (heavy on Prequel figures), and price guides. Links to toy mechandise sales & auction sites. Legos on the way.

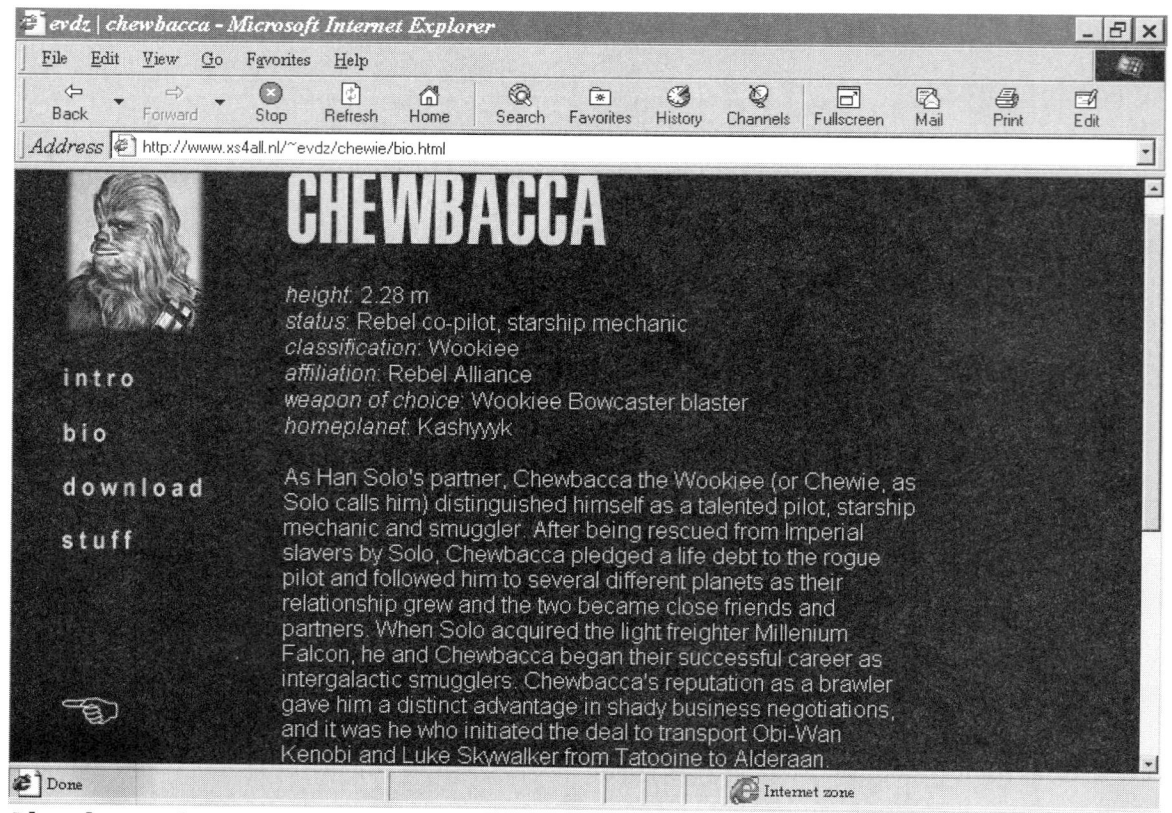

Absolute Chewbacca
www.xs4all.nl/~evdz/chewie/bio.html
   Biographical information on Star Wars' favorite character, found on Erwin Van Der Zande's pages.

Add-ons, from Jedi Council Chamber
www.geocities.com/Area51/Hollow/9125/addons.htm
   Computer wallpaper - Yoda, Darth, Boba, troopers, etc - also cursors, icons, screensavers, & Imperial Code Font.

Admiral Ackbar For President
www.geocities.com/Hollywood/Studio/6290
> Why? We don't really know. Fans can view the rhetoric, sign the guestbook, read the manifesto, see the Ackbar gallery, hear sounds, see lookalikes, and meet other famous Ackbars. It's a spoof.

Admiral's Star Wars Page
www.geocities.com/Area51/Hollow/2779
> Member of the Star Wars Collective webring, the Admiral offers a nice collection of images, also a guestbook, links, Real Audio music, and a Lynyrd Skynyrd page (a big-time 1970's carryover).

Ain't-It-Cool-News Reviews
www.aint-it-cool-news.com/section.cgi?type=Review
> Ain't-It-Cool reviews all kinds of movies - from an alternative sort of perspective. They also have a news site, forums, and search feature where you can search for mentions of Star Wars.

Air Force One
www.spe.sony.com/movies/airforceone/home_swf.html
> Columbia TriStar Tom Clancy epic flic with Harrison as the angry civil-servant/President who makes his own breaks at 20,000 fee. Here's the official Sony Pictures page with "the game," multimedia, plot, bios and buzz.

Alan's Star Wars MIDI Page
www.geocities.com/SiliconValley/Pines/4928/midi2.htm
> Good variety of Trilogy MIDI's sounds and music to download.

Alan's Star Wars Page
www.geocities.com/SiliconValley/Pines/4928/index.html
> Alan's index page connects to all he has to offer: sounds, pix, MIDI's, movies, hints and codes for games (and game archives), Prequel stuff, Themes, even a chat room. Also has trivia and a guestbook.

Alec Guinness - All-Media Guide
http://allmovie.com/cg/x.dll?UID=9:01:46|PM&p=avg&sql=B29203
> All-Media Guide reminds us that Alec Guinness - old Ben - had his first starring role in "Great Expectations" - the 1946 version, then starred in '48 in "Oliver Twist." Read details of his filmography and biography here, then connect to other Star Wars people/places/things.

Alex's Star Wars Media Page
www.geocities.com/Area51/Labyrinth/8385
> Each JPEG image from either the Rebels or the Imperials section is followed by a WAV or MIDI sound file - this mixed media page is set up as a scroll; pictures are image captures from the Trilogy.

Alien Vocalizations
http://buteo.colorado.edu/~yosh/psi/system2/sounds
> A few alien noises from Star Wars in AIFF format - Jawa, Leia, Droid laugh, also a WAV of Jabba's laugh. Length and format are listed for each.

All About Episode 1 Racer
www.next-generation.com/jsmid/news/6205.html
   Next Generation Online Magazine (gaming) got ahold of the Star Wars team members who put together the pod race sequence. They talk about how the pod race was turned into a game for Nintendo 64 and the PC.

All-Media Guide
http://allmovie.com/cg/x.dll?UID=9:01:46%7CPM&p=avg&sql=A179455
   Did you think "Star Wars: Episode 1 - The Phantom Menace" was "bright, fast, dynamic" or "low key, calm, slow"? Rate it 5 Stars. At this site, not only do you get information and the good, main links, you also get to submit your feelings about the film's qualities. The site is searchable!

All-Media Guide Star Wars
http://allmovie.com/cg/x.dll?UID=9:01:46|PM&p=avg&sql=A46636
   AMG rates Star Wars 5 Stars - High Historical Importance, High Production Values. Site gives all details, cast, related movies, awards, plots lines, oh-wow data. Translates into other languages. Vote on movie quality. Who was that "Detention area officer?" (Malcolm Tierney)

Amara's Cantina
www.flyingarmadillo.com/cantina/index.html
   A "must see!" Pop-outs open as you investigate the image; click on house of skywalker for RTP (paper dolls), original art for Amara's excellent galleries (Trilogy, Prequel & MUSH), humorous cartoons and song lyrics. Good artist = good pages! Respect copyright request.

American Graffiti
www.lucasfan.com/amgraf/index2.html
   An unofficial site, this has a good collection of pictures and what-not from George Lucas' first hit movie, American Graffiti (1973). The $750,000 budget film with then-unknowns like Cindy Williams & Richard Dreyfuss grossed nearly $200M and opened the way to Star Wars.

Amusement Enterprises
www.aeigames.com
   This site features video and computer games for a company in the Pacific NW; click on "Computer Room" and scroll down to find the Banner Links to all the computer game company biggies and electronics hardware providers. Also game news and connections info.

An Appeal to the Tolerance-Challenged
http://members.aol.com/candyfish/appeal.htm
Droids are our friends, Droids are our friends, Droids are our friends, Droids are our friends. Here's why we should respect them! Droids are our friends.

Anakin Skywalker, Slave Boy 👁
http://meltingpot.fortunecity.com/greenwood/487/char/anakin.html
The Prequel Spoilers web site has excellent background material on EP1 characters, including Jake Lloyd's young Anakin: "I'm a pilot, you know, and some day I'm gonna fly away from this place."

Anakin's Hovel Set Plan 🖼
http://members.xoom.com/_XOOM/mb_starwars/anakin/index.htm
Blueprint of Anakin's house which was used for designing the movie set at Leavesden Studio in England. The various areas of the house are described. One catch: this site is in French.

Anakin's Rebel Base 🖼 👁
www.geocities.com/Area51/Labyrinth/8664/noframes.html
Varied collection of movies, photos, computer goodies (themes, cursors), but mostly this site features a page of great scratch models (page listed separately as Powerflicker's Model Page). By Bryan and Steve (son/step-dad).

Anakin14's Ring of the Jedi
www.geocities.com/Area51/Chamber/6138/ringofjedi.html
A webring in a somewhat formative stage. If you're building a site or ring, this site can be helpful.

Anakin14's Star Wars Home Page 🔊
www.geocities.com/Area51/Chamber/6138/frames.html
Offers a lot for those wanting to build their own Star Wars pages, or join or cruise webrings. Also, links to site that sells CD Star Wars soundtracks. Variety of downloadable sounds, also scripts.

Andrew Gruner's Custom Star Wars Projects 🖼
www.mesastate.edu/~agruner/sw/custom
Power of the Force 2 customized figurines, diorama sets, custom costumes. Do a lot with figurines.

Animated GIFs Collection 🖼
www.geocities.com/Area51/Cavern/3129
A cool collection of animated GIF's from Paul Washipabano; site can be viewed in French or English. Speeder bikes, R2-D2 dancing, spacecraft, lightsabers - lots of goodies for web sites! File names include size, description.

Animatics: Moving Storyboards of Episode 1
www.starwars.com/episode-i/features/animatics/01
Official Star Wars site about the editing of movies and the Prequel, and how storyboards and scenes are managed.

Animations & Icons 🖼 👁
www.wcug.wwu.edu/~paradox/animation.html
From the Compendium's galleries pages you can download animated symbols, logos, and cool "actions" for your website or other uses. Includes Darth-morph-to-Fett and space action GIF animations.

🖼 IMAGES   🎬 VIDEO   🔊 AUDIO
👁 MUST SEE! $ SELLS STUFF   ⬛ ADULT CONTENT   🔍 SEARCHABLE
💬 CHAT ROOMS   📥 MESSAGE BOARDS   📬 MAILING LISTS

Anthony Daniels - All-Media Guide
http://allmovie.com/cg/x.dll?UID=9:01:46|PM&p=avg&sql=B16857
As C-3PO, actor Anthony Daniels "excelled." Here's a bit more about the British actor and what is known of his acting career, courtesy of All-Media Guide. Find other major and minor characters linked to this searchable site.

Art (Jedinet)
www.jedinet.com/multimedia/pics/art/index.htm
Jedinet's page needs no more title than "Art" - it offers some of the very best to be found on the Internet. Collections of Dave Dorman, Ralph McQuarrie, the Hildebrandt's, also big renderings files and a museum full of miscellaneous images. JPEG images are expandable: file and image size is given.

Art (Rancor Pit)
www.sentex.net/~dah/art
Four artists (Johnny Craig, Nathan Hoel, Nick Nugent, Andrew Hoel) who are associated with Rancor Pit have put their fan sketches and posters up for viewing (click on artist name, not autograph).

Artwork & Symbols
www.wcug.wwu.edu/~paradox/art.html
Used mainly as The Compenium's resource for roleplaying games, this has grown into major galleries of JPEG & GIF images and WAV sound clips (Prequel galleries, too). Click on the thumbnails to enlarge the pix. Includes candids, cast pix, fan art, and animations/icons.

ASCII Star Wars Images
www.civila.com/hispania/obi-juan/swascii.txt
We didn't know how to categorize this web site: it's "typed" (as in "ASCII") Star Wars images that you can use at school or download on paper, or whatever. Tricky to transfer, but you'll catch on!

Ask A Question - AllExperts.com
www.allexperts.com/tv/starwars.shtml
Neat AllEXPERTS site features savants who will attempt to answer your questions about Star Wars and especially Episode 1, The Phantom Menace. Pick your expert, or cruise to other topics and find resident experts there as well.

Ask A Question - Natalie Portman
www.allexperts.com/moviestars/oz/portman.shtml
Want to ask an expert what they know about Natalie Portman? Go to this ALLEXPERTS site and ask a Hollywood insider. (This may only be a temporary file.)

AT-AT
www.starwars.com/vehicles/at-at
Imperial walkers - At-Ats - All-Terrain Armored Transports - have a Lucasfilm page, with some specs, stock pix.

Audio Booth, The
www.smartlink.net/~deej7/audio.htm
Here you can download a number of different players for converting sound files - GoldWave 3.02, SoundApp 1.5.1, Cool Edit. Galleries here are AU/RealAudio from Harrison Ford movies - Sabrina, Indy, Fugitive, Witness, & Star Wars. Also some Jay Lenos.

Audio Recordings (Knight Hammer)
www.geocities.com/Hollywood/Bungalow/3606
The Knight Hammer site has a decidedly Imperial "look" to it, but the WAV files found here are collected from good characters as well as bad. Find over 100 sound clips, many arranged by character, with length of clip given.

AV Photo & Media Finder
http://image.altavista.com/cgi-bin/avncgi

AltaVista has about the best media finder. Here you search for images, videos, or audio. For example, type in Ewoks, click "images", and hit search - the media finder comes up with as many as it can find, then displays expandable thumbnail pix. Also, view by detailed listing.

Avanzada Rebeldo
www.ing.puc.cl/~bsq

Chilean (the country, not the food) multimedia site with sound and image files. By BeNeNO. Spanish required.

Azeroth's Labrynth
www.otn.net/mypage/azeroth/default.htm

We noticed that this site was producing Prequel news and comments, and gave Darth Maul "The Hardest Person of the Week Award." Includes reviews of video games.

Azeroth's Labrynth Comics Update
www.otn.net/mypage/azeroth/comics.html

Reviews of recent Star Wars comic offerings, with some small pix of their covers.

B Squared's Star Wars Stuff
www.synicon.com.au/sw

Australian site by Rob Brown is a top resource for info on spacecraft, especially the Falcon, Slave 1, Corillians, Xt-2400, escape pods, also for lightsabers, badges, RPG extras, and the myths of Star Wars. Has good links.

B-wing Fighter
www.starwars.com/vehicles/b-wing

Introduced at the battle of Endor in Return of the Jedi, the Rebel Fleet's B-win fighters had an unconventional appearance which could perhaps be attributed to the design preferences of Admiral Ackbar. An official Lucasfilm page with some basic info & stills, also links to other official sites.

Bad Guide to Star Wars
www.geocities.com/Area51/Vault/6031/bgsw53.txt

Star Wars Bloopers and "very interesting" facts collected up to 9/28/94 by Brandon Gillespie, but found at this URL. How come Darth's lightsaber is white (instead of red) just after he does in Obi-wan? Wasn't Han's shirt untucked in when he was frozen in Carbonite? It is when Leia thaws him.

Banners of other Star Wars Sites (Swammi collection)
http://members.xoom.com/kessel/outpost/thumbnail.html

You don't have to visit half the galaxy to see all the different Star Wars web site banners (titles) - just go here and you'll see a good sampling of them. Most can download for use on your own web site.

Barnes & Noble.com
www.barnesandnoble.com

"If we don't have your book, nobody does" says this Barnes & Noble mega-book site. Soon, they'll offer music. They offer coffee. Search by title or subject. PUSH technology can alert you to new Star Wars titles of interest. Also find software, magazines, bargains, gifts, and a kids section.

IMAGES   VIDEO   AUDIO
MUST SEE! $ SELLS STUFF   ADULT CONTENT   SEARCHABLE
CHAT ROOMS   MESSAGE BOARDS   MAILING LISTS

Battles & Events
http://members.tripod.com/Tiger887/EmpireBattles.html
This not yet complete Galactic Empire site (do they ever complete anything?) lists text of battles, skirmishes, losses, and some specifics about the spacecraft involved.

BCR (Scott Thompson) Saga of the Wind Image Archives
www.flash.net/~draegos/Archives.html
Thompson specializes in creating images for his fiction/gaming conceptualizations, collecting base images and reconstructing them in various scenarios. It's a bold idea - taking 3D game images and adding animations, graphics, renderings, etc. Also, check his linked pages.

Ben & Grovers Media Archives
www.bmartin.u-net.com/media.htm
80+ RealAudio sound files including the four movie soundtracks; files arranged by movie, then characters, droids, FX, and miscellaneous. "That's no Moon" or "Are you sure this thing is safe?" Also find 2 QuickTime videos of the Special Edition and EP1 trailers.

Ben Burtt: Sound Design of Episode 1
www.starwars.com/episode-i/features/burtt
Ben Burtt coined the term "sound design" (sic) with his work on 1976's Star Wars. This article catches up to him just before the Prequel, and talks about sound work on the movies.

Ben's Awesome Star Wars Page
www.geocities.com/Area51/Zone/7153
Canadian Ben claims to have "more sounds than we can imagine." Well, "we can imagine a lot of sounds!" MIDI's and WAV's abound! Also, scripts for the 3 Trilogy movies.

Berlin's Network
www.geocities.com/SouthBeach/Lights/5679/index.html
Although not a Star Wars site specificly, we found Berlin's Network from his Prequel site. This homepage has plenty of info on 3D, links, 3D webring connections, also games, including the site author's own. We liked the author's energy and attitude.

Bespin
www.starwars.com/locations/bespin
Official Lucasfilms site for gas planet Bespin, location of Cloud City and where we find Lando Calrissian, old friend of Han Solo. Click on the pix for 6 full-color stills of Bespin, Cloud City, etc.

Bespin 2 Multimedia
www.marua.com/bespin/index3.htm
New in late April, this Marua Sector multimedia site connects to other web sites that have a ton of resources, so we expect this one will grow in summer '99. Plain backgrounds take a bit of getting used to (that'll change, too).

Best of Meco
www.live-wire.com/record-reviews/frame/m/meco/best-of.html
Meco was the instrumental group that had a solid hit with the disco version of Star Wars - remember? Here, find a 54 second download of that, said to include music from the Cantina Band. This is a collector item made for Mac AIFF or MPEG. Includes other Meco songs.

Best Samuel L Jackson Home Page
http://member.aol.com/gifhack/main.html
Expected to be the official Samuel L Jackson home page. You'll find his bio, filmography, and images and sounds from movies such as Pulp Fiction; "AK-47; when you absolutely positively have to kill every mf in the room." News and links to interviews and movies.

Big Kourt's House of Star Wars, X-Files, Star Trek & Used Hubcaps
www.geocities.com/Area51/Lair/7558
Title clues you in - this is definitely a self-serving fun site (not for kids), with a few unusual sound files and author's select pix. Light mix of X-Files and Trek, too. One sound file describes this page: "what a piece of junk!"

Biker Scouts
www.starwars.com/characters/biker_scouts
Although they work for the Empire and trash up Endor, the Biker Scouts rate their own official Lucasfilms site. General background material and a couple action shots are here.

Bill's Dagobah Page
www.geocities.com/Area51/Dimension/6975/starwars.html
Good mix of sound and video pieces from Return of the Jedi, but not much to do with Dagobah exclusively. Links to similar sound/video sites for Hoth, Mos Eisley Cantina, and Star Wars generally.

Bill's Star Wars Page
www.geocities.com/Area51/Dimension/6975/starwars.html
Bill's Page is divided into four sections: main page, Hoth, Dagobah, and Mos Eisley Cantina, each with the appropriate sights, sounds & links. Survey and webring connections, too. Bill's index includes Back to the Future, Wonder Years, & Metallica pages. What a mix!

Blake's Ultimate Star Wars Site
www.geocities.com/Area51/Shadowlands/4351/index.html
Good variety of sights and sounds, also QuickTime video files and the usual questbook, pix, etc., but also links to EverQuest and a Toys page. We are left to speculate about Blake's "Angie" love tribute.

Bloopers (Jedinet)
www.jedinet.com/multimedia/blooper/index.htm
Each Trilogy flic is examined for mistakes - bloopers! The results are listed here (but no pix). One drawback is this: these nitpik lists can ruin the watching of the movies. You're distracted by the errors - you know they're coming. We know it's hard, but please make your movies tighter, Mr. Lucas.

IMAGES   VIDEO   AUDIO
MUST SEE!   SELLS STUFF   ADULT CONTENT   SEARCHABLE
CHAT ROOMS   MESSAGE BOARDS   MAILING LISTS

> Do you like me enjoy, behind the scenes and cut scenes images? Publicity shots, bloopers, production sketches and other pictures you never see just watching the movies? Congratulations!, you've come to the right place. With aprox. 400 images in the archives - I hope you have time to stay a while!

Blueharvest.net Star Wars Images
www.blueharvest.net/imageswww.blueharvest.net/images
   Excellent galleries of magazine covers, Star Wars spoof comic strips, MAD magazine covers, Star Wars Christmas images, blooper shots, close-ups, PR pix, new Dockingbay 94 photos, also schemes, Miscellaneous scenes, section, and, most of all, a Salacious Crumb section.

Blueharvest.net Star Wars Videos
www.blueharvest.net/video
   49 Video clips from movies, TV, auditions, lost scenes (where C-3PO gets destructive with a warning sign), public service safety instructions, Chewie's MTV lifetime achievement award, Energizer Bunny commercial, Wicket vs. the Dragon, TROOPS, Taco Bell, and original FX.

Boba Fett
http://members.aol.com/Fett15m/Fett.html
   Boba Feet is considered the coolest of characters; find out why and read his background. Also, Mandalorians, Boba's ship "Slave 1," and some good-sized images.

Boba Fett & Darth Vader Galleries
www.geocities.com/Area51/Shadowlands/4918/gallery.html
   Galleries for Boba Fett and Darth Vader images are linked to the TIE Fighter Hangar Bay web site.

Boba Fett - Ultimate Star Wars Multimedia Page
www.geocities.com/Area51/Crater/3234/fett.html
   JPEG picture gallery of Boba Fett from the Trilogy & Special Editions, also a couple WAV quotes (remember: Boba only had four or five movie lines total!) and an animated GIF of his ship Slave 1.

Boba Fett at the Smithsonian
www.geocities.com/Area51/Vault/3227/index.html
   From the camera of Chris Coleman - Boba Fett figure from the exhibit at the Smithsonian Museum.

Boba Fett Fan Club
www.bobafettfanclub.com
   Archives, collectibles, convention schedules, comics, bios, pictures, editorials and more is found at this site dedicated to bounty hunter and Han Solo nemesis Boba Fett.

Boba Fett's Awesome Homepage
www.geocities.com/Area51/Lair/2192/Home.html
   It is awesome, R2, it is! Good collection of Boba JPEG images from movies, comics, cards, figurines, also a video clip of Boba's "lil accident." This frames site also turns up pages of Boba history & stats, also to the Guide to Bounty Hunters, and more. Impressive pictures!

Boba Fett's Backyard
www.geocities.com/Area51/Stargate/9082/index.html
   Under construction at time of publication, this site is intended for Prequels, sequels, and information on the original Trilogy. Check for updates; they should be good.

Boba Fett's Bungalow
www.geocities.com/Area51/Nebula/9901/bobafett.html
   Biography information on Fett is from official sources, they say! Gives vital stats, picture gallery, 4 sound clips, and 2 video clips. We didn't find the Bungalow, but we did see Boba's spacecraft in action.

Boba Fett's Home Sector
www.geocities.com/Hollywood/Set/5760
   Boba Fett's Home Sector is a geocities jumping off point for a variety of topics (via links), particularly to all five scripts, the Musical, quizzes, humor, and more. This site has a high volume of visitors.

Boba Fett's Lair
www.geocities.com/Area51/Vault/3227/lair.htm
   A Boba Fett directory page on geocities.com by Chris Coleman, with links to other interesting sites such as the Smithsonian exhibit pictures. Full of Boba Fett stuff.

Boba Fett's Page
http://members.tripod.com/~Rowlandc
   Basically this is a searchable link list and Star Wars message board by Canadian CJ Rowlands. Boba Fett is not featured, however. He must be away hunting Han Solo again.

Boba Fonts
http://starwars.fans.net/bobafonts
   Davide Canavero resource site has a calendar, his novels, as well as cursor & font collections for your computer. Unzip the fonts for downloading - very up-to-date typestyle collection.

Bogus Star Wars Homepage
www.cinenet.net/~agrapha/StarNet/SW.html
   JPEG images, commentary, Star Wars news, and info on the FX (effects) for the Special Edition versions of the Star Wars Trilogy. There's some Prequel news. Learn the differences between Special Editions and the originals.

Bond's Star Wars Page
http://home.tampabay.rr.com/bond/starwars.htm
   Bond is into Quake as well as Star Wars - his site has some interesting action scripts; we hope he adds more. Links to webrings. Features an animated Boba Fett.

IMAGES   VIDEO   AUDIO
MUST SEE!   SELLS STUFF   ADULT CONTENT   SEARCHABLE
CHAT ROOMS   MESSAGE BOARDS   MAILING LISTS

Boober's Star Wars Galaxy
http://home.fuse.net/mckee/frames.htm
> Variety! News, Games, Downloads, Humor, Trivia, Awards, Links & Webring, Survey, Message Boards - how does he do it? Impressive listings of games, clues, and how to's. Multimedia includes over 625 sounds.

Books - the force.net Expanded Universe
www.theforce.net/books
> Tremendous resource for information on Star Wars books, novels, reading items for young readers, guides, pop-ups, movie adaptations, behind-the-scenes glimpses, price guides, and news. Illustrated with GIF & JPEG images.

Books Section of Hydrospanner
www.hydrospanner.com/books
> Book reviews and surveys - and, submit your own reviews. This Hydrospanner site also features a book news section with book cover pictures, timeline (promised) and links to Star Wars book sites.

Bossk's Homepage
www.geocities.com/Area51/Dimension/9216
> Information and a tribute to Bossk, the Trandoshan bounty hunter who specializes in tracking down Wookiees. Also, image galleries of vehicles, characters, aliens. (formerly Nathan's Home Page)

Bounty Hunters
http://people.a2000.nl/tvdbrink
> Searchable gallery/collection of Star Wars Bounty Hunters compiled by Tim van den Brink. Links to videos, 3D, & Bounty Hunter Guild. Site may have completed its "construction."

Bria's Retribution, Flagship of the Rebel Commander
www.geocities.com/Area51/Nebula/8247/sum.html
> Mara Jade unicorns, comments on the Han Solo Trilogy and spoilers, also fan fiction and Han pix area are all found on Bria Tharen's homepage, part of the Han Solo-ists webring.

Britt's Boba Fett Site
www.geocities.com/Area51/Quadrant/2581/frmemain.html
> Says "Welcome to the best site to learn everything you want to know about Boba Fett." Nice movie sequencers on main page, also instructions on how to build a Fett costume, short video clip plus downloads of the Prequel trailer. Includes Fett bio & future appearances, armor & weapons.

C-3PO
www.starwars.com/characters/c-3p0
> Protocol droid C-3PO has his own official Lucasfilms page, with pixs, general background material.

C-3PO's Starpages
www.surfnet.fi/~zargon/swchan/c3pos.html
> C-3PO is an absolute expert as dispensing "information to please" - not always the best information, but not often wrong, either. Here he answers other Star Wars character's flaky queries.

Cantina, The
www.the-cantina.com
> Launch yourself into the sites and sounds of the Mos Eisley Cantina, the character-filled watering-hole for creatures the universe over. Cover page lists other news of interest, from Star Wars to Internet Freedom issues.

Capeman's Prequel Homepage
http://members.aol.com/capeman69/index.html
News, pics, rumors, cast & character information about Episode 1, The Phantom Menace.

Capeman's Prequel Production Pictures
http://members.aol.com/CapeMan69/pic.html
Candid photos reportedly taken during Prequel filming, in Tunisia. Photos: interiors, character posings, equipment.

Captain Needa's Star Destroyer
www.geocities.com/Area51/Rampart/5559
Info on Imperial Fleet operations and Captain Needa's ship. Site is part of the Imperial Navy group for roleplaying, hosted by geocities and Andrew. A few good star destroyer pix, also scenario information.

Cards (Jedinet)
www.jedinet.com/multimedia/pics/cards/index.htm
"We've been all over the universe, and we've seen a lot of things, but we've never seen an all-powerful card page that controls everything" - except that this Jedinet collection comes close. ANH Yellow, ESB Red, ROTJ Red, Galaxies, Topps, & miscellaneous Ralph McQuarries.

Cards - A Prequel Message
http://thephantommenace.co.uk/postcard
The Phantom Menace United Kingdom site offers up a variety of 12 Prequel greeting cards which you customize and send via e-mail. Cool!

Carrie Books
www.saunalahti.fi/~margot/books.htm
Find 3 Carrie books, cover pictures, and relevant comments on Margot's Carrie Fisher Page. Postcards From the Edge, Surrender The Pink, Delusions of Grandma. Carrie: "I never would have been so arrogant to assume that I could write, although I had that secret ambition."

Carrie Fisher (Lycos Network)
www.lycos.com/entertainment/celebrities/celebs/Fisher_Carrie.html
Lycos Entertainment's Carrie Fisher page is a great place to find out all about Star Wars favorite Princess. Have access to some vital stats (Carrie is an intelligent Libra-Scorpio in astrology), her claims to fame, links to her official sites and some fan pages. Searchable!

Carrie Fisher Website
www.carriefisher.com
Super Carrie Fisher pages here! Biography, filmography, pix and more pix, autograph, also news, addresses, chatroom, message boards, guestbook, survey. Join the mailing list. Check "Special page" for her latest interview.

Carrie Photographs (Unofficial Carrie Fisher Homepage)
www.offsoho.com/carrie/html/8photographs.html
4 Photo sections of sub-pages (JPEG & GIF) of Carrie: B/W, B/W Star Wars, Color, Color Star Wars. Very nice.

IMAGES   VIDEO   AUDIO
MUST SEE!   SELLS STUFF   ADULT CONTENT   SEARCHABLE
CHAT ROOMS   MESSAGE BOARDS   MAILING LISTS

Carrie Videos (Unofficial Carrie Fisher Homepage)
www.offsoho.com/carrie/html/8video.html
Collection of video clips of Carrie in QuickTime format. Includes clips from her Star Wars audition, Saturday Night Live corny Obi-Wan Kenobi bit, Austin Powers, and her comments on the slave bikini.

Cartoons - Droids & Ewoks
www.lucasfan.com/animated/animated.html
Ewoks and droids both had their own TV series, just like Star Trek. At this LucasFan.com site, you can find pictures and videos of the cartoons, all organized and well-presented. You don't have to wait til Saturday morning!

Cast & Characters (Prequel)
http://members.aol.com/capeman69/cast.html
Early list of Prequel cast and rumors and info about them. Page is composed by Capeman69. Rumor: James Earl Jones will only do Vader voice-over in Episode 3.

Cast Lists - Knight Hammer
www.geocities.com/Area51/Chamber/4182/cast_tpm.html
Even the Imperials have cast lists from the Star Wars movies - this lists each movie and the actors twice, once under the character and again by real name (Imperial-types have trouble separating the real from the fictional).

CCG: The Imperial Domination Sites List
www.webring.org/cgi-bin/webring?index&ring=empire
47 sites from the Empire Star Wars Customizable Card Game Ring is primarily attuned to SW:CCG game playing.

Celebrity Message Boards (Lycos Network)
http://boards.lycos.com/cgi-bin/WebX?13@32.1eteaz6maFa^2@.ee6b348
Can't promise the above URL address is correct, but it got us to the searchable Lycos Celebrity message boards (or try the alternate URL). Find your favorite celebrity and sign in and do postings or read them. A deluxe rumor-mill.

Cg-Char Mailing List for 3D CG Character Animators
www.cg-char.com
Here's the listings for the 3D artists who specialize in character graphics. Also, there is a discussion field. We doubt that rank amateurs are welcomed, but those with a sincere interest can try to join in.

Characters of Star Wars Official Index
www.starwars.com/www.starwars.com
Subject Directory web page by Lucasfilms from which most Star Wars characters are linked - from Auntie Beru to Wicket the Ewok. Essential background material is one click away.

Chat Server - Echo Station Interactive
www.echostation.com/chat
Brings contributors to the Star Wars universe online for you to talk to. You'll find a schedule of appearances, also archives of previous chats: producer McCallum, artists, writers Michael Stackpole, Jeanne Cevalos, Ann Crispin.

Chewbacca Galleries (Taz's)
http://seconn4.yoda.com/~vader97/chewie/chewie.html
Two JPEG picture galleries of Chewbacca the Wookiee in all sorts of scenes. Files are a little slow to load, but worth it. Also, see Taz's other character galleries via his main page.

Chewbacca Homepage, The New
http://users.ids.net/~mtavares/chewie.html
Modern Chewie site that runs Java applets. Gallery is filled with many best-ever Chewie images. WAVs sound files list an assortment of growls, also Han's Fuzzball and "it's not wise to upset a Wookiee" quotes. In Miscellaneous, find autographs of Mayhew, Prowse, Baker & Bulloch.

Chewbacca the Wookiee
www.starwars.com/characters/chewbacca
Lucasfilms page for Chewbacca, compadre to Han Solo. Like all official character Pages, text and info is a bit thin and pix are limited but well-posed, but it is easy to link to other official sites. Click on Chewy for a full-color still.

Chewie's Web Page
www.music.uh.edu/~chewie
Well-constructed site, with Chewie art and views. Sights, sounds, poll, news, and a new Cantina page with chat.

Chewie's Web Site Pictures & Sounds
www.music.uh.edu/~chewie/ps.html
WAV sound clips gallery from Episode 1 - "Once those droids take control - they'll take control of you", also memorable quotes from the Trilogy - "It's not wise to upset a Wookiee." Lengths of files given, with text. Also, humorous South Park sounds and Park Wars video.

Chico's Star Wars Video & Music
http://chico.simplenet.com
Video clips (and some audio) from first 3 movies, plus some great action pix, posters, and downloadable items. Miscellaneous section has clips of cast interviews, games, & other rarities. Use the frame link to the chat room.

Chiv's Star Wars Page
http://highlander.cbnet.ns.ca/~bchivari/star/star.html
Multimedia site presented by Brad Chivari, with sounds, video clips, images, also trivia, transcripts, screensavers & themes to download for your computer.

Christmas Pictures
www.jedinet.com/multimedia/pics/xmas/index.html
Jedinet's collection of JPEG images for the merry holiday season. Various Yoda Santas, C-3PO & R2s.

Cita Delle Nuvole (Cloud City)
www.geocities.com/Area51/Corridor/1431
An Italian multimedia sites with the nice airy flavor of lovely Bespin. Find downloads of MP3 audio and MPEG video here - we cannot guarantee they will be in English. Order videos in Italian. FAQ and multimedia goodies.

Classified Military Plan - Secret (Example)
www.geocities.com/Area51/Corridor/4309/secret.html
   This data could be very valuable to - to the right people. An examle of a roleplaying message page, probably useful in a game scenario. It is tech info about an Imperial 3-class Star destroyer.

Cloud City
www.starwars.com/locations/cloud_city
   Lucasfilms page for Cloud City, floating high above gaseous planet Bespin. Temporary home to Lando Calrissian, Cloud City closed out The Empire Strikes Back. We assume the city floats to this day, kinda like Las Vegas.

Clubs of Star Wars on Yahoo
http://clubs.yahoo.com/Entertainment___Arts/Movies/Genres/Science_Fiction_and_Fantasy/Titles/Star_Wars_Series/index.html
   Yahoo hosts more than 3 dozen clubs - fan clubs, message boards, Girls Only Star Wars Club, Young Jedi Knights, Bob Fett Rules, The Star Wars Bar, The Han Soloists - Take a look see!

Collecting (the force.net)
www.theforce.net/collecting
   Find hints and advance warning about many of the collectible products that are supposed to be out there. Pizza Hut, Pepsi cans (JPEG images of 24 of the 25), and an archives of news on Legos, games, hobby stuff, and more.

Comic Book (Unnamed)
www.geocities.com/Area51/Corridor/7410/pg1.html
   Don't know if the artist forgot to name it or if he's just waiting for a suggestion or encouragement. An original Star Wars comic book venture - your comments are welcome.

Comics & Covers - Thrawn Art Gallery
http://empire.res.wabash.edu/art/comics/index.htm
   Colorful collection of JPEG images of Star Wars comic books and covers. To find more covers here, click on the thumbnail; it opens a new image. See Shadows of the Empire, Golden Age of Sith, X-wing Rogue Squad, Heir.

Comlink, The
www.outer-rim.net/multimedia/sounds.htm
   Awards good Star Wars sites and "profiles" them, and for older sites, puts them in an archive called the "garbage chute." Lists the "comlink" and Star Wars sound of the month. Sounds archives arranged by subject/character.

Compendium, The
www.wcug.wwu.edu/~paradox/images/hyper
   Hard to describe: too much information about all aspects of Star Wars & roleplaying. Characters, powers, history, EP1 galleries, huge image galleries, commentaries, scripts, downloads, chat, holonet, hardware, game info.

Completely Phat Star Wars Site
www.perfekt.net/~snoopy/video/video.html
   Site says: all movies located on a T3 server - your leech should run at light speed. Can't guarantee it, but this site has Special Edition videos, EP1 Trailer Version 3 (2:11 min.), :35 seconds IMAX Destroyer, & Pepsi commercial.

Complete Star Wars Prequel Page 🖼 👁
http://outland.cyberwar.com/~smad//Prequels.html
> This lively Prequel site was formerly the Star Wars Prequel Pics page and has now expanded, boasting a super "running news" section (with archives). Site includes pictures, "speculation," cast list, links, and "I don't get it" (Q's & A's about continuity in the Trilogy).

Complete Star Wars Timeline
www.swdatabase.com/pages/time.html
> This timeline says when things happen in the grand scheme of Star Wars. It is also a database that can be used for writers of fan fiction, and for fans generally. Entries by title, type and time. List by Mark "Rogue Leader" Wieck.

Completely Unofficial Star Wars Encyclopedia 6th Edition 🔍 👁
www.mindspring.com/~bobvitas/swenc.htm
> Stumped on what a M-g2 is or the Mayagil System? Find out in the Encyclopedia. Alphabetized; easy to search, it lists planets & races, cast & crew, chronology, timeline, numerics & arcana. Updates often.

Computer Generated Artwork (the force.net) 👁
www.theforce.net/Skystation/artscrn.html
> Computer generated original art works - and very good. This is the first of many pages that link via theforce.net Skystation site. Images appear to be signed (copyright implied). (See also "CG" profiles.)

Concerts - Star Wars Episode 1: The Music
http://members.es.tripod.de/Befan/Episode1music_Concerts.html
> Collection of scheduled concerts for John Williams or Star Wars-related symphonic or pop music. Dates, times, featured performers, links, Tanglewood schedule, also whether the concert is sold out.

Conduit 9
www.conduit.utah.edu/program.html
> Utah University non-profit club sponsors Sci-fi events, live roleplaying games, local Sci-fi movie showings, miniatures, models, story contests. Keeps atop sci-fi hot topics & CONduit conventions in Salt Lake City area.

Continuum, The
www.the-continuum.com
> Variety of online games and flight simulators (no Star Wars when we visited; there should be some there now).

🖼 IMAGES   🎬 VIDEO   🔊 AUDIO
👁 MUST SEE! $ SELLS STUFF   ADULT CONTENT   🔍 SEARCHABLE
CHAT ROOMS   MESSAGE BOARDS   MAILING LISTS

Conventions (the force.net) 👁
http://theforce.net/main/cons.shtml
   A tight calendar of Star Wars related events - confabs from Plano, Texas to the Big Apple Comic Book Show.

Coruscant Project at Ord Mantell 🎬
www.geocities.com/Area51/Lair/8349/txindex.html
   An index page for the history, pix, and movie clips on Coruscant - looks like it could be a great place.

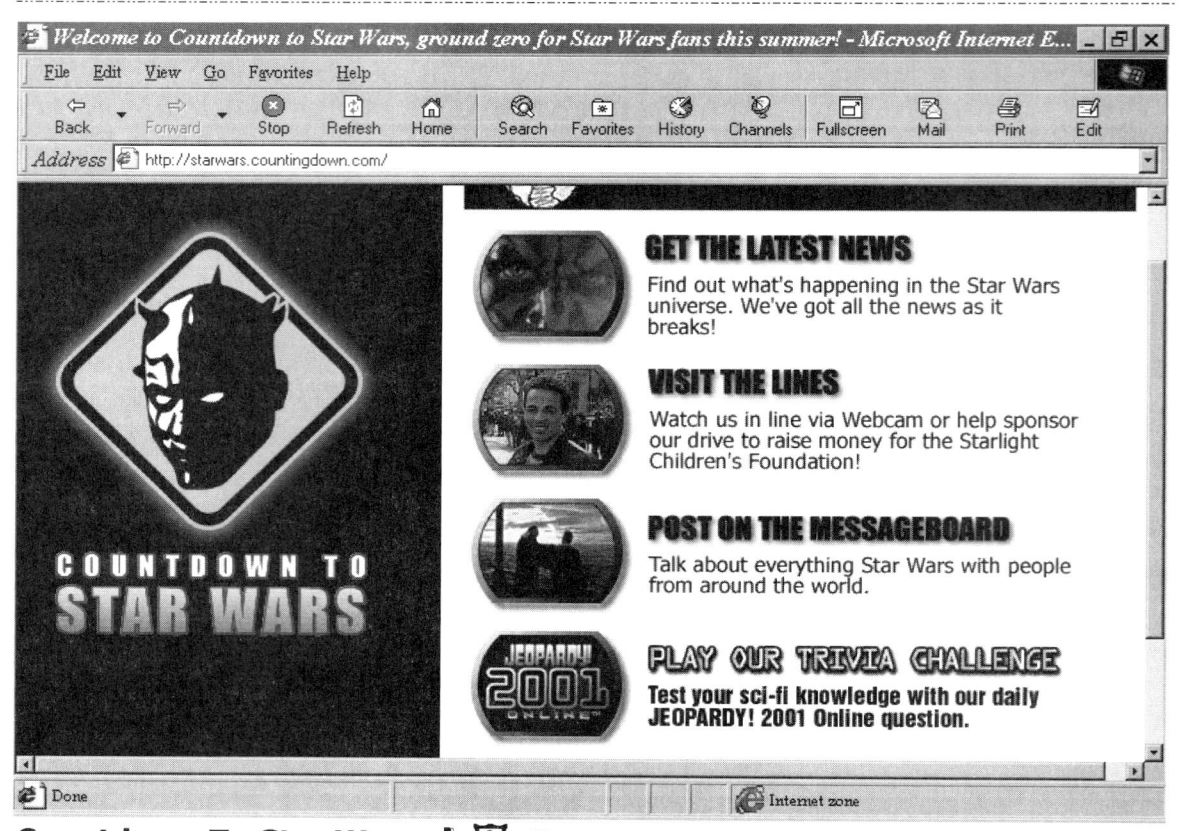

Countdown To Star Wars ⚓ 🏛 👁
http://starwars.countingdown.com
   The countdown to the launch of Phantom Menace is over. Some crazy guys who specialize in "countdowns to openings" did put up this site with "Star Wars countdown news, comments, media stories, etc." It became huge.

Countingdown Star Wars Forum ⚓ 👁
http://countingdown.com/starwars/forum
   Before the Episode 1 opening, this site was so busy it was hard to get on. Forum is operated by countingdown.com group who listed about 100 forums plus live computer access from the line at Mann's Chinese Theater Hollywood.

Covers to Star Wars Products 🏛
http://members.xoom.com/kessel/outpost/cover.html
   There's a gallery for everything else, why not a gallery of covers for Star Wars video tape boxes? There's also a cover to a Dave Dorman Star Wars art book.

Crazy Star Wars Galaxy ⚓

http://clubs.yahoo.com/clubs/thecrazystarwarsgalaxy

It's not a gang - it's a club. Belushi said that. This club, sponsored by Yahoo, lets you join and post and read messages that are like taking a walk in a wild galaxy of Star Wars, they say.

Creative Impulse, The

www.cwrl.utexas.edu/~daniel/309m/project4/christal/lucas.html

Is George Lucas merely a filmmaker? The question is expanded upon and "the creative juices" analyzed in this thought-grinding article/essay by Daniel Christal, John Sumpter, & David Morse. This is a good Lucus tribute.

Clicket.com Star Wars Gallery $ 🖼

www.clicket.com/clicket/swgal/swgal.html

Full-serve costume site makes shopping/ordering easy. Find adult, kid, and new Prequel Costumes here (kid Jawa, Yoda, Tusken Raiders), also posters, ties, life-sized stand-ups, Chromart collectibles.

Criminal Organizations in Star Wars, The Index to

http://index.echostation.com/crime.html

Since the Imperial Empire is concerned mostly with power, it's not surprising to find a vast criminal underground at work as well, operating in the shadows like a Russian mafia. Here's a list of those who smuggle, take bribes, and profit illegally - or try to. (May be shut down by authorities)

Crossover Universe

http://pages.prodigy.com/crossover

Crossovers are when you combine elements of one subject with elements of another, usually with humorous or satirical results. As you can image, Star Wars has more than its fair share of faux pas to exploit. Find pages that feature them, with commentaries, also other shows.

Cult of Piett Member Sites

www.piett.org/link.html

Admiral Piett had the unenviable task of serving under Darth Vader - a sure way to a quick end - so it's only fitting the Piett be somehow immortalized on the web - by a number of international sites! Here's the Cult Linklist, along with other tributes to Star Wars bit-part warriors.

🖼 IMAGES   🎬 VIDEO   📢 AUDIO

👁 MUST SEE! $ SELLS STUFF   ADULT CONTENT   🔍 SEARCHABLE

🗣 CHAT ROOMS   📥 MESSAGE BOARDS   📬 MAILING LISTS

Cultural Abstractions Index
http://index.echostation.com/cult.html
So, you don't know what to wear to an Ewok festival, much less what to expect at their Sascension Ritual of the Hoods? In addition to cultural mores, find slang from other languages at this site. A "Xeno" is a rude term for an alien, so don't say it in polite society.

Cursors & Icons
www.jedinet.com/multimedia/windows/cursors/index.htm
The wee liddle things for your computer. At this Jedinet resource site you'll find two zipped icon files to download. Imperial vehicle icons might discourage others from messing with you and your computer.

Da Quotes
www.geocities.com/Area51/Chamber/4182/quotes.html
Found on the "Imperial" Knight Hammer site, these quotes are arranged by topic, i.e. Yoda, the Force, love, "responsibility," about father & son, also the characters' quotes. Many quotes accompanied by a WAV sound file.

Daala's Quarters
www.geocities.com/Area51/Chamber/4182/admiral.html

Why aren't there more Imperial female officers? Here's a page for Imperial Admiral Daala, found via the Knight Hammer Imperial web site. Fearing that we might see something we shouldn't, we didn't view her statisitcs, quotes or images pages, although you might.

Dagobah
www.execpc.com/~zerob/Dagobah.html
It IS a cool site, R2, it is! Main page lists actors and their credits, also TV Now links that list shows and times when that actor appears this month. Master Yoda has much more - news, clippings, Prequels, pix, other surprises.

Dagobah Official Site
www.starwars.com/locations/dagobah
Lucasfilms site for swampy planet Dagobah, home of Yoda in Empire Strikes Back. Page is a bit thin with only a couple pix, some local links, and a little background material on the small, wise Jedi.

Dagobah - or - Yoda, The Jedi Master
http://207.79.146.3/employees/jamieb/art.htm
We're not sure what the site name is, but we are "sure" of the excellent galleries of JPEG images of posters, covers and original art collections of Dave Dorman, Ralph McQuarrie, John Alvin, Drew Struzan. Also has a miscellaneous artists collection. File sizes are listed.

Dagobah System, The
http://members.aol.com/Yoda328/index.html
Renamed William Barefoot's Home Page, this sports a small pix gallery; more on the way. Leaning toward Yoda.

Daisy Hill Village
www.angelfire.com/fl/yubcantina/daisyhill.html
Want to join an Ewok village, and you live in the England? At publication time, Daisy Hill village is in its infancy - but that's how Ewok villages start - small. Anyone can visit.

Daniel Feith's Star Wars Videos 🎬
www.germany.net/teilnehmer/101/78382/Star-Wars.html
 Find a selection of QuickTime Videos on this German site. File names are in German - there's a surprise in store when you view these files.

Danny's Super Star Wars Page 🖼️ 🔊
www.geocities.com/Area51/Comet/3947/index.html
 Substantial collection of pix and sounds in MIDI format including J. Williams' Star Wars music theme.

Dark Horizons 🎬 👁️
www.darkhorizons.com/index2.html
 Australia's Garth Franklin provides video trailers, news & rumors, '99 film index, weekly reports (UK, US, AUS), reviews, release dates, film archives, box office figures, TV guides (X-files, Buffy, Xena), & place to submit info.

Dark Horizons Film Trailers 🎬 👁️
www.darkhorizons.com/trailers/index-n.htm
 General collection of almost all movie trailers, including the Wing Commander commericial and the Prequel trailers. Download the various movie players here. Frequently updated.

Dark Horse Comics $ 🔍 👁️
www.dhorse.com
 Great official comic book source for Star Wars, with feature stories, archives, and related Sci-fi titles.

Dark Hunters 🖼️
www.homestead.com/DarkHunters/index.html
 Enter if you dare, smugglers and internet spies! These reborn bounty hunter pages open with a big pic of a death star. Inside you'll find good graphics, bounty hunter lore, bounty hunter poll, guestbook, bios and more: Imperial Spy Network webring, webring FAQ, form, & sign-up.

Dark Lords of Sith
www.method.org/sith
 As part of the Sith online family of pages, here you'll find biographies of Darth, Exar Kun, and links to other evil Sith characters whom you wouldn't want to meet in a dark alley. No pix, however. Rats!

Dark Lords of Sith Trivia Test 👁️
www.geocities.com/TelevisionCity/Stage/5455/swtrivia.html
 Winse & Cameron's trivia test features three levels - Farmboy trivia (easy), Flight Cadet trivia (kinda harder), and Jedi master's trivia (fanatics only). Opens with an excellent large Darth Vader photo.

Dark Rising
http://home.sol.no/~mgrambo/index2.htm
>Not a very active site, this does have galleries of movie clips, sounds, and photos, also a news section and survey results. Seems to editorialize. True to its name, site frames are dark, but subject matter isn't.

Dark Side of Star Wars
www.geocities.com/Area51/Vault/2674/index2.html
>Don't worry, the title is the darkest thing about this Johan Lundin site. Links to several webrings and a modest collection of sounds. Also, find scripts and a variety of off-site links.

Dark Side Rumors
http://sw.simplenet.com/darkside
>E-mail in your rumors or just your wild and whacky observations - editorialize, wax prophetic, or rationalize your butt off - or just share something you heard. Everyone else here does. Goes from current comments, back 2 years.

Dark Side, The - Jedi Academy Lesson
www.jediacademy.com/dark.htm
>No, Bill Gates is not the Dark Side (on the contrary, his MicroSoft company has enabled us to have our own PCs, letting all enjoy Star Wars on the Internet). Jedi Academy presents the Dark Side page to comment on the evil of evil, something that all Jedi (and humankind) need to be aware of.

Darth Vader
www.starwars.com/characters/darth_vader
>Lucasfilms page for Darth Vader, with general fictional bio and official links to other dark side characters and locations - links to short stories about better characters as well. Click on Darth's photo for his official color still.

Darth Vader Galleries (Taz's)
http://seconn4.yoda.com/~vader97/darth/darth.html
>Taz has arranged 3 galleries of JPEG images of Mr. Vader - sir! Images take a while to load; quality is quite good.

Darth Vader Song, The
http://198.70.186.7/enterhtml/live/Kidz/vader.html
>Can you sing me a song about Darth Vader, asks a little boy. The answer comes in a song in AVI file format, courtesy of Megapis Enormous. It takes a look at the "good vs. evil" thing.

Darth Vader's TIE Fighter
www.starwars.com/vehicles/vaders_tie_fighter
>The stand-out design of Darth's personal TIE fighter makes it recognizable as the Imperial craft that almost saved the original Death Star from destruction - almost. Like the other official pages, this one is not deep in specs or pix.

Dash Rendar's Star Wars Universe
www.angelfire.com/wi/SciFiPlace
>Dash Rendar has his own spaceship; it look a lot like the Falcon. Usually, Dash is off "on some wild, idealistic crusade" so this page is not always as smooth as it should be. It used to have a lot of spunk.

Dash's Star Wars Mania
http://members.tripod.com/~Dash88/index.html
Solid collection of Trilogy images, animated pix and sounds, also good collection of nit-piks from Trilogy movies.

Dash's Star Wars Mania Nitpicks Page
http://members.tripod.com/~Dash88/nodead.html
Here's a list of all the little mistakes and bloopers from the movies, called nit-piks. Next time you watch the movies, watch for these mistakes.

Dave's Star Wars HUB
http://empire.res.wabash.edu
Choose high or low graphics versions to access resources such as Thrawn's art gallery, New Republic Intelligence HQ, Holonet Booth, Vader's Castle, or the search field. Site from Wabash Univ. IN.

David Jansen's Star Wars Page
www.strw.leidenuniv.nl/~jansen/sw
No longer maintained, but has good basic links (arranged by category) to go along with its galleries of sounds, images, and "fortune cookie" quotes - like a Star Wars quote of the day.

David Prowse - All-Media Guide
http://allmovie.com/cg/x.dll?UID=9:01:46|PM&p=avg&sql=B57960
His voice wasn't used in Star Wars, but his presence was - read about British actor David Prowse and his filmography on the All-Media Guide Database. Could you spot him in "A Clockwork Orange?" He played Frankenstein, once; also was a champion weightlifter.

Deak's Den
http://frodo.hiof.no/~deak/audio/miniwav.html
Good selection of WAV sound files from the Trilogy. To get to the MP3s, go to bottom of the page and click on "MPEG Audio Layers3, 52 files." Link to 11 MIDI music files and 3 Sun audio files. Segments described, sized.

Death Star I
www.starwars.com/locations/deathstar
It's not a planet, it's not a star - it is your worst nightmare. This is the Lucasfilm site for the thing you love to see get blown to white-hot little bits. The page isn't very tech specific; you'll see Leia in the Death Star Detention area.

Death Star II
www.starwars.com/locations/deathstar_ii/index.html
Like the first Death Star, there is an official web page for lethal Death Star II, even though it was destroyed before completion. Find basic storyline tie-ins for end scenes of Return of the Jedi, but nothing about the fabulous construction of this awesome piece of equipment.

Death Star Trench
www.starwars.com/locations/deathstar_trench
What exactly is a death star trench, anyway? Here is the Lucasfilms official "page" for that canyon that Luke has to fly down in the end of Star Wars A New Hope. Did the second Death Star also have a trench, or did the Imperial Empire learn from its mistakes?

IMAGES VIDEO AUDIO
MUST SEE! SELLS STUFF ADULT CONTENT SEARCHABLE
CHAT ROOMS MESSAGE BOARDS MAILING LISTS

Death Stars, Technical Commentaries
www.theforce.net/swtc/ds.html
So, you want to know all about Death Stars? Here you'll find just about everything you need to know - where the sub-light drive nozzles are, etc. More likely, you're interested in the size of a typical Death Star, and detail pix.

Debo's House of Star Wars WAV Site
http://houseofdebo.simplenet.com/wavhouse/starwars.html
"You're not permitted in here" and a gob-zillion other WAV sound bites from the Trilogy - 7 files for R2-D2 alone. Find Jabba's laugh and Jawa yells. "I've been waiting for you, Obiwan" - Darth.

Deck Plans (for Star Wars)
www.geocities.com/Area51/Labyrinth/6246/DP.html
Intended as a RPG game resource, this site has specs for Star Wars spacecraft including scouts, escape pods, and light freighters. Also, there's plans for a couple of new droids. Site connects to the Hidden Temple of Tharizdun (Fantastic Realms) RPG site, with dieties.

Delta Source
www.jedinet.com/delta
Jedinet has scoured the galaxy for Star Wars info arranging it in these Delta Source files. Easy to use directories include Weapons (30), vehicles, planets & locales, characters, battles & events. You can contribute to these files.

Den, The
www.theden.com
The Den (at the Daily Entertainment Network) gives you a daily rush of movie news, TV news, Sci-fi news, links to gaming news, also a survey (like: "Your favorite movie candy is?" 1answer: - sh*t I snuck in"), postings, links to a review site, and light barbs. Find a video, occasionally.

Description About Star Wars' Vessels
www.civila.com/hispania/obi-juan/ship.txtwww.civila.com/hispania/obi-juan/ship.txt
Text with straight-scoop specifications about Star Wars craft. From Obi-Juans site in Spain.

Design Originals of Episode 1; Doug Chiang's Portfolio
www.starwars.com/episode-i/features/chiang
Star Wars Episode 1 chief artist Doug Chang talks about designs, objectives, and his work generally on the Prequel. Pix are of his original art, used as samples to illustrate the official site text.

Desktop - Star Wars: A Feminine Perspective
http://members.aol.com/bananie42/desktop.html
Download & unzip these files to find 65 cursors and 140 icons for your computer. 1 typestyle: the StarVader font.

Digital Blasphemy
www.digitalblasphemy.com
This site offers 3D wallpaper, startup screens and tutorials on making 3D art. Not specific to Star Wars, the galleries include space vehicles, scenery and planetscapes.

Dioramas at Louis Inman's Fett's Place
http://members.aol.com/lfett/custom/diorama.htm
Linklist of dioramas from a number of modeling artists - Inman, Moff Peter, Brandon Vise, Gruner, Steve Myers. Click the underlined link to open the image at its webpage. See, you can do a lot with those figurines, a little poster paint, and some imagination.

Dioramas at Moff Peter's Dominion 🖼 👁

http://members.aol.com/moffpeter/www/diorama.html
Excellent collection of about 45 dioramas that incorporate Star Wars miniature figures in the hope of producing a lifelike image - not easily done by mere mortals. These look like CG but they aren't.

Dioramas Maintained by Gus Lopez 🖼

www.toysrgus.com/images-displays.html
It is a work of art to take a lump-of-clay action figure or model spacecraft and turn it into a scene that looks like it's right out of the movies, or CG. Here's collected dioramas featuring Lopez, Schloegl, Ketzer, Nitkin, Filippis.

Directory of multimedia/realvideo 🎬

www.lucasfan.com/multimedia/realvideo
Short collection of Star Wars RealVideo clips, octect-stream. Also contains a RealAudio file.

Disgruntled Ewok & Malcontent Jawas Page

http://netdial.caribe.net/~orinoco/jae.html
Actually, we didn't find them that cranky. You'll find an uplifting translation of the Ewok victory song here, also the Jawa's Nit-piks, Pointless Humor, & Useless Star Wars Activities. It's pretty useless.

DJ Rhythm's Dance Music Database 🔊

www.djrhythms.com/db
DJ Rhythm's Dance Music Database is a catalog containing a good many pop/club dance music releases of the past 3 decades. Tracks included are of a variety of musical genres, and includes Meco's Star Wars disco versions.

Don Post's Studios Star Wars Masks $ 👁

www.nightmarefactory.com/starwars.html
Great collection of Trilogy & Prequel masks - some rare - from Darth to Ewoks, also gloves for alien costumes. Limited edition collectors masks, pod helmets, deluxe trooper & fighter helmets, Queen Amidala, Palpatine, more.

Dr. Itos Star Wars Images 🖼

http://www1.iastate.edu/~dritos/pix.html
There really is a Dr. Itos at iastate.edu, and the good doctor has collected a JPEG image gallery of what he says is really big pix (big size, not big number). This has the biggest TIE fighter we've seen.

Dreaming of Mark Hamill

http://members.xoom.com/DreamingofMH
Get this: when we visited this site, the author named Celene was asking if anyone wanted to take over this great site dedicated to Mark. It was a really warm and lovey-dovie site; syrupy but nice.

Dreams of Space:
Space Art in Children's Books 🖼

http://sun3.lib.uci.edu/~jsisson/john.htm
Depictions of space in children's books of the 1950s-1970s. Includes bios on the artists and samples.

🖼 IMAGES   🎬 VIDEO   🔊 AUDIO
👁 MUST SEE! $ SELLS STUFF   ADULT CONTENT   🔍 SEARCHABLE
CHAT ROOMS   MESSAGE BOARDS   MAILING LISTS

Droid Files - Tech Specs
http://members.aol.com/candyfish/droidfiles.htm
> From Cathy's Droidshrine, here's the details on C-3PO and R2, also pix. C-3PO is gold except for his knee joint down, which is silver? R2 has developed the ability to lie - pretty good for a little guy, huh?

Droidcentric Art & Fan Fiction
http://members.aol.com/candyfish/gateway.htm
> Like its mothership page (Droidshrine), this is the C3-PO & R2-D2 droid repair shop of fan fiction, pictures, images, and droid-isms on an eye-piercing orange/skyblue/tan background. These must be official droid colors.

Droids
www.starwars.com/droids
> The Lucasfilms page for robotic creatures from A-Z. Not all the droids in Star Wars lore - just the key ones in the movies, like Too-OneBee, medical droid, the non-human miracle working expert who keeps Luke up and running.

Droids-Weapons (Star Wars Force Graphics)
http://plaza.harmonix.ne.jp/~m-falcon/c-3po.html
> Poster images (JPEG files) of droids, lightsabers, blasters, denonators - find excellent images on this Japanese site.

Droidshrine - Oh, Thank The Maker
http://members.aol.com/candyfish/droidshrine.htm
> Dedicated to R2 & C-3PO, the most ignored heroes in the universe - until now! Droidshrine's wonderful author Cathy has editorials, Prequel news, forum, tech files, fan art/fiction, droids & more droids! Not fancy - just droids!

Droidstuff
http://members.aol.com/fishdroid/Droidstuff.htm
> Found on the Droidshrine site, here's an eclectic collection of ha-ha droidstuff. Not everyone has an Anthony Daniels autographed picture - this site does!

Droopy McCool's Star Wars Page
www.geocities.com/SunsetStrip/Disco/1283/starwars.html
> Image gallery of GIF pix from the Phantom Menace. Also, black and white pix of the four main characters: Jake Lloyd, Natalie Portman, Ewan MacGregor, Liam Neeson.

Duel of Darth Vader & Obi-wan Kenobi Video
www.telecom.csuhayward.edu/~aleung/dv_ken.mov
> Video clip of the famous light sabre duel of Darth Vader and Obi-Wan from Star Wars A New Hope.

Dune Sea
www.starwars.com/locations/dune_sea
> On planet Tatooine, the only place more inhospitable than the Jundland Wastes is the Dune Sea on this Lucasfilms location page. Click on the image at the left to go to the full-color Dune Sea picture with herding bantas.

E187vader's Favorite WAV & AU Sounds
www.geocities.com/Area51/Vault/6782/wavs.html
> Site title about says it all. Files are mostly Vader clips: "No disintegrations." Also Han, Yoda, Lando, Emperor, and Leia's acid lines, like: "The more you tighten your grip, the more star systems will slip through your fingers."

E187vader's Special Edition Page
www.geocities.com/Area51/Vault/6782/special.html
A very-seldom visited pix gallery of Special Edition GIF and JPEG images. Here you'll find the dancers at Jabba's palace and other shots not seen in the original Trilogy.

E187vader's Star Wars Empire
www.geocities.com/Area51/Vault/6782/frames.html
Opens with Vader's favorite picture - him putting the choke on the hapless Commander Antilles at the beginning of A New Hope. Not a high traffic site, it does have Special Edition JPEG image gallery and WAV & AU sounds.

EarthStation1's Movie Sounds Showcase: Star Wars WAVs
http://earthstation1.simplenet.com/starwars.html
"You are part of a rebel alliance and a spy" - and a host of other Trilogy WAV sound files. The format is a bit unusual: click on the moviemaker/man to open a sound. "Your powers are weak old man."

---

eBay
www.ebay.com
eBay is arguably the largest online auction service. Type in "Star Wars" in the search field - we generally get 8000+ hits on Star Wars items for sale. You may want to make your search more "specific." Buy or sell here.

---

eBay Listings: Star Wars Toys
http://listings.ebay.com/aw/listings/list/category751/index.html
Auction off or buy Star Wars action figures, collectibles, toys, Yoda furbies, new or vintage items - our last visit here found 136 big pages (not counting the non-kid stuff)! You want it? "It" is probably here.

Echo Station
www.echostation.com
Echo Station ranks as one of the top Star Wars sites and a "must see." Home page has news, new departments, new books, plus pages on everything - almost. Find a crossword, 3D, roleplaying, free e-mail, events, ICQ, store.

Echo Station Event Guide
www.echostation.com/events/index.htm
So, except for some movies, you haven't experienced a Star Wars in-person event in awhile - or not ever! Have you been stuck on Dagobah!? Here's listings of events in the US and internationally, with prices, times, details.

Echo Station Interactive Store
www.echostation.com/shop/index.htm
To make it easier to find Star Wars toys, books, music, novels, collectibles, action figures, games, software, movies, kid products - everything - all in one place, Echo Station put together this great Star Wars Outlet Mall.

IMAGES   VIDEO   AUDIO
MUST SEE!   SELLS STUFF   ADULT CONTENT   SEARCHABLE
CHAT ROOMS   MESSAGE BOARDS   MAILING LISTS

Edis Krad's Online Bookshop $ ♀ 👁
http://george.lucas.net/edis.htm
> This looks to be an official store for genuine Lucas and Star Wars books, also Jim Henson's No String's Attached - Creature Shop book. The site also links back to the tour of Skywalker Ranch and ILM (Industrial Light & Magic) production facilities. Search for any book through the amazon.com field.

Editorials - Echo Station Emag
http://emag.echostation.com/editorials/index.htm
> The online magazine "Emag" lets the opinions fly in their editorials! Not whacky - these writers are thoughtful and the insights give us a good view of challenges in the Star Wars universe. There's fun stuff, too, BobaFerret.

El Camino's Star Wars Page 🎬 🔊
www.geocities.com/Area51/Rampart/4264/ie4.htm
> A bit more involved than the usual geocities Star Wars multimedia page, this has links to a good photo gallery and author's favorite role-playing sites, MUDDs, music, videos, scripts and other fun.

El Camino's Star Wars Pictures 🎬
www.geocities.com/Area51/Rampart/4264/pics.htm
> 80+ character photos in JPEG format, with some GIFs. Most of the characters are covered; most are official Lucasfilm stills. Click on the blue links to open and view the pictures.

Electric GIFs 🎬
www.electricgifs.com
> Enter STAR WARS into the search field, hit search, and it will locate 25 popular Star Wars GIF image files in a second. Click on links to view, then download them to add to your own Star Wars web site.

Elite Star Wars Webring: The Best in the Galaxy 👁
www.shavenwookie.com/elitering.html
> 80 selected sites comprise this webring list, administered by Shaven Wookie. Excludes porn and hateful Star Trek sites. Sites were examined for content, accessibility, and quality. Link lists or galleries are generally not included.

Emag - Echo Station 👁
http://emag.echostation.com
> Echo Station's Internet magazine "Emag" has a Cantina-like selection of Star Wars lifestyle-related features (games, collectibles, comics) and the usual stuff you find in magazines: editorials, book reviews, pictures, humor, interviews and that catch-all: "features."

emerchandise $ 🎬 ♀
http://www2.emerchandise.com/consumer
> Ready to shop? Use emerchandise's "-Movies-" browse button to find a Star Wars movie, then hit "go." From "Category: Star Wars" you select any of the product categories. Say you want a Darth Vader cap, or a Chewbacca tie-dye t-shirt? How about a mousepad? Shop til you drop.

Emperor Palpatine
www.starwars.com/characters/palpatine
> Menacing, evil emperor Palpatine is explained somewhat on this official Lucasfilms character site. The sorry sorcerer may wish to forward his resume to the next casting for the ghost of Christmas Future.

Emperor Palpatine Archive 🎬 👁
http://seconn4.yoda.com/~vader97/emperor/emperor.html
> There is no one more evil than Emperor Palpatine - why would anyone want a picture of him? Taz has collected a gallery of over 20 Palpatine images, some from the Phantom Menace. All are disturbing.

Empire Strikes Back Portfolio 👁
www.bantha-fodder.com/esbport
   Another of the excellent Star Wars Portfolios by the masterful artist Ralph McQuarrie.

Empire Strikes Back Special Edition FAQ 🖼
www.jax-inter.net/users/datalore/starwars/esbindex.htm
   Not really FAQ pages, but commentaries called "Threadwells' List of Changes to - " -- all about the new scenes in the Empire Strikes Back Special Edition. Nice images illustrate the scene changes. The site is well organized. See similar Threadwell pages for A New Hope and Return of the Jedi.

Empire Strikes Back Transcript
www.geocities.com/Area51/Stargate/9082/Empire.txt
   Final version of The Empire Strikes back by Kasdan and Brackett, story by George Lucas.

Empire Strikes Back Video Clips 🎬
http://home.multiweb.nl/~bramenpim/staresb.htm
   Good selection of video clips from Empire Strikes Back, including George Lucas explaining and showing the new Cloud City effects, also Sci-fi Channel's commercial. The new Wampa scene is included and favorites like the Falcon escaping the asteroid cave. (Some files were down)

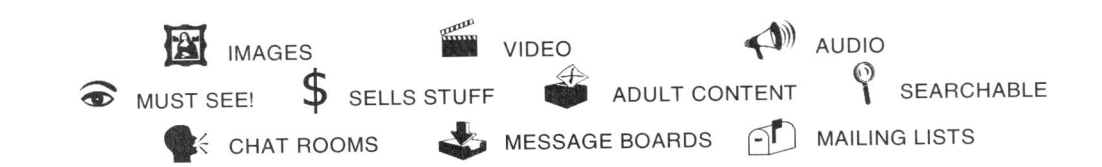

🖼 IMAGES   🎬 VIDEO   🔊 AUDIO

👁 MUST SEE! $ SELLS STUFF   ADULT CONTENT   🔍 SEARCHABLE

CHAT ROOMS   MESSAGE BOARDS   MAILING LISTS

Empire Strikes Back, The
www.starwars.com/episode-v
> Official Lucafilms page for Episode V. Here are links to other places and characters in Empire, along with pix. Find facts about the movie - good basic background material.

Empire Strikes Back, The (1980) $? 👁
http://us.imdb.com/Title?0080684
> Internet Movie db's fabulous info page gives cast, plot line, credits, genre, user ratings, and links to other entries in the database, and to an online store to purchase videos, soundtracks, books. Did you know Jeremy Bullock (Boba Fett) can also be seen playing Lt. Sheckil?

Endor
www.starwars.com/locations/endor
> Officially, The Forest Moon of Endor, home of the Ewoks. From this official Lucasfilms page you can see and read about Endor, then quickly cruise to other related official pages.

Episode 1 Characters Addresses 📪
www.geocities.com/Area51/Nebula/5101/main.html
> World's Greatest Star Wars Webpage has a growing list of addresses and autographed pix (when available) of actors in Episode 1. Write to Ian McDiarmid (Palpatine), Liam, Frank Oz, Natalie Portman, & Samuel L. Jackson.

Episode 1 Humor Pages 🖼
www.theforce.net/humor/episodei
> The force.net's Episode 1 humor page rounds up posters, pictures, and comic strips - all for a few yuks. See "rumored" Prequel focus problems, The Bart Menace, Got Milk, You've Got Maul. All in fun.

Episode 1 Multimedia (the force.net) 🖼 🎬 🔊
www.theforce.net/multimedia/epi.shtml
> The force.net is among the top collectors of Star Wars materials, so you'd expect this Episode 1 multimedia site to be top-notch. They've done a grand job of collecting one of just about everything among pictures, sounds, videos!

Episode 1 News Archives
www.sevaan.com/starwars/news/archives/index.htm
> Miss something? Here's a collection of news clips, surveys, and editorials about the Phantom Menace.

Episode 1 Racer 🖼 ?
www.gamespot.com/features/sw_racer
> Pod Racer for PC & N64 reviewed by Gamespot's Elliott Chin. Learn all about the Pod Race game: how it works, background, features, the tracks, sabotage, see screenshots. Connect to other great Gamespot sites & game stories.

Episode 1 Script Review
www.sevaan.com/starwars/news/archives/old_layout/news/scriptreview.htm
> One of many editorials found on the Episode 1 site, this is by "Moriarity" who rips Star Wars critics then gives some insightful comments about the truth behind Episode 1.

Episode 1 Widevision Cards
www.sevaan.com/starwars/fanart/topps.htm
   JPEG image collection of Topps Episode 1 Widevision Cards created by artist Savaan Franks.

Episode 1: Phantom Menace Ship & Vehicle List 🖼
http://theforce.net/prequels/oldPreq/ships/ships.shtml
   A Star Wars movie wouldn't be complete without cool ships & hardware. This Force.net site collected old & new vehicles pix, data, schematics, and other spy information before the Phantom Menace release.

Episode 1: The Phantom Menace
www.angelfire.com/sc/francis915/page2.html
   Looks like an official site, but once scrolling, it's plainly an unofficial EP1 tribute site with loads of JPEG pix and reviews of the movie characters. Has an interesting frame-by-frame of Obi-Wan aging. Sub-pages include teaser trailer pix, trailer info, rumors, and the latest news.

Episode 1: The Phantom Menace News Page
www.angelfire.com/sc/francis915/news.html
   The best way to read Star Wars news is on a starry background, right? Although this site doesn't have ALL the news, it "has it where it counts, kid." Keep those updates coming!

Episode 2 at Sci-FI Advance
http://scifi.simplenet.com/starwars/prequels/episode2.shtml
   Already data is beginning to flow in about Episode II (2002 release) of the 3-part Prequel series. Sci-FI advance is tracking news stories and floating rumors. Also, down-link to Episode III (2005 release).

Episode X 🖼 👁
www.sevaan.com/starwars
   Prequel news and subpages of juicy fan-friendly stuff: plot, script, characters, locations, editorials, news, fan art, links, even a fake Phantom Menace script that someone cooked up. A cornucopia of interesting prequel sub pages.

Essential Guide To Droids - Review
http://theforce.net/books/reviews/guidedroids.shtml
   The Essential Guide to Droids is published by Del Rey books, a division of Bantam. The page here reviews the book and shows the cover. You can link to other reviews via this great force.net book site.

Etcetera (Virtual McGregor) 👁
www.enter.net/~cybernut/ewanlinx.htm
   Virtual Ewan McGregor's virtual FAQ page (all text): his bio, filmography, facts, guestbook, even a place where you can help this pretty awesome site grow.

🖼 IMAGES	🎬 VIDEO	📣 AUDIO
👁 MUST SEE!	$ SELLS STUFF	🔞 ADULT CONTENT	🔍 SEARCHABLE
💬 CHAT ROOMS	📥 MESSAGE BOARDS	📬 MAILING LISTS

Everything I Know I Learned From Star Wars
www.geocities.com/Hollywood/Set/5760
   One-liners collected by Boba Fett/geocities; some are wisdom, others corny. You decide.

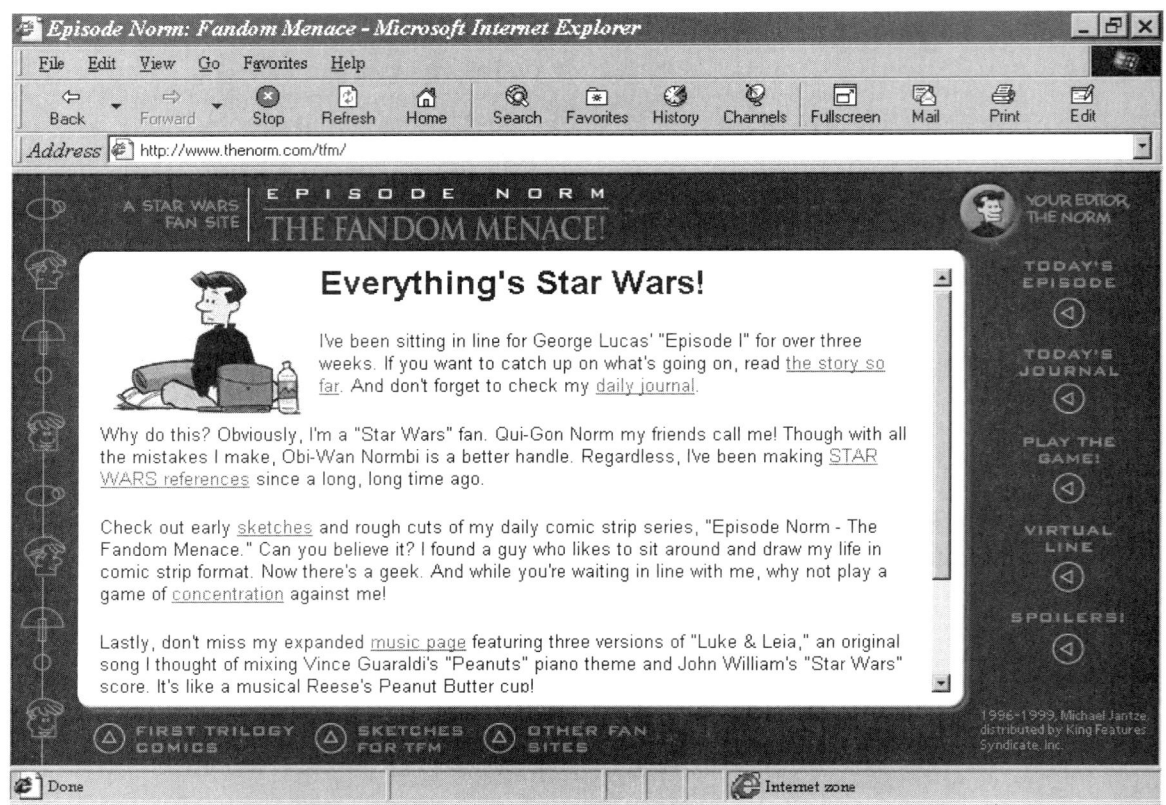

Everything's Star Wars - the norm
www.thenorm.com/tfm
   "the norm" is cartoonist Michael Jantze who craves Star Wars. See his Star Wars tribute pages of his cartoons, his Star Wars diary, his sketches, and a "concentration game." See his "spoilers page" for his humorous top-secrets!

EW's Top 25 Actors of the 90s - Samuel L Jackson
http://cgi.pathfinder.com/ew/features/minisite/90s_actors/0,2566,16-16,jackson.html
   Entertainment Weekly's page for Samuel L, listing him in conjunction with Entertainment Weekly's top 25 actor nominees for the 1990's. Find a photo and short article with personal bio material.

Ewan MacGregor
http://ucs.orst.edu/~harraha
   Some might expect more when visiting here, but there's enough of his Star Wars stuff and Ewan background to make it worthwhile. Click on the Ewan picture, then find his bio, filmography, images, also merchandise sites.

Ewan McGregor (Lycos Network)
www.lycos.com/entertainment/celebrities/celebs/McGregor_Ewan.html
   28-year-old Ewan's career is on the rise; find the basic background stuff about the Scotsman here at his Lycos Entertainment/Celebrity site. He's married. Find links to official Ewan sites, also fan sites, as well as his claims to fame, birthday, etc. Site is searchable.

Ewan McGregor Gallery
www.geocities.com/~ewanmcgregor/gallery
> Reputedly the largest collection of Ewan McGregor photos, this features magazine covers, Ewan inspired art, and 156 images (from Japanese commercials to hip fashion 'zines). A random section includes art of unknown origins.

Ewan McGregor Greeting Cards
www.geocities.com/~ewanmcgregor/postcards/card.html
> Valentine's Day, Happy Birthday, Missing You and three more Ewan greeting cards for you to personalize and e-mail to a friend/lover/chum/fan/relative. Found on the Ewanspotting site.

Ewan Multimedia
http://ucs.orst.edu/~harraha/multi.htm
> Multimedia page devoted exclusively to the new Obi-Wan - Ewan McGregor. He's exposed in his Obi-wan role - well, not exactly exposed. Videos and sounds are also expected here.

Ewanspotting
www.ewanspotting.com
> Unique geocities "unofficial" Ewan McGregor site starts with a simple pull down menu; inside are a mini-galaxy of Ewan-things. Big pix galleries, postcards, desktop images, but hardly a hint of Star Wars (that should change).

Ewok Adventure, The (1984)
http://uk.imdb.com/Title?0087225
> Made for TV movie that kids and adult fans fell in love with in 1984. Find out more about this Ewok epic, via the Internet Movie Database. Who played Widdle? (Tony Cox). Aubree Miller played Cindel. Burl Ives narrated.

Ewok Warrior Headquarters
www.angelfire.com/al/cybertrees/dwf.html
> Ewok lore and Ewok enemies list, hosted by Deej. Get the scoop on Ewok culture. Find a picture of Han on a stick, and another of our furry Ewok friends.

Ewoks
www.starwars.com/aliens/ewoks
> Rough resourceful furry-beings on the forest Moon of Endor rate their own official Lucasfilms page. Here are some stock pix and background material, and links to other official Star Wars pages.

Ewoks - Star (Marvel) Comic Books Series
http://207.237.121.181/starwars/ewok01-06.html
> Colorful gallery of GIF images for the 16 Star (Marvel) Ewok Comics. Site is sponsored by Star Wars Comics. Search the onpage links to find other Star Wars comics.

Ewoks [Star Wars: various titles] - TV Series 1985-87
http://us.imdb.com/Title?0088515
> "Ewoks are the almost unbearably cute 'n' cuddly 'teddy bears with spears' seen in the third 'Star Wars' movie, 'Return of the Jedi'," says Scarlett-30 on the Internet Movie Database page for the animated Ewok TV adventure series. Learn facts & cast info, also purchase videos.

IMAGES   VIDEO   AUDIO

MUST SEE! $ SELLS STUFF   ADULT CONTENT   SEARCHABLE

CHAT ROOMS   MESSAGE BOARDS   MAILING LISTS

Ewoks Stink - What Ought to Happen to Ewoks
www.silcom.com/~pruth/ewok.html
It's hard to believe that not everyone likes Ewoks, the real heroes of Return of the Jedi. Sam's Star Wars page lists reasons why Ewoks stink, and what should be done with them. Disagree? E-mail him!

Ewoks Story
www.foxhome.com/animated/html/ewstory.htm
Fox entertainment's cuddlly online storybook about the Ewoks, with animated GIF images. Great for children's reading and viewing. Also find a coloring book and children's Ewok projects.

Ewoks: The Battle For Endor (TV/Movie, 1985)
http://us.imdb.com/Title?0089110
Made for TV animated movie about the Ewoks of Endor; find out about the production, its cast, and find the book to purchase (video may be available). This site had a negative review; Ewok fans can submit a much better one.

Extreme Star Wars Site
www.angelfire.com/co/qavind/index.html
Animations, scripts, background text (great if you need a report on the Millenium Falcon, etc.), pix, links to webrings, trivia, and more - a very good variety!

Eye On Episode 1
http://starwars.tierranet.com/episode1/frames.html
Once upon a time Little Yoda's World and Zombie Film Review (Gordon & Roa) got together and made an Episode 1 page. It turned out pretty good, as you can see. Find news, cast & crew info, pictures.

Eye On Episode 1 - Cast & Crew
http://starwars.tierranet.com/episode1/frame4.html
Do you need the Episode 1 character's name, actor who plays the character, and a picture of them? Good - most are here, certainly all the main ones. Check out the crew page to find out who did what.

Eye On Episode 1 - News & Rumors
http://starwars.tierranet.com/episode1/frame3.html
The authors collected news and photos from foreign sources, then added sublinks to pre-release pix, and piled of the details. Click on "Past News" for - past news, or submit your own news. We liked the free-form newswire scrolling of this page. Click on the line of text to view the accompanying picture.

Face to Face with the Masters
www.theforce.net/jedicouncil/interview
Collection of interviews with "masters" like Rick McCallum, Michael Stackpole, Kevin Anderson and heavyweights Jeanne Cavelos, Warwick Davis, and Star Wars Men Behind the Masks - Mayhew, Bullock, Baker.

Fan Art Museum (the force.net)
www.theforce.net/museum
Collection of art from various contributing artists; arranged into Prequel and Classic sections.

Fan Created Art (Echo Station Interactive)
www.echostation.com/art/index.htm
There's a lot of absolutely knock-out Star Wars original fan-art floating in cyberspace, but we have to believe that this Echo Station JPEG image gallery is about the best.

Fan Fiction by Brendon Wahlberg
www.theforce.net/fanfiction
　　This superb force.net site turns Brendon Wahlberg's collection of fan fiction into a blockbuster event - just look at the size of those banners! A dozen titles are featured. The Ebony & Jade text is illustrated.

Fandom Menace
www.fandommenace.com
　　Main page lists action figure, toy and merchandise news by date, such as: Darth Maul & Jar Jar towels found at Target April 14. Site has good lists and pictures of toys as they were found in stores and on the web, etc. This page also links to sites where you can make purchases.

Fett Files, The
www.geocities.com/Area51/Vault/3227/index.html
　　A Chris Coleman Boba Fett/geocities site, this links to interesting bounty-hunter stuff (weapons, ships) and also to reviews of Star Wars books, comics, and games.

Fett Net
www.bobafett.net/page1.htm
　　Have a Boba Fett and bounty-hunter fetish? Fett news, Fett lore, Fett filmography, Fett cards, comics, Fett links, even a Prequel Hunt. A "must see" site, and good submissions are welcomed.

Fierce Battle of Endor Video
www.telecom.csuhayward.edu/~aleung/fight.mov
　　QuickTime video of the Battle of Endor.

Fighter Gets It In The Trench
www.telecom.csuhayward.edu/~aleung/trench.mov
　　Video (QuickTime) of fighter craft winging it - until destruction - in the Death Star trench.

Filk Songs (Amara's Cantina Humor)
www.flyingarmadillo.com/cantina/starfun/filk/filk.htm
　　I'm a Jedi And I'll Whine If I Want To (sung to It's My Party), and Take A Walk on the Dark Side (sung to the Lou Reed classic Take A Walk on the Wild Side).

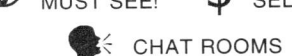

Film 100: 32 George Lucas 👁
www.film100.com/cgi/direct.cgi?v.luca
> Listing Lucas as 32 in their rankings (Speilberg 82; 1 is Mr. Lauri Dickson who invented basic movie techniques), The Top 100 Lucas bio walks you through George's film and cultural accomplishments. Did you know Francis Coppola backed George L's THX-1138 movie in 1971?

Film.com $ 🏛 🎬 🔍 👁
www.film.com
> Movie resource site: download video clips of movies, see the clip of the day, buy videos, read the latest news, read reviews of various titles, and find what's in theaters now. Features G2 players, soundtrack cinema, videos for kids & family, and the Screening Room.

Filmthreat Online ⚓ $
www.filmthreat.com/Welcome.htm
> Filmthreat describes itself by saying it is "independent, cult, underground, alternative film, Hollywood Satire and no BS." Yet, they sell stuff and are connected to the "pastel" the den.com. Sections include "Hate Mail" (a forum).

Force Powers
www.wcug.wwu.edu/~paradox/force.html
> All who are familiar with the Jedi also know of the force - do you? Here is a web page devoted to the power associated with "the force." This page is a resource for roleplaying games, but everyone can do with the valuable information here and be more of a Jedi.

ForceCollectors.Com 🔍 👁
www.forcecollectors.com
> Site is designed to help Star Wars collectors navigate the various online auction sites. Search by item or by category - figures, posters, books, memorabilia - or search by price range. Sell off that old land-speeder, or that old droid with the bad motivator.

FORCE.NET - Your Daily Dose of Star Wars ⚓ 🎬 🔊 👁
http://theforce.net
> The dosage is huge - site rated the BEST! Daily & Prequel news, news about comics, books, collecting, games, also a holonet, a newsletter, surveys, forums, links, sounds, 2much2mention. Great links, very current. Everything is fine here, just had a slight weapons malfunction.

Forcethis Mailing List 📫 🔍
www.forcethis.com/list.htm
> Subscribe and you will have access to a growing number of e-mail subscribers who are interested in any number of aspects of Star Wars. List service is brought to you by marua.com and forcethis!

Fort Tusken 🖼 👁
www.iqw.clara.co.uk/index.html
This UK site includes Star Wars inspired art work by Paul Smith, and plenty of movie gallery pix to choose from, especially from Episode 1 The Phantom Menace.

Forum FAQ 👁
http://jedicouncil.net/forum/faq.html
Would you like to participate in a Star Wars forum but want to know more so that you don't offend others and look like a nerfherder? Good. Check this FAQ page to get "educated" in the basics about forum pages.

Frangisco's Star Wars PC Themes 🖼 🔊
http://coyote.accessnv.com/fasalvo/sw/theme.html
Find Star Wars stuff to add to your own computer's Windows - wallpaper, pix, sounds, phrases, icons.

Frank Oz - IMDb $ 🔍
http://us.imdb.com/Name?Oz,+Frank
Frank Oznowicz - better know as Frank Oz - is a wiz at creating muppets, muppet movies, being part of Sesame Street and directing childrens' shows. He's brought us Yoda. Here's his professional career and Oz vital stats.

Freak7's Star Wars Realm
www.geocities.com/Area51/Zone/2365
This site should improve; it promises bloopers, humor, more Episode 1 material. Also features Quake.

Free E-mail (Imagine Games Network)
www.ignmail.com
Do you play a lot of computer games and want a "gamer's" e-mail account for free? At this site you can get your e-mail without charge and enjoy all the advance features on a secure e-mail server.

Free E-mail - The Rancor Pit
www.sentex.net/~dah/mail.html
Rather new e-mail system promoted by the Rancor Pit group and supported on the Sentex system. Here you can get your free e-mail address - it claims to be faster than most e-mail systems!

Free Resources from Dave Labbett 🖼 🔊
http://users.netmatters.co.uk/davelabbett/free/resinfo.html
Tired of those Star Wars "Space" backgrounds? Here are plain yet different backgrounds for site builders, including space without stars and one that looks great as a Tatooine sand background. Find AIFF sound files for the Jawa yell, lasers, and The Shining.

FTP Directory / Bladerunner 🖼
ftp://ftp.sunet.se/pub/pictures/tv.film/Bladerunner
Ford fans: visit this Swedish University resource site for Bladerunner GIFs and JPEGs. Main directory has Clear and Present Danger, Dr. Who, Apocalypse Now, Tron and dozens of other movie classics.

IMAGES   VIDEO   AUDIO
MUST SEE! $ SELLS STUFF   ADULT CONTENT   SEARCHABLE
CHAT ROOMS   MESSAGE BOARDS   MAILING LISTS

FTP Directory / Star Wars
ftp://ftp.sunet.se/pub/pictures/tv.film/Star_Wars
Good sized gallery of photos & art courtesy of a Swedish university archive site. Click on the name of the image you want. Most are stock photos, but there's a good variety.

FTP Echo Station
www.echostation.com/multimedia
Echo Station allows you to sign up for access to its humorous send-off collection of FTP files, then you can download and enjoy them. Let's see, hmmm. Here's some titles: Macbeth, The Odd Couple, Troops, Death of a Jedi, and Mos Eisley Multiplex.

Galactic Empire Data Bank
www.iaw.on.ca/~btaylor1/index.html
Information on Imperial & Rebel strengths and spacecraft, also bounty hunter vessels and craft used by other persons & groups. Take a shuttle to the Dark Forces Pharoah and find rebel fleet estimates and tactical questions.

Galactic Senate, The
http://starwarz.com/boards
If you're going to be in a Star Wars forum/discussion group, why not be a galactic senator?! What a great idea. Sign up and create your profile, then join the talks, which are pre-arranged. Use the menu to view past discussions.

Galaxy Software $
www.nwlink.com/~gareth
Gareth's selection of Star Wars-related computer games is available through him, and at reasonable rates. If you need a game he doesn't have, you can probably find it through a linked game web site. Gareth also presents news and links to his other scroll pages.

Games & Sport Index (Echostation)
http://index.echostation.com/games.html
Found at Pablo Hildago super index site, here you will find all the games that Star Wars citizens play. Find organized sports like shockball, wallball. What do you say after a perfect 23 in the popular card game Sabacc?

Games - the force.net Expanded Universe
www.theforce.net/games
Claims to be the latest Star Wars games news - it is a sweet site for finding news, pix, publications, and details on the big commercial game stuff. Also has monthly archives to rummage through.

Gamesa Cards (Starwarscards.net)
www.starwarscards.net/gamesa.htm
Small Gamesa "Cookie Cards" were distributed by Sonrics in Mexico (division of Pepsi) and are somewhat of an oddity (therefore, a collectible) in the US. If you've them, then you've got something that could become very valuable. Click on the Ewok pictures to get to the card image scans.

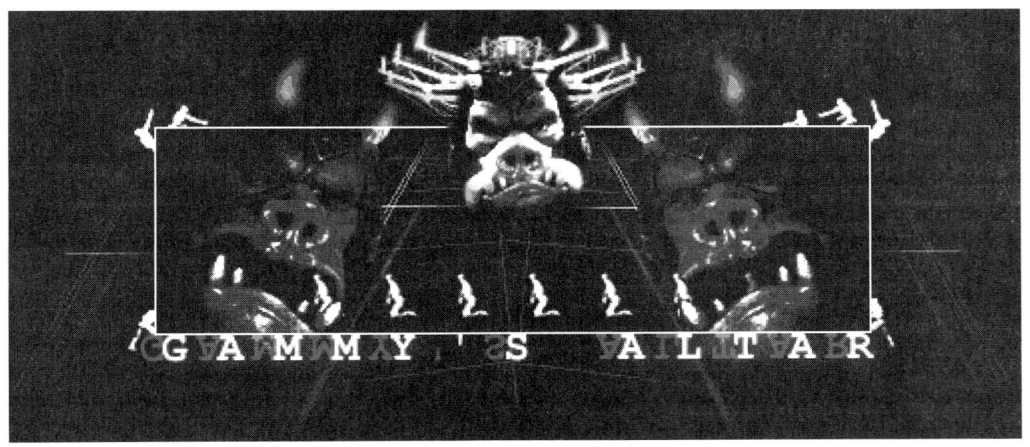

Gammy's Altar
www.toshistation.com/gammy.htm
> Another sick (but that's okay) Toshi Station site, this featuring Gammy, who is one of the disgusting pig-like alien guards in Return of the Jedi. Bent humor here also pigsNspace, Gammy, Mork & Mindy icons. Why? Who knows.

Garindan's Book Reviews
www.geocities.com/Area51/Shadowlands/4918/bookrev.html
> Books and reviews by "Garindan Kubazanian, information broker at Mos Eisley," who also is connected with a good Imperial-type site, TIE Hangar Bay.

Gary Kurtz - All-Media Guide
http://allmovie.com/cg/x.dll?UID=9:01:46|PM&p=avg&sql=B98317
> All-Media Guide gives some details of Star Wars producer Gary Kurtz' career. He also produced The Empire Strikes Back and two of our favorite motorhead flix: American Graffiti and Two-Lane Blacktop. How much cruisin' did he and George Lucas do, anyway?

Generic Star Wars Page, The
www.geocities.com/Area51/Corridor/9410
> Good selection of RealAudio clips (interviews, promos, fan music), also good multimedia links such as the Pepsi Vader/movie usher duel commercial, Trailer Parks, and other Sci-fi videos.

Geographic Links - Shaven Wookie
www.shavenwookie.com/swlinkslocate.html
> Is there a "system" somewhere in the Star Wars galaxy that you didn't find in this book? Then, name the system! Open this alphabetical link list and you just may find the location you're looking for.

George Lucas (Lycos Network)
www.lycos.com/entertainment/celebrities/celebs/Lucas_George.html
> Need basic info on George Lucas, creator and director of Star Wars? This Lycos Entertainment/celebrity Lucas page is a good place to start. Here are his basic vital statistics and claims to fame. He's a Taurus with an Empire! Search field and good links are available here.

George Lucas - All Media Guide
http://allmovie.com/cg/x.dll?UID=9:01:46|PM&p=avg&sql=B100308
All-Media Guide's George Lucas page gives his biographical info, years active, movie genres, a translation option, and good links to just about everything connected with Mr. Lucas. Gives his awards and rates his movies for quality. Won best film 1978 at British Academy Awards!

George Walton Lucas Jr.
http://us.imdb.com/M/person-exact?Lucas%2C+George
Internet Movie Database (IMDb) biography/filmography site for George Lucas, creator and director of Star Wars. His birthdate, films, acting, TV appearances, skills, credits, accomplishments are listed.

Get Ready for Star Wars
www.excite.com/events/star_wars
Excite is one of the top search engines and it (like aol) has put together an entertaining and informative Star Wars site, rich in media news, poll, and high-interest sub-pages (most link onsite). Good place to visit for finding the more-common but well-trafficked Star Wars linked sites.

GH Moose Star Wars Pictures
www.dsu.edu/~denholmr/StarWars.html
Small, exciting JPEG gallery of spacecraft pix, some renderings, 3D, models and some from video; all very cool.

Gonkite's Groovy Grotto & Glossary
http://members.aol.com/gonkite/index.htm
Glossary of Star Wars terms. What's your favorite gonkulator? Find out here and all about Gonk - that box-like droid. All Gonk scenes and deeds are listed, and many are listed as "Divine." You will also find Gonk WAV files (Gonk & other's sound clips).

Gothic Skywalker's Medieval to Mark Hamill Page
www.geocities.com/TimesSquare/Dungeon/3913
This unusual site has a thing about tie-ing in Gothic/Renaissance stylings and Star Wars, also mentioning that the Force is borrowed from Aikido and Buddhism. Cool! A refreshing change from the usual. Useful in role playing.

Gothic Skywalker's MUSH Page
www.geocities.com/TimesSquare/Dungeon/3913/mush.html
Star Wars roleplaying is the name of the game. You emulate a character and slush your way through the game/lifestyle/role/fantasy. Some say it's kinda like acting, only you get to make up the script as you explore. This site touches on aspects of it all.

Governments & Institutions Index
http://index.echostation.com/gov.html
Do these governments and institutions remind you of any of our own? Here's a list of what can be found in the way of governing bodies in the Star Wars universe, discovered in Pablo Hildago indexes (site was partly down).

Graham's Star Wars & Homepage
www.angelfire.com/ga/glf/index.html
Found nice Prequel pages here, also surveys, weekly box office report, and the great pic of Bart Simpson as young Anakin. Sounds and pictures are pretty much the standards, but this is a relatively new site and it should grow.

Guerre Stellari
http://users.iol.it/betv/gs.html
This Italian index page links you to Cloud City, a good Italian site. There's also news of upcoming Star Wars conventions, and pages on Bespin - but you need to know Italian.

Guide to the Ewoks Cartoon Series 👁
www.mvhs.srvusd.k12.ca.us/~ehall/ewoks.html
   Here's a good list of the Ewok cartoons: each episode's author, plotline, date. Remember "Party Ewoks" where Kneesaw's celebration is crashed by motor-cycle gang-like creatures? Revisit Wicket, Teebo, Latera, & Ewok friends. Site by Evan; excerpts from John Snyder's article.

Guide to the Star Wars Universe
http://bobafett.metrolink.net.au/guide
   Alphabetized list of sites, but not a large list. Sites are rated, however, with click-to links.

Gungan Din - Article EW Daily News
http://cgi.pathfinder.com/ew/daily/0,2514,1308,insidelookatmore.html
   How does George Lucas come up with names such as the ones in Star Wars? Read this article by Steve Daily on EW Daily News. Lucas heard "Gundan" in the cries of a 3-year old child.

Han Solo
www.starwars.com/characters/han_solo
   Page from the official Lucasfilms main site that breezes over this main character, played by the star who shines as bright as Star Wars itself. We really liked Ford first as Milner's nemesis in American Grafitti. Click on the pic for a larger color still of Harrison as Han.

Han Solo Archive 🖼 👁
http://seconn4.yoda.com/~vader97/han/han.html
   Han is so photogenic that Taz's web site has collected five JPEG image galleries of him! The galleries are good quality, featuring Han images from across the galaxy, but they may take a while to load.

Han Solo Condemns Me to a Digestful Fate Video 🎬
www.telecom.csuhayward.edu/~aleung/fett.mov
   Downloadable QuickTime video of Han sending Boba Fett into the mouth of the Sarlaac creature at the Pit of Carkoon. Did you know that Boba manages to escape?

Han Solo-Ists 📬 💬 🖼 👁
www.hansolo-ists.freeservers.com
   "Hi, I'm Rabeya Solo, a wannabe Jedi, and I am truly, madly, deeply, in love with Han Solo." The author's comment appears to be true; she's collected an excellent tribute to Han on her pages, including a webring, a multi-page gallery of Han images, also offers a chat room, guestbook, more.

Hanger, The ⬇ 💬 🖼
www.jedinights.com/hangar
   Very new gaming site that features Prequel games Pod Racer and The Phantom Menace. For each game you'll find info, screen capture images, previews, cheats and levels. Site also has a chat room, forums, suggestions page, help, any game news fit to print.

🖼 IMAGES   🎬 VIDEO   📢 AUDIO
👁 MUST SEE! $ SELLS STUFF   ADULT CONTENT   🔍 SEARCHABLE
💬 CHAT ROOMS   ⬇ MESSAGE BOARDS   📬 MAILING LISTS

Hardware Wars - IMDb $ ♀

http://us.imdb.com/Title?0077658

Called "crude but highly entertaining," this is the Internet Movie Database page for Hardware Wars, the 1977 take-off of the original Star Wars. Wookie monster is a brown cookie monster and Artie-Deco turns out to be a vacuum cleaner. Yes, collectors can even purchase it.

Harrison Ford (1) $ ♀ 👁

http://us.imdb.com/Name?Ford,+Harrison

Internet Movie Database's page for Harrison lists all his movie/TV profession credits with links. Did you know he was in an episode of "Kung Fu" (1974) and played a character named "Mr. Harrison"? Some vital info here; birthdate/place. Good site for info searching; it also provides an online store.

Harrison Ford (Lycos Network) 📢 ♀ 👁

www.lycos.com/entertainment/celebrities/celebs/Ford_Harrison.html

Lycos Entertainment page for Harrison Ford (Han) gives his vital statistics, other official sites (movies), claims to fame, and links to chat, books and message boards about him. Site offers general news, comments, & rumor page.

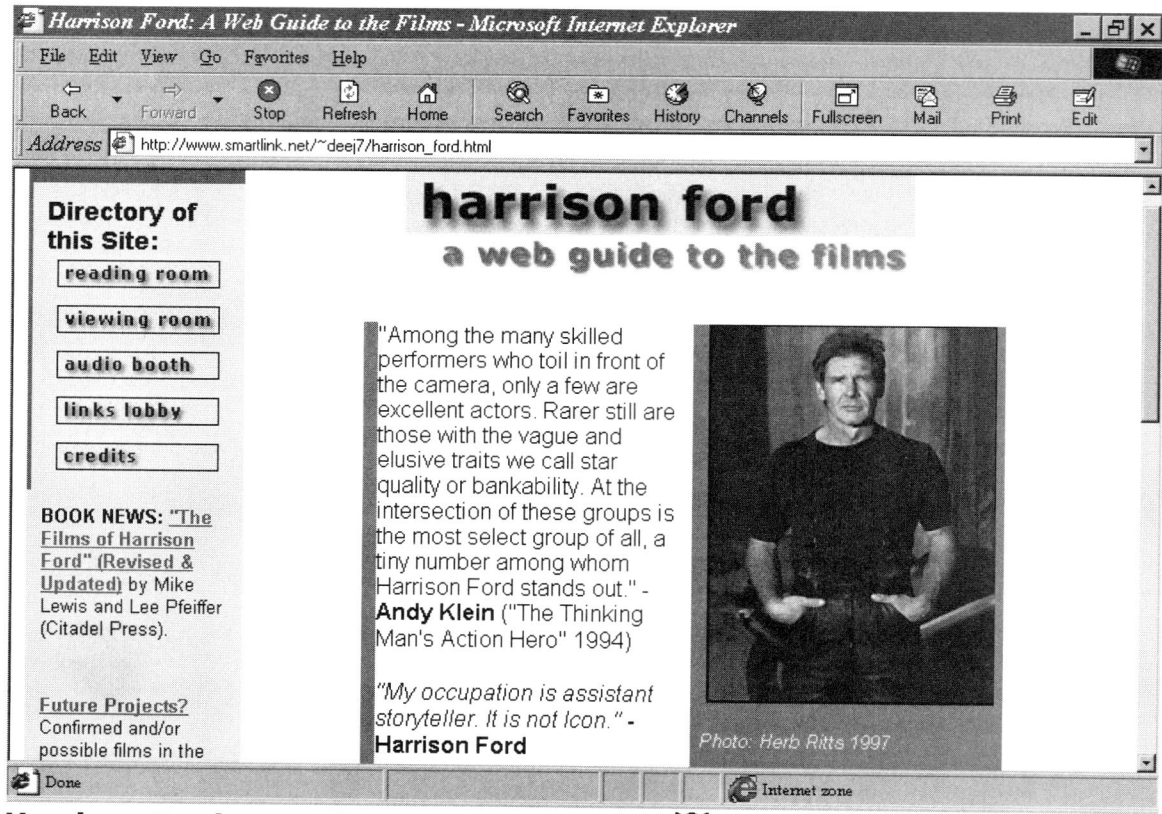

Harrison Ford - A Web Guide to the Films 🎬 📢

www.smartlink.net/~deej7/harrison_ford.html

"The Science of Harrison in the Movies" should be the real title here. Find a reading and viewing room, audio booth, book news. This page may be too matter-of-fact for small children.

Harrison Ford - Viewing Room 🎬 🎞 📢 👁

www.smartlink.net/~deej7/pix.htm

Deej's great gallery of Harrison pix from most of his movies, plus pr shots, candids, artwork, book art, posters, and, get this, the original GIF Hanimation (where he's shrugging after capturing troopers).

Hasbro - Making The World Smile $ 🔍
www.hasbro.com
Kenner/Hasbro Toys main site where you find new Star Wars toys as well as all the toys they offer.

Hasbro Cool Stuff 3D VR Collectibles
www.hasbrotoys.com/coolstuf.html
Hasbro Toys uses QuickTime to show off some favorite toys in 3D video.

Hear Mark
www.chez.com/jedinat/sounds.html
Natalie's Mark Hamill "Hear Mark" page is a tidy sound collection of Mark quotes from the Trilogy, plus Mark doing impressions of Yoda and Harrison on LNWCO (Late Nite with Conan O'Brien).

Heat.net Online Gaming
www.heat.net
That's right: fast free online gaming! Good portal and info site for computer gaming, with 100 or so games online, also calendar of events, news, top-5 games, personalization, tourneys. Many call this the best game site on the Net.

Heir to the Empire
http://books.echostation.com/heir.html
So, what happens after the Return of the Jedi - does the story just end? Not according to Timothy Zahn, who offers up this book. We present it on its book/novel page to please those who have to ask the question, "What next?"

Hello There Video of Obi-Wan Kenobi
http://users.why.net/radrock/sounds/hello.avi
Short downloadable AVI video of Obi-Wan's introduction - "Hello there" - to R2-D2 in Star Wars.

Here Come The Jedis!
www.geocities.com/SunsetStrip/Alley/7028/swhctj.htm
Humorous parody take-off of the Prequel renamed Here Come The Jedis. Things are a little out of hand - Seinfeld's Kramer seems to make his way into most of Doug Anderson's derivative works.

HGWizard's Multimedia Archive
www.geocities.com/Hollywood/Hills/1792/opening.html
Movie clips, pictures and sounds, but several sub-pages were not complete when we visited.

HGWizard's Star Wars Movie Clips
www.geocities.com/Hollywood/Hills/1792/movie.html
QuickTime video gallery, mostly action movie clips, except for maybe Chewie growling.

Hi-Impact Photo Gallery - Star Wars
www.armory.com/~paladin/gallery/starwars/starwars-c.html
Get "costumed up" and take a few pictures - your own Star Wars party should look so good. JPEG images here will give you some ideas for costumes and scene set-ups.

IMAGES   VIDEO   AUDIO
MUST SEE! $ SELLS STUFF   ADULT CONTENT   SEARCHABLE
CHAT ROOMS   MESSAGE BOARDS   MAILING LISTS

Hollywood Online - Star Wars The Phantom Menace $📷 🎬 🔊
www.hollywood.com/starwars/main.html
> Hollywood Online puts up a fast-paced Star Wars page, with a weekly character bio, and features like celebrities telling their favorite Star War stories. Enter contests, visit the online store, check galleries of photos (characters & Premiers), interviews, videos, trivia & more fun.

Hollywood Online Database 🔍 👁
http://moviepeople.hollywood.com
> Drop in a celebrity name or film title in the white search field, hit submit, and you've accessed the great Hollywood online database. Once found, click on the name for bio infomation, etc. Find movies lists, Hollywood players - also search by top movies and top celebs.

Hollywood Online George Lucas 🔍
http://moviepeople.hollywood.com/people.asp?p_id=P100308
> Bio, filmography, awards of George Lucas, compiled from the Hollywood Online Database. Click on George's birthdate to get a list of others born on the same date. Did you know that George was into auto racing, wrecked, then retreated to college and began studying filmmaking? That's right.

Holocards 👁
http://outer-rim.net/card.html
> Pick and personalize an online greeting card to e-mail. The variety of cards and topics include Friendship, Romance, Birthday, Sorry, Support, Happiness, Departure, & May The Force Be With You's. Some cards are animated. Customize, and really express yourself.

Holocron, The
www.infinet.com/~schieltz
> If you're wondering what happened to the great Holocron site and all its great GIFs, you may want to inquire via e-mail. When we last visited, The Holocron had closed its doors. Sorry.

Holonet (the force.net)
www.theforce.net/holonet
> Good place to find news that is submitted by fans - also video-clips, audio files of speaking engagements, interviews, the whole 9 yards. Here we found audio of Mark Hamill speaking at a university. Check the monthly archives. You can comment via the Jedicouncil link.

Home THX Product Database 👁
www.thx.com/consumer_products/av_equip.html
> High-tech THX entertainment products for your home are available - home theatre systems! Search on this page for manufacturer and product category - DVDs, receivers, speakers, etc.

Hoth
www.starwars.com/locations/hoth/index.html
Lucasfilms official page for ice planet Hoth, with pic of Luke on a Tauntaun. It will leave you cold.

House of Skywalker Luke & Leia Paper Dolls 👁
www.flyingarmadillo.com/cantina/fashion/leia/leia.htm
That's right - paper dolls of Luke (complete with clothes) and Leia (not yet complete when we visited). Basic Luke comes in his Boba Fett undies and you print out and put on all sorts of costumes from all the different movie locations. From Amara's Cantina (visit it!)

How to Build a Stormtrooper Costume 👁
www.studiocreations.com/stormtrooper
Everything you need to know to create a lifelike stormtrooper costume - vacuumform table building, creating a body cast, detailing, trooper photos, FAQs. Links to the Imperial Stormtrooper webring, of course.

HTML Files of Interest to Educators
http://users.hub.ofthe.net/~mtalkmit/VRMLsearching.htm
This VRML resource site contains a "gallery" of resources for VR and 3D modeling and web site building. It'll make sense to you, but didn't to us, because we still rub two sticks together to get online.

Humor; Entertainment Cell (Boba Fett)
http://pweb.netcom.com/~fragger/load_humor.html
This Humor page on the Entertainment Cell is an evolving site - formerly listed as a Boba Fett site and still maintains some Bob Fett characteristics.

Hydrospanner 🖼 🎬 🔊
www.hydrospanner.com
Very nice looking web site with news, humor. Go to the "Prequels Probe" section for latest humor JPEG pix (Prequel Beanie babies stand, Hooters restaurant, and more) and "Damit Anakin" video GIF. Also, there's a place to submit your Prequel things that others shouldn't be without.

I Don't Get It 👁
http://outland.cyberwar.com/~smad//getit2.html
Page is now officially "closed," but it lists lively speculations about some of the odd incongruities of the Star Wars Trilogy. Each of the three is analyzed, and comments are made by fans with savant-like powers of observation. May the force be kinda nearby, maybe.

Ian's Incredible Star Wars Page 🖼 🎬 🔊 👁
www.airnet.net/pcusers/ianspage
We liked the energy and selections on this multimedia page, especially the "Thank you Mr. Lucas" poster. Good links, sounds, icons, pictures, scripts, MIDI sounds, guestbook and FAQs.

🖼 IMAGES	🎬 VIDEO	🔊 AUDIO
👁 MUST SEE!	$ SELLS STUFF	🔍 SEARCHABLE
💬 CHAT ROOMS	📥 MESSAGE BOARDS	📪 MAILING LISTS
	⬆ ADULT CONTENT	

Icon Collection - Star Wars
www.airnet.net/pcusers/ianspage/SWicons.zip
More than 300 icons in a WinZip file. These can be downloaded and used as icons on your computer.

ICQ list; Star Wars (Echo Station Interactive)
www.echostation.com/icq/index.htm
ICQ mailing lists are relatively new and growing too fast for us to accurately keep up with. We found that Echo Station (a portal) would appear to have a good ICQ list, and so its web site is presented here.

ICQ Soundpack, Irc Script Pack, New Star Wars Font
www.jedinet.com/multimedia/windows/misc/index.htm
Instead of the standard ICQ sounds, why not get the Star Wars ICQ sounds? Here, also, is the new Star Wars font, and the Irc script pack of humorous lines from the Trilogy to enliven your chat sessions.

Images of Episode 1
http://plaza.harmonix.ne.jp/~m-falcon/Image_of_Episode1.html
Star Wars Force Graphics page for Episode 1 includes JPEG images of posters and stylized Phantom Menace pix.

IMHFC International Mark Hamill Fan Club
www.markhamill.com/home.htm
After being offline for awhile, the IMHFC is back. Here's the inside story on Mark's life and career, also lists his personal appearance schedule, credits year by year, and has knock-out photo collages.

Imperial Executor
www.angelfire.com/ny/ImperialExecutor/index.html
Imperial Executor is the name of a new Imperial Cruiser - and like most Imperial projects, always seems to be under construction. 15 short homemade animations by Bill Smith are available, also trivia and links to chat rooms.

Imperial Fleet Schleswig-Holstein
http://members.xoom.com/ADAM_IFSH
IFSH is a German site with resources for Imperial craft, insignia, pictures, videos (in German, which should add something) & webring. Pictures are original art, mostly sketches, by members in this site's Phaeton club.

Imperial Funnies
www.flyingarmadillo.com/cantina/starfun/starfun.html
Amara's colorful cartoon collection called Imperial Funnies is definitely worth viewing! Link back to her other pages for more pleasant fun surprises. Respect copyright request.

Imperial Intelligence Agency
www.angelfire.com/ab/ewok/starwarsframe1.html
Roleplaying games resources that also serves as background material for various Star Wars movie characters, with fictionalizations attached to them. Not only are Imperial characters found here: there's rebel & freelance personnel, also freelance ships, other categories, and news.

Imperial Navy Technical Database
www.geocities.com/Area51/Shadowlands/4918/tech.html
Specifications and pix of Imperial Fleet warcraft, guided by Admiral Torran (see a picture of him with stormtrooper). Info on TIE Starfighter, Interceptor, Bomber, also Assault Gunboat. More is promised in the future.

Imperial Officers 🖼
www.geocities.com/Area51/Corridor/8727/imperial_officers.html
Big JPEG images of evil Imperial officers, collected by Taz. These pix will sober you right up, Achtung! Includes Darth putting the choke on that mouthy Imperial Death Star know-it-all.

Imperial Outpost 🖼 🎬 🔊
http://members.theglobe.com/bobafett66
"Because he's holding a thermal detonator!" and other sounds are found on this very high-tech multimedia page, with encryption tricks. Find pictures, sounds, downloads, music, video clips. Downloads of games, themes, icons.

Imperial Pictures 🖼 👁
www.geocities.com/Area51/Corridor/4312/imperial.html
Nice big JPEG shots of Darth (and some of the emperor) including a wide angle view of Darth putting the choke on an unlucky Imperial commander. Use the alternate URL to find other Imperial officers.

Imperial Power Web Ring
www.geocities.com/Area51/Dunes/3630/IPWR.html
Yes, this 12-site ring is decidedly "Imperial" - Save the Emperor above all others!

Imperial Rhapsody, The
www.geocities.com/Hollywood/Set/5760
Queen's Bohemian Rhapsody is transcribed into "The Imperial Rhapsody"using Lando, Han, Leia - a bit of a stretch but at a karaoke party it'd be a nice departure from Queen's overplayed version.

🖼 IMAGES   🎬 VIDEO   🔊 AUDIO
👁 MUST SEE! $ SELLS STUFF   ADULT CONTENT   🔍 SEARCHABLE
CHAT ROOMS   MESSAGE BOARDS   MAILING LISTS

Imperial Shipyards
http://members.tripod.com/~Dolmyn/shipyard.htm
Data and JPEG pix on warcraft under Imperial control. FYI: TIE Defenders can accelerate at the rate of 30 MGLT/second! They are not manufactured in China.

Imperial Spy Network
www.angelfire.com/mo/StarWarsImages
Good picture gallery of spacecraft, also sounds - "Laugh it up fuzzball" - and some animations (Vader morphing into Boba Fett is 1). There's trivia and good links, but we didn't find spies.

Imperial TIE Fighter Hangar Bay, The
www.geocities.com/Area51/Shadowlands/4918
"Serve the Emperor above all others" suggest this Imperial multimedia site. Good links to tech data, Boba Fett & Vader galleries, pictures, books, Royal Library, some music, "a survey" and guestbook. Updated weekly - usually.

Imperials Uniforms, Insignia, Logos, Technical Commentary
www.theforce.net/swtc/insignia.html
In addition to explaining Imperial Insignia and logos, this site has comments on Imperial Uniforms: stormtroopers, navy, starfighter, and others. Also lists sources, methodology, etc. Just click and go. Most subpages have pictures.

Index (by Pablo Hildago) Hosted by Echo Station
http://index.echostation.com
Databases divided into books: 1 = Characters & droids. 2 = Vehicles, vessels, businesses, 3 = Aliens, creatures, science/nature, health/medicine, supernatural. 4 = Places. 5 = Hidden Essentials like culture, governments, military, battles, media, food/drink, games/sports.

Index of data/video/avi/Movie Trailers/Star Wars
www.burbclave.net/data/video/avi/Movie_Trailers/Star_Wars
AVI video clips/files directory. Most are 1995 Trilogy pieces, with length given.

Index of Multimedia Sounds.star.wars
http://info.fuw.edu.pl/multimedia/sounds.star.wars
University resource sound file for Star Wars with AU/RealAudio files. Not deep, except for the Darth Vader clips.

Index of Waves/Star Wars
www.ug.cs.sunysb.edu/~bouzakij/waves/Star_Wars
More WAV sound clips! "You may fire when ready" - "So, you think you've been treated unfairly?" Other gems are all listed alphabetically with file size. It's not a big sound resource, but easy to use.

Injuries to Darth Vader
www.theforce.net/swtc/injuries.html
We all know that Darth Vader - by the end - was more machine than man. How did he get that way, and what exactly were the injuries? This site tells all the gory details and includes X-rays.

Insignias
www.jedinet.com/multimedia/pics/insignia/index.html
Jedinet's collection of Insignia is certainly useful for creating your own authentic looking Star Wars costumes, or for decorating your web site.

Institute For Impure Science - Star Wars
www.ifis.org.uk/p.cgi/multimedia/starwars
   Videos of Trailers (theatre and TV) and parodies ("Troops" and South Park's "The Little Menace") in various formats: QuickTime, AVI, MOV - zipped and unzipped - all for your viewing pleasure.

Internet Movie Database (IMDb)
http://us.imdb.com
   Want movie or moviemaker info, details, bios, credits, news, box office happenings, what's new and what's cool in the movie biz? IMDb probably has it and more. Search by title or name (use "more options"), also lists openings.

Internet Role Playing Society
http://irps.engr.ucf.edu
   Down for re-construction when we visited, this should be back and offer the same great resources and free membership in online RPGs. Offers an E-zine, too.

Interviews (with authors & obscure characters)
www.lucasfan.com/interviews
   LucasFan.com interviews as many Star Wars characters and authors as the site owner can find to talk to him, like Femi Taylor who played a Oola the Jabba Palace dancer in Return of the Jedi. Most interviews also have pictures.

Interviews - Hollywood Online
www.hollywood.com/starwars/interview/interview.html
   Hollywood Online Entertainment site lists Star Wars Interviews in 3 formats: articles, videos, and audio. These are fairly current, with new interviews being added often.

IRC RPG Resource; Star Wars (Echo Station)
http://rpg.echostation.com
   Echo Station now hosts this RPG site, including the Star Wars RPG booklist, RPG updates, sounds, game cheats, humor, PC & miniature galleries, banners, links and webrings. Site also has a running Roleplaying news column.

Jabba The Hutt
www.starwars.com/characters/jabba_the_hutt
   Lucasfilms page for villainous crime lord Jabba the Hutt who eventually gets his (his weight would have got him anyway). For what it's worth, click on Jabba's pic for the full-size pin-up version, perfect for the refrigerator door.

Jabba The Hutt Archives
http://seconn4.yoda.com/~vader97/jabba/jabba.html
   Yuck! A memorial JPEG picture archive of Jabba The Hutt! This file will take some time to load, which isn't surprising considering Jabba's slovenly girth.

Jabba's Palace
www.starwars.com/locations/jabbas_palace
   Lucasfilms' official page featuring Jabba The Hutt's crime-infested den, and one of the few places to find a scantily-clad Princess Leia. Click on the pix to get to full-size palace stills from the Trilogy.

IMAGES   VIDEO   AUDIO
MUST SEE! $ SELLS STUFF   ADULT CONTENT   SEARCHABLE
CHAT ROOMS   MESSAGE BOARDS   MAILING LISTS

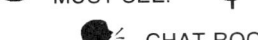

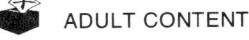

Jabba's Palace - Outer-Rim Multimedia
http://outer-rim.net/multimedia/sounds/Palace
   Download a slew of villainous sounds from Jabba's Palace from this Outer-rim multimedia page. "Bo shuda" and droids crying in pain! Click to other files at this great, modern Star Wars site: music, videos, images, scripts, and Winfiles. "Now you're Bantha fodder." - Jabba.

Jabba's Palace Movie
www.telecom.csuhayward.edu/~aleung/jabba's.mov
   QuickTime video of Jabba's Palace, with dancers from the Trilogy Special Edition.

Jacen Solo's Homepage
http://members.tripod.com/~jacenp/mainpage.html
   Not-your-usual Star Wars pictures montagued on 2 sub-pages. Find sounds, webrings, & Spawn sub-page.

Jake Lloyd (1) - IMDb
http://us.imdb.com/M/person-exact?Jake+Lloyd
   At just 10 years old, Jake Lloyd again hits it big in Hollywood with The Phantom Menace. Find what else he's appeared in at his Internet Movie Database (IMDb) web page. Jingle All The Way, for one, and 3 Episodes of TV's ER, among other gigs. Born 5 March 1989.

James Earl Jones - IMDb
http://us.imdb.com
   URL for Internet Movie Database's page for James Earl Jones is too long, so go to the site above. In "Search for title/name" type in " James Earl Jones", click on "name" - hit "Go." This takes you to his filmography page. Once there, click to find other interesting items or search for other actors.

James' Star Wars Page
http://webhome.idirect.com/~maguda/starwars.html
   Not the usual multimedia page. Find StarWars game codes, X-files the game, Wu-Tang Clan Page, Star Wars MIDI music collection. Also, in the archives, find Dune Sea map and a R2 Unit diagram.

Jar Jar Binks, Gungan Outcast
http://meltingpot.fortunecity.com/greenwood/487/char/jarjar.html
   Jar Jar's voice is a combination Jamaican/Italian. He has an eight-foot tongue, and he's completely computer-generated - all this and more is revealed on Jar Jar's page on this Prequel Spoilers web site.

Jason's Star Wars Page
http://http.tamu.edu:8000/~jpc6754/starwars.html
   Inactive but has Boba Fett pix, other graphics (JPEG's, GIFs), and a few sounds: Han - "That's what I'm afraid of."

Javval's Star Wars Page
www.multiboard.com/~jhowarth/starwars.htm
   Who's Javval? He's the bastard son of Jabba the Hutt. Javval's fictional autobiography starts: "Greetings fellow sentients." Site is rather old but has photo galleries for episodes 4-5-6 and a good number of MIDI sound files.

Jawa Force & Wampashit
www.lortaphanble.com
   Lorta Phanble Studios offer up Jawa Force Comic and Wampashit magazine "By Fans, For Fans." Both are humor/parody publications online; equally unsuitable but worth a peek. Steer young-ungs away from Leia pin-up.

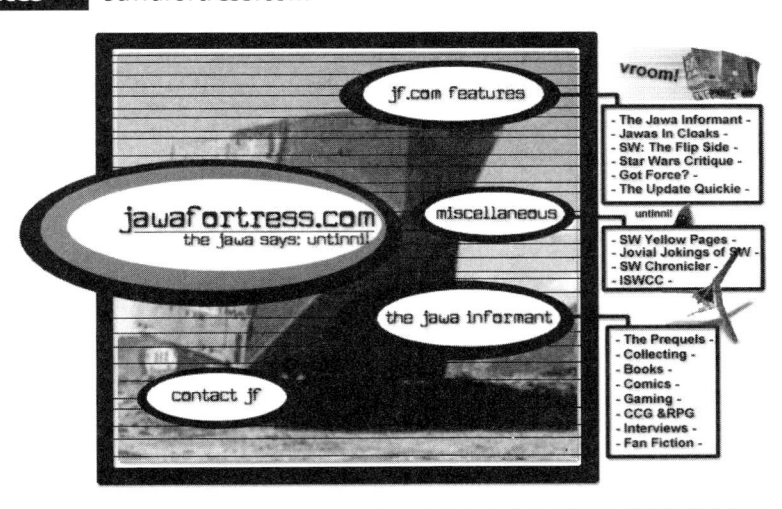

jawafortress.com

www.jawafortress.com/index2.html

This great looking web site was in the "formation stages" when we visited, and it was soliciting for cool jawa helpers - website builders. Jawas like to keep busy, as you know. This site looks great.

Jedi Academy

www.jediacademy.com/force.htm

Everything a good Jedi should know is explained on Jedi Academy's sub-pages: saber combat, the force, Jedi lessons. Also find Jedi Forums for posting messages, Jedi Chat, and inside scoop on the evils of the Dark Side.

Jedi Academy at Yavin IV

www.nerf-herder.com/jedi

Once inside, you can move around and check out the different pages and the information that's offered. We found very nice images and the trip through the site is like an adventure. Hold on R2! Hope your computer is up-to-date!

Jedi Archives

http://listen.to/thejedi

Short Link List, alphabetized but not categorized nor are there site profiles. Best feature may be the picture of Yoda with quill pen in hand.

Jedi Base

www.bestweb.net/~fett

Click on Luke to get to index; find the usual stuff (links, chat, webring, scripts, top 25, e-mail) and, surprise - a good gallery of McQuarrie & Dorman artworks, audio gallery, but few Jedi specifics. Developing a game section.

Jedi Base Audio Files

www.bestweb.net/~fett/audiomain.htm

Audio gallery of WAVs and MIDI sounds files from the Trilogy.

IMAGES   VIDEO   AUDIO
MUST SEE! $ SELLS STUFF   ADULT CONTENT   SEARCHABLE
CHAT ROOMS   MESSAGE BOARDS   MAILING LISTS

Jedi Base Galleries
www.bestweb.net/~fett/davemain.htm
Dave Dorman and Ralph McQuarrie art works; a section each for these 2 great Star Wars painters.

Jedi Council Chamber, The
www.geocities.com/Area51/Hollow/9125
Site is heavy on "kisses" including a video of a Luke-Leia kiss. Jedi Council Chamber also has good collections of audio files, pix, and goodies for your computer, and the usual multimedia site stuff - scripts, awards, news, links.

Jedi Domain
www.geocities.com/Area51/Shadowlands/3543
Jedi of the month plus other Jedi-type entertainments: humor, trivia, message boards, art gallery, Kenner collectibles files, and news.

Jedi Knight Clan Legacy
www.starwarz.com/swlegacy/clan/frameset.html
What a group. First, they are dedicated gameplayers, having friendly tournaments and events among themselves. Second, they've become actors and video producers by pooling resources and putting together the Star Wars Legacy video project. Now that's something.

Jedi Knight Qui-Gon Jinn
http://meltingpot.fortunecity.com/greenwood/487/char/quigon.html
A lot was known about Qui-Gon before the Phantom Menace opened - here's the inside scoop and some of the major quotes, all from the Prequel Spoilers web site.

Jedi Knights Homepage
http://members.aol.com/Myau84/jedi.html
Text pages with selected images from the Trilogy that illustrate the benchmarks of Jedi-being. Jedi award, bios of some familiar Jedis, lightsabers, The force and the dark side explained.

Jedi Mark's Place
www.geocities.com/Area51/Hollow/9125
Definitely a tough guy site - space motorheads - with sub-pages for bounty hunters, vehicles, animations, and a link list that actually tells you what you'll find on the link sites!

Jedi Paradise Episode 1
http://members.aol.com/bigeoz/JPhome.htm
Find Special Edition and Episode 1 pages here, also a poll, trivia, links to new merchandise and Star Wars news updates, and Big E Oz quips like "Titanic will sink for the last time." We didn't know it was still afloat.

Jedi Paradise Multimedia for Star Wars & Phantom Menace
http://members.aol.com/bigeoz/multimedia.html
   Lively page of videos (mostly trailers), JPEG pix, music. Hi-Res picture section. Linked videos include Troops (takeoff on COPS) and SimWars, a real mockery. You'll like the straight-up clips, too.

Jedi Society
http://members.aol.com/Myau84/society.html
   This page will link you to a number of other sites with "Jedi" in the title. Are they real Jedi's or just puttin' up cool looking sites? Explore, then decide.

Jedi Trivia
www.fortunecity.com/tattooine/lucas/66/jt-index.html
   Four levels of Trivia - 1.Jawa/easy, 2.Stormtrooper/medium (hmmm, we would have thought that Jawa would be medium and stormtrooper easy), 3.Bounty Hunter/hard, and last, 4.Jedi/very hard. Maybe you'll make it to the hall of fame. The text is rather dark and a bit hard to read.

Jedi's Planet
http://members.xoom.com/jediplanet
   Italian Guerre Stellari (Star Wars) site with Wallpapers and excellent artworks by Ray Traced.

JediKnight.net
www.jediknight.net
   Not all Jedi are in the movies - some are game players. Find them, also gaming news, hosted sites, forums, fingers, servers, online games. Featured are Jedi Knight, Mysteries of the Sith, Rogue Squadron, X-Wing Alliance, Force Commander, and the NEW Prequel games titles.

Jedinet
www.jedinet.com/frame.htm
   By the fans for the Fans, Jedinet is one of the bigger Star Wars sites; its huge collections of pages & info makes this a good portal. Its chat room should be more active than most. News is very current. Find message forums, literature, and humor pages.

Jedinet Pictures
www.jedinet.com/multimedia/pics/index.htm
   May be the finest collection of JPEG Star Wars images online. Well organized; each sub-page gives expandable thumbnails, file size, pix size. Topics include Art, Christmas, Insignias, Imperials, Media, Places, Rebels, Cards, Technical, Falcon, Logos, Sabers, and more.

Jedinet Software
www.jedinet.com/software
   Awesome software section of Jedinet: find news & reviews of games, also items for your computer. See screenshots from games. Download demos & patches. Has great archives of game demos, articles, & reviews. Links to major Star Wars game sites. Cheat codes will soon be available.

Jeffrey Zeldman Presents
www.zeldman.com/toc.html
   This site, which is full of useful sitebuilding information and links, contains a lot of downloadable images, including "disturbing desktop patterns" and "web art."

IMAGES   VIDEO   AUDIO
MUST SEE!   SELLS STUFF   ADULT CONTENT   SEARCHABLE
CHAT ROOMS   MESSAGE BOARDS   MAILING LISTS

Jim Butt's Star Wars Page
http://members.accessus.net/~wbutts
The Jukebox and picture pages make this a solid site. Also, find trivia, past Star Wars Questions & Answers. View this site in frames or no frames versions.

Jim's Star Wars Chronology
www.gis.net/~mcfadden/jmm/swhome.html
Are you lost in space AND time? Here's where you can find the right time - when things happened and some background about events. Look by event or a book or story to find out when it happened in the scheme of things.

John Dykstra - All-Media Guide
http://allmovie.com/cg/x.dll?UID=9:01:46|PM&p=avg&sql=B88556
Find out more about this academy award winner for best visual effects at his All-Media Guide page. His credits include Battlestar G., Star Trek: The Motion Picture, Batman Forever, Firefox, Batman & Robin. Only person nominated for academy awards for both Star Wars & Star Trek.

Join the Campaign
www.jax-inter.net/users/datalore/starwars/campaign.htm
We've included this rather unusual page in the productions section because the page author (Jay Pennington of Threadwell's Techdome) makes some comments (some quite movie/technical) about what, technically and story-wise, might be added to the Trilogy flix.

Jon's Fly-By-Night Sci-fi Image Gallery & Sound Archive
http://web.wt.net/~jquick/archive.html
Two screens: one for images (mostly stock pix) and another for WAV audio files. Features more than Star Wars - also Star Trek, Sliders, Independence Day, Buffy - TVS, and a couple fantasy Sci-fi shots.

Journal of the Whills - Miscellaneous: Imperial City
www.geocities.com/Hollywood/Set/8008/misc.html
Prequel page features some early concept pix of the Imperial City on Coruscant. The new color JPEG images are compared to the McQuarrie original concept images. Early black & white illustrations.

Journal of the Whills Cast of the New Trilogy
www.geocities.com/Hollywood/Set/8008
How wrong we all can be! This page is old, and, obviously, it hasn't been updated because you find casting errors: Kate Winslet is on the list; Gregory Hines rumored as Windu. But they got McGregor, Neeson, and Portman right!

Journal of the Whills Star Wars Prequel Trilogy
www.geocities.com/Hollywood/Set/8008/prequels.html
Open pages for Episodes 1, 2, 3, also find pages for characters, casting, effects and art. Miscellaneous page features Coruscant. Effects and art include photos from the England studio, with George Lucas on hand.

Juan's Star Wars Site
www.civila.com/hispania/obi-juan/english.htm
Obi-Juan's (Juan Antonio Gil Lopez) Spain Multimedia site has English and Spanish versions, both are well-organized, top-notch. Includes pages of animations, videos, images, sounds, and downloads of desktop software. Text files include species descriptions, bios, screenplays, histories, and more.

Jundland Wastes
www.starwars.com/locations/jundland_wastes/1_bg.html
Call it a desert, call it the badlands - it's the official Lucasfilm page site for Tatooine's Jawas and Sand People. Don't go it alone here. Click on the pix on the left to go to a full color still, with magnificent sunset - like Arizona.

Kave, The 🖼️ 🎬 🔊
www.educ.kent.edu/~kdevine/movies
Collection of QuickTime and MOV videos of the Prequel Trailers, some in stereo, also MPEG. Includes the Special Editions, and Trilogy trailers. Adding to the fun is MP3 audio files of the Imperial March, including Metallica's. See Lego images, toys, and powerpoint calendar.

Kaya Cloud's Star Wars Clip Art 🖼️ 👁️
http://members.tripod.com/~KayaCloud
Jedi Graphics page with nice clean originals of R2-D2, X-wing, AT-AT, and Han's blaster.

Kenny Baker - All-Media Guide 🔍
http://allmovie.com/cg/x.dll?UID=9:01:46|PM&p=avg&sql=B3418
At 3 feet 8 inches tall, actor Kenny Baker was a cinch to play R2-D2 in Star Wars - and in other flix such as Time Bandits, Dressed to Kill, Mona Lisa, Amadeus. This All-Media Guide page gives Baker's bio and filmography. This searchable site also links to other Star Wars people.

Kessel Run
www.kesselrun.com
Under construction when we last visited, but if the site is anything like the opening graphic, "we should do well."

Kevin's Angle On Things - Why . . . Be a Jedi Knight 👁️
http://orion.it.luc.edu/~kriorda/angle.html
Observations of the Star Wars myth with real life, simply stated in 5 sections. "Jedi appeal to me not only because they had strange and wonderful powers, but because they portray a simple, elegant poise" - "Philosophy of knowledge, self-exploration, and harmony with nature."

Knight Hammer 🔊 🔍 👁️
www.geocities.com/Area51/Chamber/4182/index.html
An Imperial site, but it is one of the "nice" ones. Learn about Admiral Daala, the movie cast & characters, and find audio recordings, images, word puzzles, quotes, briefing room, also survey, timeline, links, search engines, best ofs, webrings, awards.

Kyle's Star Wars Web Site 🖼️
www.angelfire.com/ca2/starwarslover
New in March '99 and under construction. Stock photo collection so far, with a few model pix.

🖼️ IMAGES	🎬 VIDEO	🔊 AUDIO
👁️ MUST SEE!	$ SELLS STUFF	🔞 ADULT CONTENT	🔍 SEARCHABLE
💬 CHAT ROOMS	📥 MESSAGE BOARDS	📫 MAILING LISTS

Lake Washington Online
http://lwo.lkwash.wednet.edu
On the main page of this .edu site we found the Prequel Trailers in high-res stereo QuickTime file format. Low-res is also available.

Land of The Prequels
www.the-mattman.com/starwars
The Phantom Menace "News" business is booming - this site has late news (but not up to the minute), a pretty nifty gallery section of images, also pages for characters and "the plot." Expect to see more pages and updates.

Lando Calrissian
www.starwars.com/characters/lando_calrissian/index.html
Lucasfilms' official page for Lando Calrissian, with background material on the character, but none on Williams (true to all official character sites). Lando is introduced in Empire Strikes Back and turns hero after a questionable start; click on his picture for a good close-up of Billy Dee Williams.

Lando Calrissian - The Suavest Man In Space
www.geocities.com/Area51/3642/lando.htm
Generally, a humor site (try to avoid the Colt 45 sub-page) that also is a tribute to Lando, with info, a trivia, a few pix from the movies, Landometer, also downloads of fonts, some rare, some not so rare.

Lando Calrissian Adventures
www.ozemail.com.au/~alkenned/starwars/swlcst.htm
Here's a summary of the Del Rey adventure book titles "Lando Calrissian & The StarCave of Thon Boka." From here you can move forward or back to other Lando and Han Solo adventure books by Del Rey Publishing. Reviews here are X-cellent but book cover pix are small.

Lando Calrissian, Boba Fett, & Jabba The Hutt Books
www.geocities.com/Area51/Portal/7365/swpages/Lando.htm
Star Wars Universe lists books and shows their covers on this page of Empire Strikes Back and Return of the Jedi's coolest characters - Lando, Boba Fett, and that slug Jabba. From this page you can find other Star Wars books for Princess Leia, Han Solo, Luke, & Darth.

Lando's Star Wars Galaxy
www.geocities.com/Area51/Chamber/5094/index.html
Surprisingly good site for Lando Calrissian lore, once into it. Click on "Information about me" for Lando talk, vitals. Get into JPEG image galleries of Lando friends and favorite pix. Download two Star Wars fonts from the main page. Connects to Kramer and Han Solo webrings.

Lars Family, The
http://seconn4.yoda.com/~vader97/lars/lars.html
Luke's family unit in Star Wars met an unfortunate end at the hands of Imperial stormtroopers, but not before this image gallery of the Lars family was compiled by Taz.

late night with you kung fu colt daddy L Silky
www.toshistation.com/lizard.htm
　　Leia gets the treatment, as you shall see, at this Toshi Station humor subpage. Enter at own risk. Page rates 1 Colt.

Latest Scoop - Star Wars News from the Source
http://home1.gte.net/filter1/starwars/index.html
　　This site was the first we found that honored Star Wars fan Steven Curnow, age 14, killed at Columbine HS, Littleton Colorado, April 20, 1999. This site organized a ticket stub drive and a petition to get Decipher to create a Star Wars CCG card in Steven's memory.

Latest Star Wars Comics News
www.theforce.net/comics
　　theforce.net's easy to use news page for comic book fans, with lists, facts, figures, pix (small), news archives, and linking pages to Dark Horse (reviews, previews, release schedules) and Marvel Series.

LeeboMan's New Star Wars Site
www.angelfire.com/co/LeeboMan
　　Site promotes active involvement - a poll, chat room links, etc. Strong point is sound files. Find some rare clips. Downloadable animations (letter/stormtrooper's helmet and more) available for computers. A Simpson's fan, too.

LeeboMan's Star Wars Sound Page
www.angelfire.com/co/LeeboSounds/index.html
　　Small but interesting sound file collection: Homer Simpson & Mr. Burns lightsaber duel, droid quotes from the Star Wars X-mas Special and other Star Wars MIDI music condensed.

Leia Quiz
www.saunalahti.fi/~margot/quiz.htm
　　Margot's Carrie Fisher page has this great Carrie/Princess Leia quiz. Take it and see just how loyal a fan you are! "What were the last words Leia said in the Trilogy?" "How did Leia's foster parents die?"

Lesser Known Rebels
www.geocities.com/Area51/Corridor/8737/rebels.html
　　Taz pix collection of rebel heroes (some nameless) in JPEG format. Some images are big and/or wide (X-wing hanger bay). Some are from foreign film versions or promos. We don't recommend calling Admiral Ackbar a "Lesser Known Rebel" - he's running for president, you know.

Let The Wookie Win
www.shavenwookie.com/ccg
　　CCG - Home page for Let The Wookie Win card game by Chris Hawkins and Matthew Ting.

Letterman Digital Center at the Presidio
www.lucasfilm.com/presidio
　　At the newly opened Presidio (San Fran.), the Letterman Digital Center is intended to house the Digital Training Center. Through this page you find out about the center, educational ops, and get to other Geo. Lucas Companies.

Liam Neeson
http://starwars.com/cast/neeson/index.html
   Official Star Wars cast site for Liam Neeson - "a venerable Jedi knight." Here's Liam's professional background, awards, and filmography combined.

Liam Neeson (Lycos Network)
www.lycos.com/entertainment/celebrities/celebs/Neeson_Liam.html
   Lycos' Entertainment/Celebrity page for Liam lists his top claims to fame, a few vital statistics (Liam's the same age as Mark Hamill and me), and official and fan web sites. Search for more from this site.

Liam Neeson - All-Media Guide
http://allmovie.com/cg/x.dll?UID=9:01:46|PM&p=avg&sql=B52070
   Liam Neeson's career has been one of steady growth, which you can see in his filmography at this All-Media Guide site. Liam is 6ft 4in tall; find out about him and other Star Wars people at this searchable site. Remember him in High Spirits? This page offers language translations.

Liam Neeson Appreciation Pages
www.geocities.com/Hollywood/Set/6510/index2.html
   Portions of this official-looking Liam Neeson site were down when we visited (no e-mail, no mailing lists) but filmography and bio pages were accessible. Hopefully, you'll find many additions in 1999.

Liam Neeson Fact Sheet
www.eonline.com/Facts/People/Bio/0,128,157,00.html
   E-Online Fact Sheets list actors' bios, filmography, and stories, but not quite as deeply as some of the other fact-crammed databases. Yes, William Neeson was born into a humble background in Northern Ireland.

Liam, Liam, Liam!!!!
http://members.tripod.com/~BASKERTON/Liam.html
   Not all web pages heep tons of praise in tribute - this page doesn't cut Liam any slack, asking the question: "Why have you made so many bad movies, Liam?" Yet, the site author applaudes Liam's kilt movie (Rob Roy) as superior to Mel Gibson's (Braveheart).

License Plates
www.theforce.net/tfnnews
   Photos of people's Star Wars License Plates collected by theforce.net on their TFN news pages. Jar Jar in California and Drth Mal in Ohio have arrived.

Lightsaber Pictures
www.jedinet.com/multimedia/pics/sabers/index.html
   Jedinet collection of color and black/white JPEG images of lightsabers being used in Trilogy movie scenes, also models, displays, and close-ups. Phantom Menace ones may show up any day.

Lightsaber Technology
www.wcug.wwu.edu/~paradox/forcelight.html
   "This is the weapon of the Jedi Knight." The Compenium has put together an information page on this hand-held weapon - and you can also link to other weapon and "force" pages at this powerful web site.

Lightsabers - Jedi Knights
http://members.aol.com/Myau84/sabers.html
   Diagram and description of a basic lightsaber. FYI, Adegan or Ilum crystals were the types most commonly used in the construction of ancient lightsabers.

Lightsabers Text
www.angelfire.com/oh/gavinda/lightsaber.html
Basic background about the most elegant of weapons - the lightsaber.

Links to the Star Wars Galaxy
www.shavenwookie.com/swlinks.html
Shaven Wookie's exhautive (1500+ sites) alphabetical list of Star Wars links; categorized but without site profiles.

Liquefy
http://grind.isca.uiowa.edu
In addition to dry university stuff, the fans at University of Iowa put up QuickTime movies to download - Prequel Trailer, Teaser, also the TROOPS Series and Trooper Clerks videos.

Literature (LucasFan.com)
www.lucasfan.com/literature.html
What are fan's artwork doing in a Literature section? Who knows! Here you can find out about Lucasfilm's Alien Chronicles, expanded novels, Star Wars & Indy books, Star Wars lit news, audio books, and most of all, comics! Has a rating system; for instance: 1 Death Star = Bantha fodder.

Lithographs - Limited Edition $
www.tncmagic.com/starwars/00litho.htm
12 original lithographs - "Rebel Base" can be signed by Mark Hamill - are available through tnc universe. Find small JPEG images for each. Click on left menu bar to view other collectibles, including figurines, playsets, cards.

Liz's Book Reviews
www.geocities.com/Hollywood/1165/books.html
Reads, reviews and rates many of the recent Star Wars books.

Locations: Prequel Planets
http://meltingpot.fortunecity.com/greenwood/487/places/planets.html
The three major planets featured in Episode 1 appear here - Tatooine, Naboo, & Coruscant - along with info about them and JPEG image galleries. Part of the Prequel Spoilers suite of web pages.

Logic - The Whill Journal
www.geocities.com/Area51/Stargate/4465/logic.htm
What will the next 2 Prequel movies have in them? The Whill Journal speculates on what we're likely to see in 2002 and 2003. Click/link to each of the next Prequels/Logics. Find good rare JPEG images among these pages.

Logos (Jedinet)
www.jedinet.com/multimedia/pics/swlogo/index.html
20 color logos from the Trilogy, including 4 versions of "A long time ago in a galaxy far, far away," all in JPEG format on Jedinet. Some logos are quite rare.

Lord Vader's Australian Collectibles
www.corplink.com.au/~hatten/lord.htm
As important as the bootleg Star Wars collectibles and collections that we don't see in America is the list of Australian Dates to Remember. Site is not very busy, so you could probably make them an offer they can't refuse.

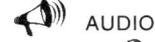

IMAGES   VIDEO   AUDIO
MUST SEE! $ SELLS STUFF   ADULT CONTENT   SEARCHABLE
CHAT ROOMS   MESSAGE BOARDS   MAILING LISTS

Lord Vader's Lair

www.geocities.com/Area51/Cavern/4897/vader.html
   Short movie clips, sounds, links, and Star Wars downloads for your computer - but where's Darth?

Lord Vader's Lair Computer Stuff

www.geocities.com/Area51/Cavern/4897/misc.html
   Desktop themes for MS Plus, also Special Edition Wallpaper and start-up/shut-down images.

Lord Vader's Lair Movie Clips

www.geocities.com/Area51/Cavern/4897/frmovie.html
   We didn't find Darth at this site, but did find many great QuickTime MOV and AVI video files.

Lost Scenes Compiled by Roderick VonHogen

www.virtualedition.com/lost_scenes/index.html
   Collection of images from original Star Wars framed in a theater setting - some are good out-takes, others are just plain blurry. In "a malfunction,", a droid spews smoke. Don't touch it - you'll break it.

Lucas & McCallum on Location in Italy Interview

www.swdatabase.com/newpics/transcript.txt
   Star Wars principles George Lucas and Rick McCallum talk about filming in Italy and about their plans for the Prequel itself. Believed to be July 25, 1998.

Lucas Companies

www.lucasfilm.com/companies_top.html
   Are you interested in employment opportunities with Lucasfilms, licensing, or curious about other businesses under the George Lucas banner? Find a brief background and links to each Lucas company.

Lucas Learning $

www.lucaslearning.com
   George Lucas has spun-off several companies: Lucas Learning is intended for teachers, schools, and students who use Star Wars materials or teaching tools. Find FAQs, company and resources pages.

LucasArts Entertainment Company $

www.lucasarts.com/menu.html
   LucasArts official site for their licensed game products. Get ready for Star Wars: Episode 1 The Phantom Menace and Star Wars: Episode 1 Racer, the first interactive games based on EP1. Also, see X-wing Alliance & Rogue Squadron and visit the company store.

LucasArts Press Room

www.lucasarts.com/pages/IndexAnnouncement.main.html
   By reading about what LucasArts says to the press about its games, you should get a good idea of what their games are about. When you get the game, you'll already know about many of its features.

Lucasfan.com
www.lucasfan.com
If George Lucas has a part in it, it's probably listed (and illustrated) here! Sub-pages include Lucas' films, interviews, literature, news, and humor around him - and an excellent television section.

LucasGames
www.lucasgames.com
The LucasArts gaming source. LucasGames Network pages: JediKnight, RogueSquadron, X-Wing Alliance, & Indy Jones. Game news, previews, forums, chat, industry links. Site is searchable. Find demos and surveys.

Luke & Leia Musical Piece
www.thenorm.com/tfm
Cartoonist "Norm" and Scott Leonard get together to produce this MIDI musical piece that mixes Vince Guaraldi's Peanuts piano theme with John Williams' Star Wars score. May the "good grief" be with you. Click on it near the bottom of Norm's Everything Star Wars page.

Luke Skywalker
www.starwars.com/characters/luke_skywalker
Official Lucasfilms character site for Luke Skywalker, with links to other familiar Star Wars screen characters and hardware. Thin, but this page is a good encyclopedia-like bio for the fictional leading character. Click on Luke's photo to go to the official full-color still image.

Luke Skywalker Galleries (Taz's)
http://seconn4.yoda.com/~vader97/luke/luke.html
Luke Skywalker images (most are JPEG files) are arranged in three individual galleries - one for each Trilogy movie. It takes a while to download, but the quality is good.

Luke Skywalker Movie Theme
www.winfiles.com/apps/98/themes-movie-q.html
Would you like Luke Skywalker on the Windows of your PC? You can download files that feature him as a Windows Theme. In fact, you can download several Star Wars & Phantom Menace themes from this alphabetical directory. Because he's the best, Luke's the last one in the file.

Luke Skywalker Ring of Dreams
www.webring.org/cgi-bin/webring?ring=lukefans;index
Webring of 10 sites - all appear to be tributes to Trilogy hero Luke Skywalker, many rich in resources.

IMAGES — VIDEO — AUDIO
MUST SEE! — SELLS STUFF — ADULT CONTENT — SEARCHABLE
CHAT ROOMS — MESSAGE BOARDS — MAILING LISTS

Lycos Star Wars Mini-Guide
www.lycos.com/entertainment/scifi/miniguide/starwars.html
   Let's get behind the latest Star Wars! This Lycos site is starting to warm up (they were a little cool at first, like the experts who under-estimated Star Wars back in '77!). Site has good links, backgrounding goodies, & is searchable!

Lyrics to YODA (by Weird Al)
www.geocities.com/Hollywood/Set/5760
   Weird Al Yankovic's tribute to Yoda using the tune for the Kink's anthem "Lola." Sorry, no music, just the words.

Mailing List Summary (Echo Station)
http://mail.novatech.net:81/guest/RemoteListSummary/SWML
   As it is one of the largest Star Wars sites, Echo Station has compiled a mailing list that is open to subscriptions, with immediate or digest delivery daily.

Main Characters (& Minor Characters) Prequel Spoilers
http://meltingpot.fortunecity.com/greenwood/487/char/clist.html
   Before the opening of A Phantom Menace, the Prequel Spoilers web site had compiled excellent background material on the characters, including minor ones. Find quotes and vital information here. Tidbit: it is possible that Anakin is the result of a bizarre, mutant virgin birth.

Making of Episode One
www.starwars.com/making
   Video diary by assistant director Lynn Hale about the making of Episode 1 from the film creators' perspectives. Uses RealVideo, and includes seven video segments. Moviemaking story by Hale.

Mandalorian Portfolio
http://scifi.simplenet.com/starwars/prequels/portfolio/mand/mand.html
   Mandalorians - read about their history, their rite of passage, society and role in the Prequel Trilogy at this Sci-fi Advance site. Much of this material comes from The Clone Wars MUSH.

Many Faces of Harrison Ford
www.geocities.com/Hollywood/Hills/2080/ford.html
   Basic bio, facts, filmography - hey, Harrison attended but flunked out of Ripon College in Wisconsin, the birthplace of the Republican Party. The site author promises to add video clips and pix.

Margot's Carrie Fisher Page
www.saunalahti.fi/~margot/cf.htm
   Margot's pages have a flair for the dramatic and a sharp appearance. Features Carrie facts (Carrie has a brother: Todd), filmography, books, good Leia quiz, pix, guestbook, and links to other Carrie sites.

Mario's Star Wars Page
http://andrix.biophysics.mcw.edu/mariusz/mario/starwars/starmain.htm
   We thought we were getting a big fancy web site here, since the URL is to a biophysics lab at MCW.edu, but it turns out the site's best feature is 3 Special Edition Posters, scripts to the Trilogy, and Yoda song lyrics to YMCA.

Mark Hamill (Lycos Network)
www.lycos.com/entertainment/celebrities/celebs/markhamill.html
   Lycos Entertainment Page for Mark Hamill (Luke) gives a few vital stats (did you know he went to High School in Yokohama, Japan?). Lists his claims to fame and other fan sites. A Lycos search field helps you find more info. A good start site for Luke research! He's a Libra.

Mark Hamill - All-Media Guide
http://allmovie.com/cg/x.dll?UID=9:01:46|PM&p=avg&sql=B29931
All-Media Guide's page for Mark Hamill, a.k.a. Luke, gives his entertainment career bio and filmography. Remember him in one of his first roles on General Hospital or in Sarah T,: Portrait of a Teenage Alcoholic?

Mark Hamill Mailing List
www.chez.com/jedinat/list.html
A message board for those who appreciate Mark Hamill, his wonderful work, and most things connected with him. Good place to exchange Mark-isms. It's non-commercial; sponsored by Natalie (see her other great Hamill pages)

Mark Hamill Quotes
www.chez.com/jedinat/quotes.html
Mark is very candid in talking about Star Wars. Here you can find some very insightful quotes and stories. We liked his garbage-smasher scene story. Also, Mark comments on the ackwardness of shooting the Yoda scenes: "So, I'd be talking to a yardstick going "Why can't I be a Jedi?"

Mark Hamill Rare Images (Gothic Skywalker's)
www.geocities.com/TimesSquare/Dungeon/3913/mark.html
We don't know where Gothic Skywalker got these family photos of Mark Hamill - maybe they aren't really Mark. You decide. Baby pix onward.

Martin Bond's Episode 1 Site
http://members.xoom.com/_XOOM/mb_starwars/index.html
Prequel site in French (no English) features video trailers, trailer images and an excellent page describing Anakin's house, with a set-design blueprint. This French (or French Canadian) site features wonderful Prequel Wallpaper.

Martinez Brothers Star Wars page
www.geocities.com/Area51/Dimension/5951
Martinez Brothers are teens and have put together a solid site of sounds, MIDIs, pix (GIFs/JPEGs), videos (gives size of file), scripts, links and humor links, also bios for 8 Star Wars characters.

Marua Sector
www.marua.com/index2.html
A very small portal, but we rate it as potentially a very good one (considering the excellent contributions to this relatively new web site thus far). Not all sections are operating, but the Prequels, multimedia, interactive features, jukebox and especially the 3D are fairly solid and worthwhile.

Masks - Star Wars
www.anniescostumes.com/swmask.htm
Full-head covering latex masks, including aliens, Boba Fett, Greedo, Stormtrooper, Tuskan Raider, Yoda, a part-plastic Darth Vader, and Admiral Ackbar. Link back to costume accessories, props, ordering, and other movie costumes. Do you need a 7-ft high Darth Vader Statue? Find it here; you'll need to sell your house to afford it.

Massassi Order
www.hta.nl/php/Jan.Jacob.Mosselaar/swring.htm
Variety and depth makes this Netherlands site worthwhile: downloads galore, themes for computers, book list with synosii, abundance of WAV sound files, images, models, games, storyboards, archives and pages for Episode 1.

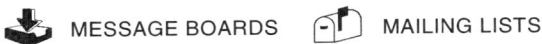

Massassi Order Pictures
www.hta.nl/php/Jan.Jacob.Mosselaar/mmpict.htm
>Collection of 520 JPEG images arranged by categories: Emperial (sic) forces, Rebel forces, Aliens, Planets & Vehicles. Most are Trilogy pictures, with some Special Editions. Click on thumbnail image to expand the picture.

Massassi Order Schale Models
www.hta.nl/php/Jan.Jacob.Mosselaar/swmodel.htm
>Since this is a foreign site, we assume the world "Schale" is a misspelling of "Scale Models." None-the-less, this site is in English, with 14 pages of cool shots of vehicles and spacecraft models.

Mastering 3D Graphics (M3G) $
www.mastering3dgraphics.com
>A new realm of 3D tutorials is upon us - become a member and then become an expert at 3D graphics, get newsletter and technical support. Click on "Galleries" at bottom of the message page and find great 3D artist samples and their e-mail addresses and sites!

Masters of Teras Kasi
www.game-junkie.com/Reviews/Playstation/StarWars_Fight/SWMOTK.HTM
>Star Wars: Master of Teras Kasi is a Playstation Game. Here it is reviewed by gaming expert "The Professor". Find some AVI video samples of the game itself. Includes move lists and gallery of JPEG images captured from the game. The Professor wasn't too impressed.

Matt Busch Original Art (the force.net)
www.theforce.net/museum/g_mattb
>Matt Busch's top-notch collection of 14 colorful originals found on the force.net rates its own page. Click on the thumbnail images to enlarge them to their full spendor.

Matt's Home Page
www.geocities.com/Area51/Rampart/6867/starwars.htm
>In development when we visited, Matt's home Page had limited information on the Prequels, also the scripts for the Trilogy, some links, and a James Bond page. More should be available later in 1999.

MaulNet.Com
www.maultnet.com
>New site for evil - Darth Maul news, products, proliferation, propaganda, also trailer video downloads, survey, and page for Maul merchandise, also artist Ray Park file, and found articles. Check the Maultimedia section for humor and tons of images. Worship the Maul.

MaulNet.Com: Maultimedia
www.maulnet.com/maultimedia
>A Maul-titude of Prequel Darth Maul images, humor pieces, html clips, JPEGs, and "At last we will reveal ourselves to the Jedi" quote downloadable in 4 formats: AIFF, NeXT/Sun, RealPlayers, Riff. Excellent covers and some behind the scenes pictures.

MaulRats.com $
www.maulrats.com
MaulRats sounds like Mall-rats, and you'll think you're in a Star Wars action figure "mall" here. Latest news and lots of pages of new, classic, and vintage Hasbo and Lego products. Check out the MaulRats.com fun page, too.

MAW Installation
www.premier.net/~exar/MAW2.htm
Collection of multimedia including WAV sound files, Special Edition pix, also sections for characters, booklist, bloopers, ships and vessels. Find downloadable icons for your computers or website.

McLaurin's Center of Knowledge
http://members.xoom.com/maclaurin386/index1.htm
From this very high-tech (Java applets) index page you can access Star Wars, also Star Trek, Bond...James Bond, and Emma (Spice Girl) pages. All pages are very good, with very solid galleries. Star Wars includes humor, video, photos, sound files and more.

McLaurin's Star Wars Movies
http://members.xoom.com/_XOOM/maclaurin384/starwars/movies/movies.html
More than 30 AVI and MOV files are found on this very good multimedia site by Peter McLaurin.

McLaurin's Star Wars Site
http://members.xoom.com/maclaurin384/starwars
This eExtremely high tech Peter McLaurin Star Wars site has most all the onscreen tricks.

IMAGES   VIDEO   AUDIO
MUST SEE!   SELLS STUFF   ADULT CONTENT   SEARCHABLE
CHAT ROOMS   MESSAGE BOARDS   MAILING LISTS

Mfalcon's Star Wars Outpost
www.geocities.com/Area51/Zone/9049
> Opens with posters of first 3 movies; also features photos and MIDI music files. Vote for your favorite characters and submit your site for the MFalcon Award.

Microsoft Flight Simulator 98 Star Wars Ships
http://members.xoom.com/Startroop1/Ships.html
> This simulator may be all over the galaxy afterwhile; this is the first site where we encountered it. Choose to fly a TIE fighter, Interceptor, X-wing or other craft. We didn't fly it - you might! Active-X WAV files in zip format.

MIDI Files (Jedinet)
www.jedinet.com/multimedia/midi/index.htm
> Download any of these 24 MIDI format music files from the Trilogy & Special Editions. File lengths are not given, but we would assume the quality and lengths are standard or above. Includes Jedi Rock from the Return of the Jedi Special Edition. Has all the themes we could think of.

MIDI Music by Scott M Leonard $
www.geocities.com/TheTropics/Shores/5972/midimusic.html
> Arrangements and originals by Scott Leonard in MIDI format, suggested for play using Beatnik (downloadable free plug-in). Arrangements are inspired from the movies, games, & Disney; originals are Hoth Echo Station, Jedi Academy Theme, Star Vipers.

Mike Bonnell's Computer Wallpaper $
www.mikebonnell.com
> This site offers an impressive array of wallpapers for Windows, many inspirational or space themes. Graphics are computer-generated and most are free to download. Choose the size of graphic to download based on monitor size.

Mike Gartley's Miscellaneous Page
www.ma.iup.edu/~tzqf/star/misc.html
> Collection of magazine covers & paintings featuring Star Wars. Find a Kellogg's C-3PO cereal box!

Mike Gartley's Poster Page
www.ma.iup.edu/~tzqf/star/poster.html
> Movie posters, book posters, foreign posters, and art posters.

Mike Gartley's Star Wars Page
www.ma.iup.edu/~tzqf/star/starwars.html
> Images of ships, characters, posters, magazine covers and art; also galleries of sounds, MIDI music themes, movie scripts. Arranged in convenient subject directories.

Mike's Star Wars Pages
www.ece.orst.edu/~volzmi/starwars
> Well-organized page by Mike Volz is "big," with directories of files of videos (MOV, AVI), sound clips (WAVs), scripts, images, music (MIDI, AIF), desktop themes, icons, wallpaper, humor "stuff" with the file size listed. Good images collection on the main page, including a large star destroyer.

Millenium Falcom - Ship of Riddles
www.synicon.com.au/sw/mf/falcon.htm
> "Escape pods" on the Falcon - no way! Here's B-squared's (Robert Brown) exhaustive look at anything and everything about the most famous Star Wars spacecraft. The collection is top-notch and the perfect place to look for Falcon info, tech stuff, images.

Millenium Falcon
www.starwars.com/vehicles/millennium_falcon
    Official Lucasfilms page for Star Wars most personable spacecraft, captained by Han Solo and Chewbacca. It's a Corillian stock light freighter with "special modifications" and termperamental qualities. Click on the pix for full-color stills of Star Wars' pancake in tinfoil. Limited specs are given.

Millenium Falcon (museum piece)
www.geocities.com/Area51/Vault/3227/index.html
    Photo of Han Solo's Millenium Falcon from the 1998 Star Wars exhibit at the Smithsonian Museum.

Millenium Falcon Pictures
www.jedinet.com/multimedia/pics/falcon/index.html
    About 100 JPEG images of the Millenium Falcon interior & exterior from the Trilogy. Size of file and pix are given. Most images are big. Click on thumbnail to expand to full size. Collected by Jedinet.

Millenium Falcon Text
www.angelfire.com/oh/gavinda/falcon.html
    FAQs about Han & Chewbaca's - and, at one time, Lando's - spacecraft. Good informative reading about this YT1300 cargo vessel, but no pix.

Millenium's End
www.fadproductions.com
    Millenium's End is an ongoing video-documentary project by fadproductions (J Cioletti?) in Hi8 video format. The subject: the fans and the impact of the web on Star Wars, and vice versa. Read about the project here and comment via e-mail. Site is part of the Starwarz group.

Monopoly Star Wars CD Win95
www.shopper.com/prdct/955/561.html
    shopper.com site posts the various online places where you can purchase the Star Wars version of the Monopoly Game. It is a CD game that you load in your coffee-cup holder. Good things about this site: you can comparison shop and search for other products.

Monument Square Home Page
www.geocities.com/Area51/Lair/3373/home.html
    The Monument Square main page links easily to images, sounds, humor (recommended), and trivia.

Monument Square Humor Page
www.geocities.com/Area51/Lair/3373/humor.html
    New Star Wars words for popular tunes ("Blast, Loot, Pillage, Burn" to the Mouse Club theme; Yoda meeting Luke to theme of "YMCA"), rejected marketing tie-ins, and files of sexually slanted lines.

Monument Square Sound Collection
www.geocities.com/Area51/Lair/3373/sounds.html
    "Well, I'm glad you're here to tell us these things." Collection of Trilogy quotes; a small number MIDI music files.

More Comebacks To Another Stupids List
www.geocities.com/Hollywood/Set/5760
   Once upon a time, due to the poisoning nature of the weak stories and characters, certain misguided Trekkie sub-factions launched a stupid list. Through this Boba Fett/geocities site comes snappy, wonderful come-backs to "the stupids," once again making the universe a joyous place.

More Star Wars Humor
http://rpg.echostation.com/humor/swjokes.html
   Collection of 10 Star Wars humor files, including Various Beers from the Star Wars Universe, Star Wars do-it-yourself Novel, Star Wars Sexually-slanted Lines ("Curse my metal body, I wasn't fast enough"), song parodies, RU Rebel Alliance Material, and the ubiquitous top 10's.

Mos Eisely Cantina Chat Room
www.angelfire.com/co/Timecruiser/StarChat.html
   Internet Chat Exchange (ICE) chat room found via Timecruiser's web site. Are aliens in this Cantina chat room?

Mos Eisley Cantina
www.geocities.com/Hollywood/Set/7355
   Colorful pages with access to a Jukebox, photo gallery, video vault, humor, and a biting top ten page of why Star Wars is better than that other Sci-fi thing.

Mos Eisley Cantina Diorama
http://members.iquest.net/~sohair/hyperspace/cantina/page0.html
   So, what would the Cantina actually look like - the layout, that is? Star Wars modeling artist (or is he just a guy who takes playing with Star Wars figurines to the extreme?) has created a Cantina diorama that gives you a new perspective on this most-famous watering hole.

Mos Eisley Humor Page
www.geocities.com/Hollywood/Set/7355/hah.html
   Star Trek takes a beating here, big time. So sorry, Trekkers.

Mos Eisley Photo Gallery
www.geocities.com/Hollywood/Set/7355/photo.html
   Opens with a Star Trek Sucks poster - tells you something about this comic-book like page. Humor, Boba Fett tribute, but no Mos Eisley Cantina stuff was found when we last visitied.

Mos Eisley Spaceport
www.starwars.com/locations/mos_eisley
   Official Lucasfilms web page for Mos Eisley Spaceport on planet Tatooine. A couple of rather good locations stills are found at this site. Click on the pictures for full-view enlargements.

Mos Espa Marketplace
http://mosespa.starwars.com/books
   Mos Espa is the market on Tatooine AND the place where you can purchase official Star Wars products and books. Site reviews featured books, new items and bestsellers. Search for books by author or title. Links easily to sub-pages for toys, collectibles, gifts, and magazines.

Movie References
www.jedinet.com/multimedia/references/ref-movies.html
   Star Wars-isms show up a lot in other movies: site lists them, from Marty McFly to Apocalypse Now. Did you hear them say "That sounds like we ran over a wookie" in American Graffiti - four years BEFORE Star Wars came out? Did you catch Tim Burton's reference in The Three Muskateers?

Movie Review Query Engine (MRQE): Star Wars Episode 1 🔍 👁

www.mrqe.com/lookup?^Star+Wars:+Episode+I+(1999)
Searches the web for reviews of your movies of choice. MRQE also offers links to other resources such as Internet Movie Database and "Reel."

Movie Themes - WinFiles.com 🖼 🔍

www.winfiles.com/apps/98/themes-movie.html
From this WinFile.com Movie Themes site, you click on "Movie Themes Q-Z" which takes you to a page with a multitude of themes packages, including one for Phantom Menace. Scroll through to find a number of Star Wars Theme packages. Luke's at the end. Find X-file and Star Trek themes too.

Movielink 🔍

www.movielink.com
What's playing where, what dates, at what time, and names of theaters. This American Express sponsored site lets you search by theater, movie title, search by star & movie type, and by time. Wow. Mix in a pic o' the week, new movie sites, trailers, and other movie details!

Movies - A Feminine Perspective 🎬

http://members.aol.com/bananie42/movies.html
No, not the mushy stuff. Plenty of MOV files from the Trilogy, also Trilogy trailers and Special Editions videos. Link back to the main page for a host of other features and a tribute/bio on Princess Leia, also computer gear, GIF image files, and online fun.

Movies - AVI & QuickTime 🎬

http://pweb.netcom.com/~fragger/movies.html
Galleries of videos from the Trilogy in either AVI or QuickTime formats. Includes the targeting computer, Ewok yells, R2 getting blasted. Sorry, there is no player to download.

Movies.Com 🎬

www.movies.com
This site contains information regarding Touchstone Pictures films that are "Now Playing" as well as those that are being released in the near future. You can watch QuickTime trailers for these films.

Movies: Star Wars Video 🎬

http://pweb.netcom.com/~fragger/movies.html
Video clips - approximately 20 short movies in QuickTime or AVI format (found on Netcom links), notably the duel between Vader and Obi-Wan, Jabba's Palace with dancers, and more.

Moyers Interviews Lucas In Time Magazine 👁

http://cgi.pathfinder.com/time/magazine/articles/0,3266,23298,00.html
Veteran television journalist Bill Moyers interviews Star Wars icon George Lucas about the meaning within Star Wars and the Phantom Menace and their social influences, etc. On Darth Maul/Vader: Moyers: "He's us?" Lucas: "Yes, he's the evil within us." Not me, baby.

MSN Star Wars Web Guide
www.musiccentral.msn.com/movies/StarWars/StarWars.asp
   Microsoft Network's Star Wars Entertainment Main Page is a portal that mainly clicks through to commercial sites for Star Wars videos, books, toys, collectibles. Find Prequel news, links to top 10 sites, and fun & weird sites too.

MST3K Version of "A Galaxy Not So Far Away"
www.geocities.com/Hollywood/Set/5760
   MST3K - Mystery Science Theatre 3000 (they roast sci-fi tomes on the tube) - once engaged in a Star Wars vs. Star Trek cross-over show premised on poor fashion. Clearly, Trek loses out big time. Figure out the transcript!

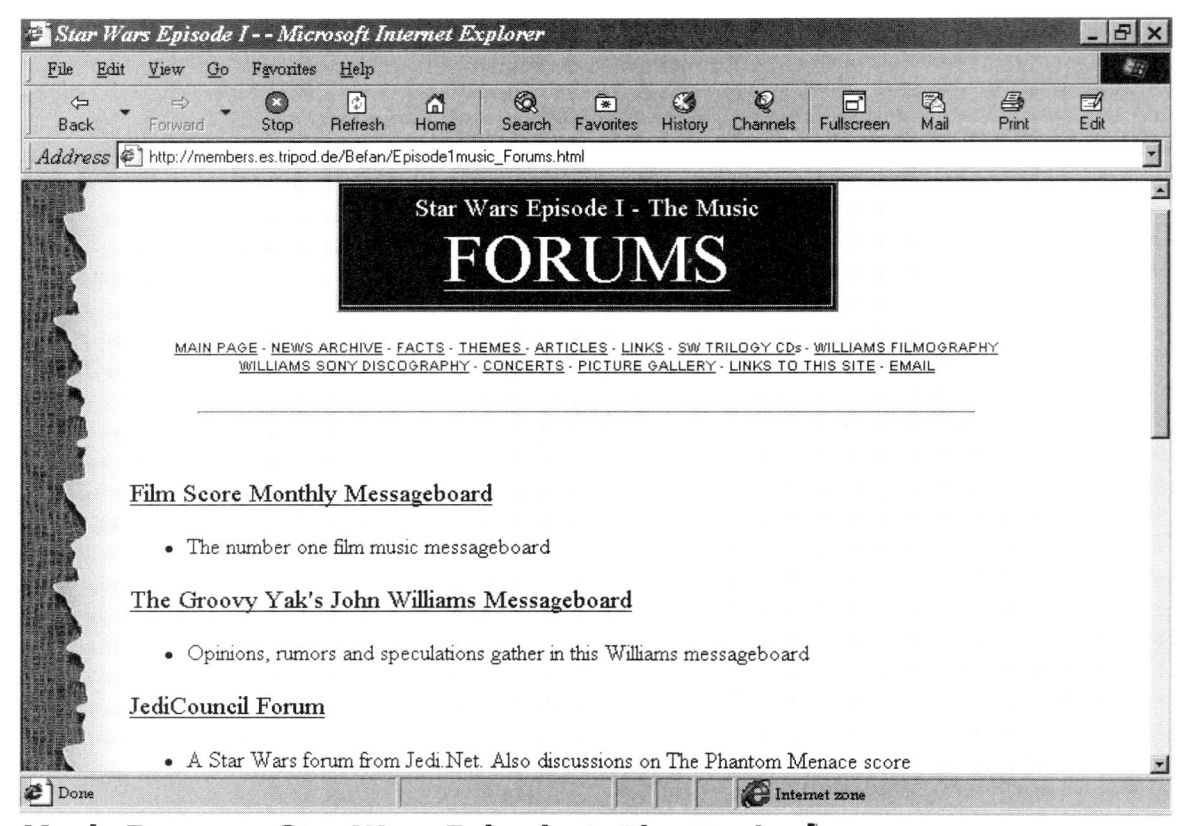

Music Forums - Star Wars Episode 1: The Music
http://members.es.tripod.de/Befan/Episode1music_Forums.html
   There are no less than 9 Prequel/music related forums accessible from this web site. Post and read messages on film scores, John Williams, heroic film music club, and the John Williams discussion list and other music forums.

Music References of Star Wars
www.jedinet.com/multimedia/references/ref-music.html
   We all know Weird Al did the song "Yoda," but did you hear the Madison WI band named Mos Eisley? Here's a list of other Star Wars references that have popped into the music world from rap to Korn to Spice Girls.

My Quicktime Star Wars Video Library
http://weber.u.washington.edu/~sbode/starwars/clips.html
   Hot collection of QuickTime videos from A New Hope, Empire Strikes Back, and Return of the Jedi maintained at a University of Washington student's page.

My Star Wars Experience
http://seclab.cs.ucdavis.edu/~wetmore/camb/hope
What if you were an "extra" in the Special Editions - wouldn't you want to have your own website to tell everyone about it? Sure you would. And you'd have some pictures of yourself with stormtroopers!

My Star Wars Web Site
www.geocities.com/Area51/Cavern/5033
Features galleries of popular Star Wars music MIDI's and pictures, also links to a chat room.

Mysterious Characters
www.fortunecity.com/tattooine/lucas/66/bio-index.html
Bios and photos from the Trilogy of such photo-op mystery characters as IG-88, Bossk, Zuckuss, 4-LOM, Greedo, and, of course, Boba Fett. Found on JF's Star Wars Trilogy pages.

Myth in Star Wars - What Makes Star Wars Special?
www.synicon.com.au/sw/myth/myth.htm
Collection of articles and stories that detail some of the key themes within the Star Wars stories: George Lucas' vision, classic elements, japanese influence, the role of history, Journal of the Whills, the Prequels, and more that helps you focus in on the essence of Star Wars.

NaboOnline
www.naboonline.com
Wonderful resource site from Sci-FI Advance: each Prequel movie has its own page, there's mailing lists, fan fiction pages, book & toy info, picture gallery, cast lists, and portfolios (Mandalorians & Palpatine). Trailer videos and posters promised.

Natalie Portman Fan Club
www.natportman.com/fanclub
Found on the official NatPortman.com site, here you can join her fan club and find and exchange info about Episode 1's biggest and most-attractive star. Also a good source for mailing lists of Portman fans.

Natalie Portman Filmography
www.geocities.com/Hollywood/Lot/7181/filmography.html
We like this Stakawaka Filmography page for Natalie Portman because it includes a color picture of her in each ot the movies she appears in. Also find co-stars and pix files.

Natalie Portman Image Gallery
www.natportman.com/images
Hundreds of JPEG images (stills, scans and video captures) from her movies, Episode 1, also some movie posters (Mars Attacks). This site connects to her main web site.

IMAGES   VIDEO   AUDIO
MUST SEE! $ SELLS STUFF   ADULT CONTENT   SEARCHABLE
CHAT ROOMS   MESSAGE BOARDS   MAILING LISTS

Natalie Portman Photo Gallery
www.geocities.com/Hollywood/Lot/7181/natpics.html
>Over 100 Natalie Portman JPEG images. Click on the thumbnail on any one of the six pages to expand your favorite Natalie pic!

Natalie Portman's Hang Out
http://ucsu.colorado.edu/~vuong/Natalie.html
>An older biography page dedicated to Natalie, so you can find images of her in her pre-Prequel days. According to this ExclamAZN site, she's born June 9, '81 in Jerusalem, but moved to D.C. at age 3. Her dad's a doctor. The Hang Out links to other female celebs.

Natalie's Mark Hamill Homepage
www.chez.com/jedinat/site1.html
>Natalie has a good collection of Mark Hamill files - a filmography, WAV sounds, a funny insightful quotes page, articles, mailing list/message boards, guestbook, webrings, pix, pix and more pix, a "what's new" page and chat.

Nathan's Star Wars Page
http://members.aol.com/nathan224/starwars.html
>A new video clip is promised each week on Nathan's aol site. Some pictures, sounds, links, trivia, survey, animated gifs, awards and good link to Star Wars novels.

NatPortman.com
www.natportman.com
>Natalie Portman's home page gives her biography, a gallery of images, some Prequel videos (trailers in QuickTime or RealVideo), and also lets you join her fanclub and post messages. Please do.

NetJunction Games
www.netjunction.com/starwars/games.htm
>Gallery of 5 games in Zip format - X-Wing, Tie Fighter, Dark Forces, Yoda Stories, Super Star Wars.

NetJunctions Movies
www.netjunction.com/starwars/movies.htm
>A dozen QuickTime videos listed with time length and file size, including new Special Edition Jabba Scenes and several of the Death Star, also trailers and "making of" clips.

NetJunctions Pictures Pages
www.netjunction.com/starwars/gallery.htm
>Small but impressive picture gallery: includes posters, B/W photos, sketches, poses, and classic shots.

Netjunctions Sounds Page
www.netjunction.com/starwars/sounds.htm
>"I've made a lot of special modifications myself," and other memorable sound clips in WAV format.

NetJunctions Star Wars Tribute
www.netjunction.com/starwars
    Opens with Leia in her classic Empire pose. Enter the rebel base and find good solid galleries of sounds, pictures, video/movies and game downloads.

Network's Star Wars Page, The
www.geocities.com/SouthBeach/Lights/5679/starwars.html
    Berlin's Network Prequel Page features a photo gallery of images from the Prequel, also old cast list and news, and links to his active 3D page and to Kenner Cantina.

New Mythology - the Star Wars Trilogy
www.dom.net/wrd/new/ref/sw
    Dominic Sagolla examines myth & archetypes: Slicer/Hacker hero, Savior/Messiah, Rebel model, oppressive order, old man/father history figure, battles, family bond, transformed evil. For actors, does it all come down to being photogenic? Mythology links, structured fabulation concepts.

New Republic Multimedia
http://thenewrepublic.8m.com/cgi-bin/framed/2478/starwars2.html
    Rather than arranging the many media each to its own page, all the media appear on one page here - WAVs, JPEGs, scripts, MIDI sounds, wallpaper, themes, screen savers, icons, humor - and some Prequel images. New Republic's main site is game related (see New Republic, The).

New Republic, The
http://thenewrepublic.8m.com
    Not sure where this web site is going. New Republic seems to be a gaming cadre, dedicated to Star Wars games, with webring links and E-mail circle, but it also has a "force-ful" multimedia section.

New Star Wars, Episode 1
www.starwars.com/episode-i/features/intro
    Destined for the archives, this is the official pre-release web site for Episode 1, and includes good backgrounds on the cast, production features and other interesting PR. Compare this to what you see in The Phantom Menace.

New York Times Flashback Review (on countingdown.com)
http://sabbeth.com/~menace/nytreview.htm
    Copy of the original New York Times 1977 review of Star Wars by reviewer Vincent Canby: "lot of explosive action and not a bit of truly disturbing violence." A very favorable review, of course!

News Stand - CHUD (Cinematic Happenings Under Development)
www.chud.com/news.htm
    Cinematic Happenings Under Development's News Stand page churns out Tinsel-town news, opinions, & rumors. We call it CHUD because we can't remember what CHUD stands for. Occasionally CHUD tosses in cool pix.

IMAGES   VIDEO   AUDIO
MUST SEE! $ SELLS STUFF   ADULT CONTENT   SEARCHABLE
CHAT ROOMS   MESSAGE BOARDS   MAILING LISTS

Newsdroid 👁
www.newsdroid.com
> Headline and lowline news for Star Wars Fans - and very up-to-date! News clips arranged by category: Prequels, comp games, books, comics, toys, board games, CCG, fan sites, affiliates, editorials, satire, also an archives and a place for feedback. This site has its own music.

Nightmare Factory Star Wars Childrens Costumes $
www.nightmarefactory.com/starwark.html
> Children's Trilogy costumes, also linking pages to Adult costumes, masks, accessories, props & collectibles. Also, flashlight style lightsabers.

Nintendo 64 Code Center ⚓🗣 ⚐
www.n64cc.com/MAIN.HTM
> Yes, this is where you find Nintendo 64 info for all of their games - there's also chat, message boards, download areas, translations, polls, contests, hot pics, and game links.

Nocturne's Pulp Fiction 🖼 🎬 🔊
www.skipnet.com/~nocturne/pulpfiction.html
> Movie that made Samuel L Jackson a fan icon, this site has a knock-out "Interesting Facts" section (briefcase combo is 666; rumor has it the case contained an Oscar; more!) along with Pulpy Themes, JPEG pix, video clips.

Not so long ago, in a movie theatre across the way 🎬
www.varsanyi.com/dennism/aboutme/starwars
> Captures a KGW Northwest News interview (on AVI video) with someone who blows the reporter away with his knowledge of trivia details about Star Wars.

Novels of Star Wars (Thrawn Art Gallery) 🖼 👁
http://empire.res.wabash.edu/art/novels/yjk.htm
> Excellent Thrawn art gallery collection of JPEG images of Star Wars Novels, especially the full-color covers. Click on a cover to open up more covers and titles. Find Zahn, Stackpole titles, short stories fiction. No text, but images are out-of-this-world.

Novels' Timelines
www.geocities.com/Area51/Zone/9015/books.html
> Info on some of the more popular Star Wars novels and the time periods in which they occur.

Now & Then 👁
www.usmo.com/~starwars/now&then/now&then.html
> It's not easy being a minor character - some characters have had a rough time making it outside of Star War, in the real "entertaInment" world. See what "other" gigs Yoda, C-3PO, Bossk, Greedo, and Chewie have had to endure.

NSX Digital Gaming Site
www.digitalnsx.com
> X-wing Alliance game demo IS here; NSX news on scheduled NvT competitions, other communiques.

Obi-wan Kenobi
www.starwars.com/characters/ben_kenobi
Official Lucasfilms page featuring pix and general history of Jedi master Obi-Wan Kenobi, better known as Ben Kenobi, played by Alec Guinness, and later by Ewan MacGregor.

Official Creatures
www.starwars.com/creatures
Star Wars is full of unique creatures. Here you will find them on the official Star Wars Lucasfilms page, searchable by type of creature or character name.

Official Dave Prowse Website
www.daveprowse.com
Starwarz.com hosts the official Dave Prowse site, where you can e-mail and directly worship the awesome one who played Darth Vader. Guess what: not one pic of him as Darth appears in his gallery! Refreshing! Site includes bio, filmography, candids, fan club info, appearances, Prowse news.

Official Unofficial Star Wars Web Site
www.powerup.com.au/~crono/new_page_1.htm
Multimedia site with miscellaneous files (Leia when we visited once, but different next trip through) and pop-up Star Wars questions. You may learn that a website can mirror your computer's files.

Official Weapons
www.starwars.com/weapons
Official Lucasfilms page that alphabetically lists and links to all the weapons found in the movies.

On The Mark $
www.geocities.com/Hollywood/Set/7029/otm.html
Although this page is quite old, it lists lists of Star Wars and Mark Hamill fan club Memorabilia, also other lists like Indiana Jones and Star Trek. We cannot guarantee how current this site is.

Online Gaming - Kalidor Squadron
http://kalidor.echostation.com
Echo Station hosts the Kalidor Squadron Online game, which consists of black op scenarios. We didn't play (we always get blown to smithereens), but you can (Go to "bridge"). Group is based on LucasArts' X-Wing simulator.

Original Art by Me & Mine
www.geocities.com/Area51/Corridor/7410/art.html
Original sketches on Star Wars theme by a father/son duo. Yes, they've put together a comic book, too. Not fancy, but there's none of that sappy Imperial sofa neon art stuff.

Orin_J Kingdom
www.gogs32.freeserve.co.uk/page1.htm
Had trouble getting to this United Kingdom multimedia site - it could grow. WAV sound files are largely Darth Vader quotes - "You have failed me for the last time" etc. Also, Fetts, sabers, and great Imperial MIDI music. Truly on the dark side. Downloadable desktop stuff is cursors/icons mostly.

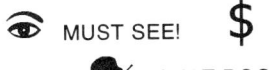

IMAGES   VIDEO   AUDIO
MUST SEE! $ SELLS STUFF   ADULT CONTENT   SEARCHABLE
CHAT ROOMS   MESSAGE BOARDS   MAILING LISTS

Orionsaint Presents Images from Episode 1
www.angelfire.com/ok2/orionsaint
Collection of very wide Episode 1 JPEG images from Orionsaint's site. Click on the thumbnails to view the pictures in full size/full color.

Our Generation - The Den
www.theden.com/den_ourgen
Oo-teeny! Spring '99 Den Daily Entertainment Network "Our Generation Study" of 16,499 US residents asked "What's the heroes of our generation?" Luke = 1 ahead of Jesus, Michael Jordan, Martin Luther King, & our parents! Spielberg beat Gates. Dilbert tied Stern. Most Important Media: Internet.

Palace of the Raider King
http://members.tripod.com/~KingOfTheRaiders/Frames.html
Find icons and a few other computer goodies and downloads, picture section is GIFs, mostly of the Falcon. Not palatial. Appears to be a mirror of the Realm of the Dark Jedi site.

Palpatine Portfolio
http://scifi.simplenet.com/starwars/prequels/portfolio/pal/palpatine.html
Sci-FI Advance's collection of information about the immensely powerful and doubly evil Senator Palpatine. Remember: he's only an aspiring senator in Episode 1, an evil emperor in Return of the Jedi. Bad no matter how you cut it! Read about his personality and rise to power here.

Pants of the Mind's Eye
www.powerup.com.au/~jdc/pants.htm
May be the best Star Wars party game - the idea at the "Pants" site is to substitute the word "pants" in a familiar Star Wars quote: "I find your lack of pants disturbing." In the game, any substitute word can be a keyword; players have to use the keyword in a Star Wars quote.

Parody Song: Star Wars Cantina.mp3 (to tune of Copa Cabana)
ftp://comedy:archives@24.65.86.38/Song%20Parodies
FTP downloadable MP3 of the Star Wars Cantina song, sung to the tune of Copa Cabana. To go directly to this file, open your FTP utility, then add this to the URL above: (Parody of Copa Cabana) Star Wars Cantina.mp3

Parody Video: Episode 1 Trailer 'A' - Special Edition
http://sabbeth.com/~menace/specialedition.htm
Knock-out video spoof of the Star Wars Trailer, produced by the fanatics at countingdown.com and including the contributions of a variety of Star Wars followers and web site hosts. It is: "What All the Fuss Was About - 4,236 frames of fan animation."

Path Not Taken, The
www.flash.net/~draegos/path/main1.html
BCR Production's (Scott Thompson) has developed a fiction that is also a game, calling the project Star Wars, The Path Not Taken. It floats along on the web, growing. We have to watch this out-of-the-internet-mist development.

PC & Miniature Galleries
http://rpg.echostation.com/gallery/gallery.html
Three interesting galleries which are useful as resources for miniature battles and modeling includes. Includes pen & ink sketches, good collection of miniatures (with color mini-pix), and inspiring tips on how to turn useless household toss-outs into useful power generators, reinforced bunkers, speeders!

Peter Cushing - All-Media Guide
http://allmovie.com/cg/x.dll?UID=9:01:46|PM&p=avg&sql=B16338
All-Media Guide lists Peter Cushing's - Grand Moff Tarkin (powdered when the first death star explodes) - extensive filmography as a villain and horror movie icon. This site also gives his biography and links to acting "connections." Cushing starred in The Curse of Frankenstein.

Peter Mayhew - All-Media Guide
http://allmovie.com/cg/x.dll?UID=9:01:46|PM&p=avg&sql=EPeter|Mayhew
Here's the All-Media Guide's page on Peter Mayhew (Chewie) and his filmography - do you remember him in Sinbad and the Eye of the Tiger (1977)? Did you know he was an editor too?

Phantom Menace - The Characters As We Know Them
www.allexperts.com/tv/swchar.shtml
The "we" is the experts at ALLEXPERTS.COM. They explain the Prequel characters, with a good dose of humor mixed in. Anakin Skywalker: "a little boy with a Bill Gates haircut and attitude to match."

Phantom Menace Action Figures
www.continet.com/aaronsmagic/pretoys/phantom.htm
Aaron Johnson's site includes pages and price guides for new EP1 action figure castings - wasn't that a bit quick for pricing out collectibles? No matter - the die is cast. Whoa, a double-entendre!

Phantom Menace II Society
www.geocities.com/~noahklein/phantom.html
Different take on some famous Star Wars dialog, and not for children. Offers its own RealVideo cartoon: Creditor.

Phantom Menace Mania
http://get.to/jedi
Good multimedia site featuring Episode 1 images, pix, video clips, sounds ("Anakin Skywalker, meet Obi-Wan Kenobi"), cast list and even a chat room. See their "Stuff" page for big pictures of new products and other "finds."

Phantom Menace Mania Chat Room
http://pages.preferred.com/~whitesk/starwars/chatroom.html
Chat Room especially designed for discussion of Episode 1 and the Prequels, but you can probably say anything you want, from "woo-woo" to "jar-jar." Brought to us by PhanMenMan.

Phantom Menace Movie Poster $
http://ucaswww.mcm.uc.edu/english/hall/sw1.htm
The URL says its an education site, but it turns into Cyber-Cinema (with a PO Box a couple doors away from ours in Tempe, AZ!) who appears to be the home of the $20 movie poster. The Episode 1 poster of young Anakin may be a tad more. Other movies and other Star Wars posters are on their list.

Phantom Menace RPG Screens
www.planetjedi.com/hangar/TPM/screens.html
Phantom Menace the game is full of great computer-animated action - here's a gallery of JPEG image screen captures and sketches from the game.

IMAGES   VIDEO   AUDIO
MUST SEE! $ SELLS STUFF   ADULT CONTENT   SEARCHABLE
CHAT ROOMS   MESSAGE BOARDS   MAILING LISTS

Phantom Menace Site, The
www.users.wineasy.se/doot/starwars/index.html
Somewhat of a typical Phantom Menace fan site except for the gigantic character poster it borrowed from another web page. English version of this Swedish site has spoilers, cast lists, images, videos, some reviews, interviews, news and Queen Amidala sub pages, also links to a chat room.

Phantom Menace UK
www.thephantommenace.co.uk/naboo.htm
TPMUK is a sharp mini-portal based in the United Kingdom, with Star Wars news from around the world (Travel), also great international links (Japan), also galleries of images, greeting cards, diaries, toys, games, and Prequel cast list. Add yourself to their mailing list to receive news and updates.

Phantom Menace UK Images
www.thephantommenace.co.uk/pics.htm
United Kingdom site that takes a different approach by offering JPEG images and photos under the categories of Craft, Promo, Toys, Trailer, Cast, and Zipped Files.

Phantom Menace.com Wallpaper
www.the-phantommenace.com/wallpaper.html
Earliest available wallpaper images from the Phantom Menace. We especially liked the young Darth and the double-lightsaber for our computers.

Phantom Menace.com, The
www.the-phantommenace.com
This promising site is a "selected" link lists arranged by movie and categories. Images are of toy "exclusives." Also, find Prequel wallpaper, webrings and a guestbook. They solicit sites to link to.

Pictures: Boba Fett & Others
http://pweb.netcom.com/~fragger/art.html
A Netcom-linked picture site heavy with Boba Fett images. Links to Jim Henson (Muppets) sites.

Pit of Carkoon
www.starwars.com/locations/pit_of_carkoon
Official Lucasfilms page for the infamous Pit of Carkoon on Tatooine (home to the Sarlacc creature), Jabba the Hutts final resting place, and an all-time favorite place-to-avoid. Actually, it's a pencil sharpener, we think.

Planet Indy - Home of the Fans
http://indyjones.simplenet.com
Indiana Jones, of course! You won't want to miss this site if you're a Harrison Ford fan. In addition to movie pages, you'll find a forum, chat, newsletter, merchandise, fan icons, Indy at Disney, books, autographs, goofs, trivia, and, of course, the Indy Quiz! Indy love!

Planet Jedi
www.planetjedi.com/main.html
New game site developing into a super-power site. Gaming news (by date or topic), screencap pic 'o day, plus a survey and place to submit news. Also find previews, forums, store (amazon & beyond), essentials, downloads, FTP, site hosting, good links to 3D sites.

Planets (of Star Wars) Technical Commentaries
www.theforce.net/swtc/orbs.html
This text, pictures, charts and tables site from the force.net lists the original nine Star Wars planets and gives all the details of each (includes Coruscant but not Naboo when we visited the site). If you have a planet question, the answer is likely to be found here.

Pod Race Reporter Homepage
http://podracereporter.listbot.com
This ListBot site will provide you with Star Wars news updates - more than you can imagine! Reports (many from the countingdown guys who post the pod race) give times, details - just click and read.

Pod Racer Screens
www.planetjedi.com/hangar/PR/screens.html
Here's JPEG images from the Pod Racer Game to give you some idea of the scenarios and quality of the game.

Porkins Central
http://web.qx.net/red6/Porkins/index.htm
Jek Porkins - you might recall - is kind of a hard-luck Star Wars character - like South Park's Kenny. Porkins gets his own web page, though, and what a page it is. Truly a tribute to a man who - well - needs a tribute! You must read the Hootkins On Film (Porkins) interview.

Poster Pictures, Star Wars
http://empire.res.wabash.edu/art/posters/index.htm
May be one of the best poster sites on the web; arranged by Trilogy title and also a file with Ewok movie poster, Immunization, Coca-Cola Vader & Star Tours posters, Whelan's Yoda, large space battles. Images are JPEGs.

Power of the Force
http://welcome.to/star.warz
May be in the process of adding a little more depth, but this site does have alliance spacecraft downloads, Episode 1 commentary, guestbook and message boards.

Power of the Force 2 Action Figures
http://oneclick.ucr.edu/chamber/aflist/swlist01.htm
Listing of action figures from Admiral Ackbar to Zuckuss. Site links to Univ. California and the Carbon Freezing Chamber web site. Also links to other "action sets" sites.

Powerflicker's Model Page
www.geocities.com/Area51/Labyrinth/8664/models.html
Cool Pix of various Star Wars models and displays by powerflicker (Steve of Dallas). Find background material about Hoth, shuttle Tyderian, Tie fighters and more. This connects with Anakin's Rebel Base.

Prequel Art Originals (the force.net)
www.theforce.net/museum/g_prequels
Gallery of original art for the Prequel collected by theforce.net. Includes poster concepts and an early wallpaper collage. We expect this site to expand with good quality contributions.

IMAGES VIDEO AUDIO
MUST SEE! SELLS STUFF ADULT CONTENT SEARCHABLE
CHAT ROOMS MESSAGE BOARDS MAILING LISTS

THE PREQUEL CENTER

Prequel Center
www.theprequelcenter.8m.com
   Site has some news and updates, and promises a DVD center, collectibles page, images and media.

Prequel Crew
http://theforce.net/prequels/oldPreq/crew/crew.html
   The Force.net's site that lists Phantom Menace moviemaking crew - the people who make the magic happen - and links to their bios/filmographies. The "Crew news" has some hot tidbits now and then.

Prequel Editorials
www.jedinet.com/prequels/senate/editorials/index.htm
   Prequel mania - good or bad?! Here's a selection of fun, sometimes biting editorials collected by Jedinet's Qui-Gon (a major Star Wars guru) over the past year.

Prequel FAQ (Jedinet)
www.jedinet.com/prequels/faq
   Prequel page of "Frequently Asked Questions" on Jedinet.com. When we visited, it was "Version 5.6" - and still adding more and more info, most seems basic (so far!). French version available.

Prequel Images from Rancor Pit
www.sentex.net/~dah/prequel/images.html
   Click on the color thumbnail picture to enlarge the Prequel image to its full JPEG image size. Good variety of location pix, though most are labeled and should be downloaded only for personal use.

Prequel Locations
http://theforce.net/prequels/oldPreq/locations/locations.shtml
   Spies (real ones, we guess) were sent to snoop around the UK Star Wars studio - they returned all sorts of reports. Info has also been collected about the fictional planets. So, you will find candid pix and lots of detail text here.

Prequel News
www.execpc.com/~zerob/Jediside.html
   Linked to Master Yoda's Dagobah page, here you can find news article links along with tags and comments, and usually, a picture from the publication it appears in. The archives are accessible.

Prequel Pics Page
http://outland.cyberwar.com/~smad//pics5.html
   Originally this was a great stand-alone image page; now it's "part of a larger world" of the Star Wars Complete Prequel Page. JPEG images here are in these files: Teaser/Trailer Pics, Pics from the Set, and Preproduction Pics.

Prequel Rumors
http://members.aol.com/capeman69/rumors.html
   Collection of Prequel rumors, news, and facts gathered and packaged online by Capeman69. Here's an interesting fact (we guess it's a fact, but don't know for sure): Qui-Gon also means Ying-Yang in Chinese.

Prequel Spoilers
http://fly.to/prequel-spoilers
Of course, there isn't much to "spoil" about "Episode 1: The Phantom Menace" now that it's in theaters, but once upon a time this page "ruined" the story for just about anyone who visited. The plot was revealed, the places, vehicles, the pix, and questions were answered.

Prequel Spoilers: Questions
http://meltingpot.fortunecity.com/greenwood/487/questions/answers.html
Answers to questions like: "is Jake Lloyd really a bad actor?" and "How do you really pronounce Qui-Gon Jinn?" and "So, just how do the Jedi operate?" From the Prequel Spoilers web site.

Prequel Storyline, The (the force.net)
http://theforce.net/prequels/oldPreq/plot2.html
Episodes 1-3 stories outlined, followed by a timeline of when central characters were born. Yoda's oldest, but you'll have to access this site to find out that Chewiee's 2nd oldest. Oops! There are some spoilers, so if you don't want to spoil your movie experience, close your eyes while you read.

Prequel Trilogy & Special Edition Homepage
http://washington.xtn.net/~robf/sw.htm
This ancient site takes us back in time to '96 or so, with a '95 interview with George Lucas about his "upcoming Prequel plans." Guess what's coming: Special Editions! Site was so old it says "will not support Internet Explorer."

Prequel Vehicles
http://meltingpot.fortunecity.com/greenwood/487/vehic/vlist.html
Long before the Prequel opened, the Prequel Spoilers' web site revealed the vehicles and spacecraft, with pictures, illustrations and their specs. A size comparison chart is also found here.

Prequel Watch on Jedinet
www.jedinet.com/prequels
Colorful news presentation scroll livens up the late-breaking Prequel news, which is already exciting enough thanks to high-enery Jedinet crew who compile it. Get in on discussions at Jedi Council Chambers (forums) and Jedinet Chat. Print a calendar from the Fun/Fandom page.

Prequel Yoda
http://members.aol.com/CapeMan69/yoda.html
Pictures of the clay Yoda model (what! Yoda's not real?!) made for the Prequel - he looks a tad younger.

Prequelmania
www.geocities.com/Hollywood/3188
Malaysia site (in English) contains much of the more common Internet Prequel materials, news and pix - all the stuff everyone in the world "needs" to know - so should you! Author(s) like to tell jokes in the humor sub-pages.

Prequels UK
http://members.tripod.com/Jona82
Another strong British Prequel site, this features pages on Episodes 1-2-3, multimedia images, a feedback section, and discussion features: news, chat and boards. Best feature may be the blocks of text info on Episodes 2 & 3.

IMAGES VIDEO AUDIO
MUST SEE! SELLS STUFF ADULT CONTENT SEARCHABLE
CHAT ROOMS MESSAGE BOARDS MAILING LISTS

Prequels, The
www.wavefront.com/~chad/starwars/prequel/index.htm
> We like the set-up of this Prequel site - author Chad calls it a "lo-fi approach" and hopefully he'll expand it with more quality images and rumors as the year progresses. This is the first site we visited that noted that Ewan's uncle played Wedge Antilles in the first movie.

Prequels.com, The
http://theprequels.com/main.htm
> Wonderful Prequel page with lots of pix and additions. Picture gallerys are JPEG images set-up as landscape cards; the Sci-fi section hits Wing Commander Web, Star Trek, and Space: Above & Beyond. Find movie release news AND Star Wars news, fun archives, poll and trailer video.

Princess Leia
www.starwars.com/characters/princess_leia
> Official Lucasfilms page for Leia Organa, better known as Princess Leia. This site has three very good pix of Fisher as Leia, but, she always takes a great pic. Text is storyline/background, but a bit thin.

Printed References
www.jedinet.com/multimedia/references/ref-books.html
> Star Wars-isms make their way into a lot of author's books - Tom Clancy, Richard Bach, Clive Cussler, Arthur C Clarke, and into Foxtrot or Pinky & The Brain. List is incomplete - it would take volumes to pinpoint all Star Wars references in print over the past 20+ years.

Production - Echo Station Interactive Store $
www.echostation.com/shop/amazproduct.htm
> Books about the "how to's" of producing movies and the Star Wars series - and books about the major contributors, artists, and other "production" specialists. Brought to you by amazon.com & the Echo Station Store.

Production Paintings, Star Wars
www.cadvision.com/geoff/swimg.html
> Eight fantastic paintings were located here when we last visited; these make great wallpaper for your computer or enjoy them for your own viewing pleasure.

Prologue to the Imperial Trilogy
www.geocities.com/Hollywood/Location/1657/harkov.html
> Read the beginning of an unauthorized novel set in the time period between Splinter In the Eye and Star Wars, and based on the bad guys perspective. Inspired by the game TIE Fighters. The Empire is striking back, again!

Queen Amidala, Monarch of Naboo
http://meltingpot.fortunecity.com/greenwood/487/char/amidala.html
Queen Amidala is 14 years old - and other vital facts about Natalie Portman's character in The Phantom Menace can be found here. Quotes and background material from the Prequel Spoiler site.

Question of the Month
www.angelfire.com/co/Timecruiser/StarQuiz.html
You get one shot and one shot only - cause there's only one Quizlet question per month on this Timecruiser site. But, it's a question you probably have to check videos or the Web in order to answer.

Quizzes from the Boba Fett Home Sector
www.geocities.com/Hollywood/Set/5760
Just to "challenge" you, a number of Star Wars trivia categories are found on this Boba Fett site.

R2-D2
www.starwars.com/characters/r2-d2
Official Lucasfilms page for astromech utility droid R2-D2, as lovable as he is handy, and true star of the Trilogy (born in the Prequel, and already a hero). Stock pix and general R2-D2 background material available here.

Race & Species Descriptions 👁
www.civila.com/hispania/obi-juan/species.htm
Alphabetically arranged texts about the many weird, wonderful and sometimes vile aliens found in Star Wars. This is found on a Spanish site, Juan's Star Wars Site, available in English or Spanish. FYI a Hutt is from planet Varl.

Raith's Page of Star Wars Art 🖼 👁
http://www2.cybernex.net/~flip1/images1.htm
Fabulous galleries of Star Wars meshes divided into pages for The Rebellion, The Empire, Other Objects, Weapons, & Gallery. The Galley has great multi-craft pix. Amazingly, all are created by one man, using models and info resources collected from other similar web sites.

Rancor Pit, The
http://fly.to/rancorpit
New site with a contributing staff that produces editorials, reports, maintains archives, supports an e-mail system and chat room as well as Prequel & Star Wars news, Image gallery, Fan Fiction section, contests/trivia, forums, art, webrings. A growing site!

Randy Martinex Star Wars Gallery 👁
www.citcomputers.com/randy/starwars.html
This Oil Pastel/Water Color/Prismacolor on Bristol (6) 1997 Star Wars Series by Kansas Citian Randy Martinez rates as true art pieces. People: Go - See! Enjoy! Now do we get an original, Randy?

Rassmcon
www.shavenwookie.com/rassmcon
If you frequent Usenet groups like rec.art.sf.starwars.misc (or other Star Wars groups), would you like to find out where you can ACTUALLY meet (for "reals") the people you only communicate with through cyberspace? Sure you would - here's a schedule.

🖼 IMAGES	🎬 VIDEO	🔊 AUDIO
👁 MUST SEE!	$ SELLS STUFF	⬧ ADULT CONTENT	🔍 SEARCHABLE
💬 CHAT ROOMS	📥 MESSAGE BOARDS	📪 MAILING LISTS

Ray Traced (Jedi Planet)
http://members.xoom.com/jediplanet/page3.html
   Fabulous! Stellar Ray Traced art works are collected on this Italian Jedi Planet site.

Real Audio (Jedinet)
www.jedinet.com/multimedia/realaudio/index.htm
   24 RealAudio tracks from the Trilogy. Files are downloads. Tme lengths are given in the index: Star Wars theme is 5:22. Yoda tells Luke what a Jedi is: 33 seconds. Includes most memorable themes.

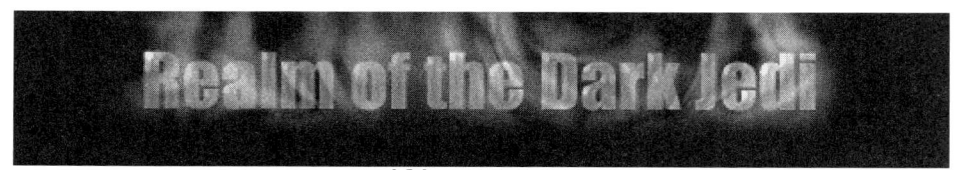

Realm of the Dark Jedi
http://members.tripod.com/~DarkJediCD/enter.html
   Enter the realm through this intro page and choose frames, aol, or no frames. Links to official page, web building tools, downloads (same as Palace of the Raider King!). Site author has put together a stellar poster. Worth seeing.

RealVideo John Williams Interview
http://theforce.net/cgi-bin/tfn.cgi?action=getstory&storyID=2008
   You can launch the Interview of conductor John Williams by Scott Young of NE Cable News. Starting by talking about music generally, Williams soon discusses music in The Phantom Menace, calling it "the best yet."

Rebel Alliance Insignia
www.theforce.net/swtc/domino.html
   Do those insignia on rebel officers mean anything, or are they just decorations? Silly question - of course they mean something, and this page explains them. This page also serves as a logo gallery.

Rebel Chat.com (toys/collectibles)
www.rebelchat.com
   There's chat rooms for eveyrthing, even Star Wars toys and collectibles. Sponsored by Philip Wise's excellent Rebel Scum toys site. Let's talk toys!

Rebel Fleet
www.starwars.com/locations/rebel_fleet
   Official Lucasfilms page with pics and light text describing the Rebel Fleet at the end sequences of Return of the Jedi. Like most locations in the official sites, it is limited, but does have a panoramic pictures of the fleet looking out through the docking bay (click on the pic for an enlarged image).

Rebel Scum.com Up To Date News (Collectibles) $ 💬 🖼 👁

www.rebelscum.com
Philip Wise's Rebel Scum site has more than toys and product up-to-date news - it has or links to new toy pix, latest photos, action figures, Galoob, Bend-ems, Lego, customs figures, collector's collections, Rebel chat room and good toy links and contests to win stuff - and more!

RedFive85 ⬇ 🖼 🎬

www.geocities.com/Area51/Quadrant/4210
"I've gotten much better performances out of my aliens this time," says Lucas in RedFive85's news and articles archives. George means they look and act a lot better. We got a laugh (but not a belly-bursting har-har) out of the Rumors. RedFive85 is no longer being updated -- however, the site's archives are worthy of viewing.

RedFive85 Rumors 🖼

www.geocities.com/Area51/Quadrant/4210/rumors.htm
The Before Star Wars Timeline gives "when" things happened from YB (Yoda's Birth) up to 20 BSW (Luke on Tatooine). Rumors are about who was considered for the Prequel, but couldn't, wouldn't, shouldn't. Kate Winslet as Queen Amidala/Padma? Her arm is as big as Nat Portman!

Reel.com - The Best Place To Buy Movies $ 🔍

www.reel.com/cgi-bin/nph-reel.exe?OBJECT=welcome.html
Search for the movie "you're looking for, and if you like, they're for sale." 100,000 movies; Star Wars always seems to be prominent (Star Wars A New Hope headed up the top 10 VHS sales for an eternity) and easy to acquire via the Star Wars Store. Use movie map or the quick search features.

Religion, Star Wars The 🖼 👁

http://hamp.hampshire.edu/~elwF94/planet/test.html
This site has 14 pages, each with theme about real life, and each uses a Star Wars scene as an example: grace, the test, temptation, dreaming, friendship, compassion - all things that a Jedi should know.

Remembering The Past: Early Drafts of Star Wars 👁

http://theforce.net/prequels/oldPreq/anhvsepi.htm
Ron Vitale article about the "curiosities" of the early, early Star Wars scripts compared to what we're seeing today in the Prequels. Good history and background of how Star Wars unfolded.

Return of the Jedi

www.starwars.com/episode-vi
Lucasfilms site about Episode 6, Return of the Jedi, with page links to the interesting features of this third movie.

Return of the Jedi (1983) - IMDb
http://us.imdb.com/Title?0086190
> Internet Movie db's fabulous info page gives cast, plot line, credits, genre, user ratings, and links to all other features of this database, and to a store to purchase videos, soundtracks, books. Did you know the working title (used while shooting to disguise the production) was "Blue Harvest"?

Return of the Jedi Script
www.geocities.com/Area51/Stargate/9082/Return.txt
> Transcript for Return of the Jedi, titled "Revenge of the Jedi" by L. Kasdan & G. Lucas

Return of the Jedi Special Edition FAQ
www.jax-inter.net/users/datalore/starwars/rojindex.htm
> Here's images and comments on all the new scenes in the Special Edition of Return of the Jedi. Not really in a FAQ page format on this planet, but it may be one in other systems. Connects to excellent Threadwell web sites.

Return of the Jedi Video Clips
http://home.multiweb.nl/~bramenpim/starrotj.htm
> See Vader throw the Emperor over the edge again, and a host of other Return of the Jedi video clips in AVI or QuickTime format. (Some files were down when we visited.)

Review of NPR's Dramatization of Star Wars
http://members.xoom.com/kessel/outpost/nprreview.html
> Did you know there was a very detailed 6 1/2 hour radio version of Star Wars on National Public Radio? Yes, and Hamill & Anthony Daniels did their own voice roles. Here's a review of "Star Wars The Original Radio Drama."

Richard Edlund - All-Media Guide
http://allmovie.com/cg/x.dll?UID=9:01:46|PM&p=avg&sql=B88665
> Four-time Academy Award winner for special effects achievements, Richard Edlund helped make the Trilogy a visual masterpiece. This All-media Guide site gives his bio and filmography: Richard also worked on Raiders, Poltergeist, Ghostbusters, Die Hard, Alien 3, and a slew more.

Roderick Vonhogen's Virtual Edition
www.virtualedition.com
> Virtual Edition lets us see side-by-side comparisons of the virtually-created movie images versus the real life scenes. Here's pages of Prequel images, the Trailer video, Star Wars lost scenes, and best of all, Time Tours.

Rogue 8's Media Vault
http://members.xoom.com/rogue88/mediavault.htm
> Great collection of MIDI music, also WAV sound files by character (zipped with description & size of file), scripts (with extras), also see Rogue 8's programs section for great fonts and downloads, like logos and themes.

Rogue 9's Animations
www.geocities.com/Baja/Mesa/4807/index2.html
> Brecht's collection of animations: Jawa, death star, B-wing, Imperial shuttle, and a couple more. The frames also link to solid galleries of pictures and sounds.

Rogue 9's Star Wars Web Site
www.geocities.com/Baja/Mesa/4807/index2.html
> Sights, sounds, animations, scripts, and even some cool downloadable Star Wars typestyles are available. Frames and non-frames versions. Join X-wing Squadron Webring here, messageboard and link list.

Rogue Squadron Screenshots
www.roguesquadron.net/screenshots.html
> Would you like to see some action images from the game "Rogue Squadron?" Here's a page of JPEG images from the game - right click your mouse on them to expand them to full size.

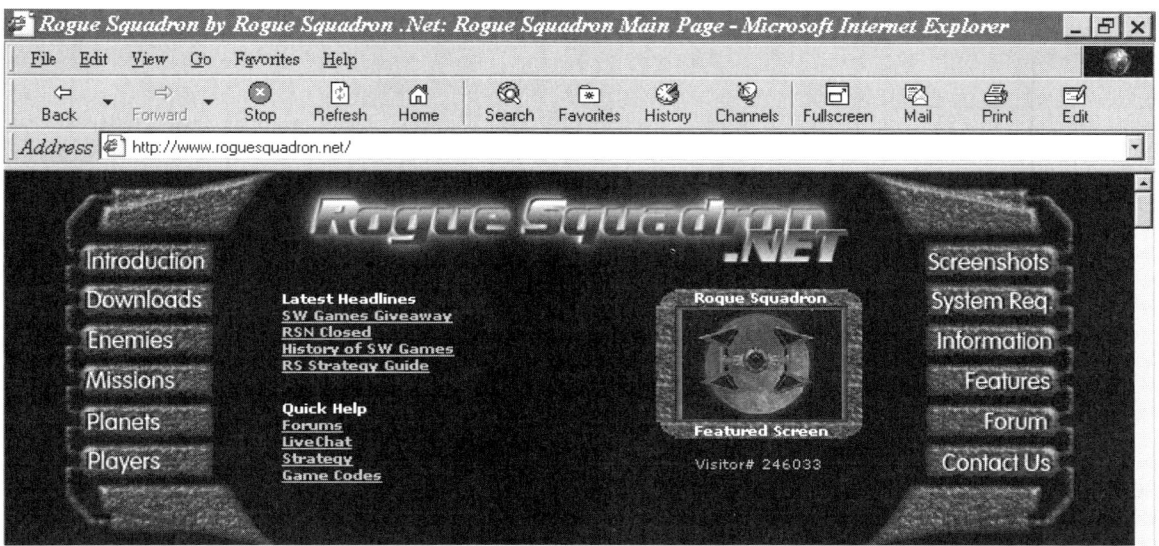

Rogue Squadron.Net
www.roguesquadron.net
> THE site for info and resources for the Rogue Squadron game, with pages for enemies, missions, planets, players, codes, screenshots, also features, a forum, news, demos, and game background. Find downloads of Rogue Squardon stuff for your computer screen and desktop.

Role Play: Mind's Eye (Echo Station Emag)
http://emag.echostation.com/roleplay/rpg1009.htm
> This Gamesmaster's thoughts on the Star Wars RPG is actually a good review of the state-of-the-game as of 1999, and also is a good place for beginners to get acclimated to the role-playing world. This Echo Station Emag article is by Mike Mistele, with a link to his site (see web page bottom).

Roleplaying in a Star Wars MUSH
www.cae.wisc.edu/~steiner/mush/site/rp/roleplay.htm
> Not familiar with how MUSH roleplaying games work? Well, here's a page that will get you started in the Star Wars MUSH. Roleplaying is kinda like being in "character," yet a lot of "different" things can happen. That's part of the adventure of it.

Rouge Leader Star Wars Page
http://members.tripod.com/rougeleader1/Starwars.html
> This site is "buggy," but it has a couple of our favorite pix, also links, webring, & MIDI music.

Royal Library - Star Wars Fan Fiction
www.geocities.com/Area51/Shadowlands/4918/fanfic.html
> Fan fiction stories with a picture to illustrate many of them. Features original and McGinnis stories.

RPG Revised & Expanded Rules - Star Wars
http://rpg.echostation.com/updates/updates.html
> Here's an online rulebook for roleplaying games (we hope that they change the color scheme on this subpage before it ruins YOUR eyes). Also at this update site you can back into other game updates at Echo Station, also Masterbook/D6 Stats Conversion, and copier percentages.

Ryan's Star Wars Pictures
http://members.spree.com/sci-fi/swrealm/Pictures.htm
> 135 images (JPEGs) in 15 pages arranged in categories. Wow! Characters, aliens, locations, Phantom Menace pix, also jokes, bounty hunters, spacecraft. Find new Jabba's pix in "Miscellaneous"- we guess that's where he belongs.

Ryan's Star Wars Realm
http://members.spree.com/sci-fi/swrealm
> Busy page with weekly trivia, good-sized picture file, webrings, links, chat room, Prequel page and link to free StarWarsRealm E-mail and clubs. Vote for your favorite spacecraft and characters. A lot of fun online activity!

Ryan's Star Wars Trivia Page (Interactive)
http://members.spree.com/sci-fi/swrealm/Trivia.htm
> Gives a weekly prize (a Star Wars Monopoly Game for instance) to the first trivia contest winner who gets 10 of 10 correct. Track Ryan's update schedule and you may hit right when a trivia game opens.

S - Pete's Movie Page.com
www.petesmoviepage.com/s.html
> This is the "S" section of the alphabetical listing of Pete's Movie page.com, so you'll find QuickTime video files for all sorts of movies beginning with "S" - find the Star Wars trailers (Original, Special Edition, EP1, & Macbeth)

Saber Combat (Jedi Academy)
www.jediacademy.com/saber.htm
> If you dropped an open lightsaber on the floor, would it burn a hole through the spaceship? At this site are lessons on how to properly handle the "most elegant of weapons." Has an archives of past lessons.

Salacious Crumb Homepage
www.madbbs.com/~salaciouscrumb/INDEX.HTM
> Find a picuture of that creepy monkey-lizard here, but not much other info about him/her/it. This is a game site for Swords of Chaos and for the page author's musical group named - Salacious Crumb.

Sam Davatchi's Page
http://perso.club-internet.fr/willow/Index.html
> Interesting site with a slant on fan rights, also plenty of useful sub-pages and commentaries. Opens with Lucasfilms Strikes Back Poster, which clues you in. Images found here are good quality. Find comic strips, thoughts, trivias, and image updates (will e-mail you information on new ones).

Samuel L Jackson (Lycos Network)
www.lycos.com/entertainment/celebrities/celebs/Jackson_Samuel.html
> Samuel's page on Lycos Entertainment/Celebrities Guide, with some statistics for Jackson, his claims to fame, official sites, fan page links. The Guide is searchable.

Sand People
www.starwars.com/aliens/sandpeople
> Official Lucasfilms page for planet Tatooine's Sand People, a nomadic tribe of nere-do-wells and scavengers, easily scared. Click on the photo at left for an official San People picture, if you dare.

Schematics Collection (Taz's)
http://seconn4.yoda.com/~vader97/Schematics/schematics.html
Huge collection of schematics for all types of spacecraft and gear. Files are GIFs in Corel 5.0 and are somewhat big, since these are photo images not line drawings. Background material for modelers.

Sci-fi Movie Clips
http://graffiti.u-bordeaux.fr/MAPBX/roussel/anim-e_03f.shtml
Wow! Spacious (and we mean Space-ious) collection of Sci-fi movie clips from this French site, including Fifth Element, Star Wars, Bladerunner, Dune, Lost In Space - and stuff you haven't seen! AVI and QuickTime formats.

Sci-Tech: The Net Feels The Force (BBC)
http://news.bbc.co.uk/hi/english/sci/tech/newsid_217000/217090.stm
"The release of the trailer for the first of the Star Wars Prequels is attracting huge attention on the Internet" starts this 11/98 British Broadcasting article. That was for the Trailer - what about the movie BBC? You can search this site for other Star Wars related BBC articles.

Science & Nature
http://index.echostation.com/ysci.html
Index of all things scientific and natural found in the Star Wars Universe. Say, for instance, you're playing a RPG and someone says they have "yagarian aleudrupe." What do you do? answer: take them; they're an edible delicacy!

Science of Star Wars
www.theforce.net/jedicouncil/interview/cavelos.shtml
Interview with Jeanne Cavelos, astrophysicist. Read her comments about her experiences and her book. The force.net site includes a pic of a big lizard on the author's head - great if you're not into reading and like reptiles.

SciFI Advance
http://scifi.simplenet.com
Newest rumors, info and pix from upcoming science fiction movies and series. We found 3 Star Wars categories here: Wing Commander, Star Wars Special Edition and Prequel Trilogy as well as Batman, Indy IV, Earth 2, Armageddon, Babylon 5, and Aliens.

Scott O'Hair's Hyperspace
http://members.iquest.net/~sohair/hyperspace/menup.html
What would a scale model of Control Room 327 look like, or what is the floor plan of Mos Eisley Cantina, or the Freezing Chamber? Artist Scott O'Hair makes models (to scale of Kenner figurines) to give us a new perspective.

Screen Savers
www.jedinet.com/multimedia/windows/savers/index.htm
Jedinet collection of 17 different Trilogy movie screensavers which you download and use to protect your computer. There's a rotating Leia in her slave gear, dollar bills with Vader's face on them, exploding/reforming Vader image, Christmas Yoda, and Dave Dorman specials.

Screensaver Plaza, Star Wars
www.dukus.com/swsp/index.html
Really clean, informative site from Craig Dukus where you can download a number of different screensavers for Windows, including screensaver images from the Prequel and Trilogy, also humorous ones. Includes a screensaver FAQ page, utilities, a link list and awards.

IMAGES   VIDEO   AUDIO
MUST SEE! $ SELLS STUFF   ADULT CONTENT   SEARCHABLE
CHAT ROOMS   MESSAGE BOARDS   MAILING LISTS

Screenshots (Jedinet Software Pages)
www.jedinet.com/software/screenshots/index.htm
> The cavernous Jedinet site offers many great subsites: this page is a super gallery of screenshots captured from a variety of great Star Wars-related games. Find JPEG images from JediKnight, Shadows, Force Commander, Rebellion, Rogue Squadron, TIE Fighter.

Screenshots.net
www.screenshots.net
> Want to see what the great new Episode 1 games Pod Racers and The Phantom Menace look like? Here's GIF images taken from these realistic computer games. Fnd other games like Quake on this searchable image database.

Scripts (Jedinet Collection)
www.jedinet.com/multimedia/scripts/index.htm
> Features A New Hope's five versions, also Empire Strikes Back Final & Return of the Jedi 2nd draft, plus Tales of the Jedi CD adaptation of the comic book series, and Dark Horse comic series Dark Empire 1 & 2.

Scripts - Star Wars
http://members.xoom.com/scriptkeeper/scripts.htm
> Collection of 10 Star Wars scripts including one that claims to be Episode III, but the site author (Matt) doubts it. He should know. You decide. Find the Holiday Special script.

Search Engines (Knight Hammer)
www.geocities.com/Area51/Chamber/4182/search.html
> On the Imperial Knight Hammer site, we found search fields to search in (2 didn't work when we visited). In the biggest search field, you choose AltaVista, Excite, HotBot, Yahoo, Infoseek, Lycos or AOL to browse. Another field lets you search geocities; another connects to a link list.

Second Prequel - What's Next
www.allexperts.com/tv/swprequel1.shtml
> Small page about what the "experts" at ALLEXPERTS.COM think will happen in the next episodes. In other words, they don't have the official storyline, so they made up what they think is a humorous one.

Sector 827 (obscure title)
http://swwa.webjump.com/books/book.html
> About 50 Star Wars books and their covers, including X-wing series, Thrawn Trilogy, Star Wars info books and others too good to categorize. Click on a book title to go to bookstore ordering.

Senate Vote, The
www.theforce.net/jedicouncil/surveys
> The good things about this force.net survey site are that it is big and the archives shows the survey results on a variety of questions/topics. You are now a "Senator," so cast your vote! Which Trilogy characters would you most like to see in the Prequels? Answer: young Han Solo.

Shadows of the Empire Pictures
www.jedinet.com/multimedia/pics/sote/index.html
> Extensive JPEG image gallery on Jedinet which is dedicated to the Shadows of the Empire series. Includes original concept art, covers, cards, captures and color panels.

Shaven Wookie LTD 👁

www.shavenwookie.com

Shaven Wookie (Chris Hawkins) has organized a fantastic subject directory of sites, newsgroups, characters - he lists a lot of sites that we simply could not fit in this book. Also, find pages on the Sith Trilogy, fashions, novels, editorials, games and a ton of stuff.

Shell & Desktop Tools 🖼 🔍

www.winfiles.com/apps/98/shelldesk.html

Not only can you find a huge assortment of Win95/98 desktop goodies for Star Wars and other topics, here you can get information on how to manage and use them, also start-up and shut-down screens, cursors, virtual desktop managers, font management tools.

Ships in the Star Wars Universe 🖼

http://members.xoom.com/kessel/outpost/ships.html

To build a cool Star Wars web site, first you start with some stars, then add your favorite spacecraft. Get JPEG and GIF images of them at this Swammi "Ships" site. Some are animated. Find Walkers here, although they can't fly.

Signs That You May Be A Complete Star Wars Addict

www.geocities.com/Hollywood/Set/5760

Exhaustive list of indications that you're living a little too vicariously, Star Wars fan! One sign: you think that John Williams is the greatest composer that ever lived. (He is, I tell you!) Found on the Boba Fett/geocities suite of Star Wars sites. See also "You're Not a Star Wars Junkie Until")

Simon Ray's Star Wars Files 🎬 🔊

www.fairfield.demon.co.uk

AVI and QuickTime Trilogy videos, also a small sounds file are available from this United Kingdom site. It was under construction when we visitied; by now the files should have grown.

Sir Steve's Action Online Chat Room (Toys/Collectibles) 💬

www.sirstevesguide.com/chatroom/chatroomgl.html

Yes, chat rooms for Star Wars toys are popular, open to young and old alike. Here you can share with others who have an interest in Star Wars goodies. This room even has an "ignore" feature that lets you tune out ick people.

Sir Steve's Star Wars (Collectibles) Guide $ 💬 🔍 👁

www.sirstevesguide.com

Hasbro, Micro Machines, trading cards, Prequel toys - that's just the feature items! Find news, forums, classifieds, calendar of events, chat, hot links, a poll, and Boolean search field. A kid safe site.

Sith Lords Star Wars Quiz

www.geocities.com/Hollywood/Location/1657/quiz.html

Everyone has their own version of Star Wars trivia; this is the Lords of Sith's version. Sith-agories go from easy to hard (only true dark siders would know the most difficult answers). Vote for your favorite villains in the survey.

Sith Powers

www.wcug.wwu.edu/~paradox/sithpowers.html

Sith Powers are something you might use in roleplaying games (which is the intent of this page, we assume), not something you'd use too much around the house. Still, you can learn a lot about these rather dark powers here - like electronic manipulation or the aura of uneasiness.

🖼 IMAGES   🎬 VIDEO   🔊 AUDIO
👁 MUST SEE! $ SELLS STUFF   ADULT CONTENT   🔍 SEARCHABLE
💬 CHAT ROOMS   MESSAGE BOARDS   MAILING LISTS

Skystation Lounge
www.theforce.net/Skystation
>Once into it, Skystation has Prequel CG images, wallpaper, and animations requiring ActiveX (downloadable at this force.net site). Don't be afraid: it's not real like a movie - it's computer generated.

Skywalker Ranch Tour
http://george.lucas.net/prologue.htm
>Did you know, even Ronald Reagan was refused admission to Skywalker Ranch, the palace of moviemaker George Lucas. But, now you can take an online tour, also learn about LucasArts, young Indy, and ILM.

Skywalker's MOV's & MPG's
www.usmo.com/~starwars/mov&mpg.html
>Variety of about 30 clips are found here. They're small and often short in length - movie clips; not animations.

Skywalker's Star Wars Page
www.usmo.com/~starwars/index.html
>The Now & Then feature of minor Star Wars characters make this site worth the visit; also find multimedia pages of sounds, images, short movie clips/animations, galleries of art by Dorman and McQuarrie. Humor page features movie out-takes, comic humor, and blooper dialog.

Smithsonian Museum Exhibit - Star Wars: Magic of Myth
www.geocities.com/Area51/Vault/3227/index.html
>Collection of photos taken by Chris Coleman (Boba Fett/geocities) at the Star Wars exhibit at the Smithsonian Museum. Gallery includes Leias gown, Han gear, trooper gear and plenty of Boba Fett.

Snowstorm Software.com Gallery
www.snowstormsoftware.com/gallery.html
>Scroll down to nearly the page bottom to find 3 sub-files for Star Wars VRML models. Look further and find connections to Star Wars VRML and 3D info. One page lets you convert 3D to VRML.

Sound America A New Hope
http://soundamerica.com/sounds/movies/J-S/Star_Wars/A_New_Hope
>100+ sound files in WAV format from A New Hope. Some are long, some short (all are listed alphabetically and with file size), from Chewie growls and alien chatter, to "You've taken your first step into a larger world."

Sound America Empire Strikes Back
http://soundamerica.com/sounds/movies/J-S/Star_Wars/Empire_Strikes_Back
>Big collection of WAV files of sounds, quotes, and conversations from Empire Strikes Back. C3PO: "Excuse me, sir, might I ask what's going on?"

Sound America Return of the Jedi
http://soundamerica.com/sounds/movies/J-S/Star_Wars/Return_of_the_Jedi
>100+ WAV sound files from Return of the Jedi. Hear Ewoks, aliens, R2-D2, Chewie and other memorable quotes and sounds. C3PO: "Oh no! The rancor!" Also, check Sound America's main Star Wars page via the page link.

Sounds - Jedi Council Chamber 🔊
www.geocities.com/Area51/Hollow/9125/Audioi.htm
We thought this was a rather good, thoughtful collection of audio quotes, also some MIDI music. "When 900 hundred years old you reach, look as good you will not." - Yoda.

Sounds - Spynals Star Wars Site 🔊
http://members.xoom.com/Spynal/sounds.htm
Arranged by Star Wars character, you'll find over a dozen WAV sound clips for each one, plus a good JPEG pic of each character. The list includes Han, Luke, Yoda, R2, Leia, Darth and even some villains. Luke: "This is your last chance: free us or die!"

Sounds; Star Wars - from Entertainment Cell 🔊
http://pweb.netcom.com/~fragger/media.html
Sounds from Star Wars in either MIDI (tunes) or WAV (phrases, etc) files linked through the Netcom Entertainment Cell. Includes 12 music themes and over a dozen downloadable phrases. Ah, the wisdom of Yoda! Find other cool things to put on your computer.

Space Depot 24
www.geocities.com/Area51/Vault/4910/space.htm
Good example of a Star Wars site in 1997. The downloads page has screensavers, icons, other computer gear, also MIDI & WAV sound files (most are short quotes). The Main site offers early-era links. Active in the game Diablo.

Spaceballs - IMDb $ 🔍
http://us.imdb.com/Title?0094012
Mel Brooks teams with actors Rick Moranis, John Candy, Dick Van Patten, Joan Rivers and other yuksters to create this 1987 Star Wars spoof. The cheap humor was a bit too ridiculous for most, but Spaceballs is probably the biggest grossing parody. You can purchase it. Find movie and character database links here.

Special Edition Annotations 👁
www.theforce.net/swse
Sadly, the images used to illustrate Paul Ens' excellent annotations about the Trilogy Special Editions are thumbnails, so, except for the titles/banners, there's not much in the way to download unless you like 'em really small. His commentaries are stellar, however. Definitely worth reading.

Special Edition Screen Shots 🖼
http://members.aol.com/T65Pilot/speced.html
GIF images from each of the Trilogy Special Editions - the new scenes, like the Sarlaac creature's mouth, the risque dancers, a better Bespin. Screen shot quality isn't the best, but some images here cannot be found elsewhere.

Special Editions, The 🖼 🎬 👁
http://scifi.simplenet.com/starwars/special_edition/index.html
Although they are now overshadowed by the Prequels, the Trilogy Special Editions (Episodes IV, V, & VI) were very special releases, featuring many new scenes and FX most of which are noted in the JPEG image galleries. Video clips and release information about the Specials are also found here.

Speculation
http://outland.cyberwar.com/~smad//spec55.html
A sub-page of the Complete Prequel Page, "Speculation" examines and ponders about how the myths and heroes interplay in the Prequel and the overal Star Wars story. The themes and theories are also looked at; comments by George Lucas are featured.

Speeder Bike Chase Video
www.telecom.csuhayward.edu/~aleung/speeder.mov
QuickTime video clip of the speeder bike chase on the Endor Moon, from Return of the Jedi.

Spynals Star Wars Site
http://members.xoom.com/Spynal/home.htm
A wonderful, eclectic high-energy site, built on a simple scroll. Good image and sound files, multi-levels of trivia, forums, chat, "your comments," Star Wars font (for you computer), survey, power searching, HTML downloads (for site building, promos), and a store for purchasing CDs & books.

Stakawaka's Natalie Portman Page
www.geocities.com/Hollywood/Lot/7181/natalie.html
Big tribute page to Natalie covers her acting career, and generally makes her an actress and person who knows no equal. The large image gallery includes a variety of Natalie poses from over the years.

Star Backgrounds (Swammi Collection)
http://members.xoom.com/kessel/outpost/background.html
Space backgrounds for use on web sites - mostly black backgrounds with white stars - what else? Also a Star Wars logo on, guess what? - black background with white stars. Keeping with the theme, there's Han in carbonite.

Star Destroyer
www.starwars.com/vehicles/star_destroyer
Official Lucasfilms page for the wedgelike giant warships of the Imperial Fleet, symbols of over-indulgent military spending and iron-fisted domination. These Star Destroyers are fairly-well described here, but we're left to speculation about what else is contained in these death-dealing machines.

Star Park

Star Park
www.jedinet.com/starpark
"A long time ago, Oh my God! You killed Kenobi!" Ultimate Star Wars/South Park crossover page, with comics and FAQ. Join in the competition and shut that Cartman up.

Star Seeker: Star Wars Episode 1
www.starseeker.com/films/1999film/starwars.htm
A basic linklist database. Star Seeker gets you into the movie title, then gives "the scoop," stars, director, merchandise, official sites, some fan sites, movie industry resources, abbreviated newsgroup lists and links to the Star Wars Trilogy. Links to 9 search engines.

Star Trek (*what's that*?) & Star Wars Jokes
www.geocities.com/Hollywood/4256/jtrek6.html
You've probably seen most of these put-downs & retorts before (unless you watch it a lot, you probably won't "get" the Star Trek sections). Submit a joke if you dare. Malaysia web site - in English.

Star Wars (1977) - IMDb
http://us.imdb.com/Title?0076759
The original Star Wars is rated the top movie by Internet Movie Database users (and everyone who knows a great movie when they see it!). Find the facts here: plotline, credits, cast, other names, and also purchase a video, soundtrack, books. FYI: Special Edition is 4 minutes longer than the original.

Star Wars (A New Hope) MP3 Sounds
www.psyc.canterbury.ac.nz/pgrad/carr/starwars.html
"Your friend is quite a mercenary. I wonder if he really cares about anything, or anybody." Find this and other MP3 files, which are downloadable or streamable from this New Zealand Site.

Star Wars (Hollywood Liz)
www.geocities.com/Hollywood/1165/starwars.html
Main page for Hollywood Liz who reviews books and reports Star Wars news including Prequel news and pix, and also offers WAV sound files from the movies.

Star Wars (Videos)
www.students.dsu.edu/hilleste/starwars.html
Educational site has a collection of AVI and QuickTime videos arranged by the 3 Trilogy movies, including trailers. See Greedo get blasted, again, and Boba Fett have a bad day. QuickTime player is downloadable here.

Star Wars - Arts et Culture: Cinema et Video: Films
http://recherche.toile.qc.ca/quebec/qcart_ci_films_starwars.htm
French Canadian site that lists a variety of Star Wars-related web sites in the french language.

IMAGES VIDEO AUDIO
MUST SEE! SELLS STUFF ADULT CONTENT SEARCHABLE
CHAT ROOMS MESSAGE BOARDS MAILING LISTS

Star Wars - The Prequels
www.nwlink.com/~gareth/starwars.htm
> Gareth von Kallenbach designs game software and has put up a Prequel JPEG gallery that has great variety, with pix that are not found elsewhere. Scroll down to get to the gallery - Gareth's comments (worth reading) are on top.

STAR WARS - Welcome to the Official Site
www.starwars.com
> Inside scoop from Lucasfilm Ltd; facts and trivia about the series, storylines, charactors, actors and production, with good images, official links, and lots of cookies. Official news, foreign languages, archives, connections to marketers and more are found at this portal MEGA-site.

Star Wars 3D Gallery
www.ipr.nl/sw-3d
> A blast from the past: Cool 1996 3D modeling site of Roland Rotherhofer of the Netherlands. This is some of his original stuff; later creations are found in the 3D Modeling Alliance pages. This site has the "Shut down or else" Hoax letter that circulated in 1996. Question: Why can't Dutch people spell?

Star Wars A New Hope Special Edition FAQ
www.jax-inter.net/users/datalore/starwars/anhindex.htm
> Not truly a FAQ page, this Threadwell suite of A New Hope pages comments on all the new and changed scenes, and uses some rather nice images for comparisons, including the scene where some claim you can see actor Kenny Baker inside R2 (you can't).

Star Wars Accessories, Props, & Collectibles $
www.nightmarefactory.com/starwarz.html
> Many collectibles here are the expensive, one-of-a-kind variety - Boba Fett Replica is $4250 - but there are more reasonable collectibles: maquettes, lifesize cardboard standups, metal collector card sets. Accessories include lightsabers, logo pins, and a Falcon keychain to make your car run better.

Star Wars Archives by SWKID
www.paulshome.cjb.net/swa
> Many of the GIFs are animated; they and JPEG images are suitable for website builders to download. Files of WAVs and MIDI sounds, also to download. Star Wars Kid's site also links back to his regular site where you can find html and computer consulting info.

Star Wars As Seen On TV
www.lucasfan.com/swtv/index.html
> Lucasfan.com's collection of Star Wars characters' appearances on TV over the millenia, like Star Wars on The Donnie & Marie Show. You may be more interested in the Ewoks! Has news updates, guestbook, also cut scenes files, promos, commercials and musical parodies.

Star Wars ASCII Art Collection
www.lstock.demon.nl/swlaunch2.html
> There appears to be no end to what you can create with a computer keyboard - over one hundred Star Wars ASCII-created art objects are here, arranged in files of easy, medium, hard, and HTML.

Star Wars Book Reviews
http://people.clemson.edu/~jvalice/starb.htm
> Reviews, ratings, and descriptions of Star Wars novels, including books by Anderson, McIntyre, Stackpole, Zahn and others. Updated only to 11/97.

Star Wars Cantina 🗣📷🎬🔊
http://members.tripod.com/~ss_star_wars/index.html
   There's plenty of variety here, but the files aren't deep in number. Includes sounds, images, movies (videos), author's ICQ, chat, links to a club and programs for a couple Star Wars games - but where, exactly, is the cantina?

Star Wars Central
www.geocities.com/Area51/Vault/3891
   What if you had to click your way through security checkpoints, images, and use a little imagination to find what you're looking for? Do what you're told and find rebel & imperial tech information, also webrings and surprises. More promised by author P. Scheid. Check his old site for sights, sounds, pix.

Star Wars Classic Costumes (Annie's Costumes) $
www.anniescostumes.com/starkids.htm
   Yes, they have Prequel costumes (adult), along with traditional Trilogy Halloween costumes in adult and child sizes. Be Luke in an orange X-wing flight uni. Inexpensive Leia wig. Masks. Expect child Prequel costumes soon. Flashlight lightsabers in white, green, red, or blue.

Star Wars Collectibles (tnc Universe) $📷
www.tncmagic.com/starwars/00masks.htm
   New Prequel costumes & masks, CCG game sets are a specialty. Find figurines, playsets, art, replicas, multimedia products, apparel, novelties for parties, mugs, posters, even vintage collectibles. Masks & costumes include Obi-wan, Queen Amidala, Qui-Gon, & Mr. Darth Maul.

IMAGES   VIDEO   AUDIO
MUST SEE! $ SELLS STUFF   ADULT CONTENT   SEARCHABLE
CHAT ROOMS   MESSAGE BOARDS   MAILING LISTS

Star Wars Collective ⚓🖼
http://starwars.interspeed.net/index.shtml
  The best feature thus far of this developing web site is the Art of Yonk JPEG renderings found in the Exhibits section. Click on "SW Fan Images" to get to the exhibit. Site also offers forum, poll, editorials, webring, and Prequel section with downloadable EP1 Trailer (Fan Version).

Star Wars Comics Price Lists
http://207.237.121.181/starwars/swcprices.html
  What's your old collection of Marvel Star Wars Comics worth just about now? Here's a price list from the Star Wars Comics people. Also find pictures, Ewoks issues, and Annuals.

Star Wars Customs.com 🖼
http://members.aol.com/awyant3477/index.htm
  Here's the challenge: take your Star Wars figurines and develop "sets" and scenes for them based on a location in any of the movies. Make it as realistic as possible. This is a diorama. Snap pictures; display them on your web site.

Star Wars Database 📪⚓📢🖼❓👁
www.swdatabase.com
  Day-by-day reports on the Star Wars world, e-mail service, message boards, lists, chat room, all types of Prequel and Trilogy files, plus valuable links to special features like comics, cartoons, fan fiction, quizzes, collectibles, games, encyclopedia, autographs, and more!

Star Wars Database Interviews
www.swdatabase.com/pages/interviews.html
  Find actor Terrance Stamp talking about his role as emperor of the universe in the Prequel, also Rick McCallum talking to a Dutch magazine about Prequels. Peter Mayhew is heard from. Check for updates!

Star Wars Database Message Boards 📪⚓❓
www.swdatabase.com:8080/~swdbase
  Here you can get e-mailing lists of those who are involved in message board activities as well as participate yourself. For instance, create a mailing list of fan fiction names, or get in with roleplayers, trivia folks, etc.

Star Wars Database Prequel Cast
www.swdatabase.com/prequels/cast.html
  Not only the cast, but some of the other actors who were up for the parts! Read about characters and their relationships. Data is pre-1999.

Star Wars Drawings 👁
www.geocities.com/SoHo/Gallery/9741/STARWARSPage.htm
   Tim Wilson's drawings rate a special notice, and not just because pencils are becoming a lost instrument. Gallery of a dozen JPEG images (check the Tusken Raider and Anakin Skywalker pix). Check Tim for permission to use.

Star Wars Drinking Game, The
www.geocities.com/Hollywood/Set/5760
   This game is played the way other drinking games are played - with lack of moderation. Start the Trilogy on tape; it's time to drink when you're prompted by certain keys, like "I had a bad feeling about this," or there is a tremor in the force, or someone's hand or arm gets cut off.

Star Wars Driving/Steering Wheel Virtual System 🖼 🎬 🔊
http://iml.millersv.edu/html.stuff/wtkstuff/wheel.dir/wheel.html
   Resource page for VRML of Star Wars, which also links to downloads of MPEGs for 3D. Find 3D death star, TIE fighter, sound clips, MPEG movie clips and links to other VRML pages.

Star Wars Episode 1 - The Music ⬇ 🖼 🎬 🔊 👁
http://members.es.tripod.de/Befan/Episode1music.html
   If it has anything to do with Prequel music, you'll probably find something about it here. Music news, John Williams links, concerts, videos, a music survey, downloads, themes, articles, CDs, pictures, internet radio show, and some killer music links.

Star Wars Episode 1 - The Phantom Menace Game 🖼 🔍
www.gamespot.com/features/sw_phantom
   For PC and Playstation, this game is reviewed by Gamespot's Moira Muldoon. You become one of the four Jedi characters and play your way through scenarios that mimic the EP1 storyline. Reviewer describes the game, gives hints, talks about the developers and ideas. Plenty of screenshots!

Star Wars Fan & CG Art 🖼 👁
http://empire.res.wabash.edu/art/cg/index.htmFAN
   One of the few pages featuring magic eye Star Wars images, also a large assortment of Computer-generated art - scenes, ships. Other files connected with this site are very big, if not fabulous! Check out the CG scenes.

STAR WARS FAN FICTION

Star Wars Fan Fiction
http://sw.simplenet.com/pages/fanfiction.html
   Fan fiction titles listed by author and title, with comments, also, instructions on how to submit your own stories, poetry, and find mailing lists. Categories are original Trilogy, Prequel, Old Republic, and New Republic (future).

Star Wars Fan Mail Addresses
www.geocities.com/Area51/Nebula/5101/fanmail.html
   Want to write a letter to your favorite Star Wars Trilogy actor? Here's their professional addresses, along with autographed picture (if available), courtesy of the World's Greatest Star Wars Webpage.

Star Wars Final Draft by George Lucas
www.geocities.com/Area51/Stargate/9082/Newhope.txt
   Subtitled "Journal of the Wills," this is George Lucas' 4th draft of "Star Wars, Episode IV, A New Hope," 1/1976.

Star Wars Fonts
http://members.xoom.com/scriptkeeper/fonts.htm
   Unzip and download these Star Wars fonts from Matt's Fonts page: Battlestar, Jedi, Masterforce, Merlin, Star Vader, Star Wars. Jedi & Masterforce also come in "hollow." WinZip program is on link.

Star Wars Force Graphics
http://plaza.harmonix.ne.jp/~m-falcon
   An arsenal of sharp graphic images, most as posters. Also find a gallery of craft works models pix. A Japanese site, but has an English version.

Star Wars Force Graphics Posters 🖼 👁

http://plaza.harmonix.ne.jp/~m-falcon/poster_art1_boba.html
Sharp JPEGs and GIFs Posters, including Boba Fett Bounty Hunter, The Dark Lord, and others on the dark side of the force - also a Yoda, an Escape, and Tatooine posters. More poster images are linked to this Japan site.

Star Wars Galaxy (a) 🖼 🔊

www.geocities.com/Area51/Chamber/1458/frame1.htm
You'd expect anything with a title "Galaxy" to be big; geocities sites are somewhat limited by size, however. Strong point of this site is its good-sized pictures gallery. There is also a few MIDI music files, some WAV sounds, stock posters and links.

Star Wars Galaxy (a) Pictures 🖼

www.geocities.com/Area51/Chamber/1458/pics.htm
Mostly characters and figures in familiar poses, also a number of spacecraft pix, all in JPEG format.

Star Wars Galaxy (b)

www.geocities.com/Area51/Vault/6031/star_wars.html
Like traveling back in time. This geocities Star Wars Galaxy site is a bit older than the (a) version (a different author). You may wish to check here to see if is updated to 1999 - when we last visited, the last update was 1/98! You may look for games, but the "files" section has the best stuff.

Star Wars Galaxy Webring

www.webring.org/cgi-bin/webring?ring=tswg;list
Operated by the large Starseed Webring Group. From here you can link to a few of the better rings.

🖼 IMAGES   🎬 VIDEO   🔊 AUDIO
👁 MUST SEE! $ SELLS STUFF   ADULT CONTENT   🔍 SEARCHABLE
CHAT ROOMS   MESSAGE BOARDS   MAILING LISTS

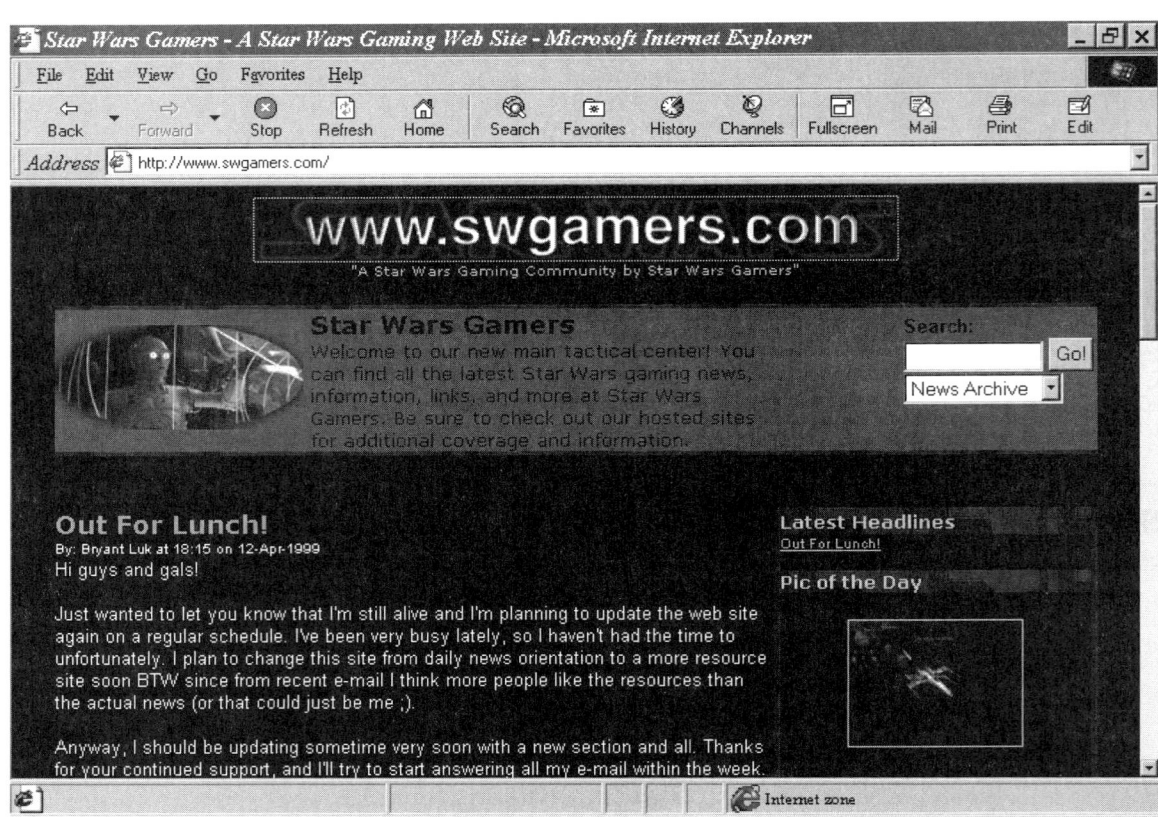

Star Wars Gamers
www.swgamers.com
>   For Star Wars game players. Here you will find news, Episode 1 games, patches, online demos, game upgrades, and lots of X-wing Alliance info. Use the search feature for news archives and links list.

Star Wars Games Cheat Codes
http://rpg.echostation.com/cheat/swgame.html
>   So, this is where you find those hints about how to get around the hard stuff so that you can look like a true champ! Many of these files are also FAQs (Frequently Asked Questions). A couple files have a note that says "This file won't help much!" Thanks, fuzzball.

Star Wars Gear
www.gogs32.freeserve.co.uk/gear.htm
>   An Orin_J Star Wars site - or should we say "a dark side site" since this is oozing with Imperial and Vader "gear." Luagh at the "goofing Death Star," or resist. Perhaps you won't. Sweet collection of Imperial animated GIFs.

Star Wars Geek Code
www.sevaan.com/starwars/news/archives/old_layout/news/code.htm
>   Guy Puzey of the UK devised the ultimate Star Wars Geek Poll where you create your own codified transmissions that tell all about your preferences. Once created, you can attach the personal code to your E-mails. Some will know "the code," - the "uninitiated" won't.

Star Wars Graphic Magic
www.geocities.com/Hollywood/Theater/3518
New site that allows you to submit GIF images you've created. Yours may be voted "Gif 'o the month." You will find a few the site author created, too. Links to Macromedia Flash, a GIF creation tool site.

Star Wars Humor
www.geocities.com/Hollywood/Set/5760
Solid Star Wars humor page! Find editorial page-like cartoons, also links to other humor pages.

Star Wars Icons
www.tem.nhl.nl/~veen606/eicon.htm
Icons from games Rebel Assault, Dark Forces, TIE Fighter, and Yoda Stories. Choose English or Dutch version.

Star Wars III, Fall of the Republic
www.geocities.com/Hollywood/Lot/6700/fallofr.txt
Fiction movie script by John L Flynn. We don't know if screenplay is/was seriously considered.

Star Wars Index to Characters
http://index.echostation.com/char.html
Alphabetical listing of Star Wars characters. Find descriptions of every name you've ever heard and then some - roleplaying information and sources as well. For Droids, click on lefthand index "Droids." Use this lefthand index to get to other subject pages. Updated frequently.

Star Wars Index to Health & Medicine
http://index.echostation.com/med.html
Of course, health and medicine is highly advanced in Star Wars - how else could Darth Vader continue on? Here you can find out all about treatments like rejuvenating bacta fluid, droid surgery, and other wonders of health care.

Star Wars Index to the Supernatural
http://index.echostation.com/super.html
The soul of Star Wars is "the Force" - here you can find it and Sith Magic, Ewok beliefs, Old Ways, Empeth & Eternity crystals, and an assortment of "the supernatural." Sources are listed. This site was somewhat limited when we visited. Hopefully it is fully operational now.

IMAGES VIDEO AUDIO
MUST SEE! SELLS STUFF ADULT CONTENT SEARCHABLE
CHAT ROOMS MESSAGE BOARDS MAILING LISTS

Star Wars JPEG & GIF Pictures
www.geocities.com/Area51/Corridor/1086/sw.html
The site author has taken the time to "rate" the multitude of JPEG and GIF image files, which are arranged by movie, and file size is given. Animated GIFs are described as well. Includes a couple favorite sound files: "Bad feeling" and "It's against my programming to impersonate a diety."

Star Wars JPEGs & GIFs Image Files
www.geocities.com/Area51/Corridor/1086/swimages.html
Nicely rated by author Adams and arranged by movie title, this gallery includes GIF and JPEG image files with sizes. A picture of the week. Includes many video box cover art and movie posters. Some images are "not found."

Star Wars Legacy
www.starwarz.com/swlegacy/frameset.html
This site is creating a series of videos in the Star Wars genre which are set 60 years after the Battle of Endor. This project is ongoing and is created by fans, not by official Lucas folks. Find other videos to download here, and web page of new production art for the Legacy.

Star Wars Legacy Download Videos
www.starwarz.com/swlegacy/video.html
Features Teaser Trailer videos to download in MPEG and RealVideo format, also an "extra special" video (which we didn't preview). Here is the RealVideo version of the CNN segment on fan videos.

Star Wars Link Engine
www.project-m31.com/prequels.shtml
Collections of web links (some with descriptions) for each of the four movies. This site had some links we don't (and we had some they don't). It is searchable. So, if you want, for instance, to find more Empire Strikes Back-related files, click on that movie title.

Star Wars MIDI Music
www.geocities.com/Area51/9394/movies
MIDI music files not only from the movies, but from the games Dark Forces and TIE Fighter as well. Collected from various music authors. All 71 files are also available in one 591KB zip file.

Star Wars Movie Art
http://empire.res.wabash.edu/art/movies/index.htm
Terrific Thrawn Gallery collection of art used in movie production for creating scenes, models, locations, sets, and characters. Contains Ralph McQuarrie pix, creatures, locations, death star, Jawa Fortress and Jabba's Palace. Others show Tatooine, Hoth, Bespin, and especially Coruscant.

Star Wars Movie Clips
http://168.229.236.7/~cc/movie.html
10 AVI format videos from the Trilogy with length given. Lots of conflicts, fighting and explosions. Also links-back to MIDI files, MP3 Audio Tracks, WAV files and pictures.

Star Wars MP3 Audio Tracks
http://168.229.236.7/~cc/mp3.html
MP3 music files from Empire Strikes Back and Return of the Jedi, including the Jedi Rocks Special Edition musical number in Jabba's Palace.

Star Wars MUD & MUSHes
www.radeleff.de/swmudlist
At the English version of this German site, you'll find a directory of Star Wars MUSHes, Muxes, MOOs, MUDs, and upcoming and closed events of the same roleplaying nature. Sites are listed by URL and Telnet; some sites are detailed, which helps you select which ones to visit.

Star Wars Multimedia
www.cadvision.com/geoff/sw.html
Moderate-size list of links to other Star Wars related sites. List is arranged by general topic including newsletters, mailing lists, info, characters and places, company sites, and there is a large list of sounds and picture web sites.

Star Wars Multimedia Archive
http://people.clemson.edu/~jvalice/star.htm
Lists and reviews a number of Star Wars books, also features an archive of JPEG & GIF images. Site galleries include MIDI music and WAV files of quotes.

Star Wars Multimedia Database
http://members.aol.com/am54g/sw/index.html
This site promises more categories (images, Prequels), though the software/multimedia section (click on "windows") is up and has new screensavers, wallpaper, and icons, many of them from the Phantom Menace. These can be downloaded to your computer for your enjoyment.

Star Wars Multimedia Headquarters
www.nerf-herder.com/swmhq/index.html
A Nintendo-like opening page for sites by Steve Lelinski lets you access other pages by clicking on character icons in the overhead view of the "HQ" illustration. Galleries of pix, videos, music and sounds are surprisingly deep. Also, webrings, awards, modeling, toys, and fun playset pictures.

Star Wars Multimedia HQ Games
http://nerf-herder.com/swmhq/games.html
Variety of downloadable games for young (k-12), medium (cool teens) and old (relics from around when Star Wars first came out). The TIE Fighters file is just a demo; most other games are complete.

IMAGES   VIDEO   AUDIO
MUST SEE!   SELLS STUFF   ADULT CONTENT   SEARCHABLE
CHAT ROOMS   MESSAGE BOARDS   MAILING LISTS

Star Wars Multimedia HQ Sounds
http://nerf-herder.com/swmhq/sounds.html
"But I was going into Toshi Station to pick up some power converters," Luke whines, and common sound bites like "Everything under control - situation normal." WAVs quotes (also Jabba laughing and Jawas screaming) and usual MIDI music files.

Star Wars Multimedia HQ Still Pictures
http://nerf-herder.com/swmhq/pics.html
Find picture files for characters, ships, and smaller files of icons, drawings, Boba Fett. A few pictures are black & white; spacecraft images are fairly common but some character shots are rare. Thumbnails or text-only versions.

Star Wars MUSH
www.cae.wisc.edu/~steiner/mush/site/index.html
If you're brave enough, if you're fan-atic enough, if you're ready for the plunge - you might want to start here for entering a Star Wars MUSH fantasy/game/role/adventure/trip. Now under new management, this site looks well organized. "Take a step into a larger world."

Star Wars MUSH Mailing Lists
www.cae.wisc.edu/~steiner/mush/site/mailing.htm
Roleplaying games need communication here, also several e-mail lists for MUSHes, each serving different functions and aspects of the game. Get at these lists by subscribing (explained at this site).

Star Wars Pictures (Clemson .edu)
http://people.clemson.edu/~jvalice/starS.htm
Alphabetical lists of GIFs and JPEG image files, including Special Edition pieces. Selection is big, not huge; lots of action shots. Site hosted by Cornell Univeristy and last updated 1/97.

Star Wars Prequels
www.execpc.com/~zerob/Dataside.html
An archives of Prequel news and views listed day-by-day. See history being made. This site attaches to Master Yoda and his great Dagobah site.

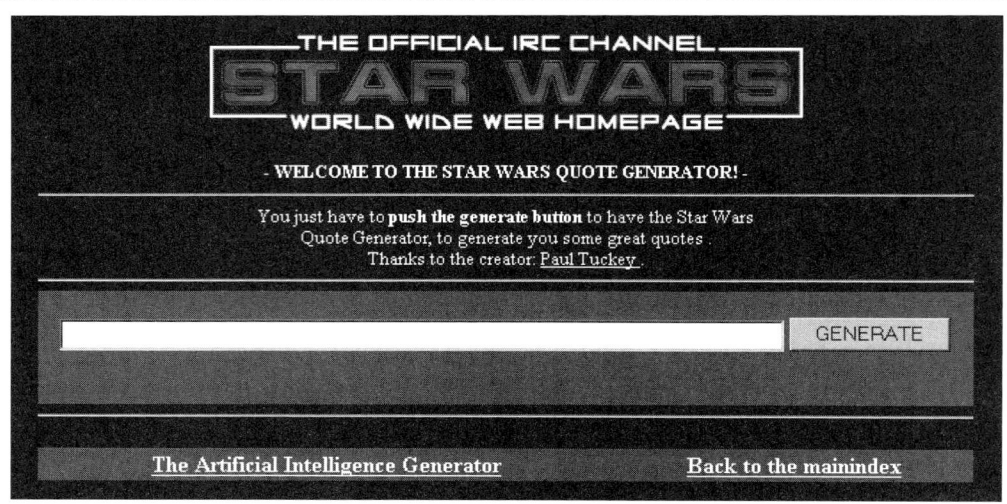

Star Wars Quote Generator
www.surfnet.fi/~zargon/swchan/quote2.html
Press the "generate" button and up pops a Star Wars quote - "Don't get all mushy on me!" - "Wars not make one great." - "Look at the size of that thing" and hundreds more, we guess.

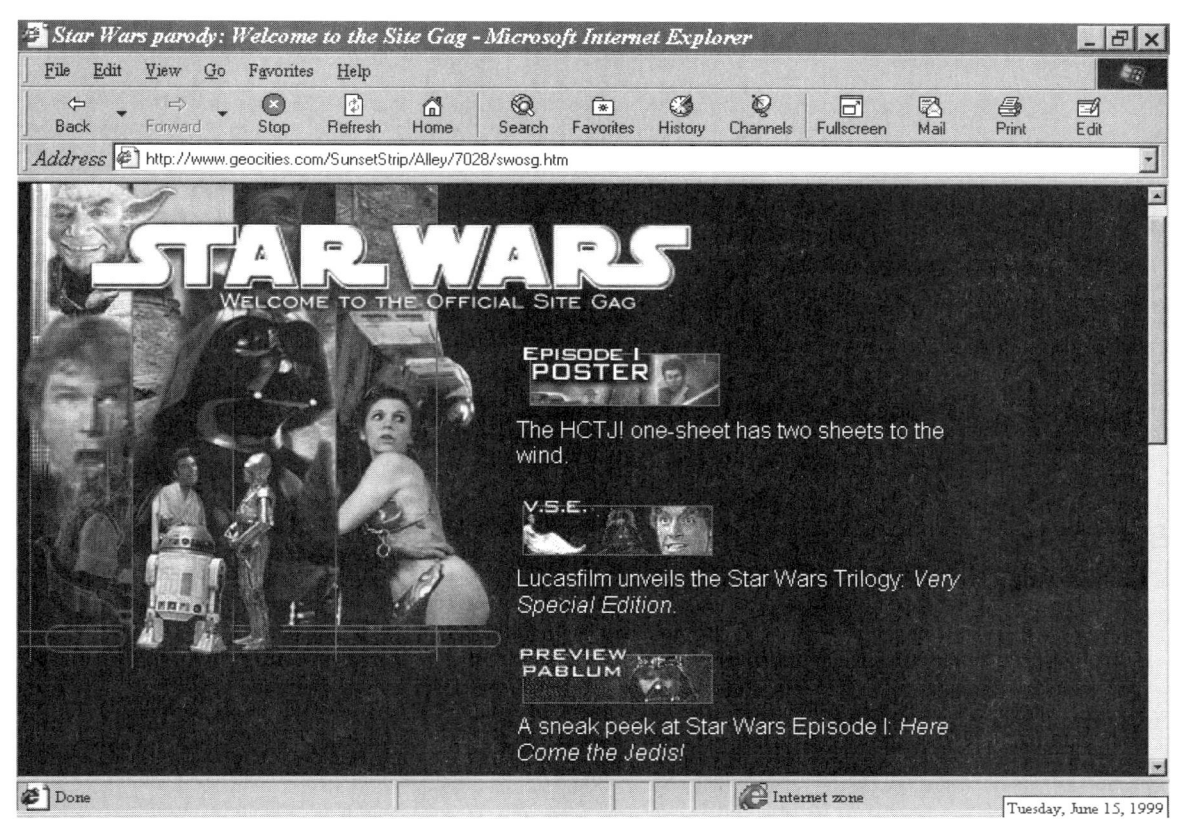

Star Wars Sight Gag Site
www.geocities.com/SunsetStrip/Alley/7028/swosg.htm
Parodies on Star Wars collected by Doug Anderson.

Star Wars Sound Mix Comparison
www.jax-inter.net/users/datalore/starwars/soundfaq.htm
Star Techies and others with sensitive ears will listen closer next time due to Jay (Threadwells Techdome) Pennington's astute observations and comments about the sound mastering. He lists sound and character line changes that have been made from version to version.

Star Wars Sound Page
www.xs4all.nl/~meelberg/index.html
Sounds are arranged by character, including quips by Luke, Yoda, Han, Darth, Leia, C-3PO, The Emperor, and Boba Fett. Only 6 MIDI music files were found, but you'll recognize them all.

Star Wars Sounds
www.strw.leidenuniv.nl/~jansen/sw/sound.html
"Great shot - now don't get cocky" and other audio quotes, with Kb size. This Dutch site was not updated since the clone wars (1996). About 50 WAV files are arranged by movie title.

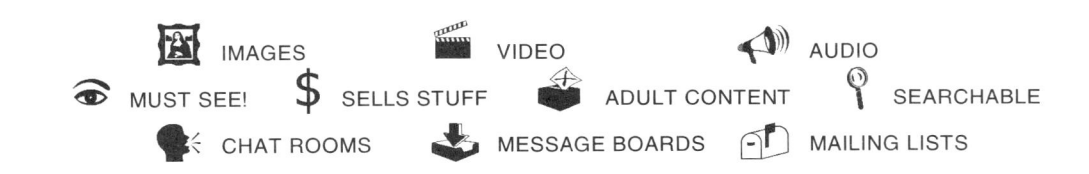

Star Wars Sounds (Carroll)
www.3-cities.com/~yogi/starwars.htm
Selection of WAV sounds, mostly Yoda quotes and Vader one-liners like "Impressive" and "Don't make me destroy you!" Also, the lightsaber power up and down sounds.

Star Wars Sounds (Clemson .edu)
http://people.clemson.edu/~jvalice/starS.htm
Approximately 30 audio quotes in WAV files. The MIDI music files include Star Wars Medley and most of the familiar favorites. Site is on the Clemson University system.

Star Wars Sounds (Imperial)
www.aaronklaassen.com/starwars/swwavs.htm
Collection of WAV sound files of quotes from Imperial characters, and a few of the desperation and ominous quotes from A New Hope main characters: "I felt a great disturbance in the Force" - Obi-wan. "What a piece of junk." - Luke. The villain quotes are better.

Star Wars Sounds From --
www.pages.drexel.edu/undergrad/bzm22/starwars.html
Selection of WAV & AIFF audio files arranged by Trilogy movie title. AIFF's are few, but they're good ones - Han's "Hokey religion" quote. QuickTime videos include new Jabba/Han from the Special Edition, also familiar scenes like the jump to lightspeed, Vader, and the Trench Run.

Star Wars Spaceport
www.geocities.com/TimesSquare/Corridor/1780/swars.html
See what a site looks like when it does NOT get finished. Feel free to report empty sites, abondoned sites, or those with links that don't work to The Incredible Internet Guide To Star Wars. Use the form in this book, or visit our website, or e-mail us at websitecentral@naboo.zzn.com

Star Wars The Game
www.tem.nhl.nl/~veen606/egame.htm
Old Vector Graphic Star Wars arcade game, which was popular in video arcades (remember them?) way back when. Of course, your modern computer will make this old version run at lightspeed. Unzip the file and let 'er rip.

Star Wars The Legend
http://cicero.com.alma.edu/MCS131/mccune/4thpowerpoint/index.htm
This is a short Powerpoint slide show gallery from alma.edu Media Services. You click the arrows to view the slides, which are mainly collages.

Star Wars The Musical
www.geocities.com/Hollywood/Lot/6700/swm-scr.txt
Transcript of eight scenes from the Star Wars Musical by Kevin Bayuk, Garrin Hajeian, and John Zuckerman. We didn't find where the music is, though.

Star Wars The Phantom Menace
www.allexperts.com/tv/swplot.shtml
ALLEXPERTS.COM's experts have taken a humorous approach to explaining the storyline of The Phantom Menace - and still manage to fill us in about how the story unfolds: "Qui-Gon offers to win his freedom in a spirited game of rocks-lightsabers-paper."

Star Wars Trilogy Cards
www.geocities.com/Area51/Corridor/4323/cards.html
Taz's collection of over 30 Star Wars Trilogy trading cards, primarily from A New Hope. Cards are "widevision" and manufactured by Topps, with 2 pix per card with storyline.

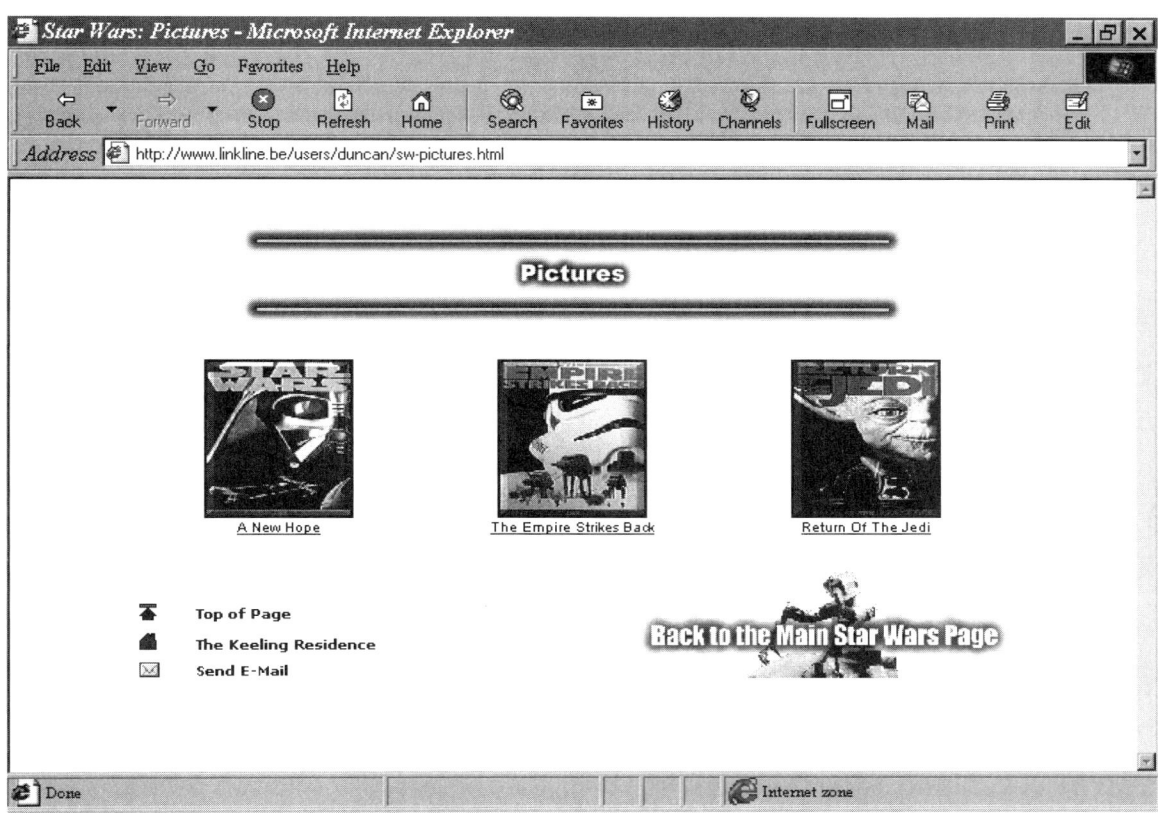

Star Wars Trilogy Gallery 🖼 👁

www.linkline.be/users/duncan/sw-pictures.html

Dozens of character shots from each of the 3 Trilogy movies, arranged by movie. Size of file is listed.

Star Wars Trilogy, The 🖼 📣

www.linkline.be/users/duncan/starwars.html

Photos, sound bites, the scripts to this Keeling Trilogy web site. All pages are arranged by the movie they were in.

Star Wars Unnamed Site 🖼

www.angelfire.com/ak/jskywalker/starwars.html

Notated as a multimedia page, this unnamed site (the closest we came to a name was Anakin Skywalkers Star Wars Page) offers expandable thumbnail pictures of Star Wars action.

Star Wars Versus Titanic

www.geocities.com/Hollywood/Theater/5049

Also known as the boycott Titanic page, the big boat and Leo D. get roasted mercilessly by a sweet author known only as "Jennifer." Rates at least a minimum visit. Don't get her riled.

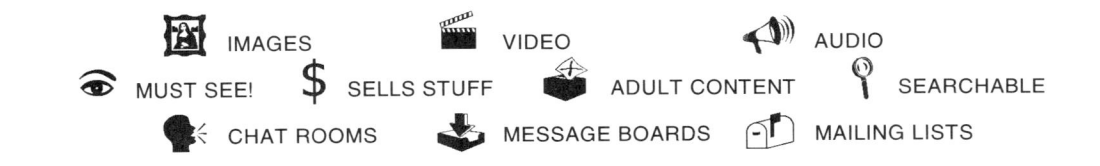

Star Wars Virtual Reality System
http://zansiii.millersv.edu/work2/starwars.dir
>Millersville University "CS373: Computer Graphics & VR" has put together a Star Wars simulator site, along with hardware advice, MPEG video clips, sounds, and an sgi demo. Click to their home page for other VRML goodies.

Star Wars WAV Files
http://168.229.236.7/~cc/wav.html
>WAV audio files of some favorite Star Wars quotes by good guys (a couple from Darth, too). Does R2-D2 say anything other than incoherent beeps and warbles? Comments and sizes of clips are listed.

Star Wars Wonderland
http://wonder.simplenet.com/sww/home.html
>Sadly, this personable site is not being updated (perhaps this Summer?!). Visit the Junk Pile for sounds, video clips, and humor files. Art gallery is mostly Ewoks; appears to be drawn by Ewoks.

Star Wars, Adventures of Luke Starkiller
www.geocities.com/Area51/Stargate/9082/swd3.txt
>Reputedly the third screenplay draft for Star Wars, dated August, 1975. Script has a lot of unknown details not found in later drafts. Note "Luke Starkiller" subtitle, obviously changed in a later version.

Star Wars: Episode 1 - The Phantom Menace
http://us.imdb.com/Title?0120915
>Internet Movie Database gives the facts on 1999's biggest movie (perhaps biggest of all time!). Cast list with great links, genre, taglines, and huge sub-data files. Submit your comments (give yourself a super A+ if this database uses it!). Purchase soundtrack and books at this searchable site.

Star Wars: Episode 1 Merchandise
http://scifistore.lycos.com
>Lycos plans to have this site up to let you find the Star Wars merchandise you're looking for.

Starbase Rickover - Computer Graphics Archives
http://cs.heritage.edu/student/newton/archives/starwars/index.html
>Gallery of Computer Graphic images, mostly spacecraft. Click on them to expand the images to their full-color majesty. Site also links back to other CG archives on other subjects found at the heritage.edu web resource site.

Starfeld 🔊
www.hydrospanner.com/starfeld
> Hydrospanner presents a "what if" Star Wars and Seinfeld's TV show were "warped" together? You'll find a humorous collection of "mixer" WAV audios - Elaine & Vader, Luke & the Soup Nazi, Red Leader & Cramer.

Starfighters 👁
http://frankg.dgne.com/swsv/starfighters.html
> Starfighters are small one or two person craft. Specifications here are from West End Games roleplaying games and, of course, from LucasArts. Many descriptions also list the original soruces, such as a crafts activities in a book, comic, or movie. A must for starfighter pilots.

Starkiller - The Jedi Bendu Script Page 👁
http://starwarz.com/starkiller/frame.htm
> Internet home of original drafts and screenplays to the Star Wars Saga. The scripts found here are downloadable; illustrated scripts are planned. From the "Writing Frame" you may wish to read the Star Wars Rejection Letters from film companies, also essays and mission statement of the Jedi Bendu.

Stars Wars First Screenplay Draft
www.geocities.com/Area51/Stargate/9082/swd1.txt
> Rough draft - the first as a screenplay - by George Lucas of the original Star Wars, 5/74.

Startroop1 Star Wars Page 💬 🖼 🔊
http://members.xoom.com/Startroop1
> Not every multimedia page has a walking At-At, chat through Xoom.com, Bob Fett, AND links to a flight simulator! See the special downloads page of author's favorites. Includes sounds, picture files, and morphing logo.

Startup/Shutdown Screens 🖼
www.jedinet.com/multimedia/windows/screens/index.htm
> Selection of 4 zipped downloadable utility screen function packages: Boba Fett, X-wings, posters, & TIE Fighters.

StarWars - a game written in Java
www.ktb.net/~rrobb/karim/stapplet/StarWarsApplet.html
> A free online game that is written in Java applets - it makes use of multiple threads running at the same time. The game reminds us of the old early '80 arcade games. This would make a super science project submission at school.

StarWarsRealm Mail
http://starwarsrealm.zzn.com/email/login/login.asp
> Yes, you can have your own StarWars Realm e-mail address - for free.

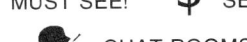

🖼 IMAGES	🎬 VIDEO	🔊 AUDIO
👁 MUST SEE!	$ SELLS STUFF	ADULT CONTENT	🔍 SEARCHABLE
💬 CHAT ROOMS	📬 MESSAGE BOARDS	📫 MAILING LISTS

Starwarz
www.starwarz.com
A collection of seven sites, these form an interesting alliance, engaged in promoting Star Wars from an alternative fans perspective. Variety of forums: most are interactive, specialized, different. Sites have video projects underway. Dave (Darth Vader) Prowse's homesite is here.

Stephen's Star Wars Den
www.geocities.com/Area51/Labyrinth/1390/index.htm
A Star Wars "Den" is like a rupus-room/home entertainment center. Here you'll find picture archives, scripts, Special Edition pictures, links to webrings and a game page to come, perhaps sounds & movies (videos). We say "perhaps" because the host for sounds & movies may have bugged-out.

Stephen's Star Wars Den Movies
www.geocities.com/Area51/Labyrinth/1390/movie.htm
Pages of Trilogy video clips in AVI or MOV format, arranged by the movie they are taken from. Size of files is listed; most are much less then 3 MB. Sounds are WAV's and MIDI's, but less in number. Also has expandable thumbnails of pix, also scripts.

Stephen's TIE Fighter Page
http://indigo.ie/~hanafin/starwars.html
Originally a resource for TIE Fighter the game, this site has grown into a good informational resource for fighter spacecraft. Section of downloads & scenarios. Has several discussion options: mailing lists, chat, message boards.

Steve's Star Wars Timeline
www.echostation.com
Steve's timeline compilation on the Echo Station mega-site indicates new additions and updates, and can be set up to inform you (via e-mail) of changes. Plus, the timeline entries are active links to the source - click and go there! You also rate the universe and read news here.

Stories by Fans
http://members.xoom.com/scriptkeeper/fanstories.htm
Read any of a number of the fan-created Star Wars stories here or submit your own. Small collection but very rare.

Stormtrooper HQ
www.ausnet.net.au/~jaseod/stormtrooper/stormtrooper.htm
Australian site had all sorts of Stormtrooper data, but it's not very active now: the mortality rate of stormtroopers is as high as was predicted. Still, this images page has great stormtrooper gear JPEG files. (Site is being updated).

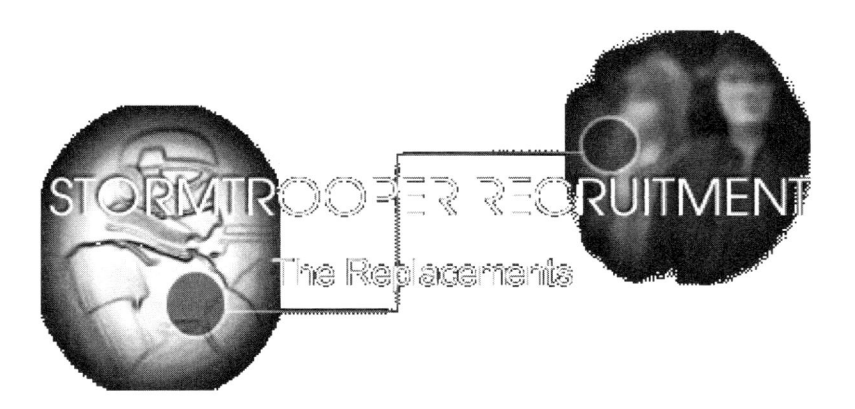

Stormtrooper Recruitment - The Replacements
http://207.136.91.134/very/x-stream
> Stealth's Star Wars site is making a new look - rebuilding as the Stormtrooper Recruitment Center. Pix and tech data of the TIE Interceptor Prototype are sharp; the rest of the site should be.

Stronghold Academy
http://mama.indstate.edu/rpg/games/weg/starwars/index.html
> The ISU Roleplaying Club game scenario resource site for Star Wars RPG games. This site also features a gamesmasters site along with the usual files for ideas, news, campaigns, and databases of characters, equipment, ships, timelines, game essentials, and dice rollers.

Stv1's Star Wars Characters
http://members.tripod.com/~stv1/index-2.html
> In case you really just dropped in from another planet, here's a rundown of the characters of the Trilogy who survived (there's also a "killed-off" list for those of us who forgot that Jabba did get ka-choked by Carrie Fisher).

Stv1's Star Wars MIDI Clips
http://members.tripod.com/~stv1/index-5.html
> We didn't listen to all these MIDI music clips, but we can say there are a lot of them!

Stv1's Star Wars Page
http://members.tripod.com/~stv1/index.html
> Character bios, MIDI sounds, photos and more photos - including very nice Chewiee, Boba Fett, and Leia pictures, and Yoda doing his ET imitation. Site also features "Bond; James Bond" Goldeneye page and a quizlet.

SW:CCG Webring
www.geocities.com/Area51/5657/ring.html
> Add your own Star Wars CCG site to this webring, or cruise this webring for other game sites. It is easy to join and a quick way to find other Customized Card Game people online.

SW:RPG - Star Wars Roleplaying Game Site
http://members.tripod.com/KSantos/swrpg/index.html/index.html
> A RPG site for both the novice and experienced players. Click on what you are. Players can use this as a resource. Novices can use it as a learning tool.

Swammi's Characters in the Star Wars Universe
http://members.xoom.com/kessel/outpost/char.html
   Site of images intended for downloading onto your own web site. There's the spooky green emperor's face, C-3PO, Boba Fett, troopers, droids.

Swammi's Knicknacks & Other Assorted Images
http://members.xoom.com/kessel/outpost/kniknak.html
   Odds N ends site of Star Wars GIFs for web pages: Boba Fett logo, 20-years logo, Star Wars firebird, and more.

Swammi's Star Wars Animated GIFs
http://members.xoom.com/kessel/outpost/anim.html
   Building a Star Wars web site and need something to liven it up? Here's a good place to find some of the more common animated GIF lightsabers, E-mail, At-Ats - even a scrolling intro.

Swammi's Star Wars Bullets
http://members.xoom.com/kessel/outpost/bullet.html
   Little Star Wars stuff to decorate your web site with - we call them icons; the Swammi site calls them bullets. Yodas, R2s, X-wing, lightsaber, Falcon, death stars, logos.

Swammi's Star Wars Logos
http://members.xoom.com/kessel/outpost/logo.html
   "Logos. Why must it always be logos?" Oh, wrong movie. We were thinking of Harrison in the snake pit in Raiders of the Lost Ark. Anyway, here's more Star Wars logos than you can shake a stick at.

Swammi's Star Wars MIDIs (music)
http://members.xoom.com/kessel/outpost/midi.html
   We liked this page because it's part of the great Swammi Star Wars Outpost multimedia collection, which you should see via the Swammi's main site. MIDI files here include the Trilogy music favorites.

Swammi's Star Wars Outpost
http://members.xoom.com/kessel/outpost
   We recommend this multimedia site for its loads of categories: animated GIFs, backgrounds, banners, bullets, characters, covers, logos MIDIs, ships, posters, novels, art, reviews, humor, trivia, scripts, survey, awards & webrings links. Great sight for material for Star Wars web page designers.

Swedish University Network SUNET Star Wars
ftp://ftp.sunet.se/pub/pictures/tv.film/Star_Wars
   Alphabetized FTP directory of dozens of good quality Star Wars photos, GIFs and JPEGs images from a Swedish University site. Check the higher level directory for other entertainment files: Bladerunner, even some Star Trek!

SWMA - 3D Modeling Information
www.surfthe.net/swma/information/information.html
   Star Wars 3D Modeling Alliance has created a superb FAQs page for anyone interested in learning more about 3D modeling and their alliance. Includes general guidelines and 3D tool specifics.

SWMA - Star Wars 3D Modeling Alliance Archives
www.surfthe.net/swma/archives/archives.html
   If it was in Star Wars, there's probably a 3D model and technical info about it here, also textures, reference material. You can use models for your personal entertainment only.

SWMA - Star Wars 3D Modeling Alliance Member Directory 📬
www.surfthe.net/swma/members/members.html
World Wide Web address and e-mail addresses for Star Wars 3D Modeling Alliance members. They make the Star Wars 3D universe happen.

SWMA - Star Wars 3D Modeling Alliance 🎬 👁
www.swma.net
Dedicated to creating a 3D Star Wars Galaxy - and they have a very good start! Archives and Galleries are excellent and well-organized. Members and links lists, forum, tutorials, news, archives and 3D FAQs.

Sylvia Christina's Special Thoughts for Mark Hamill A Very Special Person ⬇ 🖼
www.yggdrasill.demon.nl/Serie01/MHHome2.htm
Sylvia HAS put together a very special page for Mark, and you are invited to visit. Find Mark's biography & filmography, a message board, newspaper clips, a slide show, fan fiction and "New" stuff.

Symbols from Star Wars 🖼
www.geocities.com/Area51/Corridor/4323/symbols.html
Taz's Logos and Symbols collection - Imperial, Republic, and Boba Fett in colorful JPEG format.

T'Bone Fenders Star Wars Universe 🖼 🎬 🔊 👁
www.starwarz.com/index.htm
"Everything for the Star Wars Enthusiast" it says, and we rate this site a portal due to its excellent set up, content, links, news, archives, and all-around fan flavor. Includes behind-the-scenes and cut scene files, interviews, Infonet reading resource, and real comments. Part of the Starwarz sites group.

Address: http://www.geocities.com/Area51/Corridor/7410/

Take a Walk Through a Splinter of My Mind's Eye:

- R2D2 pictured here was the card box made by my son and me for last Valentine's Day. It consists largely of an Oatmeal box, Paper towel tubes, half of a Plastic ball, and a working Flashlight as his front lens.
- My Sketch Book. Updated 03/FEBRUARY/99
- Links to Friends & Places. Updated 11/MAY/98
- Action Figures Updated 24/APRIL/98
- An Original Star Wars Comic.
  - Page One is up.
- My Love of "A New Hope".
- Some Prized CCG Cards.
- This site was updated: *February 03, 1999.*

Take a Walk Through a Splinter of My Mind's Eye 🖼
www.geocities.com/Area51/Corridor/7410
Big name, unusual little web site. Not a typical multimedia page: find an R2-D2 made of an oatmeal box, paper towel tubes, a plastic ball and a flashlight. Links to action figures, an original Star Wars comic, prized CCG cards.

🖼 IMAGES 🎬 VIDEO 🔊 AUDIO
👁 MUST SEE! $ SELLS STUFF ADULT CONTENT SEARCHABLE
CHAT ROOMS MESSAGE BOARDS 📬 MAILING LISTS

Tally Ho! Movie Prop Replicas - Star Wars $
www.dsctoys.com/swc1.html
   Tally Ho has a good but irregularly-stocked collection of Star Wars Trilogy Costume Prop Replicas, Helmets & Mask Replicas, and Life-Sized Figure Prop Replicas. Click back to the Star Wars Collectors page to find novelty items from bed sheets to cookie jars to X-mas goodies.

Tally Ho! Star Wars Collectors $
www.dsctoys.com/warsc.html
   Lots of categories to choose from - Bet you don't have a '70s Wonderbred Star Wars collector's card set! Find all sorts of Star Wars merchandise (subject to availability) here, including clothes, cookie jars, holiday cards, pins, displays, hats, plates, bed sheets, banks, and a whole lot more that would take forever to list here.

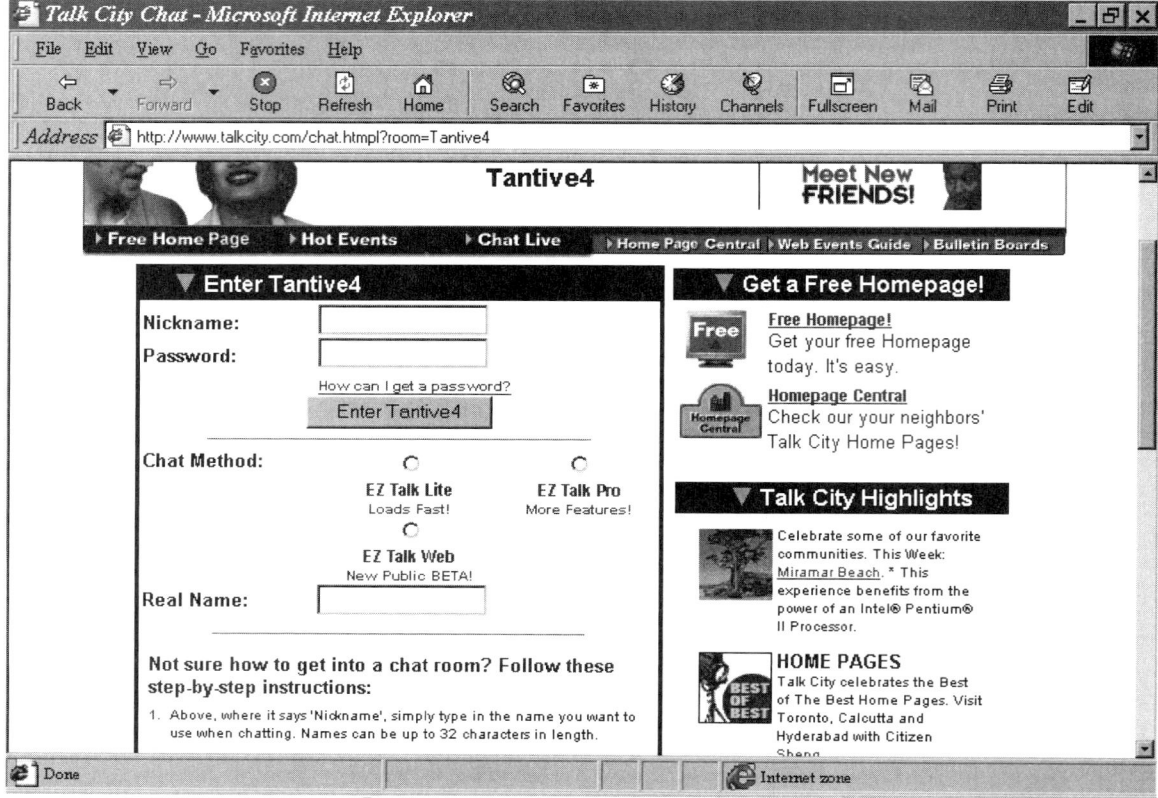

Tantive 4 Chat Room
www.talkcity.com/chat.htmpl?room=Tantive4
   Tantive 4 chat room for fans is sponsored by Talkcity, who offers EZ talks & EZ talk Web on the new public Beta.

Targeting Computer (Rogue 8's)
http://members.xoom.com/rogue888/computer.htm
   Best collection of downloadable Star Wars fonts (Ewok, Jedi, Boba Fonts and more) plus programs like Win Sabacc, Star Wars Ship Racing, old video games, also desktop themes, system logos and start-ups for computers.

Targeting Computer Quick Shot Video
http://users.why.net/radrock/sounds/trgcmptr.avi
   Short downloadable AVI video of the targeting computer used by Luke in his X-wing fighter.

Tatooine
www.starwars.com/locations/tatooine-vi
   Lucasfilms site for planet Tatooine, which appears in all Star Wars movies. Largely a desert, Tatooine is home to the Dune Sea, Mos Eisley Spaceport, the Sarlacc creature at the Pit of Carkoon, and Jabba's Palace - all are accessible via links from this page. A good pic of Jabba's sail barges is found here.

Tatooine Text
www.angelfire.com/co/gavind/tatooine.html
   Informative text on many aspects of planet Tatooine, site of memorable Star Wars action.

Tauntauns
www.starwars.com/creatures/tauntauns
   Official Lucasfilms site featuring Planet Hoth's Tauntauns. Background info and pix on these big Llama-like riding creatures of ice planet Hoth.

Taz's Boba Fett Galleries
http://seconn4.yoda.com/~vader97/boba/boba.html
   Four separate Boba Fett galleries are accessible from here. Most appear to be JPEG-image files. Very big, also takes a while to open, but well worth it.

Taz's Collection of Star Wars 3D Renderings
www.chez.com/lordvader/3drender.html
   20+ 3D renderings in winzip files. Most are spacecraft or vehicles, also R2, C3-PO, At-Ats and Darth.

Taz's Star Wars Animations
www.geocities.com/Area51/Corridor/4307/starwarsani.html
   Find animated GIFs such as the death star exploding e-mail, Darth with lightsabre, or vehicles that fly across the screen and more - a modest collection for web site builders, but a good one.

Taz's Star Wars Art Galleries
http://seconn4.yoda.com/~vader97/art/art.html
   There are 10 - count them, ten - big JPEG image galleries with 20 pix in each. All appear to be original art collected by Taz. See various size JPEG files, most in color and good quality; many are composite pix, some Prequel, some are wide angle. We cannot verify the origins.

Taz's Star Wars Movies
http://seconn4.yoda.com/~vader97/movies/movies.html
   "Now all I have to do is find this Yoda." - Luke. Over 50 Trilogy video clips in AVI video format, listed in alphabetical order. May require some time to download, but the selection is sure to please.

Taz's Star Wars Page
www.geocities.com/Area51/Corridor/4309
   Great main site by Lord Vader 97; links to individual gallery subpages of characters, posters, ships, schematics, new re-release scenes, Chewiee, Han, Boba - everyone - plus scripts, movies, music files, New Hope trading cards. (See individual lsitings for Taz's pages, adjacent.)

IMAGES	VIDEO	AUDIO
MUST SEE!	SELLS STUFF	ADULT CONTENT	SEARCHABLE
CHAT ROOMS	MESSAGE BOARDS	MAILING LISTS

Taz's Yoda Archives
http://seconn4.yoda.com/~vader97/yoda/yoda.html
About 30 good quality JPEG images of Yoda, all collected from various sources by Taz. After the long loading process, click on a Yoda picture for its full-sized view.

Tazos & Pogs
www.starwarscards.net/pogs.htm
Pogs, Tazos, stickers, even Doritos discs and cards can be found at this excellent starwarscards collector's site. Files are listed as American or International, also Vintage or Modern. This sites links to trading cards, collectible game cards, and other great resources pages.

Technical Commentaries
www.theforce.net/swtc
While these aren't actually "articles," they are useful comments and explanations of some of the elements found in Star Wars. Learn about Death Stars, Hyperspace, Astrophysical Concerns, Insignias, Darth Vaders injuries, Zoology, standard units, continuity, and more.

Technical Pictures
www.jedinet.com/multimedia/pics/tech/index.html
Jedinet's collection of technical drawings (JPEG image format) for Star Wars hardware, craft, droids, spacecraft, showing their general features. These are useful for modeling, image building, roleplaying.

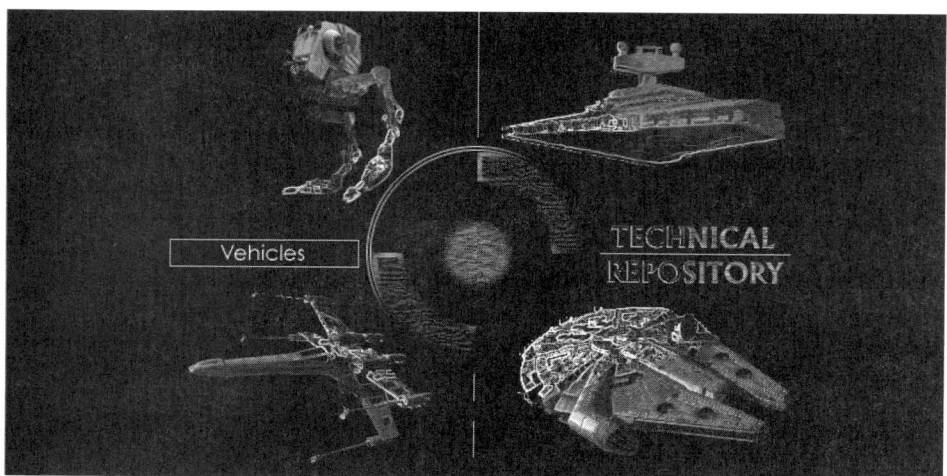

Technical Repository
www.cae.wisc.edu/~steiner/swsatellite/technic
This Star Wars Technical Repository houses information, specifications, and images of spacecraft by type, also on weapons such as At-At Walkers. Information can be used for modeling, roleplaying, or simply as a gee-whiz stop.

Technology (Official Star Wars Site)
www.starwars.com/technology
> Official Lucasfilms site that serves as a light subject directory to just a few of the more interesting devices that are introduced throughout the Star Wars series. Not too deep, this is a source of material on things such as ice chambers, hyperdrive, and Lord Vader's suit.

Ted's Star Wars Pictures
http://dvader.mit.edu/old/starwars.html
> This was Ted Weathers' multimedia page at one time; now this site on the MIT University server has a selection of wide action pix from the original Star Wars.

Television References
www.jedinet.com/multimedia/references/ref-tv.html
> ER's John Carter is referred to as "Young Jedi surgeon." Rachel dresses in the Princess Leia bikini as a Friends episode ends. Jim Carrey picks up a scalpel and says "Anyone wanna play Jedi Knights" on In Living Color. Hordes of other Star Wars TV references.

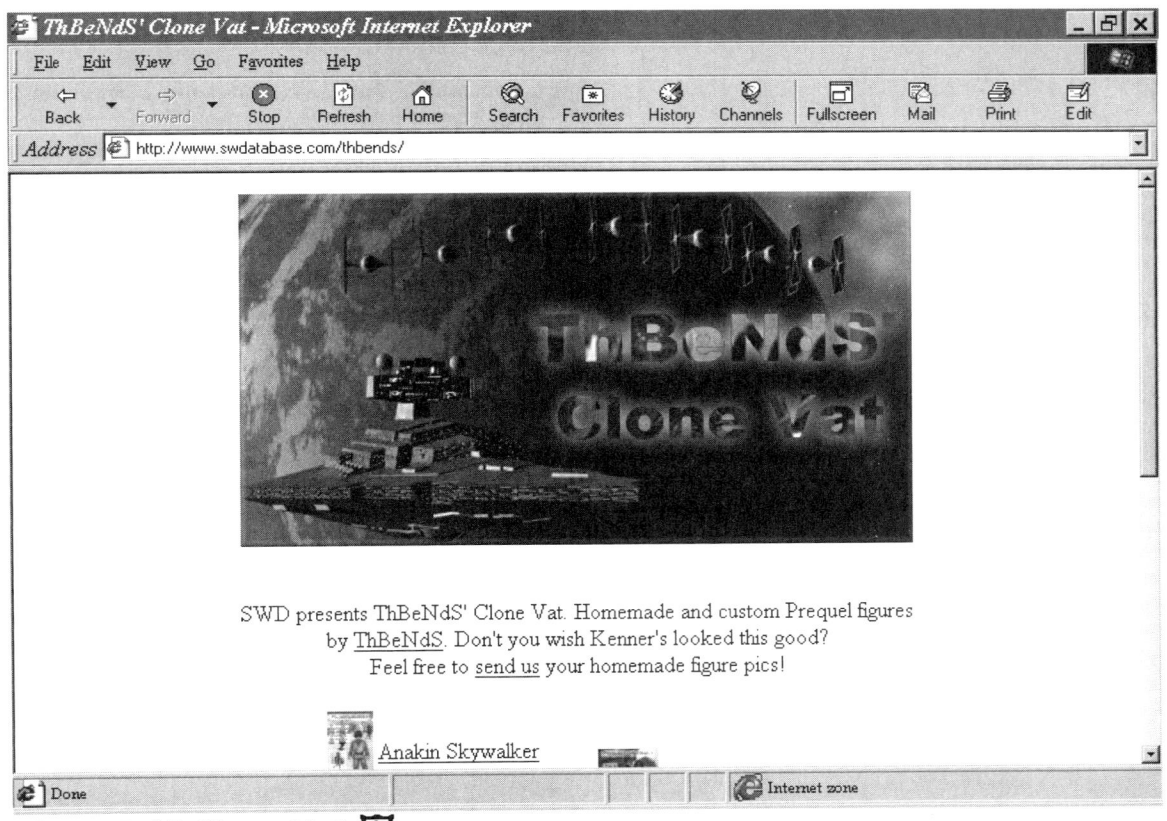

ThBeNDdS Clone Vat
www.swdatabase.com/thbends
> Excellent Prequel models site. 13 JPEG pictures of posed models look realisitic enough to spring to life. Homemade figure pictures are welcomed.

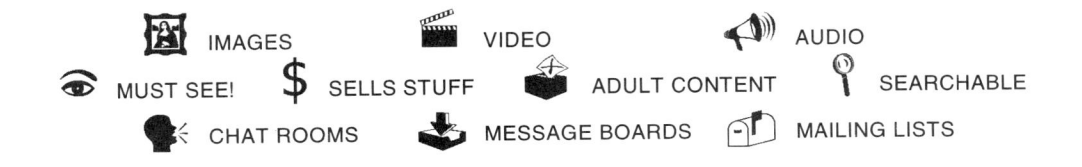

The Core
www.geocities.com/Area51/Rampart/2117
This online game group was found through the Marua Sector sites and the group (like others) are seeking new players and new scenarios. Since so many of these games are a matter of taste and personalities, you might find this ones right for you. This one looks well organized.

The Star Wars - Masthead: Adventures of The Starkiller
www.geocities.com/Area51/Stargate/9082/swd2.txt
Reputedly the second screenplay for the original Stars Wars, this is notable for the name change, the introduction of the Journal of the Whills, and other variations that changed later. George Lucas' January 28, '75 address is here.

Theatrical Trailers
www.jedinet.com/multimedia/movies/index.htm
Zipped files of trailers from the Trilogy & Special Editions sponsored by Jedinet. We didn't check, but, included are said to be the Energizer Bunny/Vader commerical, and the Pepsi promo with Vader in the theater.

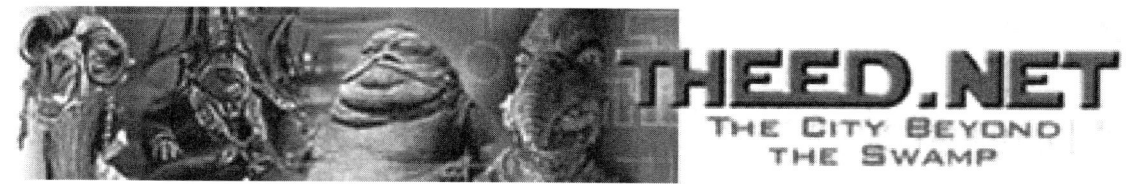

Theed.net - City Beyond the Swamp
www.theed.net
A new site in development, Theed.net does have a nice mix of editorials & news, basic Prequel FAQ (just the answers - no questions), and a launch page called "The Universe" - a theoretical map of where in the galaxy Tatooine, Naboo, & Coruscant are to each other.

Themes - Star Wars Episode 1 - The Music
http://members.es.tripod.de/Befan/Episode1music_Themes.html
90% of the Phantom Menace Score is new music. This site lists the themes we hear in the EP1, also commentaries on the new & old character themes and on the relevant music scenes in order. Links to CD track listings - scary, exciting, tender-hearted, comic, noble, and heroic music.

Third Prequel Movie: You Slice Me, I Slice You
www.allexperts.com/tv/swprequel2.shtml
ALLEXPERT.COM fields questions about Star Wars movies, and they also produce "Spoilers" that inform about the plots of movies - spoiling the excitement of discovery. But, this site is only a spoof spoiler - fictitious humor.

Thomas Star Wars Home Page
www.geocities.com/TimesSquare/4580
Dedicated to "the three greatest movies in the history of filmmaking," this 1996 Tom Hopkins multimedia site appears to be loosing a bit of its content and hasn't been updated. Hopefully, it will be.

Thrawn Art Gallery - Videos, Toys & Others
http://empire.res.wabash.edu/art/others/index.htm

Star Wars art can be found almost anywhere - here are galleries of art in promotions, video cassette boxes, toy covers, games and game screenshots, and magazines. For promotions, you can choose between Fritos, the chihuahua guys, and a soft drink sponsor.

Thrawn Art Gallery Music Collection
http://empire.res.wabash.edu/art/music/index.htm

Download any of these 75+ MP3 music files - or the one RealAudio file of the Special Edition Finale - and give a listen. Length of files are given. Did you know the 20th Century Fox fanfare was written by Alfred Newman, 1954? No, not the Alfred Newman in Mad Magazine.

Threadwell's Techdome
www.jax-inter.net/users/datalore/starwars

"Threadwell" is the name assigned to those rolling droids with spidery arms - with heads like Johnny5 from those '80s robot hi-jinx movies. Find specs and data invented by Threadwell, and also technical observations and comments about Star Wars Trilogy production, the sound especially.

THX
www.thx.com/main.html

LucasFilm THX is a technical/product arm of Lucas' business group. Here is information and products for theatres, professional products and services, retailer pages, also consumer products, employment oppportunities, and THX news and press releases.

THX Consumer Products
www.thx.com/consumer_products/index.html

Wouldn't it be great to have a THX sound system in your own home - say, your bedroom? Okay; the den. Go to this site to get info on THX systems for the home. Check press releases for standard features and hints on prices.

IMAGES   VIDEO   AUDIO
MUST SEE!   SELLS STUFF   ADULT CONTENT   SEARCHABLE
CHAT ROOMS   MESSAGE BOARDS   MAILING LISTS

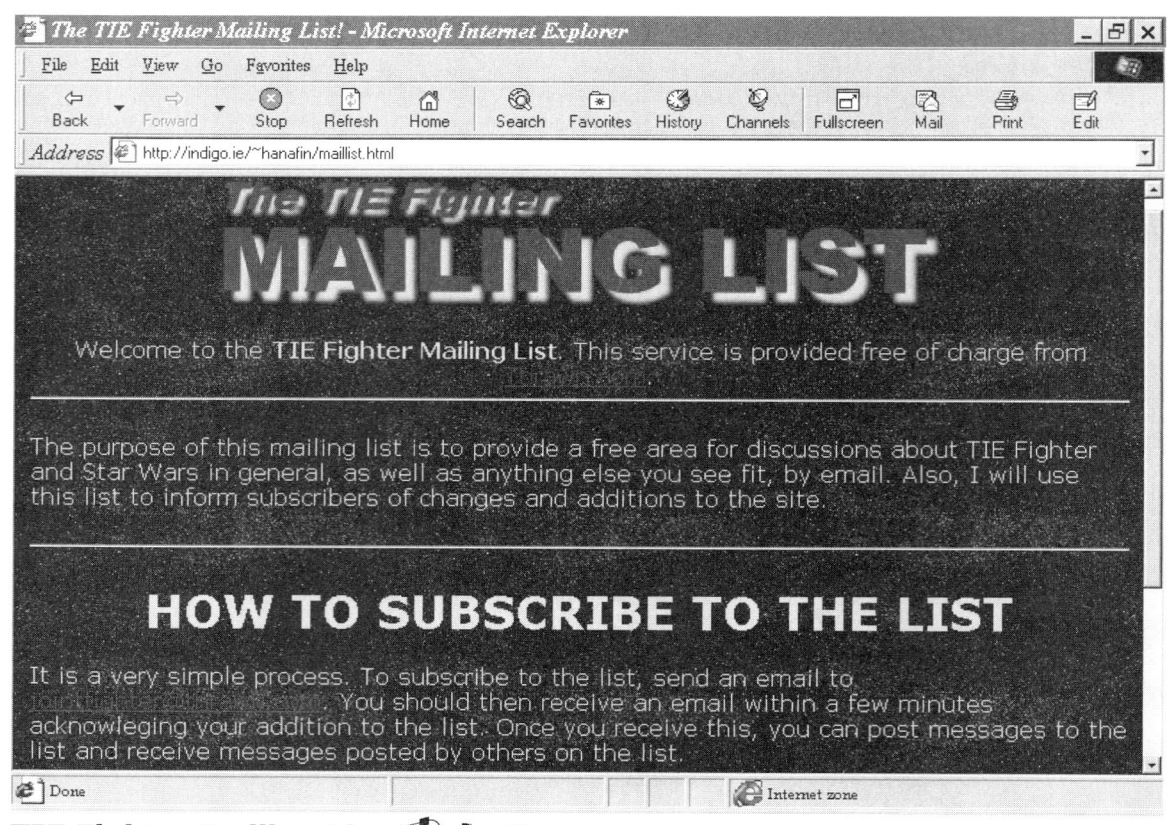

TIE Fighter Mailing List
http://indigo.ie/~hanafin/maillist.html
> Do you want to get in touch with others who share your enthusiam for Star Wars spacecraft? Here's a mailing list to join. Also, see Stephen's TIE Fighter Page for a chatroom, trivia, and more.

TIE Fighters
www.starwars.com/vehicles/tie_fighter
> As described in this official Lucasfilms site, TIE stands for Twin Ion Engine. These menacing little knats are a staple in the Imperial fleet. The site gives a general review of the TIE Fighter, and like most of the official sites, there are limited pictures, but they are expandable when clicked on.

TIE Fighters Free Downloads
http://indigo.ie/~hanafin/download.html
> Find and download utilities, single missions, complete battles, and learn how to use add-ons and more as you explore the world of space combat. Connects to Stephen's TIE Fighter Page; an excellent resource.

TIE Fighters Technical Commentaries
www.theforce.net/swtc/tie.html
> These menacing spacecraft used by the Imperial forces as air-to-air fighters are well-documented at this force.net site. Read about all of them; view most of them. Site offers more than we care to know.

TIE Interceptor
www.starwars.com/vehicles/tie_interceptor
> Official Lucasfilms page for the Empire's newly introduced TIE Interceptor, an improvement on the previous TIE Fighters that seemed to fall out of the heavens in earlier episodes. The sites gives a general run-down and offers a couple still pictures; click on them for enlargements.

Time Tours - Roderick Vonhogen's Virtual Edition
www.virtualedition.com/timetours/timetours_splash.htm
>Roderick Vonhogen's Virtual Edition Time Tours is set up like Disney's Star Tours, with droids leading you through the virtual tour in the Timespeeder. At the start page, click on time tours - away you go. May be too graphic intense for older computers and droids.

Timecruiser's Prequel Pictures
www.angelfire.com/co/Timecruiser/Menacepics.html
>An early Prequel JPEG gallery with some explanations added to the pictures - also some concept art paintings. Timecruiser seems to be up on the latest news and offerings.

Timecruiser's The Picture Gallery
www.angelfire.com/co/Timecruiser/StarPicture.html
>Has pictures of major characters in their more memorable poses - a fair collection of color JPEG images.

Timecruisers Star Wars Galaxy
www.angelfire.com/co/Timecruiser
>Multimedia site with pages (some under construction) for heroes, villains, music, chat, pix galleries, chat room, message board, Q&A, and link to Xoom software deals. Find prequel news, polaroids, art.

Timeline (Jedinet)
www.jedinet.com/multimedia/timeline/index.htm
>Year 0 starts with A New Hope (Luke, Han, Chewie rescue Leia, Death Star 1 has a "problem:"). The line goes forward and back - back to -30,000 before hyperdrive. At year 25+ we eagerly await the future - or whatever Sir George Lucas or the Star Wars Legacy group dreams up.

Timeline - Knight Hammer
www.geocities.com/Area51/Chamber/4182/timeline.html
>Since Imperial fans will want to get their information from Imperial sources, here's a Star Wars timeline that was found on the Imperial Knight Hammer Site. Now you'll know what happened when.

Tips & Tricks - Gamestats
www.gamestats.com/tips/List/All
>Wanna know tips, cheats, and tricks of Star Wars computer games Roque Squadron, Jedi Knights or for most any game for that matter? This Gamestats site "lets the llama out of the bag" and helps you play the games and "rule."

Tommy of Escondido's Alien Fonts Page
www.geocities.com/TimesSquare/4965
>This site offers a wide array of downloadable fonts based on many popular science fiction series. In addition to Star Trek, the site provides fonts related to Star Wars and Babylon 5.

Top Ten Reasons Why Star Wars Is Better Than Star Trek
www.geocities.com/Hollywood/Set/5760
>Subtitled "Star Trek Sucks," this Boba Fett linked site offersTrekkie put-down top-ten lists such as, "a Trekkie hero is some pansy running around in pastel spandex" and other gems, some witty, some base.

topwallpapers.com: Star Wars
www.topwallpapers.com/starwars.htm
topwallpers.com lets you search for wallpapers on almost any subject - the Star Wars page offers Episode 1 paper, big-as-your-computer-screen Star Wars logo, and pictures from Star Wars movies.

Toshi Station
www.toshistation.com/jedi.htm
Hip Chris Holuka humor/tribute site that takes a bit of exploring to get used to. First, check "New Acquisitions." This tunes you in. Check "Reruns" for archives of his parodies, and then Wookie Theatre for more

Totally Games
www.totallygames.com
Totally Games is the game development company headed up by Lawrence Holland, creator of X-Wing & TIE Fighter. Learn about their products, apply for a job with them, get up to speed on producing flight combat games.

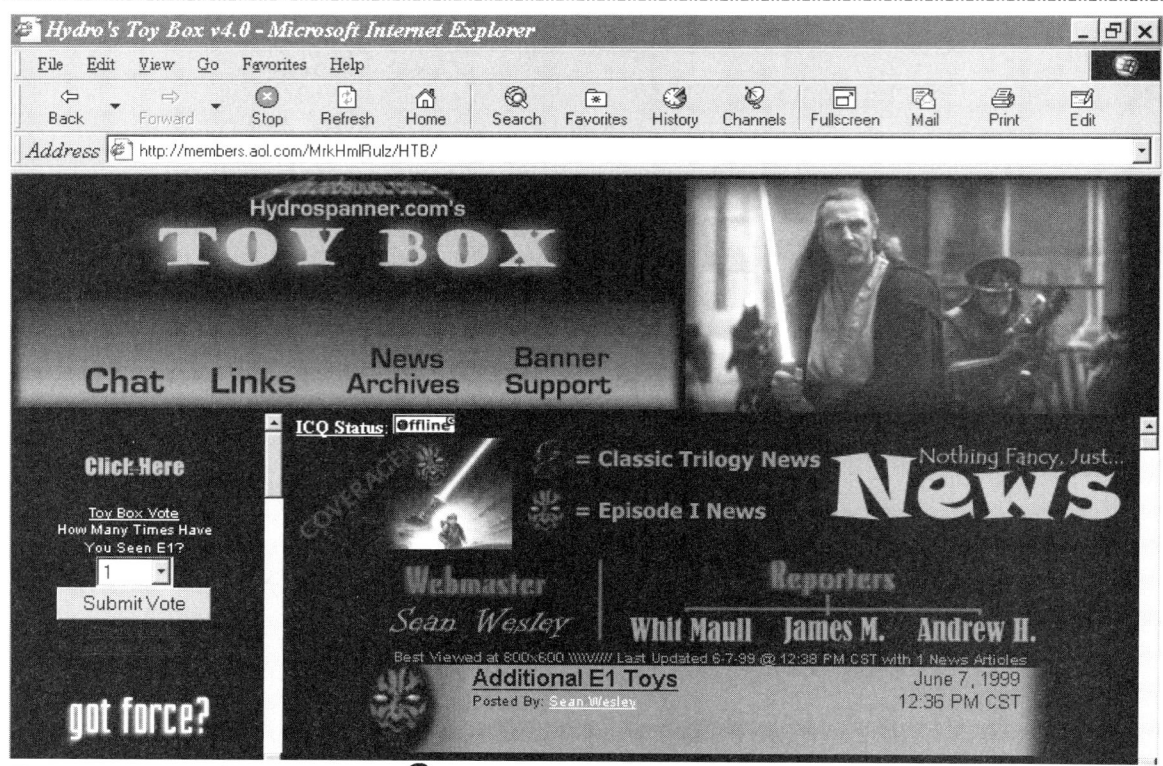

Toy Box - Hydrospanner
http://members.aol.com/MrkHmlRulz/HTB
Another good Star Wars toy site, with general toy news findings, also a chat room, nice banner links, news archives, and a survey.

Toys, Gifts, Collectibles - Mos Espa Marketplace $ 🔍 👁

http://mosespa.starwars.com/products

Official Star Wars products - "they're for sale - if you want them," - Obi-wan Kenobi. Browse by category: action figures, computer games, toys, exclusives, cards, games, models, masks, music, pins, pewter, posters, art, wearables. Also links to books and magazines. It's a searchable store!

Trading Tips

http://yakface.com/hosted/tuskentrader/tips.htm

Are you interested in trading, buying and selling via Internet Star Wars trading groups? Here's a tips page for you so that you don't look like a nerf-herder online. Click on "home" to view the Tusken Trader main site.

Trailer Mirror Lists 🎬

http://sabbeth.com/starwars/mirrorlist.htm

Lists of mirror sites offering Star Wars Trailers. Read specifications about them, file type, size, and helpful comments compiled by the countingdown.com group.

Trencher ALB's Episode 1: The Phantom Menace

http://members.tripod.com/trencheralb/index2.html

Trencher ALB - who claims to be 14 years old - has a good Episode 1 news site, updated frequently. Click on NAVBAR "Star Wars." The nifty countdown sequencer shows Prequel scenes & actors.

Trilogy Blooper Guide

www.egosystem.com/starwars/bloopers.html

Jeremy Kennedy - with plenty of time on his hands - has put together a collection of bloopers and nit-piks (some with pictures) that makes us happy that we're safe on Earth, not bumbling around in Lucas space!

Trilogy Font

http://yakface.com/hosted/tuskentrader/font.htm

A Macintosh font based on the lettering used in promotional material for the Star Wars Trilogy. Basically, it's a Bauhaus-looking ultra-bold. Get the PC version at tusken@tampabay.rr.com

Trilogy Special Edition FAQs 🖼 👁

www.jax-inter.net/users/datalore/starwars/sepage.htm

Not actually FAQs, but rather this is a suite of sub-sites that comment on all the details of the changes in the 3 Special Editions, illustrating them with movie frame captures. We feel this is one of the better treatments of all the movie scene changes to be found on the web.

Tripod's Pod Central Sci-fi Lounge ⬇ 💬 🔍 👁

www.tripod.com/pod_central/pods/sciencefiction

Tripod's Sci-fi Pod is an interactive site where you can join in chat or message boards as well as search within the Lycos system, also view the Sci-fi archives or read newsletters. Link easily to similar pods, also link to games, MP3 databases, and other cool entertainment.

🖼 IMAGES	🎬 VIDEO	🔊 AUDIO
👁 MUST SEE!	$ SELLS STUFF	⬥ ADULT CONTENT	🔍 SEARCHABLE
💬 CHAT ROOMS	⬇ MESSAGE BOARDS	📬 MAILING LISTS

Tripod's Star Wars Fan Pages
www.tripod.com/explore/entertainment/wire/wire_969531_71102_best_1.html
Tripod and the Lycos gang host many Star Wars-related web pages. Here you can find the listing of them all, their e-mail addresses, but they do not come with descriptions of what's on them. (instead, the search feature helps you find sites quickly). Links to other Tripod pods.

Trivia - Jar Jar's on Jedinet
www.jedinet.com/multimedia/trivia/index.htm
Some trivias are easy - this one isn't. Easiest of the 44 questions here is, "Who said, 'Look sir, droids.' " Tougher is "Name the Itherian in the Cantina." One obscure question is: "What does Harrison Ford do in his spare time?"

Trivia - LucasFan.com
www.lucasfan.com/humor
One of the better trivias we found even though it is mis-named as a "humor page" on the Lucas-Fan.com main index page. If you don't know the answers, use this book to help search the web for the answers at this site, then submit your answers and find out how you did!

Trivia - Star Wars Trivia on Echo Station
www.echostation.com/trivia
Ooooo! Trivia. Prizes. Scores. Get online (Sundays at 3 EST) and see if you know your Star Wars or if you're simply a scruffy-looking vacuum-head in your own wretched hive of scum and villainy.

Trivial Side of the Force
www.theforce.net/jedicouncil/trivia
8 separate trivia sections brought to by the Jedicouncil at theforce.net. A semi-daily trivia that, well, is a lil' bit up the difficulty scale. Answers are accessed immediately by highlighting the area below a question.

TROOPS
www.theforce.net/troops
TROOPS is among the best Star Wars humor/parody videos. Author/Producer Kevin Rubio & friends dressed up as Stormtroopers in the desert and acted like COPS characters. Video is downloaded in streams from numerous sites. Get scripts, FAQs, trivia, photos, and storyboards, too.

TROOPS - IMDb
http://us.imdb.com/Title?0153301
Perhaps the most successful of the home-made Star Wars spin-offs, here you can read the technical movie info about the great spoof production TROOPS, a crossover of COPS & Star Wars.

Turbolaser Commentaries
www.snowhill.com/~by
Everything you need to know about turbo-lasers & ion canons. This site also mentions blasters and lightsabers occasionally. Debate the merits of these weapons onsite. Site owner asks that you respect the copyright, please; he's spent a lot of time and effort on this topic.

Tusken Traders Trader Lists 📬 ⬇

http://yakface.com/hosted/tuskentrader/list.htm
   This site serves two purposes: 1) it lets the Tusken Trader group be known and gives links to their wants and haves lists (somewhat like a message board), and 2) serves as mailing lists of their trading group. Also, click home to check the Tusken Trader Index site.

TV Now Entertainment - Stars on TV 🔍 👁

www.tv-now.com/stars/stars.html
   TV Now will tell you when your favorite character's work is scheduled to appear on television during the week. In the search field, type in the real name of the actor or director, then hit "search," or click on one of the 3 TV screens on the right for the directories.

Ultimate Carrie Fisher Shrine

www.angelfire.com/ca/princessleia2
   Site is under construction by Libby who hopes to make this a top Carrie Fisher tribute site. We really liked the opening message, but all we found in early April 1999 was a couple links, webring and guestbook.

Ultimate Star Wars Cursors Page 🖼

www.geocities.com/Area51/Lair/3724/cursors.html
   150 cursors to choose from for your computer, all in one zip file for you to download.

Ultimate Star Wars Homepage 🖼

http://members.aol.com/gio2003/frame.htm
   This Josh & Chris site was missing files and wouldn't make our list except that it has an absolutely great collection of rendered images on its picture page. Sounds and 3D are question marks, but site has scripts & links to webrings.

Ultimate Star Wars Icons 🖼

www.geocities.com/Area51/Lair/3724/icons.html
   Four zipped files of icons are found here: characters, droids, starships, and miscellaneous. Use them as shortcut pictures, file pictures, icons.

Ultimate Star Wars MIDIs Page 🔊

www.geocities.com/Area51/Lair/3724/midis.html
   MIDI music files - nothing fancy, just click on and listen.

🖼 IMAGES   🎬 VIDEO   🔊 AUDIO
👁 MUST SEE! $ SELLS STUFF   ✚ ADULT CONTENT   🔍 SEARCHABLE
💬 CHAT ROOMS   📩 MESSAGE BOARDS   📬 MAILING LISTS

Ultimate Star Wars Multimedia Universe
www.geocities.com/Area51/Lair/3724
>It's a universe of big collections of cursors, icons, MIDIs, pix, sounds, computer goodies, virtual reality VRML, and links. Main page isn't fancy, but it'll make point 8 past light speed.

Ultimate Star Wars VRML
www.geocities.com/Area51/Lair/3724/vrml.html
>You'll need a VRML viewer to participate in any of these 10 virtual reality Star Wars locations.

Unofficial Carrie Fisher Free Banners
www.offsoho.com/carrie/html/8banners.html
>Unofficial Carrie Fisher site has a small collection of banners that are really, really Carrie-astic. Every website should have at least one of these banners to show appreciation to Carrie.

Unofficial Carrie Fisher Homepage
www.offsoho.com/carrie/html/86home.html
>Pert collection of Carrie : bio, filmography, quite nice photo galleries, her fun video clips, a few sounds, past articles archive, and"What's New"! We liked the Banners section found on the media page.

Unofficial Episode 1 Ed Bain Comics Page
http://members.aye.net/~roncole/tpmky/comic.htm
>Cartoon panels and comic strips by Ed Bain. Collected by Kentuckian Ron Cole, this is a very nice site with what looks to be Bain's complete "Standing in The Line" series.

Unofficial Episode 1 Homepage (Kentucky area)
http://come.to/tpmky
>Ron Cole site for fans around Kentucky and Louisville are, but anyone can visit, of course. This site has Ed Bain Prequel comics, also, movie news, local news, webring, links, and discussion group.

Unofficial ILM Downloads
www.ilmfan.com/files
>Small gallery of downloadable files from The FANatic, who operates an ILM-alike site. Here's where we found the Iain McCraig image of the sinking Titanic covered with Star Wars characters, reputedly given from Lucas to Titanic Director James Cameron. ILM FAQ, also MOV videos.

Unofficial Industrial Light+ Magic Website

www.ilmfan.com/index2.html

An "unofficial ILM Web site," but it looks official and seems to link to official ILM sites. Here's fairly current news, films featuring ILM images, commercials, downloads, behind the scenes secrets, employment ops. It is open to fan feedback - yours.

Unofficial James Earl Jones Page

www.geocities.com/Hollywood/1585/index.html

Tribute pages to James Earl Jones, the voice of Darth Vader. Here you can learn all about him (his screen debut was in Stanley Kubricks' Dr. Strangelove!). Includes Jones' filmography, biography, and, of course, sounds (WAVs & RealAudio). "That hairball is my son!" - Jones, from the Lion King.

Various Beers from the Star Wars Universe

http://rpg.echostation.com/humor/SWBEER.TXT

I'm sorry; this had to be included for all the speeder mechanics, foam-heads, and Lite Lifers out there - this one's for you. Includes "Lightsaber Lite: not as clumsy or random as other lagers" or Death Star Ale: "Continue with intoxification. You may vomit when ready."

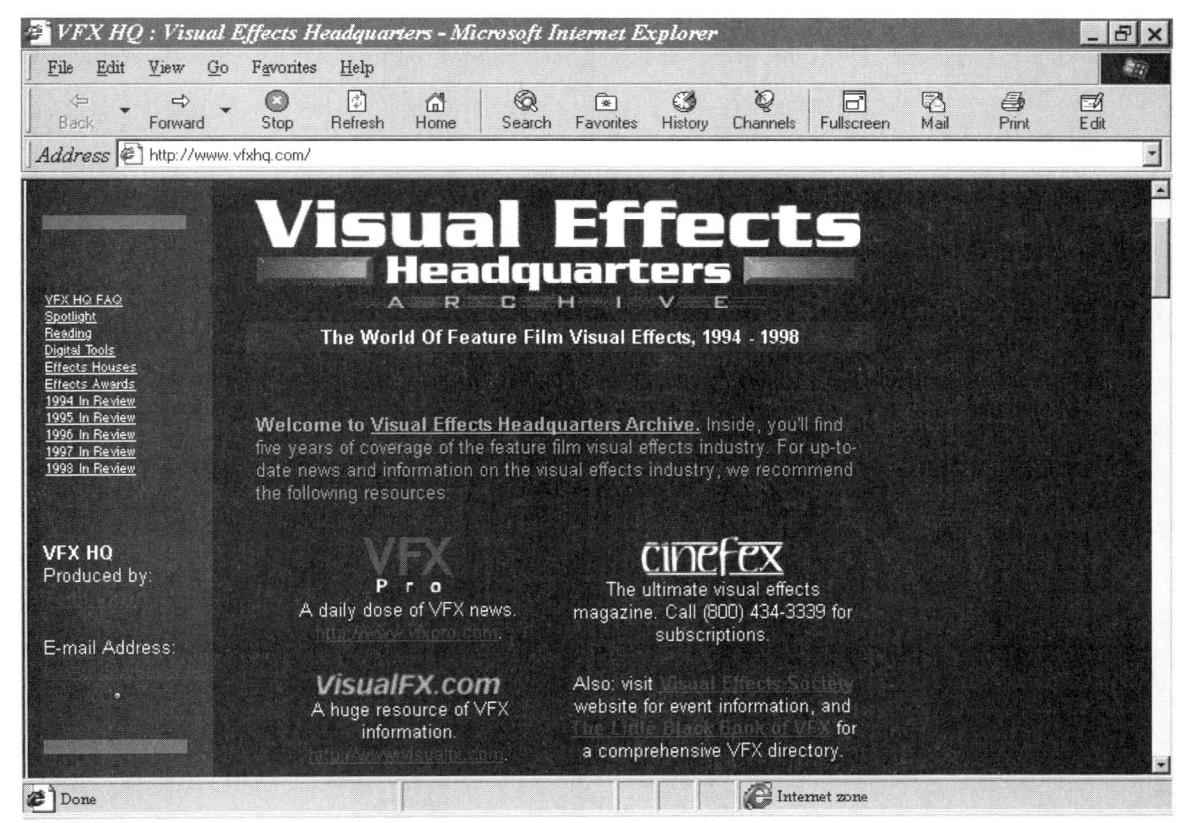

VFX HQ Archives (Visual Effects Headquarters)

www.vfxhq.com

Here are the people who seem to be on top of what's happening in movie special effects. Visit their "Best of" page (with pix!). Covers 1994-1998. Links to other resources for FX and Visual Effects society, and has daily news.

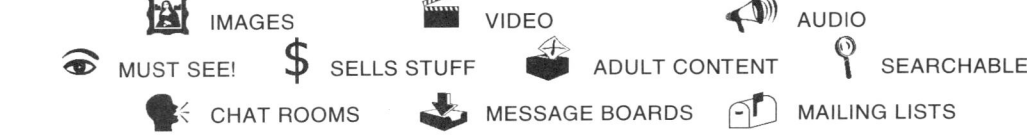

Virtual Edition Forum
www.mvpforums.com/partners/virtualedition
   This virtual reality forum looks to be more sophisticated than most and it links to Roderick VonHogen's popular site. Forum offers many customizing features - for free. Join and post messages and connect to the virtual galaxy!

Virtual McGregor
www.enter.net/~cybernut/articles.htm
   Multimedia site for rising international star Ewan McGregor. Find articles, pictures, film pix, galleries, news, sounds, screensaver, bio, filmography, survey (vote for best recent Ewan movie: Episode 1, Velvet Godmine, or, Nora.) A very interactive site.

Voodoo Extreme Games
www.voodooextreme.com
   Touted as THE "big boys site" for gamers who want more, faster, more challenging stuff! Good resource, with news, shots, archives, forums, interviews, and, of course, games. Only site still under Communist control, it says.

VRML Object Supermarket
www.dcs.ed.ac.uk/~objects/vrml.html
   A VRML resource in the United Kingdom, we found a Star Destroyer, a Falcon, a TIE, and X-wing here among the vehicles. There are links to other resources that have archives of Star Wars VRML files.

WarCraft II Sg-1 SAGA
www.geocities.com/Area51/Vault/4910/sg1.html
   A roleplaying game "under development" and the author invites you to help. Not a direct Star Wars gamesite, but here may be a chance to see how a game is created and to contribute.

Warships of the Empire, Technical Commentaries
www.theforce.net/swtc/warships.html
   This is a regular encyclopedia of Imperial flying hardware, including comments about them, technical specs, and pix. Links to all Imperial craft types. Images vary from color illustrations from comics to original pencil drawings to color photo images.

Warships of the Mon Calamari, Technical Commentaries
www.theforce.net/swtc/mcc.html
   The challengers to the Imperial Starfleet, the Mon Calamari warships are mostly converted vessels, yet, the technical specifications and weaponry show them as formidable. Find text, pix, and individual breakdowns of the spacecrafts; good for modeling and roleplaying.

Watch This - Video of Han & Leia in the Falcon
http://users.why.net/radrock/sounds/watchths.avi
   Short AVI video of Han saying to Leia "Watch This" as he attempts to move to hyperspace. Most of us know what happens next. This should be downloadable as a screensaver.

Watto's Junkyard ⬇$ 🖼 🎬 ❓ 👁

www.wattosjunkyard.com

Solid Prequel site! Plenty of images to illustrate the news and articles, also a survey, message boards, QuickTime videos, game demos, downloads. Also, connect to an online store for books, movies, soundtracks, games & toys. Prequel page has storyline, characters, vehicles, and ticket files.

Watto's Junkyard Archive 🖼 ❓ 👁

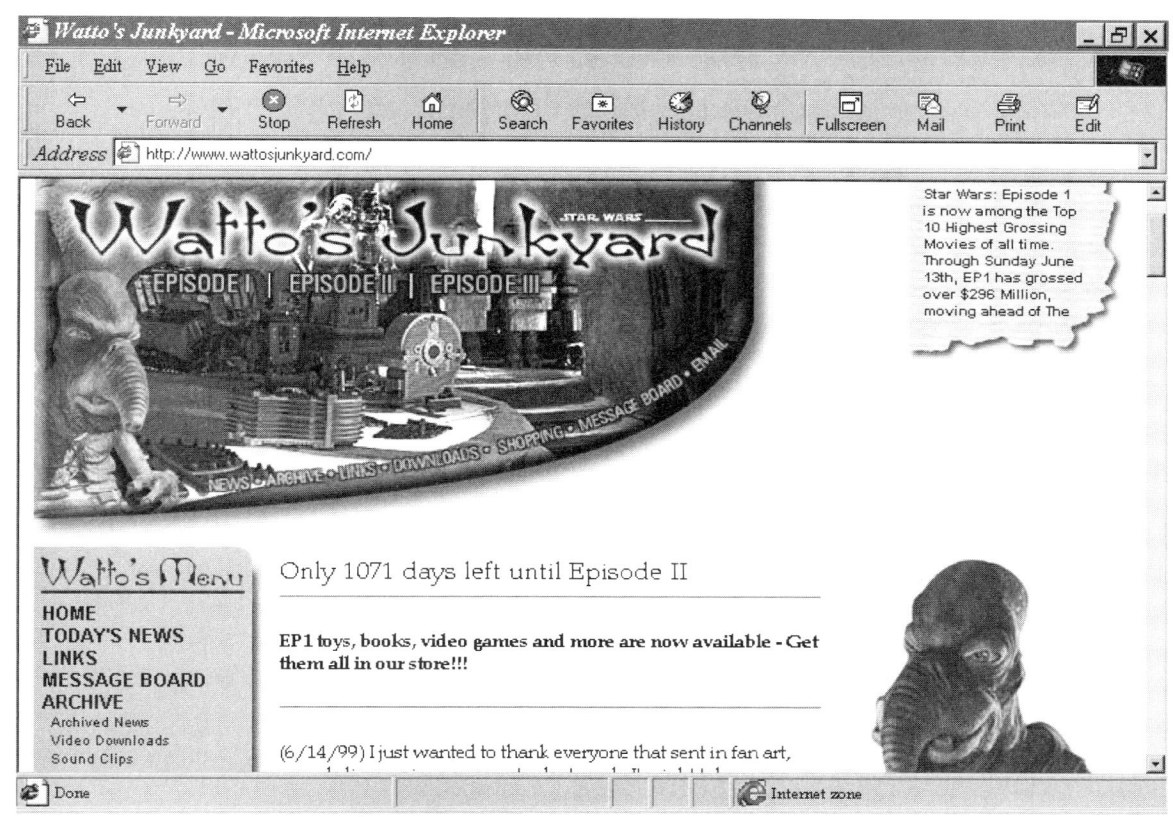

www.wattosjunkyard.com/fanart.html

Phantom Menace fan art (sketches & posters), also official posters. Text section lists Prequel articles from magazines, and includes full color JPEG images. Click Backgrounds & Screensavers to find great Prequel wallpapers, and a Darth Maul screensaver for your computer.

Watto's Junkyard Downloads 🖼 🎬 ❓ 👁

www.wattosjunkyard.com/downloads.html

Good selection of Prequel and game downloads, mostly QuickTime videos (some RealVideo) of Trailers in various formats and sizes. Here you will find the South Park and Imitation Milk parody videos, Lynn's EP1 production diary, Star Wars Game video demos and George Lucas video clips.

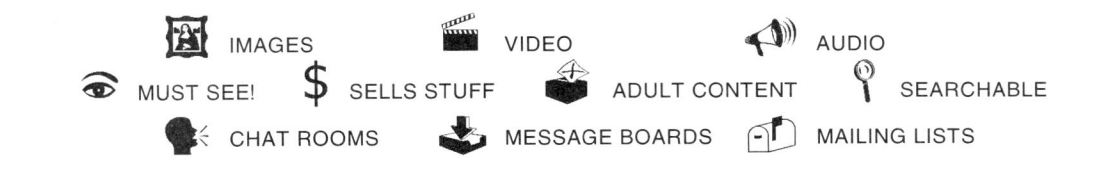

WAV Archive - RPG at Echo Station
http://rpg.echostation.com/wav/wav.html
    This WAV sounds gallery is especially designed with roleplaying games in mind. Find Salacious B Crumb laughing, C-3PO pleading "Please don't de-activate me," probe droid transmitting, etc. Plus WAV music themes, including an Imperial March on electric guitar.

WAV Central - Star Wars
www.godlike.org/frontpage/starwars/index.html
    The many WAV files here are listed with text, length, and type, so you know exactly what you'e getting. Also found MPEG Episode 1 Trailer video here, also a QuickTime Version.

WAV Files
www.jedinet.com/multimedia/sounds/wav.htm
    Jedinet's WAV sound files are arranged by characters, then topics: Darth, Han & Chewie, Leia, Luke, Ben, Yoda, C-3PO & R2, Sound FX & Miscellaneous. Size of file is given; some sections are accompanied by a picture. "There's no mystical energy field that controls my destiny."

Wave Central Star Wars
www.wavcentral.com/starwars.htm
    About 70 quotes and sounds from the Trilogy, arranged by movie title, in WAV sound file format. Length in KBs. C3-PO: "I believe sir, it says that the power coupling on the negative access has been polarized." Duh. You will find even better, longer gems.

Ways of the Sith, The
www.geocities.com/Hollywood/Location/1657/sith.html
    An ongoing magazine-like site featuring stories based on what most people consider the "villain's side," but we'll leave that up to you to judge! The Sith Ways are the path followed by Darth and Exar.

Weapons & Equipment (The Compendium)
www.wcug.wwu.edu/~paradox/weapons.html
    Weapons and Equipment is a subpage of the Compendium RPG site. Find out about various equipment - also explosives, medical supplies, fatigues, blasters. If playing, here are price lists and other "qualities."

Weapons of Episode 1
www.starwars.com/episode-i/features/weapons
    An official Star Wars site featuring pix, comments, and illustrations of Episode 1 weapons.

Web Hosting - Echo Station Interactive
www.echostation.com/hostinfo.htm
    So, you'd like to launch your own web site? Here's an example of what one Star Wars host (Echo Station) is doing to solicit and help other Star Wars fans take "the first steps into a larger reality."

WebChat's Star Wars Cantina
http://chat14.go.com/webchat3.so?cmd=cmd_doorway:Star_Wars
    WebChat operates a huge string of chat rooms; the Star Wars chat room here is among the more active Star Wars chat rooms online. Also, find a poll that relates, usually, to chat rooms.

Webring Javigator Purple Pages
www.javigate.com/Webring/PurplePages/ent/scifi_starwars.html
    The Webring Javigator helps you find webrings. The site is searchable, so you type in a topic or name. Webrings on that topic are then listed for you as "links" (but actual URL addresses are not given).

Welcome to Death Star III 🖼️🔊
www.pitt.edu/~rsest4/starwars.html
> Apparently this "Death Star III" is going to try to "explode" on us with a barrage of sounds. The WAV sound files are arranged by character or topic, and each is accompanied by a JPEG pic, just in case you forgot what Leia or a lightsaber looks like.

Welcome to Endor 🔊
www.geocities.com/Area51/Cavern/9101
> Although we didn't find any "Endor," we did find "a favorite character poll" and Trilogy MIDI music files, videos, and links to a chat room and the Hanson Punch page (that's where you get to ravage a Hanson), also webrings.

Welcome to my page of Starwars WAV files 🔊
http://members.tripod.com/~Satan15/SWars.html
> This WAV sound file page is hosted by Satan15 (a joke we assume) on the Tripod system. The selections of sound bites are arranged by character and it is heavy on Han & Darth quotes. Also miscellaneous character sound files.

Welcome To The Cantina (Gallery) 🖼️📦👁️
www.geocities.com/Area51/Corridor/8540/cantina.html
> Features lots of Cantina images (color & black/white photos, paintings) including risque pictures of dancers. Also, there's Cantina band shots, aliens, and Han getting ready to defrost Greedo.

Welcome to the Mandalorian Sector 📬🖼️🔊👁️
www.geocities.com/Area51/Cavern/5723/index2.html
> Great collection of Boba Fett JPEG pix (includes Mr. Boba's face image), sounds, and Fett facts, also his ships: Slave I & Slave II, plus information about the Mandalorians, who won't get directly involved in the struggle, but do tend to favor the rebels. Sources here are mostly Star Wars comic books.

West End Games World Wide WEG
www.westendgames.net
> THE resource for roleplaying, West End Games has recently gone through a bit of downsizing but is still the most experienced promoter of RPG resources, catalogs, and how-to's. Go to "Games People Play;" click on Star Wars.

What Does Vader's Chestplate Say? 👁️
www.theforce.net/rouser/chestplate.shtml
> Go to this force.net site and see that there are Hebrew characters on Darth Vader's chestplate. The second line is upside down (the person putting the line on didn't know Hebrew or Bocchi) but what the lines say is significant and obviously done "on purpose."

Whill Journal, The ⚓ 👁️
www.geocities.com/Area51/Stargate/4465
> The Whill journalist has put together an excellent text site with thoughtfully selected JPEG images as illustrations. Much of the site speculates on future episodes - the logic, alleged plotlines. Also, find some news, fan fiction, articles, and a forum for postings.

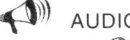

🖼️	IMAGES	🎬	VIDEO	🔊	AUDIO
👁️	MUST SEE!	$	SELLS STUFF	📦	ADULT CONTENT	🔍	SEARCHABLE
💬	CHAT ROOMS	📥	MESSAGE BOARDS	📬	MAILING LISTS

Why Luke Stinks
www.silcom.com/~pruth/luke.html
   Occasionally we have to mention the complainers. Sam's Star Wars page whines about Luke and about Ewoks. Basically, this is about what Luke couldn't do, like save Han's behind at the Sarlaac pit, etc.

Why Wedge Rules
www.silcom.com/~pruth/wedge.html
   Luke Skywalker and Wedge have a long history together, yet Wedge gets caught in the background. Here's some reasons why Wedge should be appreciated more: he doesn't hear the echoing of dead people in his brain; he's not a whiner like Luke; he helps blow up Death Star II.

Wig Outlet $
www.wigs.com/plist.html
   No Star Wars party can be without Princess Leia. Here's where you can find a Princess Leia wig. Once at the catalog page, click on "World's largest collection of costume wigs" and find "Princess Leia." Of course, you'll want to remember this as THE wig site for any celebrity do.

Willems Star Wars Homepage
www.tem.nhl.nl/~veen606/veen606.html
   Site has the old Star Wars arcade game, 3 Trilogy scripts (either English or Dutch), icon files to download, and WAV sound files of Leia, Luke, Darth, Han, Chewiee, but only 3 quotes from each.

Wing Commander Movie
http://scifi.simplenet.com/wingcommander/index.html
   Finally, a movie that is spawned by the popular Star Wars game, Wing Commander. Though you can't play it here, you can read all about the movie, view images, check the cast and movie facts. Interesting modeling pictures are also found on this Sci-FI Advance web site.

Wing Commander Prophecy
www.wingcommanderprophecy.com
   This is where you get into Origin Systems' & Electronic Arts' "Wing Commander" game. Now, can you get out? Your resistance is low - you must go forward - it is futile to resist the power of the force. You must play. You must explore. Narrated by Luke (Mark Hamill) himself.

Winse & Cameron's Episode 1 Pictures
www.geocities.com/TelevisionCity/Stage/5455/episode1.html
   When we first visited, Winse & Cameron had a good collection of Episode 1 JPEG images; most seemed to be publicity photos and trailer pix, but better things have arrived.

Winse & Cameron's Star Wars Section
www.geocities.com/TelevisionCity/Stage/5455/starwars.html
   These guys also cover Space Ghost, skiing, comedy, Aerosmith - The Star Wars section has a nice trivia challenge and stacks of Prequel photos - wherever did they get them all? We except to see more.

Wolf359
http://members.aol.com/wolfpak359
   Wolf359's pages are filled with Star Trek, Babylon 5 and Star Wars 3D graphics. The images are unbelievably realistic and well-worth viewing.

Wookie Hooky
www.geocities.com/Hollywood/Studio/9203
Whacky site is full of advice on how to skip work/school/reality in order to continue your quest to be part of the Star Wars scene. You can also log in and give away your secrets about how to break away - click the "play hooky" button. Join the e-mailing list for news!

Word Finds
www.geocities.com/Area51/Chamber/4182/hunts.html
Tired of being online? Play some Star Wars word find puzzles for a change. Here's several from the Knight Hammer Imperial site. Don't worry, the puzzles are very friendly and un-Imperial.

World 'O Chewbacca
http://members.aol.com/andrewm675/chewbacca/chewie.html
This Chewbacca tribute page has a poll where you can express your true feelings toward Star Wars greatest star. Also, under "Movies", you'll find QuickTime and AVI format videos from the original Star Wars. At this site you can also download the 3D rotating Chewie head, and his bio.

World's Best Star Wars Webpage
www.geocities.com/Area51/Nebula/5101
World's Best page doesn't take into account that it's a large growing universe full of web pages. Still, this is a nifty site, with fan mail access to Trilogy & Prequel actors, also pictures, sounds, music, Star Wars computer accessories, Star Wars vs. Titanic survey, and links to other interesting sites.

World's Best Star Wars Web Site Pics
www.geocities.com/Area51/Nebula/6259
A grab bag of JPEG image files, with the emphasis on Princess Leia and Carrie Fisher. Pix come with descriptions. There's a second pix page accessible via the World's Best Star Wars web site home page.

World's Best Star Wars Web Site Sounds
www.geocities.com/Area51/Nebula/4247
Alphabetized WAV sound files have names like "afraid.wav" so sometimes it's a guess as to what you'll get, although a true fan can feel the force and instinctively "knows."

WWWF Grudge Match
www.lightlink.com/grudge/old/ensign-stormtooper.html
The contestants: red-shirted ensigns (from Star Trek) versus stormtroopers. No gory video, but lots of fan involvement. One fan explains: "I gotta go with the Stormtroopers. Lucas is still alive, Roddenberry is dead." The real question is, is reading violent dribble online better than watching it?

X-Wing Attack Video Preview
www.hollywood.com/multimedia/movies/starwars/video/mmindex.html
Hollywood Online's "Video Preview" files of X-Wing Attack in 3 formats: Macintosh, MOV, AVI.

X-Wing Fighter
www.starwars.com/vehicles/x-wing
Most noticeable of the Star Wars fighter spacecraft, the X-wing is also one of the most documented. This official Lucasfilms page goes into detail about the X-wing (moreso than other official sites do regarding other craft), and some good stock X-wing pix can be found here.

IMAGES   VIDEO   AUDIO
MUST SEE!   SELLS STUFF   ADULT CONTENT   SEARCHABLE
CHAT ROOMS   MESSAGE BOARDS   MAILING LISTS

X-Wing vs TIE Fighter Webring
www.webring.org/cgi-bin/webring?ring=xvt1997;index
> Lists gaming sites and groups that engage in spacec ombat with TIE Fighters and X-Wings. 17 sites/groups including the Dead Kenobis, Obsidian Order Online, Gamma Squadron, Crimson Fury, and Wildcards Squadron are found here. A good resource for fighter information.

X-word Squadron Online Edition
www.echostation.com/crossword
> So, you think you're pretty perky, Mr or Ms Star Wars Know-it-all? Try these online crossword puzzles (actually, they're easy for us, but could be a real challenge for you!). Seven puzzles in all, courtesy of Rob Cashman.

XXX Pictures
http://members.aol.com/qio2003/pictures.htm
> Not x-rated, this cool page is divided into 2 parts: "movie pix" and "rendered pics." You can find most of the movie pic on other web sites, but the rendered pix will knock your helmet off. Most renderings in this collection are big gorgeous action shots.

Y-wing Fighters
www.starwars.com/vehicles/y-wing
> Lucasfilms page for Y-wing fighters. Y-wings seem to have a high mortality rate, causing us to wonder if the model makers wanted to get rid of them before they fell apart or what? The site goes into some glowing detail, pix are good, yet we're not convinced Y-wings aren't the Pintos among spacecraft.

Yahoo!: News & Media: Television
http://dir.yahoo.com/News_and_Media/Television
> In case you'll like to get away from the theatre or your computer, or if you want to catch Star Wars stuff on the tube, check this convenient Yahoo TV directory first.

Yakface's Realm $ 🖼 👁

www.yakface.com

Yakface's news was up to the second when we visited. It has most of the features the other toy/collectible mega-sites have AND some they don't: Spirit of the Force Zine, Tastes Like Jedi, Vintage Star Wars, Let the Wookie Lose (games), Tusken Trader. Connects with ActionAce.com

Yoda

www.starwars.com/characters/yoda/index.html

Lucasfilms' official page for Jedi master Yoda, complete with stock photos and general background material about him. Although not deep, this page have very good links to other official pages. Go to them you can.

Yoda - Online Psychic

www.sun-sentinel.com/graphics/entertainment/yoda.htm

The Sun-Sentinel newspaper has turned Yoda into an online psychic, giving our favorite Jedi master a humor page to gab on, IF you have the shockwave program (if not, you can download it here, then be amazed). If you wish, submit your comments you can.

🖼 IMAGES   🎬 VIDEO   📢 AUDIO

👁 MUST SEE! $ SELLS STUFF   ADULT CONTENT   🔍 SEARCHABLE

🗣 CHAT ROOMS   📥 MESSAGE BOARDS   📫 MAILING LISTS

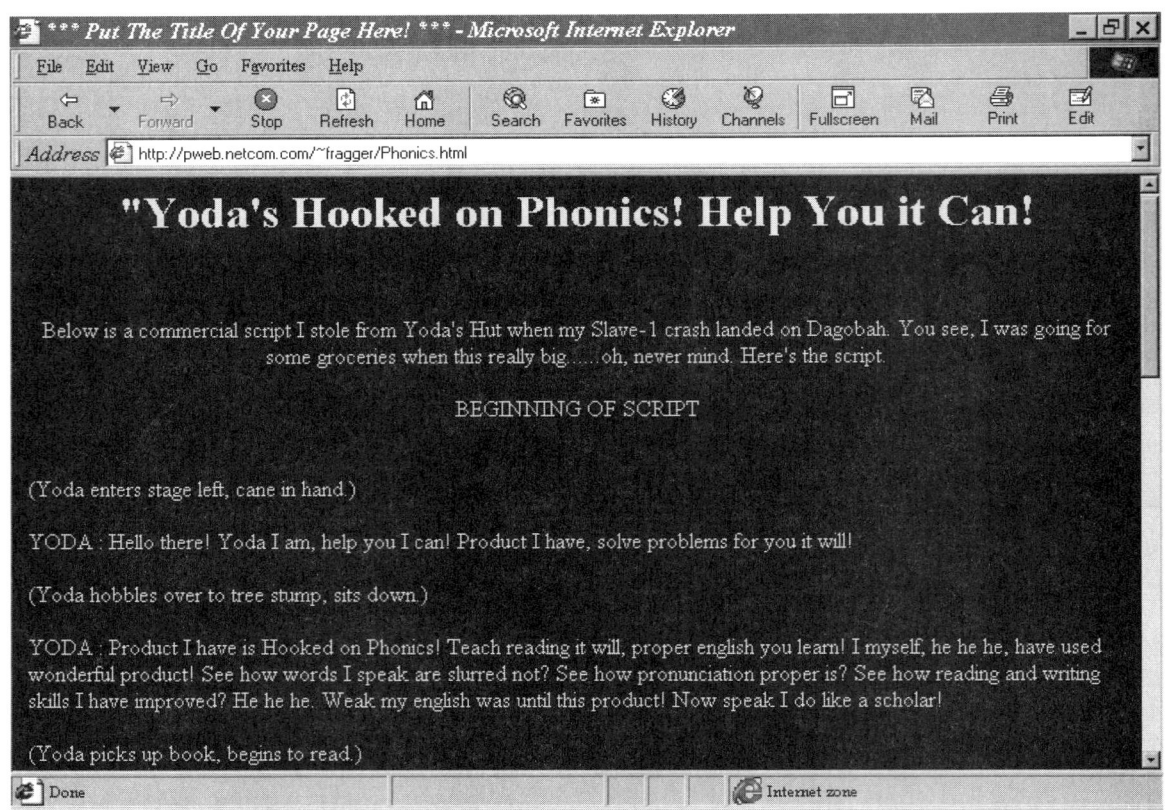

Yoda's Hooked On Phonics, Help You It Can
http://pweb.netcom.com/~fragger/Phonics.html
> On the Web, Yoda gets picked on much too often. Here Yoda is a pitchman for Hooked on Phonics, but, he tends to say things in a 'round about way, and that doesn't help his students become better at English.

Yoda's Hut - Star Wars Movie Files
http://home.rogerswave.ca/qbarnes/swmovies.html
> AVI and/or MOV video files of Star Wars, many from the Trilogy Special Editions including the CGI Jabba scene. Length of files is given, but files can be downloaded by only one person at a time.

Yoda's Swamp
http://www2.netdoor.com/~broberts/yodapg.html
> Yoda's Swamp is filled with more that the usual Yoda-ism; there's a good selection of Yoda art from many sources, also his favorite quotes, his Dagobah stew recipe, and some of Luke's training regimen.

You Are Now a Prisoner in The Entertainment Cell
www.geocities.com/Hollywood/Set/1630/main.html
> Originally stylized in a bounty-hunter Bob Fett character, this geocities site has links to many entertaining goodies, also links to scripts, videos, and surprises.

You People Should Know that My Loyalties Lie Very Firmly with the Empire
www.aaronklaassen.com/starwars/starwars.htm
> Another Evil Empire site with plenty of information about TIE fighter missions, TIE utilities, specs and wisdom from the Imperial order (author: "And I'm proud of it."). Galleries include sounds, music, a couple AVI movie clips from Hoth, and more scripts.

You're Not A Star Wars Junkie Until
http://www.geocities.com/Hollywood/Set/5760/junkie.html
> Comedy list of things (like you've called someone a laserbrain and meant it) that indicate you've had a little too much Star Wars. A companion page to "Signs You May Be A Complete Star Wars Addict."

Zaphoid's Animated GIFs
http://synergy.foo.net/~zaphoid/starwars/animated_gifs
> First of two pages of animated GIFs - exploding death star, Emperor Lightning, Falcon being swarmed by TIE attackers, dogfights, and dirty Dagobah R2.

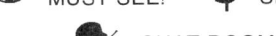

Zaphoids MS Plus Themes
http://synergy.foo.net/~zaphoid/starwars/ms_plus_themes
   Great collection of Star Wars themes, Features 29 zip files, including Boba Fetts, death star assault, empire, rebel, Endor, probe droid, jabba, jawas, and mucho more, even lil' Yoda.

Zaphoids Star Wars Fonts
http://synergy.foo.net/~zaphoid/starwars/fonts
   Downloadable Star Wars typestyles for your computer. Only two files found - wars.zip and aurebesh.zip (which the author describes as useless unless you want the Imperial alphabet.)

Zaphoids Star Wars Multimedia Extravaganza
http://synergy.foo.net/~zaphoid/starwars
   Need Star Wars stuff for your computer? Good. Zaphoid's Star Wars site is full of icons, cursors, screensavers, fonts, themes, animated GIFs, renderings, movie images, and it has the usual stuff, plus an e-mail update form.

Zaphoids Star Wars Screensavers
http://synergy.foo.net/~zaphoid/starwars/screensavers
   Download 3 screensavers in zip format here. One is Star Wars characters, two is ships, three is posters.

Have a Site You Want to Add?

Spotted a Change?

For review, send deatails about the site (including its name and URL) to

`WebSiteCentral@naboo.zzn.com`

Want to Find Out About Other Titles in This Series?

Visit us on the Web at

www.brbpub.com/iig

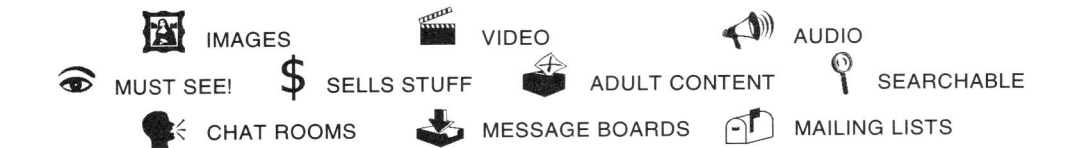

IMAGES VIDEO AUDIO
MUST SEE! SELLS STUFF ADULT CONTENT SEARCHABLE
CHAT ROOMS MESSAGE BOARDS MAILING LISTS

The Incredible Internet Guides
Facts on Demand Press

Cyberspace: The Final Frontier! Now Trekkers can go warp-speed to the Web's good stuff -- over 1500 of the best Trek-related sites. Using *The Incredible Internet Guide for Trekkers*, you can quickly find photos, scripts, sound/video clips, characters, historical perspectives, fan groups and free fun sites. Need to throw a Trekker party, send a special Star Trek greeting card, or go where no one has gone before? Start here! Included in *The Incredible Internet Guide for Trekkers* are sites for every regular cast member and character, sites for roleplaying, and sites specifically devoted to each of the Trek series! You'll find sites devoted to the Klingons, the Borg, and other alien races as well as Trek chat rooms, mailing lists, newsgroups and lots more!

ISBN# 1-889159-11-8   Pages 360

Star Wars and the Internet Have Come Together in this New Directory. Author Peter Weber covers all aspects of the Star Wars Universe: Fans, Movies, Characters, Star Wars Lifestyle topics like Games, Events, Humor, Products, News Sources, Trivias, Chat Rooms, Fan Forums. Get into Multimedia, Portals, and Galleries of Star Wars Images, Photos, Animations, 3D, VRML, Sounds, Videos & Trailers. Click to Star Wars Databases, Posters, the Best Original Art, Comics, Fan-fiction. Tour the Galaxy with sites featuring Star Wars Spacecraft, Planets & Locations, Droids, Creatures, Villains, Hardware. On the way you'll find Official Sites, Fan Clubs, Webrings, Books, Toys....

ISBN# 1-889150-12-6   Pages 360

I want ___ copies of   ☐ *The Incredible Internet Guide for Trekkers* $13.95 Plus $3.95 S/H
I want ___ copies of   ☐ *The Incredible Internet Guide to Star Wars* $13.95 Plus $3.95 S/H

Name _____
Address _____   State _____ ZIP _____
Phone _____

Fill out and mail or fax to: BRB Publications • PO Box 27869 • Tempe, AZ 85285-7869
1-800-929-4981 (FAX)
Order on the Internet at **www.brbpub.com/iig**